The Colonial Metamorphoses
in Rhode Island

REVISITING NEW ENGLAND: THE NEW REGIONALISM

Nancy L. Gallagher
*Breeding Better Vermonters: The Eugenics Project
in the Green Mountain State*

Sidney V. James
*The Colonial Metamorphoses in Rhode Island:
A Study of Institutions in Change*

THE COLONIAL METAMORPHOSES IN RHODE ISLAND

A Study of Institutions in Change

SYDNEY V. JAMES

Edited by Sheila L. Skemp and Bruce C. Daniels

University Press of New England

Hanover and London

University Press of New England, Hanover, NH 03755

© 2000 by University Press of New England

Printed in the United States of America

5 4 3 2 1

CIP data appear at the end of the book

Contents

Editors' Preface   vii

Introduction: "The Generall Having Life in Perticulars"   1

CHAPTER 1
Customary Ways and Radical Ideas in the Original Town   13

CHAPTER 2
The Colonial Governments in the Seventeenth Century   40

CHAPTER 3
Disintegration of the Communal Ideal in the Original Towns   64

CHAPTER 4
Land Promotions and New Towns   82

CHAPTER 5
Religious Association Replacing Secular   101

CHAPTER 6
The Rise of the Colonial Government and a
New Direction for Institutional Development   112

CHAPTER 7
Subduing the Conflicts over Land   137

CHAPTER 8
Town Ambitions and Town Government   153

CHAPTER 9
Sacred Fellowship in Relation to Time and Space   170

CHAPTER 10
The Framework of Government after 1738   186

Contents

CHAPTER 11
Steps toward the Private Corporation   207

CHAPTER 12
Ecclesiastical Organization and Civil Incorporation   226

Retrospect   241

Notes   257
Bibliographical Notes and Key to Short Citations   313
Index   321

MAPS APPEAR ON PAGE 19 AND PAGE 91.

Editors' Preface

Rhode Island's early history is at one and the same time the story of America's future and of its past. Whether by accident or design, the tiny colony anticipated many of the beliefs and practices that characterize the United States today. Rhode Island's inhabitants were the only seventeenth-century New Englanders to use the term "democracy" frequently and uncritically in their discussions about the nature and purpose of government. They were also the first British Americans to accept the consequences of religious pluralism as they struggled to craft and then to rationalize a church-state relationship that was like none they had ever experienced or even desired. Trial and error, restraint and persuasion, social and geographic anomalies combined with the early settlers' dissenting habits of mind to give Rhode Island the most experimental political culture in New England.

While they appeared as innovators in some areas, Rhode Islanders were cautious, pragmatic, and bound by convention in others. They were, despite their deceptively modern words and practices, seventeenth-century people who were closer to their medieval ancestors in some ways than they were to Benjamin Franklin or Thomas Jefferson. Their detractors accused them of leveling instincts, but in fact the colony's inhabitants never abandoned customary notions of hierarchy and deference. If some of their religious and political views were experimental, even radical, provincial leaders continued to rely on traditional political theory and practice to secure at least a minimal level of stability in the colony.

At times, Rhode Islanders simply copied English and Massachusetts practice uncritically. But as was the case with all of America's colonies, even when they made every effort to borrow terms, practices, and institutions from the familiar Anglo-Saxon world of their ancestors, nothing in Rhode Island remained the same for long. Despite the intentions and best efforts of the colony's founders, old values there underwent subtle alterations in meaning; old practices changed as Rhode Island's institutions confronted new realities in a very new world.

Rhode Island may be the most understudied of England's mainland colonies. Its lack of clear form, its ironies and contradictions, its spotty and disorganized record keeping have discouraged even the most intrepid historian. Blithe references to "Rhode Island exceptionalism" abound. The colony's early leaders—Roger Williams, Anne Hutchinson, Samuel Gorton—have drawn more than their fair share of attention, even if historians dwell on their idiosyncrasies rather than their representative natures. But the long period between the heroics of the founding and the Revolutionary generations has largely been ignored. Scholars have leaped from Williams and Hutchinson to Samuel Ward and Stephen Hopkins with nary a stop along the way.

Sydney James went a long way toward remedying this problem in his *Colonial Rhode Island: A History*, published in 1975 as part of the series A History of the American Colonies in Thirteen Volumes. A meticulously researched book, *Colonial Rhode Island* followed the lurching development of the four independent communities on Narragansett Bay into a fragile, tentative colony that survived almost miraculously to become one of the most distinctive as well as the most under-studied states of the new nation. Always sensitive to the possibility that the successful end was never foreordained, Syd nevertheless kept his eye on the particular ball he was chasing: the development of the instruments of government that ultimately gave form and order to a fractious society. Perhaps most important, *Colonial Rhode Island* substantially filled the gap between the founding of the colony and the coming of the American Revolution. The book went where virtually no professional historian had gone before, exploring Rhode Island's murky intramural battles over land, its currency and taxation problems, and the administrations of governors whose names had been all but forgotten by any but the most determined antiquary.

With the publication of *Colonial Rhode Island*, no one would have blamed Syd had he retired forever from the shores of Narragansett Bay, content to be the author of the best book ever written on early Rhode Island. Fortunately, he did not. Instead, he turned his attention to the project that would consume the rest of his life: the institutional development of the colony of Rhode Island. This book represents the culmination of that effort. It is not simply a history of colonial Rhode Island. It is the story of the way in which the province's founders created and then rationalized the institutions that shaped their own lives at both the local and provincial levels. With painstaking attention to detail, it follows the tortuous and uneven path Rhode Islanders took as they developed the town and colony governments, the churches and private corporations, the courts and land companies that eventually gave a semblance of order to a disorderly province.

This is a story replete with accounts of the foibles and errors, failures and even occasional successes of human beings as they struggled to survive in an untested, dangerous but potentially bountiful land. Rhode Island's inhabitants moved to the region they would call home without a set plan in mind. In the beginning, they possessed no authority from the king and received even less recognition from their neighbors. Not surprisingly, their first years were chaotic, almost anarchic, as they came as close to the Lockean state of nature as any American colony ever did. Confronted by hostile forces from without, the colony was also torn apart by its own inhabitants, who themselves were motivated by a mix of religious conviction, greed, and just plain cantankerousness. Individual inhabitants viewed one another with a suspicious eye. Towns quarreled with each other and what passed for the colony government. Religious institutions were similarly competitive until most of them eventually bowed to the inevitable, grudgingly acknowledging that no single church possessed the power to impose its own faith on significant numbers of people. Lacking any traditionally recognized sense of legitimacy, the colony's leaders were forced to devise institutions that relied on the consent—or at the very least the tacit acceptance—of Rhode Island's inhabitants.

Out of the original chaos, order of a sort finally came. Despite the colony's richly deserved reputation for quarrelsome intellectuality, its inhabitants exhibited a surprisingly pragmatic desire for system and regularity. If competing claims to land divided Rhode Island, the need to protect property rights and to build a prosperous community helped mitigate, although it surely did not eliminate, conflict. If Williams and other early leaders were often quixotic, disputatious theologians, they also hungered for a peaceful setting for their own version of Zion—and this made them practical politicians almost in spite of themselves. Laws, even when they were made, were not always rigidly enforced. Leaders often held back, doing as little as possible, hoping that their inaction would create no enemies and would buy them enough time to soften the edges of disagreement. Always they had to deal with a climate that respected dissent; always they functioned in a world beset by contingency.

Little in Rhode Island was ever straightforward. Its settlers were radical pioneers of religious liberty; yet they saw themselves as the protectors of ancient Christian tradition. The frustrating process of trial and error often conflicted with their desire for intellectual and spiritual purity and their inclination to return to first principles. In the end, pressure from England and the other colonies, the needs of a growing mercantile community, and the activities of Rhode Island's religious leaders imposed a rough order on the province. But even at the beginning of the eighteenth century, stability was not assured, and infant institutions retained only a tentative basis of support.

Significantly, the story of Rhode Island's institution building is, despite the little settlement's special circumstances, not entirely unique. Perhaps no colony had as little direction or guidance in the beginning as Rhode Island did. But all colonists, especially those who came to America in the first wave of settlement, had to face the task of creating institutions in an unfamiliar environment, balancing traditional practice and New World exigencies, religious belief and secular imperatives, public need and private interest. The difficulties inherent in the process of developing colonial institutions existed everywhere. In this sense, Rhode Island's effort to achieve order under extraordinary circumstances was in many ways the ordinary experience of all of America's mainland colonies. In this sense, too, the story of Rhode Island's halting creation of institutions that Americans today simply take for granted is a story that begs to be told, one that provides the very basis of our understanding of who we are and whence we have come.

Rhode Island and Sydney James were a natural match; to his friends and students the two seemed to share a personality defined by an ironclad personal and scholarly integrity. Syd loved detail, and he refused to succumb to the temptation to make an easy generalization. In his personal life as well as in his scholarly endeavors, he always relished the fact that humans do not operate according to the laws that historians have imposed on the past in a vain effort to make their own jobs easier. He always appreciated, even reveled in, the contingent nature of the human condition, as he made room for the quirky, the unusual, the stubborn fact that refused to be shoved into an appropriate pigeonhole.

This book reflects Syd's love of detail. It reflects as well his uncanny ability to tease out as much meaning as possible from the tiny fragments of data with which he worked and his willingness to make those generalizations to which the evidence clearly pointed. In the end, although he would surely not call this book a story of Whiggish progress, it is nevertheless, as was his earlier *Colonial Rhode Island*, an account that moves the disorganized communities of Rhode Island from near chaos to something approaching stability.

Make no mistake about it, although he died before he could shape the final manuscript, this is Sydney James's book. The research is entirely his. Who else would have had the patience to uncover, plow through, and decipher the documents and fragments of documents that went into the writing of this book? The organizational construct and the perspective are his as well. As editors, we tried to do little more than shape the whole, to pare down some of that marvelous detail, to shorten the manuscript without destroying its integrity. We gave the book a contextual dimension, comparing Rhode Island's experience to that of other colonies when the occasion seemed to demand it. And we incorporated material from an alternative version of the manuscript into the one we chose to edit for publication. We tried never to lose sight of Syd's voice—to allow him, as much as was possible, to tell his story in his own words. The manuscript deserves no less than that.

Many people have earned more than a nod of recognition for the work that has gone into preparing this manuscript for publication. Linda K. Kerber has been an enormous help. Her encouragement and gentle prodding kept us moving forward toward the project's conclusion. She was always there to give us advice and to run interference for us on numerous occasions, eliminating many practical difficulties, and making our job easier in countless ways. The contributions of Marilyn Houston, who meticulously read and edited the manuscript, have been invaluable. The History Department at the University of Iowa and the University of Iowa Foundation, especially its president, Michael New, provided much needed financial assistance as we prepared the manuscript for publication. Syd, himself, was always grateful to the Rhode Island Historical Society and its director, Albert T. Klyberg, who exhibited a sustaining faith in the project over the years. Most of all, however, we all owe a debt to Syd James, whose fascination with America's smallest colony led him to return to Rhode Island's archives again and again, getting everything just right and making this book possible.

S. L. S., B. C. D.

The Colonial Metamorphoses
in Rhode Island

Introduction: "The Generall Having Life in Perticulars"

This is a book about the changing configurations of institutions in colonial Rhode Island. I chose Rhode Island because it was small and yet had a surprising internal diversity, had a long colonial history and yet left a manageable quantity of evidence, produced a variety of public and nonpublic corporations—and because I was living there at the time. The book has a thick texture because the project, by its definition, put the importance of each element in the material on the relationship to the others. "The Generall having life in perticulars," as an early Providence man said in another connection, the separate institutions and their connections with the life they served should be viewed together.

Though the study of institutions unavoidably features the persons who held office almost to the exclusion of others, it is useful—often foundational—to the study of all aspects of life in a colony. Any society guides and in turn is influenced by its laws and institutional forms. I would argue also that the parts of the entire institutional complex at any given time influence and limit each other, that they ordinarily have a consistency of method or tone or form or justification, that they take similar directions, and that the more comprehensive forms—though not in Rhode Island during the seventeenth century—commonly lead in shaping the more limited associations.

In any case, the development of institutions in the English colonies in America had a special importance. Though many people in the Old World could take for granted the framework of village and manor, parish and guild, county and realm, nobody in America could ignore the need to create a framework where none existed to satisfy the White colonists. For years in the many English colonies founded with plans devised in the parent country, settlers resisted obeying the letter or spirit of those plans and sooner or later forced new terms on the social order. The Rhode Island founders, lacking plans formulated abroad, had to plan everything for themselves from abstract justifications for all the arrangements they made to facilitate their lives.

Accordingly, around Narragansett Bay to an uncommon extent, the institutional fabric in all its strands was an expression of the standards and aspirations of the White people who went there. It might be compared to literature as a projection of the society, though it was a social product more than literature can be. The analogy has its drawbacks, of course. For one thing, literary texts remain the same, however profoundly the words change meaning to readers in passing generations. By contrast, institutional forms designed to express one understanding of how to organize society and one set of calculations about how it might be organized undergo modification through time in order to serve new ends. With all due acknowledgment of the analogy's shortcomings, I have tried to interpret the institutional record much as one might interpret a body of literature.

I had to adopt my own definition of institutions rather than one from a dictionary or sociological treatise. For the most part, I have set aside one use of the term, meaning ceremonial observances, such as Easter, or customs like marriage. Rather, I have meant by institutions the ways in which human beings act together on a routine or recurring basis and also the organizations they form to conduct this action. Form comes to seem virtually independent of purpose, to lend effectiveness to the actions of the organizations, and to require an explanation—myth or theory—for their existence. Altogether, an institution in my use of the concept should have five traits: a social function, a recurring or potentially recurring method of collective action, a form guiding it that remains constant or nearly so, a ritualistic tone in the use of the form, and a belief that the mode of action is justified by external verities. Obviously, the list might be redivided or rephrased, but it may serve.

A human society at any one time will use an array of institutions to organize action for different ends. So the assortment of institutions will be roughly an index to the collective concerns at any given time. It follows that the array should change over time as a society's concerns change or become more demanding. Population growth alone, for example, may create a use for new kinds of local government, or increased capital in a manufacturing enterprise may create a use for a new form of business structure. But ordinarily, existing institutions change slowly, because their form and ritual seem important in themselves or because their familiarity inhibits awareness of their shortcomings. Reality, however, in the end scorns easy formulations. The interplay between forms and functions and invention will require that the historian accept what the record shows and the understanding of a given society that the record yields.

At the outset, I hoped to find out about all institutions in Rhode Island, to see how the array at one time became inadequate over time or created opportunities previously inaccessible or inconceivable. This hope proved un-realistic to some extent, especially after I learned the limits of surviving evi-dence. Most economic associations, for instance, turned out to be elusive. I discovered nothing about arrangements among men embarking on fishing voyages and surprisingly little about the mercantile partnerships that were so vital to the colony's advancement. Commercial agreements, such as those to lease vessels or pay seamen, took standardized forms obviously derived from practices used throughout the English trading world, so they revealed little about the aspirations or practice in Rhode Island. Only those enterprises that needed real estate, such as mills or waterworks, were likely to leave even skeletal evidence. Nor did most church records contain much, except for those kept by Quakers beginning in 1676. The others were kept sporadically; only scraps survive from before 1700. Separation of church and state de-prived me of the instructive wrangling over establishment. Most social or-ganizations and schools came to light only in stray allusions and a few agree-ments among the persons concerned. Only fragments of evidence came to light on apprenticeship and the militia. All kinds of basic ceremonies, from weddings to judicial etiquette, lay beyond my grasp, apart from a few skimpy reports on ordinations.

Ultimately, in spite of the ideal of comprehensiveness, I reached the con-clusion that some evidence would yield too little to justify spending time on it. I reluctantly left to another occasion some of the fiscal and military records of the colonial government, tantalizing shelves full of court records, several series of town records after the first third of the eighteenth century (when in formalities they became essentially the same), the elusive file papers lurking in town halls, and uncounted commercial ledgers and bundles of business letters.

After the founding years, Rhode Islanders wrote little that survives on their intentions or their reasons for shaping their institutions. Necessarily, I have used inference freely, drawing out explanations from the patterns of events in the documents before me as Rhode Island housewives used to draw out yarn from fibers in their hands. When the time came to wind it on the spindle, the spinner might find that the strand had uneven strength. So I have taken pains to point out where inference took over from evidence, wherever the distinction was not obvious, and to give prominence to explana-tions in documents that reduce the need for inference.

My work rests almost entirely on original sources. When I began, very lit-tle of value had been written on early Rhode Island concerning times between the early years and the revolutionary period, almost nothing on the turbulent decades around 1700. I had to learn most of the fundamentals of the colonial period for myself—and took time out to write a general narra-tive, *Colonial Rhode Island: A History* (New York, 1975), that covers mat-ters not germane to the study of institutions. Since then, the study of the founders, above all Roger Williams, has intensified; and several good articles, books, and dissertations have appeared.

As a result of what I found and what my mental traits disposed me to notice, the material came to a roughly coherent collection. The institutions under the lens of research were primarily governmental, ecclesiastical, economic, educational, and those graced by a corporate charter. I paid attention, of course, to their interrelations (at least in formal respects) and such associated relations as those between law and the family or ownership of land. During the years of research, quantitative approaches to demographics, family dynamics, officeholding, and poverty came into prominence. I saw too little documentation to allow me to try similar methods as part of my analysis and was ill prepared to use them in any case. Others have done useful work along these lines, if only on what might be called a sample scale—the equivalent of the archaeologist's trench—rather than the comprehensive one I desired.

For all the shortcomings of my original hopes, I have covered institutional history on a very wide spectrum. In the past, scholars and antiquarians examined individual institutions, such as a town, church, hospital, missionary society, or military company or the lower houses of colonial assemblies. Sometimes the resulting studies treated their subjects rather biographically, as progressing from birth through stages of development to maturity or as the inevitable exploration of a basic form. Either way produced a treatment of the past that made an institution both a self-contained entity and a slow, fumbling preparation for a modern one. Such treatments have tended to make any increase in size or complexity—or any change whatsoever—a kind of motion toward the better.

Though at the outset, I wanted to discover how one type of institution came upon the scene, I rejected any expectation that it could be seen as an isolated phenomenon and tried to avoid any supposition of linear progress or commitment to a process of change. Life in 1640 had different needs and norms than did life in 1740; one was not conducted as preliminary to the other. Without assuming that the arrangement of institutions must be functionally correct for its time—such notions have become antiquated even among anthropologists—I nevertheless thought it useful to see how far such a premise might yield an understanding of a given time and reveal where the arrangement of institutions was inadequate for the circumstances and so led to change.

On the whole, I have found myself leaning toward a dialectical rather than an evolutionary explanation. Solutions tried in one era often resulted in recourse to something that might be presented as their opposites; and they in turn, by their failure, led to the use of still another sort of opposite. (Alas, dialectical theories always suffer from difficulty in defining opposites.) Using the dialectical concept in a flexible way, I have found, often gives a coherence to the historical record. In addition to a loose use of opposition, I have shunned a choice between idealist or materialist premises in dialectic. Faith must make that choice; historical evidence does not bear it very well. Maybe it would be better to scrap the precision of dialectic altogether and look on the record as examples of the ironies of human life.

Ultimately, I find virtually any mode of connecting "cause" to "effect" figurative at best—giddy pride at worst. An interlude of pondering leads to sober thoughts. We think about a sequence of events and regard it as sensible, giving no offense to the mind, even though each new day may bring an expanded understanding of what remains unknown in the sequence. Because the superficiality of causal explanations is widely understood, it becomes possible to use them as metaphors, as expressions of a necessarily limited understanding subject to improvement. Without them, clear exposition can be all but impossible.

Having acknowledged the limitations of the research and the nondogmatic nature of the intellectual framework on which the findings were hung, I should summarize the result. What I have found in Rhode Island was a complicated record that fell into four segments, the first three characterized by salient problems and prevailing views about how to find solutions. The segments overlapped at places, partly because the end product of one was the point of departure for the next, partly because the order of events in the different sectors moved at an uncoordinated pace. Besides, sometimes setting aside simple chronological barriers allowed orderly presentation.

The first period extended from 1636 to about 1658. It began with settlement under conditions that were unusual in English colonization: absence of English sponsorship and any one predominant religion. Instead, the Rhode Island founders held several religious views, all abhorred in the parent country, and had to devise their modes of association. They did not originally intend to create new communities, doing so only when they were forced out of neighboring colonies on account of their religious beliefs. They created settlements with a diversity of social goals. They created a few churches according to their various convictions. They set up town governments to embrace the settlements.

And they felt a need to justify much of what they did. They resorted to fundamental ideas of consent—universal law, power by status, and obedience to the divine will derived either from Bible or direct inspiration—only to find that they could not achieve general acceptance of the magistrates' authority without obtaining a delegation from England, which was done after a less than ideal fashion by the parliamentary charter of 1644. Without explanation, they took land ownership, the family, agricultural practice, and the magistracy as simple facts independent of any jurisdiction. They based these, of course, on English forms and procedures. Yet they could not make Old World villages come alive around Narragansett Bay. Circumstances required revising traditional communal arrangements.

In this time of incongruous resort to iconoclastic thought and unexplained tradition, the settlers leaned most heavily on ideas when planning religious associations. They kept the hope of fellowship as an attribute of community but resolutely and daringly went where their beliefs took them, whether to exclusive churches of the predestined saints along Separatist or Baptist lines or to all-embracing formless agglomerations or convictions that no church could be formed before the millennium, which some thought was imminent. Silently they rejected the traditional social functions of religion and endorsed freedom of conscience and disconnection of state and church. They saw no acceptable anchor to clutch when religious association proved fragile, no counterpart of a governmental charter or English law or shared ownership of land. Some individuals gravitated back to yearnings for the past, if only the Puritan background, but they produced no institutional embodiment for the time being.

Whether in secular or ecclesiastical association, the simple classifications expected at the beginning gave way to the complex. Equality of householders in early Providence, for instance, exploded into a ladder of rights to land and standings in a political community. Religious fellowship, long based on the supposition of equality of souls, even in the presumed equal access to direct inspiration, generated classifications into members and nonmembers, ordinary members and those with a divine gift, as well as the differences among the many persuasions.

Altogether, the directions taken in the first years produced motion toward something quite different, and the results in turn yielded surprising consequences in the years from 1658 to 1696—in fact, conditions verging on anarchy. Definitions of towns as opposed to churches were based primarily on shared land rights as settlers. This produced disintegration rather than cohesion. Common land transactions nearly everywhere had to be separated from the conduct of other civic business, which led to independent organizations of proprietors that were often at odds with political communities. Indeed, efforts to make the most of land rights, whether derived from early purchases or new ones after 1654, led to opportunistic attempts to manipulate the political framework or scuttle it and replace it with one that was more pliant. In a long and tangled set of disputes, control over the Narragansett country became the bitterest and the likeliest to undo the colonial organization.

Moreover, the charter of 1644, even after it had been replaced by a royal one in 1663, failed to create a higher jurisdiction of any strength over the towns. The colonial authority had greatest sway in Newport, where it was intertwined with the town, less next door in Portsmouth, and far less everywhere else. Short on revenue as well as respect, it could do little more than define law for its territory and hope to see that law obeyed. Torn by conflicts over land and boundaries, its policies shifted under pressure. It could not resist invasion of the Narragansett country by neighboring colonies during King

Philip's War and seemed unlikely to keep jurisdiction after those belligerents devastated the region. Then the colonial government was replaced completely when the colony was made a county in the Dominion of New England.

Reliance on the Crown appeared to have annihilated rather than reinforced the authority behind locally chosen magistrates, to have replaced community self-government with an almost military control through officers chosen outside. Yet overthrow of the Dominion in its capital at Boston ended that effect, and a resurrected Rhode Island quickly finished its slide into dissolution. A new war left the officials in Newport barely able to organize local defense. Some towns shunned colony jurisdiction, and even more nearly ceased to function. Only a new expression of royal backing from new monarchs enabled the colony to begin undoing its disruption.

In this time of enfeeblement or disappearance of the usual political organization, smaller-scale associations gained importance. Following the lead of towns and proprietors of undivided lands, assorted enterprises like mills and ferries grounded themselves on rights to real property. Ironically, in some cases churches began to bring people together on a large scale and supply the direction to their lives that government and community failed to give. Above all, the Quakers developed by far the most effective ecclesiastical polity and gave nearly complete guidance to the members' lives. And in many small ways, people sought to bring dependability into their efforts.

As government weakened, people began to see legal or self-created rights as individual ones, rather like property instead of as attributes of association in communities. So the varieties of status multiplying in the middle of the seventeenth century fragmented into atoms or molecules. Old ideas of liberty of conscience and separation of church from state seemed sardonically metamorphosed into individualist conceptions of rights and a replacement of political association by ecclesiastical.

In the years from 1696 to 1738, however, the dissolution of society went into a dramatic and surprising reverse. Rather suddenly, an effective institutional fabric emerged, with traits both derived from and different from the earlier periods. The Rhode Island government sprang back into action and to an extent made real the central control over the territory given to it in theory by the royal charter. Only a small expression of approval from the officialdom of William and Mary prepared the way for a new relationship with the monarchy, which was neither the passive backing of a local magistracy sought in 1644 nor the direct government of the Dominion but a sort of synthesis of the two in an endorsement of the royal charter of 1663. This was accompanied by requirements to take part in wars against France, obey the English trade laws, allow the authority of royal officials in the customs house and vice-admiralty court, and permit appeals from the colonial high court to the royal privy council. With reluctance, the colonial government accepted the terms and learned to thrive with them.

It did its part with a variety of actions. It provided more than the monarchy required for the imperial wars. It gained a measure of control for the first time over the local militia within its jurisdiction. It created an adequate judiciary. It subdued the divisive contests over land by defeating most adverse claims to the Narragansett country, coming to terms with others, and driving most old syndicates of proprietors of common lands into nearly complete division of their holdings. It forced squabbling proprietors from neighboring towns to negotiate peacefully or submit their claims to the assembly.

The colonial government promoted its central authority by other measures to assert its power. If it had to give up efforts to collect a property tax, it nevertheless gradually brought about a degree of authority in town government, made towns to some extent administrative arms of the colony, and used its laws to do such things as define town boundaries and lay out and maintain a system of roads.

Key to the reestablishment and phenomenal extension of central authority was the rise of the mercantile center in Newport. As in other colonies about the same time, possessors of concentrated wealth—in this case, commercial and to a small extent landed, in the Narragansett country—made a central government the tool and expression of their strivings. The lengthening list of statutes to build roads, regulate the sale of some commodities, promote production of others, regulate ferries in Narragansett Bay, stop the debilitating conflicts over land, provide a judiciary, and, above all, create a currency served to nourish the commerce of Newport by linking it to markets and suppliers of exports. Accordingly, something like a ruling class, though hardly a class by strict definition, directed the colonial government. This emergent elite, which fused political and economic power, contrasted dramatically with the rebellious religious leadership of the founding generation. The merchant magistrates backed the new imperial relationship and flourished under it. The compromises with royal government, far from hampering commercial prosperity by confining local discretion, facilitated it by giving it access to the British world of trade. If the ambitions of Newport merchants leaped beyond their grasp, those men nevertheless looked optimistically to the future.

The implications for the towns, if less dramatic, still went far. More and more subservient to colonial law, increasingly used as administrative subdivisions of a comprehensive jurisdiction, usually stripped of control of allocations of land by their own choice or force of circumstances, and anxious to emulate Newport's commercial success, town governments lost most of the old attributes of managing communal concerns. Towns stopped trying to create and control facilities such as mills and taverns. Towns lost much of their original ability to decide who should be admitted to inhabitancy. They still could say who should get political rights but found themselves able to repel paupers only by methods prescribed by colonial statutes. Relieved of fiscal pressures by subsidies from the colonial treasury, towns let their finances drift away from collective control. As towns grew more populous, the town council gained in importance over the town meeting. In the face of increasing central control, towns in the 1730s tried anachronistically to assert a privileged condition analogous to the one given the colony by its charter. The effort flagged soon.

Along with the successful restoration of the colonial jurisdiction and its new relation to imperial authority and concentrated wealth went an introduction of traditional Christianity. Several parishes of the Church of England and of New England Congregationalists were gathered. These new organizations introduced religions at variance with the outcast faiths of the seventeenth century, bringing back the learned clergy, restoring ministerial prestige, and introducing ceremony and traditional ecclesiastical edifices.

In some senses, these developments were only the other side of the Quaker coin. The Friends had brought religious cohesiveness and discipline to some Rhode Island congregations reminiscent of the Christian past. They had maintained an antitraditional belief in immediate inspiration as the center of their faith. Yet they had built the first meetinghouse in Rhode Island. The newcomers, Anglicans and Congregationalists, had to adjust to Rhode Island's unique history of diversity and toleration. Above all, they could not achieve a connection with government such as they enjoyed elsewhere. In the early eighteenth century, even some Baptists and Quakers returned to tradition in limited ways—the Baptists by recruiting a learned clergy and constructing meetinghouses, the Quakers by putting new weight on theology and bringing their children into the faith. In short, the old and new began to converge.

And throughout the institutional fabric, the new century brought a devotion to law. The colony at last published comprehensive books of statutes. Like other New England towns, it prescribed methods of town government. It provided minimal regulation of families and mills. It established rules for the organizations of proprietors of undivided lands. It made its courts compatible with English common law. Towns framed regulations on many topics in the language of statutes. Older denominations elaborated codes of conduct and discipline, new arrivals brought their own. Associates in economic enterprises adopted the practices of the British commercial world. In short, rules and mechanistic use of them became pervasive if still rudimentary by the standards of later times. Perhaps the most characteristic expression of this approach to society and certainly the most important historically came in the use of the colonial charter as both a plan of official powers and also a definition of their limits, as an object of veneration, much as constitutions would be later.

After this era of stunning change, in the years from 1738 to the Revolution (and in many ways thereafter), the institutional pattern underwent no more conspicuous upheavals. Still, the pattern altered fundamentally, if less obviously, and in ways that became common to English America and the United States. Rules intensified; the conduct of authority proceeded further from undifferentiated and paternalistic modes of the past toward limited and defined ones. Indeed, the stress on laws and procedures, whether in government or religious fellowship or small-scale association, narrowed authority or obligations by defining them, but it left what remained more effective. In the process, individual rights, toward which Rhode Island practices had been progressing for a century, became clearer, if not clearly named, before the Revolution. Thus, the coercive and monopolistic kind of authority, from which ecclesiastical concerns had been excluded from the start and which had been plainly reduced to governmental institutions by the early eighteenth century, itself fell under restraint. It had to protect rather than infringe upon private discretion where law could not or would not impose requirements.

The colonial government, in most respects but not all, etched deeper the lines drawn in the early eighteenth century. It continued to articulate law and increase control over local government, but in its own operations it moved toward creating specialized organs. The many-sided authority of the General Assembly—the elected magistrates together with the deputies of the towns—never relinquished any of the powers or duties given by the charter. Yet it did create distinct judicial and administrative provincial institutions. The fumbling of these organs, however, led the Assembly to redivide responsibilities, notably to put its administrative subordinates under the direction of committees of its own. So the Assembly undid part of its willingness to spin off some of its functions.

On a small scale, towns followed the colony's lead as well as its directives. Still eager to foster commercial zones, they added a variety of organizations, such as workhouses or fire companies or schools, under whatever sponsorship and regulation seemed promising. As a balance to the improvisatory character of these projects, most towns insisted on codes of regulations for them.

Behind the modifications of colonial and town government lay a changed set of political realities. The enormous success of Newport's commerce brought growing population and accumulations of wealth to smaller ports around Narragansett Bay. If Providence did best, other places had equal ambitions, notably East Greenwich and Bristol. The Newport patriciate, which had learned early in the eighteenth century to court the voters of mainland towns, had to share with them the exercise and benefits of power. No longer able to manipulate mainland politicians and voters, Newport's elite had to concede more and more of a voice in colonial affairs to men elsewhere. By the early 1750s, Providence interests became sufficiently developed to challenge Newport's primacy; the colony could no longer have a straightforward policy in its internal affairs as coalitions of men with a range of purposes contended for dominance in the General Assembly. The result was two organizations much like the political parties that took shape in the United States after 1790.

Amid these readjustments of what once had seemed clear, Rhode Island's commitment to commercial enterprise and political assertiveness began to blur the distinction between government and other forms of association in ways out of keeping with earlier times by authorizing lotteries and chartering corporations. For all the contrasts between the two institutional devices, they shared the characteristic of getting from central authority a power to act by majority rule among the participants and to act as parties in litigation—that is, to enjoy an artificial personality in law.

Lotteries quickly became available for a profusion of purposes, but corporations began as methods for the Newport patriciate to promote their leadership in elite military companies, a library, and so forth. A charter gave an association the capacity to impose its own rules on its own minority and to prevent its property from being treated as undivided assets of its members' estates when the members died or fell into bankruptcy. The charter gave a security and stability to undertakings on a scale hitherto impractical. It also gave the association some insulation from the winds of party politics. Yet the corporate advantages could not be confined to the Newport leadership any more than political power could be. The colony not only gave charters to men below the upper level but also to men in other places. And it improvised forms, such as associations with some attributes of corporations but not all, for a lengthening list of aspirants.

In time, the corporate device proved flexible enough to bless the ambitions of several churches. Anglicans led the way. They wanted legal powers primarily to enforce a pew tax. But Congregationalists and even Baptists wanted charters to secure property or to define for their organizations the characteristics that would safeguard them against drift into heterodoxy. At last, the colony of soul liberty found a way to lend governmental support to religion without wetting a toe in establishment. Alone among the denominations, Quakers for the time being disdained this help, but they found their own method to approximate it.

This was a record both unique and reminiscent of those in other colonies. Rhode Island in its first century lived on the extremes: undirected from outside and all but unplanned by its White colonists, it showed what it could do strictly on its own. Yet the results of colonial strivings produced an extreme case of the descent into disarray or conflict elsewhere in English America in the later seventeenth century. Conversely, Rhode Island's rapid success in bringing itself a new and effective order after 1695 resembled what happened in other colonies but in an especially dramatic version. Most obviously, the Newport mercantile buccaneers made the institutional fabric one to serve themselves, much as did dominant economic interests in other colonies. And the subsequent elaboration of a provincial life had much in common with what happened in northern North America.

A few technical points remain to be covered. In the text, I have kept Old Style, or Julian, calendar dates except to put the beginning of a new year at January 1 instead of March 25. After Great Britain officially shifted to the New Style, or Gregorian, calendar in September 1752, the dates follow that system. In the notes, however, I have kept Old Style dates in the fullest form—that is, with double year numbers for days from January 1 to March 24. As a result, I may have got a few dates wrong, because colonial Rhode Islanders could be just as mixed up about the calendar as first-year graduate students today. But surely no horrendous reversals of sequence have resulted.

In transcribing quotations, I have kept original spelling except to expand manuscript abbreviations. I have supplied in brackets an occasional word or conjectural reconstruction when doing so would prevent a cryptic sentence.

I have chosen to capitalize most of the titles of officials of the Rhode Island colonial government but not most others. Thus, I allude to "the Governor" when meaning the one in Rhode Island but to "the governor" when referring to one of another colony. The resulting inconsistency, by which the king of England fails to rate a capital letter, in my judgment will facilitate reading.

✤ 1 ✤

Customary Ways and Radical Ideas
in the Original Towns

English people who started colonies in America commonly assumed that they could carry with them some parts of life in the Old World while replacing others—and then learned to their perplexity that neither transplanting nor reform would work as they hoped. So it was for the religious radicals who founded the four towns that eventually joined to make the colony of Rhode Island. These people differed vehemently among themselves as to what the mixture of custom and renovation should be, and they all differed from those who designed other colonies.

The first colonists around Narragansett Bay most resembled the Puritans of the adjacent colonies. Like those people and unlike early Virginians, they expected to transplant the traditional family along with many traditional practices of English rural life and commerce. Like orthodox Puritans, they planned to create nuclear towns where the residents would live godly lives as loving neighbors. That is, they had a communal ideal based on their moral tenets and their sense of what had been good in days of yore.

This ideal included traditional elements that were hard to transfer to a new setting. In the idealized English past, an array of occupations, arranged on a ladder of ranks, had created both an interdependency among the members of a community and a hierarchy of power topped by a ruling class of aristocrats and gentry. The people also formed a parish, so unity in faith and worship had blessed and lubricated the arrangement. The result was order—a complex concept compounded of functional interdependence, hierarchy, religious fellowship, and inertia—the whole intended to produce law-abiding behavior and even contentment.

The founders of the Rhode Island towns drew upon this ideal in different ways. They all wanted a diversity of occupations to create interdependence as well as a compact cluster of houses and association in work that would foster neighborliness. They counted on distribution of land to frame this system by arranging home lots and such common fields or pastures as they desired. They also expected the distribution of land to create a social hierarchy, highly differentiated or not as the case might be, just as the distribution of land in England corresponded to social rank. They assumed the village community could control the use of land by controlling use of common fields and pastures, adopting fence rules, and so forth. They assumed that special facilities, such as mills and taverns, could be expressions of their collective will exerted in the allocation of special sites or the choice of officers or the award of privileges and franchises. There would be no clear boundary to the community's self-regulation within its own territory. The towns began with meetings of men with membership rights, who might vote on any subject whatever, and proceeded to more intricate arrangements of committees and special officers as occasion required. For these men the substance of action mattered; they were less concerned about the form their actions took, imagining that they could either improvise a form or adopt an English one.

The founders, however, also turned their backs on some basic features of English village life, whether by choice or force of circumstance. They devised no counterpart of the manor and lacked a generally acknowledged ruling class; as a result, they encountered perplexing difficulties in creating a magistracy. Three of the four towns turned away from the norm of uniting all the people in one church and so lacked the means of moral suasion as a force for harmony. Founders of two towns tried to build a highly stratified society in their communities by a distribution of land. Two tried a rough equality. Neither policy was generally acceptable. Any distribution meant a creation of ranks, for land always had been the basis for the social configuration; and where the ranking lacked the sanction of time, it appeared arbitrary. Rank previously held in England created a presumption of desert in the new town, albeit a weak one. Many people wanted larger shares than they were given and saw no reason to let a town's policy stand in their way.[1]

Outsiders accused the heretic settlements of disorder and assumed the fault was with their religious radicalism. Insiders, aware of their objective record of turbulence, defended themselves as best they could. Nobody mentioned—maybe nobody appreciated—the frailty of any social configuration that was new. Imitation of the Old World past was just as much an innovation as deliberate reform. Tradition inheres in the concrete and is denatured by its conversion to abstract terms. So the Rhode Island pioneers, equipped with principles to justify their deviation from custom, found that they must also defend their imitation of English village life. Whatever they did, they would be attacked. This was true whether they proclaimed a concept of a harmonious village untainted by greed and envy or a church composed of the faithful united in strict observance of rules derived from Scripture or direct revelation. The towns at first had no framework of government or plan of society provided by backers in England—in this they were like many other places in New England at that time—and explored all imaginable basic principles for the foundation of collective authority.

Assertion of principles brought only counterassertions, followed by shifts to other principles. Ultimately, the turbulent settlers fell back on the less theoretical. They began to regard earthly forms of association as based on shared land rights, which turned out to solve little. They obtained a delegation of governmental authority from England and then continued to bicker over its use. Likewise, their disputes over the traits of a true church drove some people back to tradition. Agreement on religious liberty and a radically secular conception of government—due to principle for some, to expedience for others—quickly ruled out the use of force to restrain religious diversity but did nothing to quell contention. Until the eighteenth century, no society took shape that was cohesive and content with the framework of its public institutions.

In the founding years, the original towns independently carried on their own disputes according to their own dynamics. Even union in a single colony failed to stop the process, because the colonial government remained so precarious. It was their creation instead of the other way around; it faced hostile neighbors and received only intermittent support from London. Nevertheless, all the towns ended in operating in almost the same way, which was a variant of the common New England pattern. Each had a town meeting, a town council (instead of a board of selectmen), and a long list of specialized officers. The towns converged on this arrangement slowly and without any initial plan.

Providence

The first of them, Providence, was especially turbulent. It struggled for years with three problems that all towns had to face: allocation of land, regulation of its use, and creation of coercive laws and a magistracy. The founders had to figure out not only what to do but also how to justify it. One plan after another failed to enlist general consent. Providence rejected from the start the goal of solidifying the community by forcing all the members into a church. In the context of early New England, this rejection was as important a source of social fragility as quarrels over the distribution of land. The settlers produced a record of intertwined disputes covering most of the terms of their association.

Roger Williams and a few companions launched the settlement in 1636 with permission from the local Indian sachems but without plans for organizing a town.[2] Williams already had rejected the fundamental premise of

Massachusetts, that government should be an emanation of divine authority to shape laws in harmony with Scripture and guard the purity of churches. Instead, Williams thought God's will required humans to use political authority for strictly secular ends and to leave the churches unsullied by mundane hands.[3]

To steer the new community, Williams at first resorted to his understanding of natural law, the principles of right that guided all human societies. This alone challenged tradition. More radical still, he decided that the settlers would start as equals, so they would reject a vital element in the traditional formula for order. All the heads of families would meet to decide what direction the community should take. Williams thought families were "the foundations of government" and "a Commonweale" was an aggregation of "[f]amilies agreeing to live together for common good." As long as the cluster of families remained small, it would need no superior authority wielded by magistrates. The founders took equal lots of land for private use, beginning with narrow house lots in a row along their harbor, and decided to use the timber in common. Later they took nearby tracts of arable land, notably those in a common field to the east. Williams thought that property rights and the family were sustained by natural law. For years, he remained firm in advocating "Libertie and Equallitie both in Land and Government."[4]

Williams's ideals were not all radical, however. He cherished an ancient communal norm of trust and generosity among neighbors, a concept that he held so deeply and so instinctively that he had difficulty expressing it. Years later, hurt by an opponent's legalistic description of the town government of early Providence as "all meere nothings and nullities, [so that] . . . we livd in no order but Routs," Williams burst forth with a slightly incoherent but therefore all the more telling invocation in concrete terms: "As thus, a Neighbour takes his neighbours Axe, How, Canow, lying unused for his neede (without his neighbours Consent, being not present) and promiseth [to?] make good upon demaund any dammage or just demand. In these and other cases, where the Thing presum'd on and taken lies dead and th[e?] owner is my friend, and absent: my Neede is present and my willingnes to Satisfie all just Demaunds is professed and declar'd. What shew of Sence is there to call these Nullities?" This expostulation probably betrayed a painful awareness that neither his own egalitarian system nor its successors had brought social harmony.[5]

The founders soon altered the simple organization of heads of families, moving to one based on social contract so that single men might also have a role, and allowing the first men to control admissions and restrict distribution of land to newcomers. Williams had to give way. The masters of households began to admit single men, then required newcomers to sign an agreement promising obedience to the majority of those with an active political voice. These steps converted a natural right to govern into a political right of freemanship. At once, the men with the vote began to restrict the distribution of land and admission to inhabitancy.[6]

In a vain effort to preserve equality in the town in 1638, Williams set land rights on a new foundation. He obtained a written memorandum, approved by the Narragansett sachems, defining the extent of land for theEnglish settlement. Then he transferred the land rights to himself and a dozen first comers in two sections. One, later called the Providence Grand Purchase, was for the original settlers and those they would admit to equal shares in it and equal rights in the town polity. The other, about a quarter of the whole on the southwest (later known as Pawtuxet) was reserved for the first thirteen settlers. This partition allowed Pawtuxet grantees to move out of the original nucleus of settlement and so to sap the foundation of the community.[7]

Having departed from the principle of equality, the town multiplied the varieties of inequality. By 1646 it had admitted some men only to quarter shares in the Grand Purchase and gave them no vote.[8] It admitted still others with no share at all. Probably a few servants and drifters came into the community. Thus, within a decade Providence created a ladder of social standings.

Williams's expectation of needing no magistracy also proved unrealistic. Rather, creating a magistracy that everyone would accept became the foremost puzzle. The first attempt to solve it was by a compact or constitution called the Combination, drawn up in 1638. It created a few officers and ruled that disputes be settled by arbitration, backed if necessary by the physical force of the men with voting rights. Arbitration, the document declared, rested on "common humanetye betweene man and man," and therefore "no State wee Know of disalowes" the method.[9] Thus, they appealed once more to natural law. It was a futile attempt and failed to stop strife: the state under the Combination was the assemblage of voters, not a higher authority standing by to enforce the results of arbitration. Defiance of the Combination came to a climax when Samuel Gorton and his followers denied the town government's judicial authority and thwarted execution of an arbitration award.[10]

This challenge to the Combination led to another effort to attain legitimacy. Natural law and a covenant having failed to resolve conflict, people began to form ties to a government with acknowledged authority to exert judicial power. The first to do so were some enemies of Gorton who already had weakened their direct ties with the community by living at Pawtuxet. They despaired of the town's ability to control itself and put themselves under the jurisdiction of Massachusetts. A few of them received commissions to keep the peace in their neighborhood and began to separate their land rights from those of Providence. Faced with this alarming secession, Williams and his neighbors sought a delegation of authority from a higher source (by earthly reckoning) than their own agreement. At their behest,

Indian Owners: The lands of the Indians around Narragansett Bay cannot be mapped with precision. Although these peoples had clear conceptions of geographical allocation of rights, the rights pertained to inconstant social groupings or were in dispute. Pequots held territory west of Weekapaug Inlet, diminished after the Pequot War; Niantics owned land east of that point. Narragansetts held territory stretching north on the west side of Narragansett Bay, probably extending into modern Massachusetts and Connecticut and on the islands. Yet the significance of the term Narragansett was fluid. At all times, bands or villages within this category held their own lands. With waning firmness, the principal sachems had a species of suzerainty over them all. Unfortunately, reports of these matters come from English colonists rather than from the Narragansetts themselves. Roger Williams and Samuel Gorton dealt with principal sachems to reach primary agreements on English acquisition of land and then settled matters with local sachems. Later, the actions by local sachems came to outweigh those of principal sachems. The situation was similar with Wampanoags, who lived east of Narragansett Bay but had claims to the islands and parts of the western shore.

Providence Cession or Purchase. The exact limits of the land ceded to Roger Williams by the principal sachems of the Narragansetts, Canonicus and Miantonomi, and confirmed by their counterparts among the Wampanoags, Ousamequin (or Massasoit), fell under dispute early. All extant descriptions of the limits are imprecise. As shown here, the limit was drawn from the Blackstone River above the falls (to include the meadows in that region) to Neutaconkanut Hill to the west of Mashapaug Pond (where there was an Indian village) to a point on the Pawtuxet River to lie above the meadows on the lower reaches. This line roughly corresponds to several early statements. Other testimony includes impossible estimates of maximum distance from east to west (e.g., six miles, much farther than the Indian village lay from the Blackstone, the Seekonk River, or Narragansett Bay) and suggestions that the line from Neutaconkanut Hill somehow went approximately south while passing to the east of the Indian village near Mashapaug Pond.

Shawomet (or Mishawomet) Purchase. At the time of the purchase, most of the territory remained occupied by Indians. Only part of the northeast actually lay open to English settlement. The first settlement, begun in 1642 and soon dispersed by Massachusetts, was on Old Mill creek, which flows into Narragansett Bay just south of Conimicut Point; when the settlement was refounded in 1647, it was near the head of Warwick Cove.

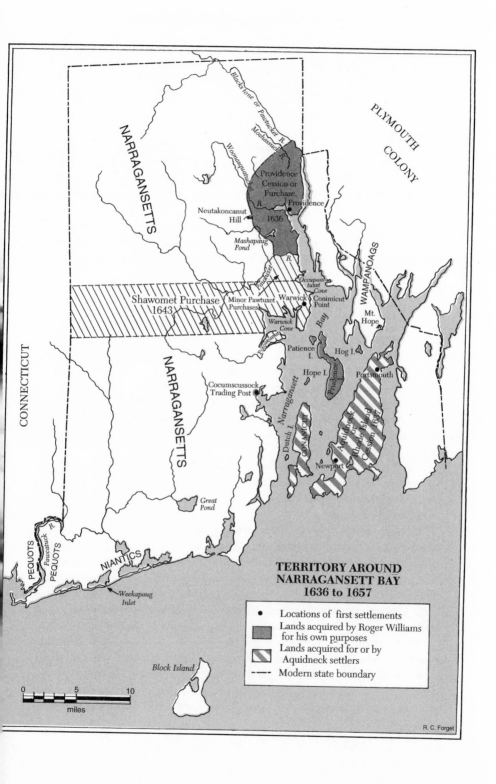

PLYMOUTH COLONY

NARRAGANSETTS

Blackstone or Pawtucket R.

Moshassuck R.

Woonasquatucket R.

Providence
Cession or
Purchase,
1636 · Providence

Neutakoncanut
Hill

Pawtuxet R.

*Mashapaug
Pond*

Shawomet Purchase
1643

Minor Pawtuxet
Purchases

*Occupass-
tuxet
Cove*

Warwick · Conimicut
Point

*Warwick
Cove*

Pawtuxet

WAMPANOAGS

Mt.
Hope

NARRAGANSETTS

Patience
I.

Hog I.

Hope I.

Narragansett Bay

Prudence

Portsmouth

Cocumscussock
Trading Post

Dutch I.

CONANICUT

Aquidneck
or
Rhode Island
Cession 1637

CONNECTICUT

*Great
Pond*

Newport

PEQUOTS

Pawcatuck R.

PEQUOTS

NIANTICS

*Weekapaug
Inlet*

**TERRITORY AROUND
NARRAGANSETT BAY
1636 to 1657**

· Locations of first settlements

Lands acquired by Roger Williams
for his own purposes

Lands acquired for or by
Aquidneck settlers

– · – Modern state boundary

Block Island

0   5   10
miles

R. C. Forget

Williams went to London to seek a royal patent, returning in 1644 with a commission of Parliament authorizing a government to embrace the four original Rhode Island towns.[11]

No government worth the name was organized under this patent until 1647, but when it was formed, it promptly gave town authority nearly a blank check. After the new colony had established a General Court or Assembly, the town was given a charter of incorporation, granting broad legislative and judicial authority to be exercised by such methods as the freemen might choose. Among other things, they created a town court and gave it procedural rules derived from English precedent. They also elected arbitrators who in effect served as an inferior tribunal. For several years, the town court acted with some success, but it made no headway against the authority that Massachusetts claimed over the Pawtuxet secessionists. It declined in importance when the colonial government (and its court) gained strength after 1655 and ended when the colonial government was reconstituted under a new charter in 1663.[12]

By then, however, Providence inhabitants were much less concerned about magistracy than they had once been and much more concerned about land. In the Old World, the pattern of land ownership had indeed been the pattern of society. Aware of this, the founders of the town had treated land allocation as a way to establish a social pattern of their own. But almost immediately they began fighting over the nature of the pattern and putting social goals in conflict with a variety of individual ambitions. The social goals suffered. By 1658, the town meeting abandoned its former efforts to control admission to freeman's status and instead tied it to a share in the common land rights. The town decided (in a vote later contested) that "all those that injoy land in the jurisdiction . . . are freemen."[13] Thus, several former distinctions were dissolved, and the original conception was reversed: instead of admission to membership in the community bringing a share of land, acquisition of land brought the vote.

Throughout this process of redefining the grounds for collective existence, the conduct of public affairs in Providence progressed from the simple origins to a town meeting complete with a number of specialized officials. At the outset, one man, designated by rotation, presided over meetings of heads of households. Soon a treasurer became useful, then an executive committee to apportion land and attend to town affairs between meetings of freemen, then a clerk, haywards (viewers of fences), judges of the town court, a sergeant to serve them, a tax collector, and so forth. Probably prompted by a colonial law, the town began electing a town council of six men at least by 1651. They directed military preparedness, levied taxes, and without known statutory authorization assumed wide probate powers. After years of delay and bitter controversy, Providence created a militia company and appointed officers for it.[14]

The town's organization was not very effective. The duties of the officers were often elastic and grew beyond their specifications. For instance, the freemen gave the judges of the town court a range of additional duties, from laying out land to examining fences and serving on the town council. Endemic turmoil undercut the power of some officers.[15]

Yet Providence managed self-government with fair success for several ordinary purposes. Like the later towns, it took for granted the power to shape its economy—and so its society—by collective decisions. It parceled out land, even if it could not enforce all conditions of title or prevent squatting or unapproved transfers of ownership. It had some success in taxation. It sponsored a few specialized occupations, such as tanning and milling. It exerted a little control over agricultural habits, though it could not impose requirements that swine be yoked and ringed. It could only make laws to allow inhabitants to collect compensation for damages wrought by unruly animals. Providence tried to effect less economic regulation than the other towns; probably the townsfolk wanted no more.[16]

By the standards of the day, Providence failed woefully in religion. Roger Williams and others among the town's founders agreed in most respects with Massachusetts Puritans. They accepted the doctrine of predestination. They thought a church should be an independent congregation and found in the Bible a guide for correct organization and worship. They concluded that a church should choose its own officers, including the minister, who would preach the gospel; administer the two sacraments, baptism and the eucharist; and supervise church discipline. They rejected both a traditional liturgy and a sacramental clergy deriving its special standing from the apostolic succession. Their worship consisted mainly of prayer, psalms, and preaching.

They differed from Massachusetts, however, in crucial ways. They repudiated the traditional parish. Nobody, they argued, should be compelled to attend worship or pay to support it. Civil and ecclesiastical authority should stay in separate spheres. The community should not exclude people of different persuasions. Williams expounded upon these beliefs at length; his neighbors endorsed them by their actions.[17]

No firm evidence survives to explain how Williams and his companions formed a religious fellowship. They were concerned with the vitality of spiritual experience and cleansing the church, not with keeping records. If he followed the English Separatists, with whom he had been aligned, he thought a simple covenant sufficient to embody a church and set four requirements for membership: voluntary adherence, including acceptance of church discipline; knowledge of doctrine, roughly in the Puritan version; as little sin as humanly possible; and repentance for that. He probably had begun to doubt the Puritan standard of a university-trained professional clergy and favored allowing the rank and file of the flock to "prophesy"—that is, preach briefly or raise questions about what the pastor said.[18]

Without the restraint of civil authority or tradition, the church proved unstable. It became Baptist when the members rejected infant baptism as a corruption of scriptural precedent. They imitated the Christian origin of the sacrament: Williams accepted baptism by Ezekiel Holliman, as Jesus had from John, and then baptised others in the fellowship.[19] This step horrified orthodox Puritans, who saw in it a repudiation of the continuity of Christianity, as it soon was for Williams, if not his companions. It was also, like the separation of church from secular government, a way to sever religion from the mundane—this time by ending the rite that had sanctified the cycle of generations.

Williams and his flock soon went in divergent directions. He withdrew from the church when he arrived at highly eccentric convictions that no true church could exist. As he read the Bible, a church could be formed to exercise discipline and elevate a pastor to administer the sacraments only by authority delegated by Christ and transmitted by his Apostles. As he read Christian history, the chain of delegation had been broken long ago by the corruptions of Catholicism. So Williams came to believe in the apostolic succession only to deny that it still existed. There could be no church until Christ refounded it, as for a few years after 1639 Williams expected him to do shortly. When his hopes faded, Williams persisted in rejecting all existing churches but thought he might preach to anybody, though not as a minister. Where once he had seen the foundation of town and church alike to be based on individual consent, he ended by seeing the two as radically different.[20]

His deserted church soon found brethren to preach. None had the college education essential for a Puritan clergyman. Nothing remains to explain how they were chosen, ordained, or defined their functions. Probably the worshippers came to regard ability to preach as a gift of the Holy Spirit and expected divinely inspired words. Surely, the new Baptist elders had little of the traditional clergyman about them.

Further novelties began to sprout up in the church. Without much controversy, the members adopted baptism by total immersion instead of affusion.[21] This procedure had been advocated already by Dr. John Clarke and Mark Lucar from Newport. But a few years later they split over the practice of laying on of hands for all believers, not just the pastor. Some interpreted Heb. 6:2 to require this rite as a sign that the power of the Holy Spirit had been extended to the new member. Presumably, they were those most likely to count on the Holy Spirit constantly to guide the Christian fellowship, especially by inspiring the ministry. Those who held out against this ceremony formed a separate church in 1652 or 1653. Their branch dwindled away by the end of the seventeenth century. Those who favored the laying on of hands for all believers endured, later becoming known as Six Principle Baptists.[22]

In its first two decades, Providence certainly had not attained tranquillity, but it had taken on some of the traits that would characterize it for many years. It remained torn by quarrels over land. Williams's goal of a society of families with equal property remained at most an ideal cherished by some of the townsfolk. The town undertook only a limited array of measures to regulate its collective economic life and often failed to enforce even these. Allocations of land allowed the families to scatter. Presumably, they did not want the tight restraint over individual preference imposed by some Massachusetts towns to enforce cooperative economic action. All the same, the Providence men began to produce enough goods to export a surplus. They also began to develop a pattern of town government that suited their minimal desires, above all for a few routine functions and the adjudication of disputes.

They had passed from one sort of settlement to another. After the explorations of principles drawn from abstract theory and the common experience of human kind had failed, they had resorted to a delegation of authority from England to create a colonial jurisdiction under which Providence would exist as a unit of local government. All in all, the first settlers of this town tried a strange mix of the customary and the radical. And the town remained unstable.

Portsmouth

In outward respects, Portsmouth, the first town on the island of Aquidneck, was begun as the opposite of Providence. Unlike the outcasts and stragglers who migrated to the head of Narragansett Bay, the men who organized the followers of Anne Hutchinson when they were forced out of Massachusetts were people of means, who planned their settlement before they arrived there. In Boston they signed a social compact that declared their intention to live under divine authority. They took for granted the establishment of a town church in the Massachusetts fashion and their power to adopt a wide range of procedures used in England. At their new home, which they called Pocasset at first, they began a process that undid much of the contrast with Providence.

In Portsmouth as in Providence, the principles upon which the settlers first relied failed to provide enough practical guidance and had to be revised and replaced. Moreover, the founders' social policies provoked opposition, more conspicuously from those men who were given little or no land and less conspicuously from those who disliked regulation to make economic behavior conform to communal ends. Portsmouth faced an outburst of extravagant religious opinions and gave up the ideal of unity in worship. Sooner than Providence, it tried to quell its internal controversy by resort to English law and an English charter.

The covenant signed in Boston in March 1638 carried to the extreme the intention to make government an emanation of divine authority. The subscribers declared, "We . . . do here solemnly in the presence of Jehovah incorporate our selves into a Bodie Politick and as he shall helpe will submit our persons lives and estates unto our Lord Jesus Christ the king of Kings . . . and to all those perfect and most absolute lawes of his given us in his holy words of truth, to be guided and Judged hereby." Although the signers invoked Jesus Christ, they cited Old Testament texts to justify their actions, texts that referred to Moses giving laws to the Hebrews and covenants between people and rulers to give power to kings in Israel and Judah.[23]

They soon adulterated the invocation of divine sanction. They resorted to earthly precedent when they chose William Coddington, the only high Massachusetts official in their ranks, to serve as Judge, an office sketched mainly as having judicial functions in Old Testament texts. He promised impartial justice "according to the lawes of God" but then went on to promise "to maintaine the ffundamentall Rights and priviledges of this bodie politick which shall hereafter be Ratifyed according unto God." In their claim of "ffundamentall Rights and priviledges" his people implied more than biblical law.[24]

Once at Aquidneck, the nineteen signers of the compact became the freemen of Pocasset—that is, the voters. They limited admission to their ranks but admitted as inhabitants those who would submit to the government. The freemen's allocation of land resulted in a society of gradations. The first distributions designed a traditional rural village with a cluster of houses and three open fields. The holdings varied greatly in size. The inhabitants obtained much less than the organizers and received no meadow rights. Even wider disparity was to come.[25]

Dissatisfaction with town government first arose against Judge Coddington's power and led to an implicit rejection of the biblical model. When the freemen retrieved some of their power, they exercised judicial functions collectively. In January 1639 they chose three elders to assist the Judge and made all four of them accountable "unto the Body once Every Quarter of the yeare," so the political community could endorse or change their decisions in the light of "the word of christ."[26]

Under the surface, the Portsmouth freemen continued to give an English flavor to their government. They appointed two English officers, a constable and sergeant, to help the magistrates. Both were "to inform of all Breaches of the Lawes of God that tend to civill disturbance." Their duties were specified in English terms. The magistrates soon were employing derivations of English procedure and concepts of crimes.[27]

The next objection to the original compact came from those who insisted not only on using English rather than divine law but also wanted to trace governmental authority to King Charles I. The source of this opposition remains conjectural, though plainly it came in part from inhabitants dissatisfied with their land allotments. Probably, Samuel Gorton advocated a secular conception of government. He insisted that Christ's kingdom was purely spiritual and acted immediately upon the individual, so mundane government, if Christians needed it at all, had to be secular.

Gorton arrived in December 1638 for his stormy time in Pocasset. He believed in direct divine revelation, which probably drew Anne Hutchinson and others to his side, but insisted that the laws and magistracy of the settlement had to be derived from the English monarch. Controversy mounted, culminating in a little coup d'état when Coddington and others were surveying the southern tip of the island as a possible site for another settlement. The Judge's opponents drew up a new covenant that scrapped reliance on Hebrew precedent and divine law. Instead, they proclaimed the derivation of laws and governmental authority from the English king and formed themselves anew "into a Civill body Politicke" in his name. To symbolize the change, they renamed their community Portsmouth. The town government became secular. The new compact was signed by men who had not been freemen before and no doubt backed the new government to obtain land rights.[28]

Though they got little enough as a result of their coup, they provoked another change in the town government. Coddington and his supporters withdrew to found Newport and then asserted their authority over both Aquidneck towns. For a few months, Portsmouth ignored this pretension. Then some founders refused to tolerate the town's reduction of inequality in land and organized their own meeting to vote themselves large lots. Next they came to terms with Coddington. He probably condoned their allocations of land; they persuaded him to abandon his reliance on divine law in favor of English authority. They accepted freemen's rights in the Newport's supra–town government, which quickly confirmed the land grants they had made to themselves. Somehow, the Portsmouth insurgents persuaded their erstwhile allies among the inhabitants to accept the new arrangement.[29]

In this episode, several square miles were carved up into big tracts, presumably for individualistic exploitation, a configuration that was quite different from the open fields that remained for the lower ranks. The direction of both economic development and social order thus shifted. The community would divide into two or more strata, with an inequality in property and a consequent growing inequality in wealth and a wide distance between residences that would undermine traditional neighborliness. For the town as a whole, adherence to the Aquidneck commonwealth during its brief existence amounted to another step away from Portsmouth's original theocracy toward the English pattern. True, the island regime confused the issue by proclaiming itself a democracy, by which it meant a government where the freemen made the laws and chose their own officers. Whatever principles they endorsed, however, these Englishmen in exile wanted certain kinds of authority formally exercised in a level above the local, as had been the case in the parent country, even if they had to create that higher level themselves. Specifically, they wanted the higher level to make general laws, organize militia, set up courts, and appoint judges. In the event, only the judiciary had much effect in Portsmouth, though Samuel Gorton defied it and derided its self-proclaimed derivation from the king as a mere pretense. For all the truth in his evaluation, he and his followers were forced to leave.[30]

The comprehensive island regime faded away after the arrival of the first colonial charter of 1644, but by then Portsmouth was through wrangling over basic principles. It moved toward the common pattern of Rhode Island town government without any intention of doing so. It never shared Providence's reluctance to create an officialdom. The anti-Coddington government of 1639 moved toward the creation of a town council when the freemen appointed a committee of eight men, including the Judge, to lay out lands and carry on routine administration and adjudication. Possibly the voters intended this panel to resemble an English county court, which combined administrative and judicial functions, but in the Rhode Island context it turned out otherwise. The freemen created other specialized officers including surveyors of highways, two men "to view the Cattell that are sould uppon the Iland before thay be transported of the Iland," a "Collector for the pore," and a clerk of weights and measures.[31]

Though they embraced the theory of a judiciary created by authority from above, the men in Portsmouth also insisted on their own consent. They installed their magistrates by using a secularized version of the reciprocal covenant that Coddington had employed to set up the judgeship. The elected officials were to promise that, "beinge Called and Chosen by the fre voate of the inhabitants of Portsmouth unto the office of a towne magistrate," they would faithfully "execute the offi[ce] of a justice of the peace . . . accordinge to the Lawes established unto us by our P[art]icler: Charter accordinge to the best" of his understanding. This done, "the towne [would] reciprocally ingage themselfes to maintain" the magistrate "in the Just execution of . . . [his] office according to the best of theire understandinge."[32]

Portsmouth, obeying colonial law, created a town council in 1647. It included three elected members, the town judges, and the resident colonial magistrates. Later, the number was reduced to six. The council assured military preparedness in times of alarm and, at least by 1655, acted as a probate court.[33] Portsmouth intended to regulate its economy for communal ends, often by allocating land with conditions attached but also by awarding franchises. A succession of town officers parceled out tracts, including shares in a common field, and frequently made grants with fence obligations or title conditional on improvement within a year. The town appointed fence viewers and made regulations on keeping up fences and pasturing livestock in order to keep crops and animals apart. In 1652 the town finally began thinking of commons as resources to be preserved. The town meeting instructed "the desposers of land" to lay out allocations formerly authorized, to set aside land for immigrants in the future, and to allot no more without unanimous consent of the inhabitants.[34] The founders of Portsmouth firmly connected land ownership with collective action, not with natural right or individual purchase in the style of Providence. Their vote created title, so they planned to put all their decisions in writing. For a time, they also required that all land transfers be subject to collective approval and recorded, but rigor declined.[35]

Portsmouth promoted and regulated commerce, essential services, and widely prized conveniences. The town used whatever method seemed expedient. The point was not correct procedure but communal control for common purposes. Regulation for the collective good, however, tended to wither, whether the townsfolk liked it or not. Among the first acts of the signers of the original compact was the grant of a privilege to one of their number, William Balston, to operate a tavern and brewery. The freemen continued to choose innkeepers along with other town officers, until the subject faded out of the town books. The founders granted a franchise for baking bread to one man, appointed an officer to regulate it in the English manner, and began to require that sellers of bread apply for a license. This practice, too, gradually disappeared. The town founders encouraged the first miller by giving him four cows, planting ground, and special rights to cut timber. When he moved to Newport, the town paid him for the mill. Before long, his successors converted the mill to private property.[36]

The town's location on an island made a ferry to the mainland vital. The town fathers appointed Thomas Gorton ferryman in 1640 and granted him an absolute monopoly. A few years later, the town meeting set aside land for a dock and a site for people and livestock to await service. The monopoly faded away, but the ferry franchise remained attached to the land. The town set a table of rates and, when Gorton refused to abide by it, transferred the franchise to John Sanford. In time, Sanford also disregarded the fee table, so the town's restrictions came to little; but for years, the freemen believed that they could control the franchise.[37]

In its first two decades, Portsmouth went through its own process of combining proclamations of principle with traditional ways of conducting English village life. On the whole, faith in principles declined, and reliance on accustomed methods advanced. The turbulence of the earliest years subsided almost into calm.

The ecclesiastical story of the settlement is short. None took shape. The search for acceptable procedures on Aquidneck was similar to that in Providence. At the beginning, the settlers shared an enthusiasm for Anne Hutchinson's interpretation of John Cotton's preaching in Boston but had no objection to the church polity of Massachusetts. They may have hoped to attract John Wheelwright to be their pastor. They wanted no separation of church from civil authority and even decided to build an all-purpose meetinghouse.[38]

They failed to produce a Hutchinsonian version of a Massachusetts town church as a result of unanticipated events. Wheelwright went elsewhere. Instead of a learned pastor, the town was greeted with a growing number of enthusiasts with widely different beliefs. These interlopers unsettled confidence that the way to establish a church was known. According to John Winthrop, Anne Hutchinson (like Williams) turned against the traditional ministry because it lacked a genuine delegation of authority traceable to Christ. By the end of 1638, Samuel Gorton arrived, with his opposition to all conventional concepts of the church and ministry.[39]

Added to Hutchinson's beliefs in direct revelation and sanctification as a phenomenon independent of justification, which had proved explosive enough already, these additional heresies turned the Pocasset community into a Babel. People there held public meetings for worship but probably had no desire for a durable ecclesiastical institution. Either the attempts to create one languished or they gave way to a mode, shortly to become familiar in England, where all in attendance prophesied, often broaching novel doctrines. Surely the function of preaching fell to nonlearned persons, and just as surely the social function of a church to unite a community in faith and values failed. Amazingly, the Portsmouth settlers, initially united by a religious cause, quickly lost their ability to agree on religious matters, and they simply dropped religious organization from their public concerns.[40]

Newport and the Aquidneck Commonwealth

Newport displayed another blend of traditional ways with reformist intentions and another series of changes in basic principles Whatever the founders had in mind when they viewed the site, they soon formed a town of their own and proceeded to make it the leading member of the two-town Aquidneck state. They tried to establish a town church, roughly on the Massachusetts model, but failed because of religious diversity. The only gathered church there suffered a succession of revisions of doctrine that led it to the Baptist persuasion and a schism. Newport's town government experienced fewer changes than the others, which is not to say that it lacked the instability so obvious in Providence. Rather, after the first few years, changes at Newport took place in the organization of the colonial government, with which Newport's civic business was uniquely intertwined.

In the progress from planning a second village on Aquidneck to creating a colonial capital, the founders of Newport made a series of alterations, most of which cannot be examined in detail because the town records from 1644 to 1679 have been lost. The men who organized the new town signed a simple and enigmatic compact. They agreed to share the costs of their project proportionally to their wealth and allowed the Judge and elders to make decisions for them "by Major voice," except that "the Judge [was] to have a Double voice."[41]Absence of a theoretical declaration to legitimize their power suggests that the signers assumed continuation of the religious foundations of the Pocasset community at that time.

In Newport a small number of prominent men held power and the bulk of the land. They envisioned a social pattern like the one that took shape in Portsmouth. For over half a year, Coddington and his friends proceeded as though they had taken the Pocasset polity, as revised in January 1639, with them. The few freemen acting together instructed the Judge and elders to hold court monthly "to heare and determine all such Causes as shall be presented." The gathering admitted new members, chose a treasurer, and a special judge for claims of damage to crops by wayward cattle. It designed a plan for distributing land, giving sizable house lots near the harbor and fields and meadow elsewhere to the settlers but leaving specific allocation to a committee. Ultimately, Coddington got the largest portion, over a square mile in all; a few others also obtained generous allotments. The recipients prospered by raising livestock for export, thus they had no need of a cooperative arrangement to cultivate land, though they did retain a nuclear pattern of residence.[42]

In the autumn of 1639, Newport revised its organization, which facilitated reunion with Portsmouth in an autonomous colony. The experiment soon failed, but it set much of the pattern for the larger jurisdiction that followed. Newport, without offering a rationale, abandoned its flexible oligarchic system in favor of a more formalized one that was described as under the authority of the English king and laws. Coddington and his associates declared that they were "the Body Politicke in the Ile of Aquethnec Inhabiting" and said they were "Naturall Subjects to our Prince; and subject to His Lawes." Thus, they agreed with their Portsmouth opponents. They even made plans to contact Sir Henry Vane, who had supported them during the Hutchinsonian uproar in Massachusetts but had returned to England and high office, to ask his help in "the obtaining off a patent of the Island from his Ma[jes]tie."[43] If they actually sent a letter, however, nothing came of it.

Reconciliation with leading men in Portsmouth, however, paved the way for the freemen of the two communities to assemble in a General Court to make further changes in their governments. They scrapped the titles of Judge and Elders and adopted a slate similar to the one in Massachusetts but carefully balanced between the two towns: an elected Governor from one town, Deputy Governor from the other, and two Assistants for each—all with judicial competence in the English style—plus several appointed functionaries.[44]

A year later the freemen unanimously adopted an opaque declaration that the government was "in favour of our Prince" but yet "a Democracie or Popular Gouernement (that is to say) It is in the Powere of the Body of freemen orderly assembled or major Part of them to make or constitute Just Lawes by which they will be regulated and to depute from among themselves such ministers as shall see them faithfully executed between man and man."[45]

Obviously, by democracy they meant primarily a form of government rather than a source of authority in popular sovereignty or equal rights for all men or an egalitarian social ideal. They began like an ancient Greek polity, where a minority of the men were voting inhabitants and the others were classified in inferior ranks. More broadly democratic qualities did appear in a few respects, however, such as the care to publicize all laws, in the actual if not theoretical reliance on active membership, and in time the admission of over half the men to freemen's rights. The rest were lawful inhabitants or so-journers. Even men in these categories were needed to perform public duties. All inhabitants were liable to selection as jurors, and all men who had resided on the island for at least twenty days had military obligations.[46]

The judicial side of the island state was the most successful and the most English. The freemen quickly established a hierarchy of tribunals. At the lowest level were "particular courts" (town meetings) with limited jurisdiction, held once a month. Appeals on civil cases lay in the next level, the quarter courts, where the magistrates presided, or the highest, "the Two Parliamentarie (or Generall) Courts," to be held each year, one in each town. There the freemen assembled would rule. In most procedural matters, judicial business followed English usage, at least in style. The quarter courts sometimes made administrative orders in the English fashion. Yet in one striking respect, the lowest and highest courts were dramatically non-English: they were meetings of freemen.[47]

At first, the General Court of the Aquidneck state tried unsuccessfully to infringe on communal self-control. It chose committees to lay out allocations for each town and provided for recording them but allowed the towns to determine by majority vote who got what. The General Court ruled that tenure on the island was freehold. It ordered the towns to perform specific tasks, such as recording earmarks. Its power declined quickly, however, perhaps as a result of failure to get a patent from London. The towns shirked their responsibilities to keep land records, and the General Court was unable to force them to do so. Soon the General Court bent to localism, adopting a vague statement confirming "all the priviledges prerogatives and liberties of the governement, state, Townes persons or person."[48]

Central authority could plan military measures even if it could not enforce them. The General Court adopted approximately the plan used in Massachusetts. It defined the obligations of soldiers, the method for choosing officers, their authority, the number of training days, and so forth. It also directed the towns to keep stores of gunpowder, bullets, match, and pipes, to be purchased at the expense of the central treasury. In spite of the air of command, however, the island government consigned selection of officers to the men in the train bands.[49]

For all the confidence apparent in the early records, the island state was shaky from the start. Coddington grew dubious of the government's future and began exploring the possibility of a merger with Massachusetts. Anne Hutchinson fled to New Netherland, perhaps because she got wind of Boston's plans to annex Aquidneck. Disturbances in Providence and Warwick, culminating in the capture of Gorton and his disciples by soldiers from Massachusetts, substantiated fears of attack by neighboring colonies. Under the circumstances, enforcement of strong central control was impossible.[50]

By January 1644, amid alarm over the invasion of the Gortonian settlement, the "Inhabitants of Newport" (not even the freemen alone) invited Providence to join the union, but the gesture came too late to accomplish anything. The Aquidneck men proposed only a general assembly and a court, not military protection. Two months later, the General Court held its last known session. Soon, Roger Williams returned from London with a charter such as the island never had obtained. Until government under it had been organized, the local courts continued to function.[51] In Newport this first experiment in a supra–town government began a mixture of the business of town and colony that lasted throughout the colonial period. Newport quickly took first place among the towns in population, wealth, and commerce and became the capital. It treated the colonial government as its own and used it to make laws that favored its own interests. Though it usually avoided formal confusion, it held one gathering in 1639 as both a "Generall Assembly" of the Aquidneck commonwealth and a particular court or town meeting. Newport men drew no logical lines between the two forms of association. The town admitted freemen, authorized a whipping post and stocks, and resolved to provide bulls for local cows. It laid down rules on control of livestock, but so did the general assembly of Aquidneck. The colony even shared the function of choosing town officers and tried to allocate land and govern the militia.[52]

Newport was unique, too, in its early creation of an oligarchy to allocate land for economic development. By 1644 the town put its undivided land under an organization of proprietors distinct from the town meeting, and they delegated control of the land to a panel of trustees. Probably the proprietors were the original recipients of allocations and their successors. Whatever the case, the organization promoted growth of commercial facilities, at first as an agency of the town government. The proprietors reserved most of the small amount of land under their control for their use in common but kept portions for public purposes and set aside a tract to be divided into small lots for tradesmen, a plan that was carried out beginning in 1667. Before then the trustees authorized holders of harborfront lots to build wharves extending into the water. Thus, Newport's founders retained their control of land after they admitted others to vote on governmental matters.[53]

Newport did more to sponsor a church and school than the other towns. Coddington and his associates formed what they expected to be a town church and called the Rev. Robert Lenthall to the pulpit. A properly educated Puritan minister from Massachusetts, Lenthall had leaned to Hutchinson's views and begun to question infant baptism and other unknown points in ecclesiastical government. Probably to help support him, the town asked him "to keepe a publique Schoole" and granted him a home lot and one hundred acres more as an endowment for the school, to encourage "the poorer sort to trayne up their youth in Learninge."[54]

The prospective town church soon failed, doomed by the spread of diverse radical views. A schism occurred, reportedly when believers in direct revelation withdrew. Lenthall departed for England at the end of 1641, and no minister of the conventional sort replaced him. In the end, the Aquidneck government adopted the only viable policy, legal freedom of conscience.[55]

Dr. John Clarke and others stabilized the remains of the church and during the 1640s made it plainly predestinarian and Baptist. They believed that adherence to scriptural precedent was sufficient authority to create a true church. Clarke served as pastor. Though a physician and not a university man, he had enough of the traditional learning to resemble a Puritan divine.[56]

No more is known about this congregation than the little the pastors in the eighteenth century could unearth. The flock had "severall Persons, able to speak to the Edification of the rest"—that is, prophesying by the members was allowed. Although there were few members in full communion, many townsfolk attended worship with them. The church, then, was a fellowship of the putative elect. The church's first historian, John Comer, believed that the original members agreed to a covenant, though he could find no text of it or of any internal regulations. While Clarke was in England, between 1651 and 1664, the church turned to others to preach and administer the sacraments. They were even less like proper Puritan ministers than he.[57]

As in Providence, advocacy by some of laying on of hands for all members provoked a schism. Introduced from Providence in 1652, the practice touched off several years of controversy, culminating in a division when the innovators withdrew. They also rejected predestinarianism and opposed restraints on prophesying by the members—and also, for obscure reasons, frowned on singing psalms.[58]

The extant documents tell little about early Newport but still present a reasonably clear picture. The town began in a rather oligarchic manner, as shown in its allocation of land and political rights. It aggressively launched the Aquidneck commonwealth and later made itself the capital of a larger colony. It began a practice of mingling town with colonial government and so escaped most of the occasions for the town as such to justify its collective authority by basic principles. It experienced the common failure to create a town church. But it used control of land to shape a society based on wide variations of wealth and an assortment of occupations calculated to produce commercial advancement rather than self-contained interdependence.

Warwick

The creation of Warwick featured the most eccentric appeals to principles to legitimize the adoption of traditional ways by a settlement without a past. In this case, the fidelity to tradition included a lasting unity in faith. After Samuel Gorton had antagonized his neighbors in Portsmouth and Providence by insisting on the nullity of all judicial proceedings except those under English authority, he was forced to create a town government on English foundations. Nevertheless, the Gortonians, like the settlers of Providence or Portsmouth, felt competent to perform certain collective actions on their own. They took the family for granted and thought they could regulate some aspects of life in their agricultural village. Their confidence was never tested, because the settlement only briefly remained outside an English framework. Besides, for decades the Gortonians could do little to smooth relations with their neighbors, an assortment of Indians, Pawtuxet Englishmen, and Dutch traders. Chronic conflict with these people helped redirect the Warwick men from solidarity around a faith and community to solidarity around collective land rights. Samuel Gorton and his growing flock of disciples founded their own settlement in January 1643. Nine leading men negotiated the Shawomet Purchase with the Narragansett sachems, acquiring a vast tract running twenty miles west from the bay just south of Providence. They hoped to reside beyond any claim Massachusetts might assert by virtue of its charter or the allegiance of the Pawtuxet settlers. Gorton explained their intention to practice their own religion and live as "free subjects to the Laws and government of our native countrey, and not unto any government extended out of its bounds and jurisdiction." Arguing that English people took their law and allegiance with them wherever they went, he and his followers refused to establish their own magistracy at Shawomet. Only the king could make a judge, and they insisted on a written delegation of authority from him.[59]

If law was a birthright but inoperative without an explicit delegation from the king, the Gortonians had to rely on what seemed to them the only alternative, anarchist ideals that outsiders might denounce as the extreme of Antinomianism. The practical effect resembled the earliest organization of Providence. Gorton insisted that God alone was their judge. He said that he and his disciples "lived peaceably together, desiring and indevoring to doe wrong to no man, . . . ending all our differences in a neighborly and loving way of Arbitrators, mutually chosen amongst us." In what he called "the order or government of Shaw-omet," the only law was "the law of God, . . . written in all mens hearts." A hostile observer reported that the Gortonians believed that "a man may judge as a brother, but not as an Officer," because as a brother he was "a coheire with 'Christ' in divine kingship." Gorton would have put it differently, because he regarded Christ's kingship as purely spiritual and regarded every major truth as the spiritual emblem of many others.[60]

But Gorton muddied the argument, probably because of lingering respect for traditional notions of order. He condemned all man-made distinctions based on rank or wealth and so implied an egalitarian society. Yet he also wrote that there is an "order set in nature in poynt of sexe, age, gifts, place, etc.," for these distinctions between human beings "are all as significant intelligencers of higher, and more noble and durable things." And he disavowed any wish to "deny the lawful use of any humane ordinances," including government in general or judicial authority in particular, when grounded aright.[61]

His followers tried to live by such ideas for only a few months before and after the disruption of their settlement by soldiers from Massachusetts, who carried seven men to jail and kangaroo trials while the other settlers fled. When Massachusetts released the seven, it forbade their return to Shawomet. Fearing another invasion, they joined the refugees on Aquidneck.[62] They returned to their land only in 1646, when they had the shelter of a colonial patent and promises of protection from Parliament's commission on plantations presided over by Robert Rich, earl of Warwick. Eventually they gave their town his name. Still, they punctiliously refrained from organizing a town government until authorized by the colony.

Quite early, the partners in the purchase planned a major subdivision, similar to the one in Providence but with the proportions reversed. They created a system of man-made distinctions such as Gorton denounced. The purchasers kept the bulk of the land in the manner of the Pawtuxet reservation and left the rest to be divided among themselves and those they admitted as inhabitants. The purchasers' portions consisted of Warwick Neck, which they began to use at once, and the vast expanse west of a line running northerly from Apponaug inlet. They admitted a few men to equal rights but never went beyond a total of seventeen shares.[63] The result seemed to be like the land system of Portsmouth or Newport, but for the time being it was not so in practice because the western part was occupied by Indians.

Between these two territories fell a zone roughly four miles from east to west, hence called the Four Mile Common or "the Towne." There, the purchasers and the inhabitants would have six-acre house lots and several divisions of arable land and pasture, as well as rights to use the remaining commons.[64] Surely the purchasers at first admitted inhabitants, who at some point gained a right to vote on further applicants.[65] Ultimately, the townsmen created over fifty shares. Even so, the acreage per share was approximately the same as for the purchasers on Warwick Neck. Thus, the partition of the Shawomet purchase created two classifications of townsfolk but differentiated more by status than by control of land. At first they built their houses near each other on either side of the line running northeasterly from the cove west of Warwick Neck. On both sides, most of the territory remained as common fields, pastures, and timber reserve.[66]

Actually, the population was diverse, which complicated the town's life for years. In addition to the usual sojourners, Warwick had suspicious English neighbors to the north at Pawtuxet; several resident Dutch traders, some of whom entered the community formally while others disdained its regulations; an Indian village near the intended heart of the settlement and another south of Apponaug inlet. All the Europeans offended the Indians, who, like most of the Pawtuxet men, put themselves under the protection of Massachusetts and sought its intervention against their new neighbors. The town of Warwick futilely tried to buy out the Indians' claims to land and prevent conflict over damage done by stray livestock in their fields.[67] These efforts accomplished little, but the chronic friction with outsiders solidified the town.

In 1647 the Warwick settlers launched a town government on the instructions of the colonial government. Drawing on their experience in Portsmouth and Providence, they proceeded more systematically than the other towns had, although some of the town's decisions were impractical in the presence of neighbors who denied its jurisdiction. Further, Warwick obeyed colonial laws more than Providence did. The townsmen, in a general meeting, chose a slate of officers that included two magistrates, four more men to join them to form the town council, a clerk, a constable, a sergeant, and a treasurer. They devised their version of a social compact and adopted the Portsmouth practice of installing their officers by reciprocal promises between officers and freemen. The town charter awarded them in 1649 stipulated nothing about the form of their government but allowed the freemen to create a town court in the Providence manner.[68]

Warwick, like the earlier towns, was as zealous to exercise control over its development as Portsmouth had been but was less successful. The purchasers planned to allocate individual holdings in Warwick Neck and a few specialized pastures and appointed men to lay out the tracts and roads. They imposed fence requirements and limited pasture rights on the common to "milch catle and Laboring Catle." Settlers with shares in the Four Mile Common, at first the same as the purchasers, proceeded in nearly the same way. They also decided to record land titles, prepared forms for documents certifying allotments, and required each recipient to build a house on his lot within one year or forfeit his status.[69]

The town meeting assumed responsibility for roads. It chose surveyors of highways and bridges to see that the other men did their share in building or mending roads. More clearly than other towns, Warwick defined the system of inhabitant labor.[70]

Warwick's regulations of its economy followed the usual lines in most respects and generally failed when they depended on voluntary action or observance of confining requirements. Measures to restrain damage caused by wayward livestock illustrate the point. Rules on keeping up fences or yoking swine accomplished little, so the town allowed aggrieved parties to sue for damages. The court was no help to the Indians, however, so the town decided to compensate them from the treasury. The town also tried to manage resources for collective use and assign land for special services, such as a gristmill, a schoolhouse, and a smithy. The record of such action was short; Warwick had a small population.[71]

Ironically, Samuel Gorton and his followers created the closest thing to a town church in Rhode Island, in spite of their opposition to the entire heritage of ecclesiastical institutions. Gorton held many religious opinions that shocked nearly all of his contemporaries. Even most of his Rhode Island neighbors who shared his belief in direct communication with the Holy Spirit rejected his views on spiritual association. He repudiated any concept of a gathered congregation, whether of the predestined elect or the populace of a territorial parish. Rather, he thought there was but one "universall Church and Congregation" composed of all humankind. Nor would he look to scriptural texts to organize an ecclesiastical institution or conduct worship. He alluded vaguely to a divinely appointed order but probably regarded it as the moment-to-moment obedience to divine direction. Gorton hardly could deny "that where two or three are gathered together in any part of the world, or at any time," for worship, they were "the true Church of Christ," but he insisted that what created a true church was not any ceremony or organization but the presence of Christ "in the midst, or in the heart of them." All worship must be spiritual, not formal.[72]

Gorton also denounced the existing concepts of a ministry, although at first, he had thought such specific roles existed. Rather, all—women equally with men—manifested the priesthood of Christ and recognized in each other's mouths the preaching inspired by the Holy Spirit. The "holy men of God speak as they are moved by the spirit of God." Later, he moved toward a concept of persons individually raised up by the spirit to constitute a ministry; he thought they should know the Bible in the original tongues, though he still held that all might prophesy, for all could interpret God's word correctly. A true minister had to speak to the whole church, humankind, or at least to "the state of every Saint of God particularly."[73]

While Gorton denied the spiritual validity of a distinction between the sexes, he recognized one between the elect and the non-elect, even though he thought it should not be institutionalized. He taught predestination and denied free choice to believe, but he did not emphasize these points. The elect would pray, glorify God, and join in worship and would do so of their own accord. Churches should not exclude the reprobate.[74]

In the absence of eyewitness reports, it is still possible to discern the outlines of Gortonian religious life. Formless it was, and probably in most respects, extemporaneous.[75] Confidence that the Holy Spirit guided them prevented the lack of regulation from disturbing the participants. They slaked their spiritual thirsts in the immediacy of religious experience. They never underwent a schism. In religion they held together as long as the magnetic Gorton remained as the benign human authority that his teachings repudiated.

Nevertheless, the community broke into conflicts that even the shared attachment to a pariah religion could not restrain. Warwick people quarreled over how to deal with neighbors who denied the town's jurisdiction. Two ramified internal disputes disrupted town business. The second of these led a saddened Gorton and several other original purchasers to offer to move away. But after two years they effected a reconciliation, and the townsfolk joined in acquiring more land along the Pawtuxet and across Greenwich Bay. The Warwick men together faced adverse claims to their new territory.[76]

Control of land and collaborative acquisition of more land had replaced a unique religion as the chief cement of the community. Warwick clearly required a secure place under the largest colonial jurisdiction that would honor its claims and refrain from persecuting Gortonians. That meant the strongest possible government under the charter of 1644.

The town could devise communal rules and often put them into effect. Its failures came partly from external circumstances, especially neighbors who opposed its government, and partly from the unwillingness of the community to observe all its own regulations. Though the townsfolk moved from a confidence that harmony would result from living by divine rule to reliance on a delegation of authority from the Crown, Warwick functioned by consent that subsisted at a level below the one displayed in votes at town meeting quite as much as it did by principles. The limits of individual willingness to abide by its decisions determined the extent of its authority and thus in a practical way determined which traditional usages would prevail.

Conclusion

Around 1658 the development of the original towns was shifting, for reasons both internal and external. Communal goals remained but no longer were sought with the original methods or confidence. Initial theories on the basis of the communities faded away, lost cogency, or were inverted. At the outset, the foremost difficulty had seemed to be legitimizing the exercise of coercive authority, whether the power of the judge or merely the right of the majority to bind the minority. Several kinds of social action had seemed justifiable, independently from the establishment of secular coercive authority. The justifications often were different and not necessarily parts of a whole. The family or the ownership of property, whether by individuals or collectivities, had seemed inherent in the terms of human life. A church could be a true one if it followed divine rules revealed in the Bible or directly to believers. Village regulation or commercial transactions for earthly well-being needed only conformity to English practice. The men of a community could regulate their lives to achieve social goals.

Experience showed that life was less malleable than they had assumed and that traditional ways lost their self-justifying quality when carried across the Atlantic. No concept of land ownership would prevent a challenge. No design of a community would make all the members observe the regulations. No formula for a church would go unchallenged where all felt free, even obliged, to keep searching for conformity to the will of God. No political theory would end disagreement over the foundation of coercive authority. The last resort, to a delegation from England—that is, to attachment to a historical chain rather than abstractions—had yet to prove its effectiveness in 1658.

A few durable elements settled out of this experience, and they had mixed implications for the achievement of order in the fullest sense, as participants were keenly aware. A social hierarchy was taking shape, but churches had to be what their adherents wanted, not what was decreed from on high; and the result was not the traditional unification of a community, except in Warwick, but rather an assortment of sects. From diverse beginnings, the Rhode Island Christians came to rely on a nonlearned leadership deemed chosen by God. For years a charismatic pastorate was the norm and remained common afterward. Where traditional sacraments survived at all, they were only for men and women admitted to membership according to standards that excluded many people. As a result, churches developed the pattern of an inner circle of fully accepted members, a larger sphere of attenders at worship, and a surrounding swirl of the indifferent. Religious liberty became permanent; government became secular in foundation.

Less that was lasting or important appeared in governmental forms. The basic design of town government—meeting, council, and specialized officers—was taking shape and would remain for many years. The resort to a higher level of authority for a framework of law and delegation of power also came to stay. The framework of law, moreover, was to embrace the family and the ownership of property, which initially had been considered independent of the collective will of the body politic. Reliance on delegated authority reversed the initial reliance on consent rising from the towns themselves. In fact, however, public authority in towns and colony depended on consent through elections and acceptance of the laws. The theory had changed more than the practice. This combination of consent to authority from above became a staple in English America. For the time being, it failed to bring tranquillity to Rhode Island. To some extent the development of the first two decades came from the internal dynamics of the towns themselves, to some extent from events outside. The initial premises in the towns provoked objections, leaps to contrasting assumptions, efforts at compromise, and eventually retreat to the town and colonial charters. From outside, the machinations of Massachusetts, Plymouth, and Connecticut to extend their borders to Narragansett Bay pushed the Rhode Island towns toward coalescence. The turbulent events touched off by the Puritan revolution in England set the conditions that governed responses there to initiatives from Narragansett Bay, whether for grants of authority, assurances of protection, or instructions. A dense population of Indians put limits on what the Rhode Island settlers might do with territory they thought they owned. The vagaries of inheritance in the Narragansett royal family plus the commerce between Indians and Whites determined the pace of sale of land to White settlers and so determined what the townsmen might buy and what competitive acquisitions they had to ward off. And as usual, the public arena was a battleground for the ambitions of swarms of people. The next chapters pursue some of these events in the larger context.

❧ 2 ❧

The Colonial Governments in the Seventeenth Century

In Rhode Island the towns came first. They designed the colonial government and altered it several times before it was replaced briefly by a creation of the English Crown, the Dominion of New England. The charter of 1644 in so many words let the inhabitants create their own constitution, and they kept revising it. They probably designed the terms in the charter of 1663 that prescribed a form of government beyond the inhabitants' ability to change it and provided for some subordination to English law and imperial government. In return for surrendering some of their control, they obtained other terms that made this subordination advantageous to the colony. The officials in London did little or nothing to shape the colonial government or make it cooperate with imperial policy. In this respect, Rhode Island was not unique. Connecticut and Plymouth had similar records. Yet Rhode Island people explored possibilities for governmental forms more widely than any others did. And the diversity among the towns often made them disagree on the operation of the colony.

The towns designed a government to be superior over them more in a theoretical than a practical sense. At first, they wanted the colonial authority to provide a code of laws, a magistracy, and an agency to act for them in dealings with nearby colonies and England. In time, they put protecting the colony's territorial jurisdiction before anything else. Always, they wanted the government to protect religious freedom, but the urgency of this need waxed and waned with perceptions of danger. The towns differed, however, in their use of colonial authority. Newport relied on it most of the time, almost to the point of making the colonial government its alter ego. Portsmouth respected colonial authority but kept town business separate. Providence and Warwick used it or defied it as they thought expedient. So outside Newport, the colony had little real power over what the towns saw as their own business.

The colonial government, therefore, was weak. Easily defied by men who thought it failed to serve their interests, it seldom could exert force in much of its ostensible territory or collect a tax or control purchases of land from the Narragansett Indians. Though in a ceremonial sense a dependency of England, in practice it depended on an uncertain consent from its citizens.

The colonial government failed to create a framework for many of the kinds of associations that people formed, even in Newport. Possibly, the inhabitants did not want it to serve that function.[1] It scarcely matters whether this failure came from the government's weakness or the colonist's preferences or absence of vision. The mainland towns could not agree to use the colony to sustain their communal self-regulation, and town effectiveness suffered. The militia, in theory a function of central authority, never was truly under central control and became a congeries of self-governing train bands or fell into decay. Institutions that once had been considered creations of communal self-government, such as mills and inns, gradually became autonomous, defined if necessary by the terms of owning the necessary land. Churches, above all the Quaker, began to provide the social matrix for many aspects of life. Without any intention of doing so, the colonial government let its people lay the foundations for modes of action that later would mark out a private sphere, into which government might intrude only upon request and only to aid or regulate, not guide or command. In the end, this development dispelled initial assumptions that collective action could shape communal existence without limit and substituted a distinctive separation of governmental from private realms. In the short term, this development fragmented association to the debility of public authority.

The Providence Plantations Charter

The inherent weakness of the Aquidneck state and the threat of annexation by neighboring colonies that opposed religious freedom prompted the appeal in 1643 for a charter to embrace Providence and Warwick. The Aquidneck commonealth never had achieved such a clear delegation of its authority nor found any other durable foundation. Still, it set the pattern for organizing the larger jurisdiction that followed under the charter of 1644.

The first charter let the people of the colony design their government. Presumably, they wanted to do so. They found it hard to agree on the nature of that design, however, and their unstable creation imitated the earlier regime by conceding more to localism than was consistent with effective central authority. Shortly, the new government broke into two, when William Coddington obtained a patent making him governor for life over Aquidneck. It reunited only after some delay when his grant was revoked. The colonial government continued to be torn between demands for direct democracy and a representative form, with the latter gradually gaining ground. When the colony at last gained something approaching acceptance from its own people, it did so less because the inhabitants agreed on how it should run than because they recognized the value of sticking together to assert their government's control over the territory specified in the charter and to preserve religious liberty. The possibility of modifying this regime again ceased because of the Restoration. A charter under the authority of a revolutionary Parliament would not do once the king was back on his throne.

When Roger Williams reached London to secure the first charter, England was in civil war, so he had to choose between approaching the king or Parliament. He chose the latter, perhaps because his sympathies, like those of other Rhode Island folk, lay with the Puritan cause. More precisely, the charter of 1644 was issued in the name of Parliament by a commission to supervise the plantation, presided over by Robert Rich, earl of Warwick.[2]

The commission incorporated the towns of Providence, Portsmouth, and Newport under the name of Providence Plantations and authorized them to erect a civil government over a territory greater than their own. The charter described the bounds as the sea, the borders of Plymouth and Massachusetts, and the westward limits of the lands inhabited by the Narragansett Indians. Thus, by any straightforward reading, Shawomet was included, though all the other limits remained misty. The commission reserved to itself only the regulation of intercolonial relations.[3]

Otherwise, the settlers had nearly unlimited freedom. They might "governe and rule themselves, and such others" as should thereafter "inhabite within any part of the said tract of land by such a forme of Civil Government as by voluntary consent of all or the greatest part of them shall be found most suteable to their Estates and Conditions." They might legislate as they liked on civil and criminal matters, provided that their laws were "Conformable to the Lawes of England so farr as the nature and Constitution of tht place will admitt." The patent specifically gave Providence Plantations the power to appoint magistrates and inflict whatever punishments the colony's laws prescribed. Seemingly, the document gave the colonists all they could want. Yet it met an opposition on the island that prevented full inauguration of a new government for almost three years.[4]

Virtually all that could be done before May 1647 was to hold public meetings of freemen. Little is known about them, apart from the choice of a few officers, who wielded no real power.[5]

Threats from outsiders undermined internal opposition to the charter. Both Plymouth and Massachusetts tried to prevent a genuine government of Providence Plantations from forming, and claimed parts of its territory, but they failed to agree on a division. Further, the United Colonies of New England (all except Rhode Island) threatened to send an army against the Narragansett Indians in 1645. Still, Coddington explored the possibility of allying

Aquidneck with Massachusetts or even placing it under the Bay Colony's jurisdiction. He styled himself Governor of the island state, but his local support fell away. He had to change course after news arrived that the Warwick commission specifically required Massachusetts to respect the patent of 1644 and firmly included Warwick in its jurisdiction.[6]

Deliberations in 1646 and 1647 led to the first, soon-revised plans for a real colonial government. Unknown men in the island towns devised the basic features of organization, derived from the Aquidneck state, and a code of laws. These men conferred with people in Providence and called a meeting of the freemen to consider their proposals at a General Court of Election to be held at Portsmouth in May 1647. Because a majority of the freemen attended, they decided they had "full power to transact." They went on to approve the plans previously formulated, perhaps with modifications.[7]

At the outset, the freemen adopted a conception of authority like that in the Aquidneck state, with the same contradictions. They acknowledged an English source of legitimacy validated by popular consent and also declared "that the forme of Goverment established in Providence Plantacions is DE-MOCRATICALL that is to say A Government held by free and voluntarie consent of all or the greater parte of the free Inhabitants."[8]

Accordingly, the freemen would make the decisions of the colonial government—at least in theory. In fact, almost of necessity they resorted to a representative form of government. They elected the colony's magistrates at an annual court of election in May, to which men who did not attend might "send their votes sealed." The secret ballot was a radical measure at the time. The meetings of the General Court between elections were to be legally meetings of the body of freemen, but the court's business actually would be transacted by twenty-four commissioners, six chosen by each town.[9]

To reconcile theory with convenience, the freemen designed the first of several experiments with procedures to give themselves direct power over legislation—a system of initiative and referendum. A town might propose a new law by majority vote. Then the town recorder would send a copy of it to each of the other towns to be voted upon. If a majority of the total votes cast favored the proposal, it would be declared a law until the next General Assembly (court of election), when a general vote on the proposal would be taken. Ordinarily, though, the commissioners would propose laws and send them to the towns to be voted on by the freemen. If a majority favored a law, as determined by the colony's General Recorder, it would be in force until the next General Assembly, awaiting a final determination there. These cumbersome methods were abandoned after one year and partly reintroduced later, but they expressed the initial, very literal use of democracy.[10]

In addition to the twenty-four commissioners, the colony had a small slate of officers chosen by the freemen at large. The chief officer had the title of President. Like the Governor in the Aquidneck regime, he was an all-purpose head of state. He had powers as a justice of the peace, as did the four assist-ants, one to be chosen from each town. They also served as coroners within their towns. Together, the five magistrates composed the bench of the General Court of Trials, with civil and criminal jurisdiction. The remaining general officers—General Recorder (secretary and clerk of the court), Public Treasurer, General Sergeant, and later water bailiffs—all had judicial functions, though the recorder and treasurer had others as well.[11]

The General Court faced a delicate question in defining the powers of the towns. A preliminary plan mentioned granting charters to them. Providence approved this idea and insisted that each town somehow have its own judiciary and power to choose and install its "perticular towne Officers" and that there "be noe inter mixture, of Generall, and perticuler Of[ficers], but that all, may knowe th[eir]e bounds, and Limits."[12]

Sensitive to such localism, the assembled freemen acted cautiously at first. They postponed the subject of town charters and ineffectually tried to direct town government as well as honor local autonomy. The General Court assigned all parts of its territory inhabited by English people to a town, though it allowed the Pawtuxet dissidents to choose whatever jurisdiction they would. The assembly required each town to do such things as appoint two surveyors of highways and designate times for mending roads, organize archery practice for men and boys, record earmarks of livestock, and choose a town council. Compliance with these stipulations was sporadic at best.[13]

On the whole, the freemen adopted the militia system of the island state. The freemen created a new organ in the town council, however, which would have a future well beyond their imagining. They saw the council first as an agency to supervise military measures, but the towns, as far as their records show, took the military regulations casually.[14]

The Providence Plantations government most obviously went beyond the island state by adopting a code of basic laws, maritime as well as criminal and civil. Like its forerunner on Aquidneck, however, the General Court drew heavily on traditional sources, for reasons that appeared briefly in the preamble to the civil and criminal code. There, the legislators endorsed the proposition "that Law is made or brought to Light." That is, law put into specific formulation the eternal principles of justice. Moreover, implicit in the sources used for the colony's code lay a more extensive endorsement of the belief that law arises from the common experience of humankind in the light of unchanging rules of right. So laws of different origins might be selected through rational choice to fit a given time and place.[15]

The legislators dealt with maritime affairs quite simply by adopting "the Sea Lawes, otherwise call'd the Lawes of Oleron," which meant the law merchant as used in England. They gave "the cheif officers in the Towne . . . powre to summon the Court and determine the cause or causes presented."[16] The new colonial government had every reason to adopt an existing mercantile law rather than invent one: commerce had to follow the practice of trading circles where the merchants wanted to do business.

The civil and criminal code that bears the date of 1647 ventured beyond a single source. While most of its provisions came from English law, probably from two digests rather than statute books, two came from the Bible and two from proverbs. Far from a complete slate even in the amended version of about 1654, which is all that survives, the laws covered constitutional points and many criminal categories but contained little on such topics as property and bonds or the court procedures. Very likely, the legislators expected the judges to adopt English usages as needed. Unfortunately, no evidence remains to show when, if, or how, the code was used in the early years.[17]

Unfinished though it was, the framework of organization and laws for the new colony made in 1647 provided a plausible start. It refined the model in the Aquidneck state and added the basic statutes on which to build.

Division and Reunion

The brave beginnings faltered within a year. Internal quarrels tore at the colony and towns. Individual inhabitants defied or ignored the central government. Towns sometimes neglected to choose colonial officials. Men chosen to office sometimes declined to serve or were excluded. The system of initiative and referendum was abandoned, only to be restored twice under modified terms. The island wanted legislation by the freemen at large; the mainland wanted a representative system, by which it would offset its disadvantages in population by equal votes in the Court of Commissioners. Three towns obtained charters allowing them self-government and then generated theories to justify their autonomy as essential to the construction of the colonial government—in short, developing a rudimentary theory of federalism.[18] Dismayed or disgruntled inhabitants continued to seek connections with other jurisdictions, such as Massachusetts or Plymouth. Those colonies, however, disagreed among themselves on which should annex the Narragansett settlements. Coddington procured a charter for Aquidneck alone with himself as governor and preciptitated a division of the Providence Plantations government into two parts, island and mainland. Even after his patent was nullified, the two sections remained at odds over policies, private disputes, and the procedure to reunite.

The events of 1648 to 1654 need not be followed in detail. Developments flowing out of the revolution in England, the intentions of the neighboring colonies, the dangers feared by the colonists from the numerous Indians near Narragansett Bay, divergent individual ideas and interests—all were manifest. Less visible sources of weakness existed as well. The lack of a specific prescription of organs of government in the charter allowed the element of consent to be overly clear and the ease of constitutional change overly great. The conflicting radical and traditionalist tendencies within the early Rhode Island towns expanded into disputes on constituting the colony. The absence of a collective purpose, other than guarding religious liberty, made the inhabitants feel free to divide or desert the government when it failed to do or be exactly what they wished.

Instructions from England accomplished little. After the schism touched off by Coddington's patent, emissaries from the two regimes claiming to continue the government under the original charter rushed to London to seek revocation of his grant. One of them, William Dyer, returned early in 1653 with an order from the Council of State addressed to leading men on the island, telling the magistrates and freemen to carry on government according to the will of Parliament, which presumably meant under the charter of 1644. Dyer and his supporters quite reasonably regarded the instructions as addressed to themselves and thought the regime on Aquidneck was the true continuation of the colonial government under the charter, so they argued that the two mainland towns should give up their separate government. The towns divided bitterly over this proposal, with the majority of freemen insisting that theirs was the true charter government and that their preference for a representative system must be the basis for reunion.[19] After months of deadlock, the island officials argued that neither side need submit to the other. Rather, the freemen could meet and reconstitute their government without deciding which part had continued the one as originally formed.[20]

This plan eventually succeeded. The superior weight of wealth and population on the island settled the argument, though other things helped. Some subsidiary disputes conveniently drifted into oblivion, while a new fear of attack on religious liberty and a new determination to keep outsiders from getting Narragansett land inspired solidarity among the original towns. Further communications from England strengthened Dyer's position. Finally, a General Assembly was held at Warwick on August 31, 1654. It adopted articles of agreement that endorsed the conduct of public business and adjudication by the various colonial governments that had operated during the past few years—even Coddington's, except for the time since Dyer's return with news of the revocation of its patent—and solemnly reestablished the colonial government almost as originally framed. The reunited colony resumed regular conduct of public business and called a special Court of Elections for September. The court elected Roger Williams as President, an office he held by reelection until May 1657.[21]

On one topic, the direct authority of the freemen to initiate or review legislation, the restored government conceded a point to the mainland towns, only to strike a compromise later with the islanders. It gave the town commissioners full power as representatives, which made the small mainland communities equal to those on Aquidneck. The island towns, which had over two-thirds of the voters, labored to restore a referendum. They succeeded in 1658, when the Court of Commissioners gave the towns twenty days after each legislative session to vote on any new law. If a majority of the freemen opposed it, it would have no force. Even with retreat from the original plan to this less cumbersome one, no record survives to show a town resorting to the procedure to abolish a law.[22]

Reunion remained precarious for a few years after 1654, however, because many old forms of divisiveness persisted. Some men objected to specific terms. Coddington was for a time unreconciled. No real loyalty to the colony prevented quarrels from being disruptive, and the freemen remained at liberty to change their form of government at pleasure. However, they agreed on the centrifugal policy of protecting town autonomy. Some men put private interests ahead of acceptance of the legality of any government. William Harris of Pawtuxet caused a stir by delivering an essay to the Court of Election in May 1655, arguing against "all earthly powers, parliaments, laws, charters, magistrates, prisons, punishments, rates, yea, against all kings and princes."[23]

Most of these threats to solidarity were slowly subdued with passage of time, a little help from English authority, the death of a few bitter men, persuasion, and consignment of touchy topics such as the Harris essay, to committees to ponder them. For example, a message from Oliver Cromwell urging unity in the colony allowed Coddington to save face as he bowed to an English ruler rather than to his neighbors; arbitrators resolved some of his disputes with them, and the colonial government dropped actions against him that had pended for several years.[24]

Difficulties lingered in the web of quarrels that included the Gortonian claims against Massachusetts, the ill will of certain Indians, and the attachment of Warwick's two coastal Indian villages and several Pawtuxet men to Boston's jurisdiction. Diplomatic efforts produced no results, but an odd incident did in an oblique way. Roger Williams, as President of Providence Plantations, urged Massachusetts to proceed against one of its Pawtuxet adherents, Richard Chasmore, who was accused of buggery with heifers. When Massachusetts tried to apprehend him, men in Providence interfered forcibly and tried to keep the accused under their colony's jurisdiction. A confusing fracas followed, but in the end, the episode showed that Massachusetts could not exercise the powers of government in Pawtuxet, and the people there quietly transfered their allegiance to Providence Plantations.[25]

With the success of reunion, the kaleidoscopic changes in the colony government came to an end. Of course, lesser changes continued, and the Providence Plantations government remained weak. Old conflicts within the colony continued, new ones appeared, external events prompted new ideas, and the colonial government had little except its modest quota of inertia to prevent the freemen from reshaping it continually. They had begun to take for granted the form of President, assistants, and equal delegations of commissioners from the largely autonomous towns. This simple form provided executive and judicial officers—indeed, a more elaborate judiciary, when added to the town courts, than was essential to a population of around two thousand at most. The judges had the air of deriving their authority from the English state. The system gave the freemen a voice in making laws. It let them elect all their officers. It recognized the primary importance of the towns. It plainly embodied the principle of government by consent, a principle the freemen had embraced by choice or necessity when establishing it. Perhaps most important, it imposed no restraint that they could not ignore when determined to do so. Laws and judicial decisions could be ineffectual, yet they served adequately for most routine purposes. Instead of disputes on basic principles, such as the authority of magistrates, the Rhode Islanders turned to legalistic bickering over procedures, defects in statutes, or jurisdictions of town as against central tribunals.

Yet the colonial government suffered from contradictions that the English charter could not entirely reconcile. As voters, the freemen were equals, whereas other indexes of standing in their lives often embodied inequality. Equality was emphasized by those who insisted that the reunion could be accomplished only by a meeting of the freemen at large, not just delegations from towns; by those who persistently favored laws to allow a general referendum on all statutes; and by the broadening franchise, which gave political rights to two out of three men by 1655. At the same time, however, the colonial government increasingly rested on equality among towns rather than among freemen; and within towns, distinctions were hardening, based on differential land rights.[26]

In practical terms, too, there were limits to equality even among freemen. Some held higher offices much oftener than others did. The older linkage had been strong in the Aquidneck towns between the exercise of power, the franchise, the grants of large lots, and wealth before immigration. On the mainland, the first settlers maintained for a time a superiority in land that often coincided with general standing in public affairs.[27] These stratifications persisted and were followed by comparable ones. Such social facts could be accepted and even used within a structure of hypothetical legal equality, provided the participants agreed on how they should fit. Disagreements, however, kept breaking out. The equalities that mattered most were within social classifications, and only one of those was coterminous with the active body politic.

The Royal Charter and Its Implementation

Most of the thinking behind the charter of 1663 has been lost, but a sufficient reason for seeking a new foundation for government was provided by the restoration of Charles II. With nothing but Parliament's authority, the colony needed the king's sanction, and it needed his endorsement of its borders before neighboring colonies could secure his approval for extending theirs. Yet when Dr. John Clarke acted for Providence Plantations in London, he sought more than confirmation of the first charter. Presumably following instructions, he obtained a specification of the rudiments of a constitution, a change of official name, stipulations of inhabitants' rights, definition of the colony's place in the English empire, and redefined borders. To his dismay, Rhode Island officials failed to back him soon enough to get his work done before John Winthrop Jr., at the instigation of his partners in a Boston-based syndicate of men organized to get land in the Narragansett country, procured a charter for Connecticut extending its jurisdiction to Narragansett Bay. Clarke still obtained a good boundary but had to accept an arbitration award that gave rise to endless trouble.[28] Many of the charter's objectives are clear, such as the intention to form a more vigorous and centralized government than the colony had had—and more so than it managed to operate.

The charter created a corporation under the name "The Governor and Company of the English Collonies of Rhode-Island and Providence Plantations, in New England, in America." Its members, the freemen and their successors, would be "a bodie corporate and politique, in ffact and name."[29] The political entity was often called the Governor and Company, by which was meant either the chief officers or the whole body of freemen.

The document prescribed a form of government rather like those of Connecticut and Massachusetts. A core of magistrates would have broad powers, from administrative to judicial, and would act as an all-purpose emergency council. When joined by representatives of the towns in a General Assembly, the combined magistrates and deputies would wield even wider authority. The magistrates included a Governor, Deputy Governor, and ten assistants elected annually at a General Court or Assembly in May by majority vote of the freemen attending. The towns would no longer send equal numbers of representatives. Rather, Newport would send six; the other original towns, four each; and any new ones, two each. The towns would choose deputies twice a year, in May and October, or oftener if necessary. Why the Aquidneck freemen gave up their preference for direct democracy remains a mystery. Surely, they supported the new system, because it could not have appeared in the charter without their approval. Maybe the gradual weakening of direct legislative power in the hands of the freemen had reflected a shift of sentiment, perhaps abetted by practicality as population increased. Possibly, the retreat from town equality in the representative assembly compensated for the complete abandonment of the referendum.

The General Assembly had broad powers, administrative and judicial as well as legislative. It was to appoint other civil and military officers and replace them as needed, admit new freemen, enact laws, establish courts of justice and serve as an appelate court, regulate elections, determine towns' boundaries and prescribe the forms of local government, buy Indian title to land, and generally control relations with the natives. In all proceedings, the General Assembly was to act by majority vote, although the majority had to include either the Governor or the Deputy Governor and six assistants. Between sessions of the Assembly, the Governor (or in his absence, the Deputy Governor) together with a majority of the assistants could set up military organizations. This arrangement allowed for emergency measures without threatening the Assembly's basic powers.

The new charter gave the colony a place in English law and the imperial structure. Following time-honored practice, it required that colonial statutes be as consonant with English law as the condition of the colony would allow. The charter ruled that Rhode Islanders might trade with England subject to English law and at all times would enjoy "all libertyes and immunityes of ffree and naturall subjects within any the dominions of [the Crown] . . . as if they . . . were borne within the realme of England." The "waste land" and coastal waters were to remain available for the king's subjects engaged in fishing. Rhode Islanders were to abide by English rules in privateering or suffer penalties for piracy. The king explicitly acknowledged that the Narragansett Indians were under his protection and required Rhode Island to notify neighboring colonies whenever it went to war with Indians and forbade the neighboring colonies to invade Rhode Island to attack Indians within its borders. And in disputes with other colonies, Rhode Island might appeal to the Crown for adjudication.[30]

In one conspicuous way, the authorization of religious freedom, the charter exempted Rhode Island from a fundamental strand in English law. It did so, however, in terms partly derived from the king's words in the Declaration of Breda. Charles II authorized the colony "to hold forth a livelie experiment, that a most flourishing civill state may stand and best bee maintained, . . . with a full libertie in religious concernments; and that true pietye rightly grounded upon gospell principles, will give the best and greatest security to sovereigntye, and will lay in the hearts of men the strongest obligations to true loialltye." He approved the famous provision, where the phrases from his declaration were used, "that noe person within the . . . colonye, at any tyme hereafter, shall bee any wise molested, punished, disquieted, or call[ed] in question, for any differences in opinione in matters of religion, and doe not actually disturb the civill peace of our sayd colony; but that all and everye persons and persons may, from tyme to tyme, and at all tymes hereafter, freelye and fully have and enjoye his and theire owne judgments and consciences, in matters of religious concernments, . . . they behaving themselves peaceablie and quietlie, and not useinge this libertie to lycentiousness and profaneness, nor the civill injurye or outward disturbance of others." He exempted them from the usual requirement to attend "the publique exercise of religion, according to the litturgy, formes and ceremonyes of the Church of England."[31]

Long and detailed though it was, the charter failed to yield the intended result during the seventeenth century. The Governor and Council seldom acted vigorously as an executive or emergency committee. The colony could not control purchases of land from Indians. The neighbors rarely observed the clauses on intercolonial relations.

Some stipulations on the form of government were imprecise and engendered dispute. Notably, the document seemed to imply a General Assembly of magistrates and deputies meeting together. Yet the rule on qualified majority votes implied the possibility of bicameralism. The officials kept the unicameral form for over thirty years but moved away from it in procedure. By 1667 the Governor and Council began meeting as a separate body in emergencies for administrative and military business. Light attendance and other disturbing elements in 1672 prompted the Assembly to rule that a majority of the deputies as well as a majority of the magistrates must be present for all decisions on "weighty matters wherein the Kings Honor is most concerned and the peopls Antient Right and Libertys most jeoperded for want of mature councill." Also, for any money bill to pass, a majority of the deputies must favor it. To justify these rules, the Assembly appealed to the example of the House of Common as the counterpart of the deputies and to the English Petition of Right of 1628.[32]

In other ways the freemen went beyond the charter, often toward continuing the previous government. Because the freemen at large were to elect the magistrates, the men of the island towns could dominate the Assembly by their majority. To prevent this, the General Assembly decided to apportion five of the twelve magistrates to Newport, three to Providence, and two each to Portsmouth and Warwick. Thus, at least two would live in each town and provide the services of justices of the peace. The Assembly also decided to allow votes by proxy, leaving the towns to decide how to conduct proxy voting. It added basic officers, which it appointed or let the freemen elect: a secretary of state called the General Recorder, a chief peace officer called the General Sergeant, a General Attorney, and a General Treasurer. For each meeting the Assembly named a moderator and a clerk, who usually was the General Recorder. These positions were carried over from the Providence Plantations government without any recorded formal decision.[33]

The first General Assembly began to regulate the judiciary. It decided that the General Court of Trials should hold two sessions annually in Newport, with the bench composed of at least six assistants, later reduced to four, and either the Governor or Deputy Governor. As the Assembly enacted nothing on the competence of the tribunal, presumably it was the same as before. The law provided also that the same judges, except that three Assistants would suffice, might be summoned as a special court between sessions to hear urgent cases brought by merchants or seamen. Although no law required it, Providence, Portsmouth, and Warwick ceased electing magistrates and so stopped holding their town courts. Instead, the Assembly allowed

Providence and Warwick to have local courts in the form of a tribunal to convene once a year in each town, with at least three assistants on the bench, to decide on civil cases involving up to ten pounds in debt or damages, subject to appeal to the General Court of Trials.[34] In other ways, the Assembly gave new towns their local courts.

In effect, changes in the judiciary overruled the original town charters. Not only did the former town courts go out of existence, but also the Assembly made the resident assistants ex officio members of the town councils, leaving the freemen to choose enough more to bring the total to six.[35]

Later, the Assembly ruled on who might be a freeman. It could do so according to the charter, but it had to respect town autonomy. It decided to admit "all men of Competante Estate and of Civell Conversation," a formula advocated by a royal commission in 1665. It would admit a man only when he applied and brought testimony to his status or when he was proposed by the chief officer of the place where he lived. The Assembly could not retain central control of the franchise, however. After some squabbles in the towns, it had to allow them to admit as freemen for local government anybody they regarded as fit for office.[36]

Likewise, the charter gave the colonial government power to create a military force. The General Assembly or, between its sessions, the Governor and Council, could choose officers. The Assembly could write general laws, but the Governor and Council had full power to meet emergencies. Still, vague terms in the charter suggested a firmer central direction than the colony actually required.[37]

In fact, only at the behest of the royal commission did the Assembly in 1665 make a show of ending the decentralized militia system that had developed earlier. Even on that occasion, the legislators bent to citizen apathy by reducing the prescribed training days from eight to six and letting each company elect its own officers. They smuggled in more local discretion by leaving towns to pay the men for service and keep arsenals—burdens the towns may well have shirked. Weaknesses appeared in the system at once, but measures to remedy them did little. From time to time, statutes tinkered with the rules or prescribed unworkable schemes to impose discipline. Perhaps the most noteworthy change of policy, first made officially in 1673, was to exempt conscientious pacifists from combat. What little evidence there is on how the militia laws were observed shows disregard of requirements on training and armaments, failure to impose fines for neglect, and even casual disuse of standard commissions for officers.[38]

The new government also attended to a few civic rituals and forms in legal documents. But the boldest decision, actually allowed by the artful language of the charter, was to sanction substitutes for oaths of office as a means to accomodate tender consciences.[39] The colony never required an oath, an astonishing provision at the time.

The freemen also demanded the itineracy of the major governmental organs through all the towns in the colony. The Court of Commissioners had been flexible in the location of its sessions. Though Newport was the home base of the colonial government, other towns insisted that the General Court of Trials and the General Assembly meet in them almost as often as in the capital for the convenience of their inhabitants. In 1669 and again in 1673, Warwick broached the possibility of having courts sit "by Course in Each respective towne so farr as the charter will allow as antiently they used to be That so the Antient rights and priveledges of the ffreemen be not Lost." Providence made the same request in 1679. Though the court remained in Newport for the time being, the General Assembly, beginning in October 1681, met in the smaller towns fairly often, though not for the annual election in May.[40]

When the new government organized, it had to reestablish the foundation of its laws. As allowed by the charter, the first Assembly declared that all the existing laws should remain in force for the time being except those in contradiction to the new charter, such as the referendum law. The following October the legislators chose the first of two committees to recommend which laws should be continued.[41] No report survives from either of these committees. Probably the older laws were modified from time to time, both explicitly in the recorded deliberations of the Assembly and by unrecorded votes entered as annotations on the records.

Years of Feeble Government

The colonial government almost at once met frustration. It faced resistance to taxation on the mainland, various internal disputes, and opposition to its jurisdiction over the Narragansett country. The opposing claims to that region came from Connecticut, which insisted on the terms of its own charter, which extended the borders to Narragansett Bay, and at most would honor the subsequent agreement between Clarke and Winthrop that allowed residents of the disputed territory to vote on which colonial government to accept.[42] When the dispute had barely begun, the royal commission tried to end it in 1665 by ruling that the land south of Warwick should be in neither colony but instead should be the King's Province, administered by Rhode Island until the king should decide otherwise. Connecticut strenuously opposed this ruling. Rhode Island wanted it revised into a still more favorable decision but never got anyone in London to make the change. So Rhode Island, as a practical matter, held fast on the validity of the royal commission's award, even after another royal commission tried to transfer control to Connecticut.[43]

A long contest over property taxes began in 1664, when Warwick balked at paying to reimburse Dr. John Clarke for his expenses in procuring the charter. At first, the town objected to its share of the colonial rate, because it had paid part of Roger Williams's way to England to oppose Coddington's patent and the island towns had not, and to the total amount because of suspicions that the figure was padded and because Clarke had received money for preaching in London. (Gortonians, like many others in the colony, thought ministers should not be paid.) Moreover, none of Warwick's representatives had been present when the Assembly voted for the rate. Then the town complained that no tax should have been apportioned among the towns until the boundaries were defined—Warwick claimed two areas under dispute—and added that its citizens had been less favored than others in access to new land.[44]

Soon sympathizers in Providence refused to pay, too. Characteristically, they resorted to political theory to defend their position. Roger Williams reported, "Some say they will pay if all doe: Some are against all Government and Charters and Corporacions: Some are not so and yet cry out against thieves and Robbers who take any thing from them against their wills." He pointed out the advantages of the charter that gave peace and liberty, freedom of religion and protection of the law, security from taxation except as authorized by elected representatives, and generally, "Libertie of Societie or Corporacion: of sending or being sent to the Gen[eral] Assembly: of choosing and being chosen to all offices and of making or repealing all lawes and Constitutions among us." To survive, the government must have a revenue. The clerk of the Assembly added his arguments for paying the tax.[45] Warwick, also characteristically, resorted to arguments based on English law but agreed to colonial policy after both town and General Assembly had executed some changes of course.[46]

The taxation controversy revealed a number of things about the new government. First, the General Assembly could not write a law and count on universal obedience. Second, it could get along on revenue from the island towns. (The only other tax imposed by colonial law was an excise on wine and liquor, collected by and for the towns.) The officials got what recompense they received from fees, except for the deputies, who were paid by their towns, if at all. Third, with neither funds nor unquestioning obedience by the citizens, the colony could not exert much force. It could pass declarative laws, adjudicate for parties willing to abide by its judgments, and speak for the colony to the empire and other colonies. That is, it could do little more than words could accomplish.

The events of 1672, furthermore, showed that changing or distracting the policy of the colonial government could be easy. The Assembly abruptly gave up militancy against Connecticut and the land claims backed by that colony in the Narragansett country. The voters put at least two advocates of concessions into the roster of magistrates and yet tried to elect as Governor a man on the opposite side, William Brenton. When he refused the job, the Assembly chose a man of still different leanings. Deputies from the towns included an assortment of views. Attempts to reduce this election to a simple opposition of sides have been unsuccessful.[47] Rather, the episode showed how mercurial or accessible to persuasion the General Assembly was. And on the dealings with Connecticut and Narragansett land claims, the government continued to waver, though it generally refused to surrender anything and so maintained a deadlock.

Such was the condition of the Rhode Island government when its control over its ostensible jurisdiction was overwhelmed by King Philip's War. That conflict brought an invading army from the adjacent colonies, a long series of campaigns by Rhode Island Indians against English Rhode Islanders and by Connecticut men (White and Indian) against Rhode Island Indians, a flight of the Whites and some Indians on the mainland to Aquidneck, the slaughter or farther flight of most of the other Indians, and an opportunistic response by the magistrates in Newport.

At the outset, the General Assembly planned neutrality but could not maintain their position. The government could not keep out invaders and prudently did not try. Soon the Governor was giving small kinds of aid to the belligerant colonies. Later, the Assembly set up a commission to organize the patrol of Narragansett Bay and post watches on the island, while other men fortified likely landing places in Portsmouth. It planned a garrison at Providence but accomplished nothing much before the Indian attack nearly demolished that town along with all other White settlements on the mainland. Then Rhode Island men began to join the final campaigns near Mount Hope, using the island as a base. At times, the Assembly could not cooperate with towns on local defense and accomodated to fact by giving retroactive approval to measures taken by "Towne Councills, Councills of War, etc., with other private orders from officers, and other ministers of justice in this jurisdiction." The end of the horrendous conflict left Connecticut forces militarily dominant in the Narragansett country.[48]

The record changed superficially for a few years after 1677, until imperial policy brought a short end to Rhode Island's independence. The colonial officials conducted themselves capably if not elegantly in dealing with a royal commission appointed during the war to settle conflicts over land between William Harris and the towns of Providence and Warwick. That is, the officials put a tolerably good face on their stalling and evasions to avoid executing the commission's rulings in favor of Harris. The General Assembly also managed to launch the town of East Greenwich in 1678, a major accomplishment considering Connecticut's opposition and military capacity. The Assembly began to receive deputies from that new town as well as two more, Jamestown and New Shoreham (Block Island), signs that the colonial government was gaining practical importance. It even began to back or regulate local government when it could do so without arousing controversy, thus establishing useful precedents.[49]

The most interesting case occurred when the Assembly stepped in to settle a controversy in Providence over the power to exclude a newcomer. The
town meeting tried to exercise the old power of a community to decide
against receiving a man it did not like. The unwelcome person would not
leave, however, so the meeting consigned the business to the council, then
reconsidered, and appealed to the Assembly for a ruling. The legislature took
the opportunity to define what a town council might do. It might require that
a newcomer post bond to ensure that the town would not be at any expense
if he should prove unable to provide for himself, or it might exclude him altogether and, if he refused to depart when duly warned, get any magistrate or
justice or conservator of the peace to issue a warrant to the town constable to
eject him. Without actually abolishing the traditional function of the town as
a body politic to admit or exclude would-be members on whatever grounds it
chose, the Assembly transferred effective discretion from the town meeting
to the council and limited discretion there. The colonial government even
managed to exert compulsion on Providence to satisfy a debt the town owed
to the General Treasurer in his official capacity.[50]

Such harbingers of effectiveness came to naught as imperial officials resolved on a wholesale change in the colonial government of New England to
put the territory under a single viceregal regime. Though the General Assembly tried a few gestures of cooperation with London, it was powerless to
deflect this plan.[51] Soon the Crown's actions against the Massachusetts charter portended similar action against Rhode Island's, to be followed by some
new arrangement dictated in Whitehall.

Rhode Island prudently sought to leave a legacy of town authority. In
1684 the Assembly passed an act in somewhat vague terms divesting the colony of its charter rights over divided or undivided land in the towns, relinquishing all claims to "the first freemen of the said Towns, their associates
and derivatives, and their heires, and assignes, for ever." Then, in 1686, the
Assembly wrote another act to empower the towns to set five days annually
for town meetings, at one of which the freemen would "elect such and so
many town officers as they shall think meet for the managing of the affairs of
their towns," and to hold other meetings as needed.[52] Quite likely, the intent
was to create what would be seen as privileges for the towns, privileges that
they could argue might not be taken away except by due process of law. As
was characteristic of the time, the Assembly's actions paired collective rights
to self-government with collective rights to land.

Into the Dominion of New England

The storm hit in 1686. Rhode Island decided not to resist the loss of its separate existence and inclusion in the Dominion of New England. First, the
commission to Joseph Dudley as President of the Council of the Dominion

put the King's Province under the new jurisdiction. Then news arrived that the monarchy had brought proceedings against the corporation under a writ of *quo warranto*. As a measure of Rhode Island's importance in the reshuffle of imperial administration, nobody informed the officials in Newport of the suit until time had elapsed for a reply to it. They wrote a submissive letter to the king, pleading for perpetuation of the colony's liberty in religion and permission for Newport to remain a port.[53]

Rhode Island became a county in the Dominion of New England, which at its greatest extent embraced English settlements from Maine to the Delaware River but broke apart before its government could settle into routine. The new jurisdiction lasted only about two years in Rhode Island, yet it beguiled a coterie of men there for much longer. They liked its authoritarian quality, its bestowal of power on the gentlemen of the place, as they esteemed themselves, without sullying them with a requirement of being elected.

Perhaps they also liked the absence of formal confinements in the conduct of public affairs. Improvisation was as marked as devotion to system, whether in the highest operations at Boston or at the county or town level. The Dominion never stabilized a means of legislation, for instance. At first, the President and Council made or revived laws by decree, then the Governor, Sir Edmund Andros, began acting almost by himself, while mentioning the prospect of an elected assembly. The new regime was intended to be centralized and even militaristic, as a means to carry out policies set in London rather than Boston. The gentlemen who held high offices expected to use them for their own ends and turned against the Dominion when they were thwarted by Governor Andros. Yet they might yearn for a counterpart in which they would have their way.[54]

The new government in Rhode Island virtually reversed the tone of the one under the charter, yet it was as nonsystematic as the central authority at Boston. When county government finally began operating after almost a year's delay, it was carried on by a General Quarter Sessions and Inferior Court of Common Pleas with ten justices, Francis Brinley presiding. The court exercised administrative and fiscal powers as well as judicial. It even wrote local laws and levied taxes.[55]

The county court, however, had to share powers both with its own subordinates and with the central governor and council. Officials at all three levels could impose taxes, for example. Likewise, all three set requirements for the towns, which remained a part of the apparatus though a minor one in theory. The governor and council made rules on town government, such as restricting meetings to one a year and requiring the voters to elect selectmen. The county court also chose town officers, allowed some of its appointees (the constables) to join with the local justices of the peace in naming surveyors of highways, and required town meetings to elect assessors. The governor and council engaged in reviews of town land rights and made awards of land within them to various petitioners.[56] This was no system.

Besides, giving orders was hardly the same as getting them carried out. At least three towns—Providence, Portsmouth, and Warwick—held more town meetings than authorized.[57] Westerly (renamed Haversham) found it could carry on extensive self-government. Towns resisted taxes imposed by the county court, beginning in June 1688. Constables did not call meetings of town voters to choose rate makers; rate makers did not serve; constables did not collect taxes. The court vainly ordered another tax, this time to be levied by the selectmen in the various towns. By the time results of this plan could have been known, the Dominion had fallen before a swift revolution in Boston in April 1689.[58] If this brief experiment proved anything, it was the futility of centralized and authoritarian government where it ran contrary to what inertia of tradition there was.

The Dominion brought a subordination to the king beyond anything imagined when Rhode Islanders had appealed to the throne before 1686. They had sought charters and resolutions of disputes but not direct control or even the disorganized control under Andros. The Dominion obviously failed to do what the previous regime had done after a fashion—make laws by consent, erect a judiciary, stabilize governmental forms, and serve the towns and land speculators in their dealings with outsiders. Nevertheless, though the viceregal government imposed an unacceptable tie to the monarchy, everyone wanted a tie of some kind. Many men learned a new lesson in the value of the charter: it could condition the link to the parent country so as to protect local interests.

Charter versus Anarchy

After the overthrow of Andros, Rhode Island fell into confusion rather like the earlier episode when the Providence Plantations government split. This time the confusion was compounded by an international war with France. The conflict soon brought privateers to the mouth of Narragansett Bay and cut off communications with London. On their own, Rhode Islanders had to try again to create the government they needed and hope for approval from Whitehall. They divided among three procedures. Some people wanted to keep the framework of the Dominion pending orders from England. That way the link to the Crown would remain clear in formal terms. Others favored a makeshift built around the essential military core, possibly with acknowledgment of the Dominion's theoretical legality. Still others, who ultimately succeeded, favored resuming government under the charter without waiting for authorization from the Crown. Their prospects were in doubt for about twenty years and particularly poor around 1694.

Action began simply. Two men, probably Walter Clarke and John Coggeshall, invited "severall prinsipall persons" to confer at Newport on May 1,

1689, on how to meet the emergency and consider "wheither our ancient priviledges and former method may not be best to insist upon."[59] The men who attended styled themselves variously as an assembly of freemen, a court of election, or a general assembly of the colony of Rhode Island and Providence Plantations and King's Province. In the last capacity, they decided to resume government under the second charter, rather as the government under the first charter had been put back together in 1654. This time, however, they justified themselves by an artful declaration to assert a relation to the empire rather than to smooth over disagreements among the towns. The self-styled assembly claimed that the colony had governed itself to general satisfaction; that the procedure under the writ of *quo warranto* never had been completed, so no formal revocation of the charter had occurred; and that the colony had voluntarily abandoned use of its privileges in acquiescence to the former king's wishes. Then they claimed that a confirmation of religious liberty by James II amounted to endorsement of the special mission of their colony and by implication its powers.[60] Thus, the erstwhile king's formula for religious freedom or toleration was presented as a contradiction of his policy on imperial government!

The impromptu General Assembly tried to restart the charter government by picking up where it had left off, with the same laws and most of the same officials. The professed object was to restore orderly administration and prepare "for defense from any Intestine Commotion or fforreighn Invasion" — that is, to serve the empire's purposes, if not by the appointed methods.[61]

Responses to this plan varied. Some people accepted the return to the charter. A few pacifists who did so declined to hold public office, however, when the war with France bore down on the colony. Some people tried to straddle the fence, such as those in Portsmouth who wrote legal documents describing the place as in "the county or colony of Rhode Island and Providence Plantations." Several towns, especially Jamestown, Kingstown, and Westerly, declined to act as local units under the revived colonial government.[62]

Some men actively opposed it. They were led at first by two, Richard Smith and John Fones, who had been justices in the county court under the Dominion and had claims to land in the Narragansett country that Connecticut backed and Rhode Island denied. After consulting with Major Edward Palmes of New London, they wrote to men at Providence and Warwick to call a meeting of representatives of the towns between the Connecticut and Blackstone Rivers to confer on military measures. Though the proposal attracted a little favor, the town fathers in Warwick concluded that the object of Smith and Fones was "wholly to subvert the present Goverment at least on the main Land and set up another by the sword."[63] Whatever the plan, it required repudiating the Rhode Island government and probably took the Dominion as its inspiration.

Opposition, however, could have other ends. To get money and ammunition and a garrison, Block Island hinted in 1691 that it might have to look elsewhere if the Rhode Island government could not help its defense. More important, Francis Brinley of Newport and some other men began schemes to get a royal governor or inclusion of Rhode Island in a larger colony.[64]

The annual election and General Assembly in May 1690 gave a false hope for success for the charter government. Deputies appeared from all towns except Jamestown. The Assembly voted to impose a tax for the king's military campaigns, however, which brought back the colony's troubles of earlier years. Only the towns attacked by French privateers, Newport and New Shoreham, even levied it. Warwick again said its share was too large. The Assembly futilely appointed men to apportion the tax within each town where the town refused and made every town treasurer ex officio "a Deputy to the Generall Treasurer."[65]

The effectiveness of the colonial government dwindled. Most obviously, it lacked the cooperation of many towns. Some would not elect militia officers, and in two places controversies prevented the men chosen for civil and military offices from assuming their duties. The General Assembly could do nothing about Kingstown except appoint a special constable and hope that his authority would be honored. It assumed probate jurisdiction in Jamestown when the local council did not exist. It ruled on a controversial election in Warwick in 1696. It caused the arrest of several men elected at Portsmouth when they refused to accept office and so persuaded three of them to change their minds. It authorized the two majors in command of the militia to appoint subordinate officers in towns in their districts where none had been chosen and to give orders for the regulation of companies that would have the same force as if given by the Assembly itself.[66] Once again, the colonial government sought a cure for disintegration in bypassing the local autonomy that it previously had to condone, and once again the cure failed.

The military organization could not be brought under control by the Assembly in 1691. The following year the trouble could be traced to the news that Sir William Phips, the new royal governor of Massachusetts, had arrived with a commission as commander in chief of all the militia units in New England. Here at last was an order from the Crown. This news inspired men to defy officers commissioned by the colony, even in Warwick, where Captain Benjamin Gorton said he would take orders only from Phips. The Assembly sent emissaries to treat with Phips, but they learned nothing. In August it hurried to appoint officers where none had been elected or to continue existing ones in their ranks, instructed them to obey orders from no one except superiors in the colony, then rushed an address to King William and Queen Mary protesting Phips's commission.[67]

The address questioned the legality of the commission, gave an official view of what was going on in the colony, and recommended a change of royal policy. The legal argument rested primarily on the charter's clauses giving control of the militia to the Governor and Company, and on clauses written after passage of the English statute said to support the Phips commission, and secondarily on the refusal of Phips to negotiate with Rhode Island officials or reveal his exact powers.

The Assembly found the key to the situation in the intrigues of men trying to subvert the restored charter government, men who claimed that "those persons commissionated by Sir Edmund Andros" should remain in office "untill some immediate order from the Crown of England." Their friends in Massachusetts got Phips's ear; he sent military commissions to be distributed by a leading Rhode Island dissident, Peleg Sanford. Most men refused the commissions, but to the colonial officials the scheme was obvious: a new grab for the Narragansett country to be achieved by defeating Rhode Island's opposition to the claims the schemers held. These intrigues were preventing the settlement of that region as well as the taxation and organization of military force needed if the colony was to do its duty for the sovereigns in war. The Assembly asked for a speedy reconfirmation of the old charter.[68]

Eventually, the Assembly's appeal to the sovereigns brought an astonishingly favorable response; yet between the hazards at sea and the press of other business at Whitehall, nothing arrived for a couple of years. Weakness and confusion persisted in Rhode Island. Surviving records surely are incomplete, but they contain no transactions of the General Assembly between June 1691 and July 1695 except for one session in August 1692, no judgments by the General Court of Trials between March 1688 and September 1693, and no entries in the treasurer's accounts between 1690 and 1695. Furthermore, records of all the mainland towns and Jamestown contain gaps. Certainly it is no accident that the basic records of the colonial government all had such conspicuous gaps at this time of troubles.

In this most extreme descent into disarray, the colonial government nearly expired. It held sway only over Newport and, in a weaker way, over the other three original towns. Of the fundamentals of its existence, only support of religious liberty went unquestioned. The charter had dubious legal standing, the borders of the jurisdiction were subject to machinations at home and in London, and the capacity of the government to serve Newport interests was close to zero. The government could not collect taxes, control the militia, hold a prisoner, keep towns in operation, or count on the authority of its magistrates' being respected. Moreover, it was quite unable to help itself. Where once it had expected to control its future by adjusting the terms or theories of political association—or later, by gaining the desired clauses in charters—by 1692 it was caught up in an international war and intrigues and cogitations in London. As the Assembly realized when framing the appeal against Phips's commission, the colony needed English backing as never before. In the end, English action saved Rhode Island, though not without requiring changes in the colony's relations to the empire.

Conclusion

The turbulent years from 1644 to 1694 took the colonial government of Rhode Island from its slow inauguration through one dissolution to nearly hopeless collapse into another. The charter of 1663 finally gave the connection to the Crown that had been desired since the 1640s to end doubt over the foundations of authority. Formally, that document made the constitution of the government an expression of royal will rather than popular consent. Quietly, the colony toned down its old democratic ways and gained some solidarity in upholding religious liberty and in frustrating adverse claims to the Narragansett country.

Yet the revised plan failed to make the new government awe-inspiring or firmly attached to the expected interests in land and commerce. The self-contained governing corporation of the Governor and Company of Rhode Island and Providence Plantations, though it set out to be what the charter implied, became even on formal terms more of a creation of the original towns. It had no capacity to enforce its court's judgments in the face of internal disputes over major land rights. Rather, it could only fend off the consequences of nonenforcement by delays and evasions.

Still, considering the government's intrinsic weakness, it did surprisingly well in keeping alive its claims to boundaries. In fact, it held its own against Connecticut, even though Connecticut dominated Rhode Island militarily. Just after King Philip's War, Rhode Island founded East Greenwich, the only town it ever sponsored on its own land grant. But the deadlock on the Narragansett claims drove the colony to an unprecedented dependency on the Crown. All parties appealed for royal backing with such determination as to make themselves unable to resist subordination to imperial authority in other fields. When James II overrode the squabbles by establishing the Dominion of New England, Rhode Island could only submit.

The Dominion lasted too short a time to have a fair test as a central government. During its brief sway over Rhode Island, it had a style almost antithetical to the charter government's yet met even more noncompliance with its authority. Its collapse opened the way to an attempt to restore the charter government. The attempt had little success for a few years. Opponents had various plans they preferred, whether keeping the Dominion or gaining union with a royal colony, but they contributed to making the colonial government the shambles they said it was by nature. A wraith of a regime wafted along in Newport while towns and individuals pursued their own interests as best they could.

Men at the time kept seeing these troubles myopically. Francis Brinley, seconded by some English officials, thought Rhode Island was populated by undisicplined people using an organization that gave too little power to the officials and put men in office who were not of the highest standing. They wanted to put wide legal authority into the hands of those with the greatest wealth, experience, English influence, and disposition to rule.[69] Yet this policy had been tried with poor results in the Dominion of New England, though Brinley and his friends refused to take the test as conclusive. The views of those who restored the charter have survived in less general concepts. Those men emphasized the charter privileges, of course, and hoped that all would be well if the monarchs reaffirmed them. But it is obvious that the defenders of the charter repeatedly traced their opposition to hostile claimants to lands in the Narragansett country and so asked the monarchs to reaffirm the rulings on the land claims that had been made by the royal commission in 1665 in terms favorable to Rhode Island.[70]

To an extent, all these ideas had validity, yet they failed to encompass all the pertinent realities. The colonial government indeed lacked a fruitful connection with dominant interests and concentrations of wealth. It could not set and hold to a systematic complex of policies while contenders for power pursued conflicting ends. The cure, however, could not be found in authoritarian control by self-proclaimed gentlemen. Local preoccupations and the accumulated experience had too much effect for that. Noncompliance in the towns stymied the Dominion as it did the charter government. Nor did self-seeking interests alone prevent order. They would seek their ends under any system. They, like many other elements in the society—small communities, militia units, owners of mills, churches, families—tended to take care of themselves first and, on the whole, well enough. They all lacked a sense of how they must fit into a larger collectivity. The government would have to form a reasonably harmonious partnership with prominent interests and form a framework to accommodate and protect all acceptable elements in the society. So far, the long-standing service of colony to Newport and the newer realization of the importance of a solid connection with England provided fixed points from which to work. It remained to be seen whether people could proceed from there.

Like the towns in the early years, the colonial government had yet to acquire the ring of power—the combination of taxation, legislation, and force joined together by a political faith and the confidence that rewards would flow from them. The faith had to assure people that the government was rightly grounded in a source of authority and would act justly; the rewards had to come in the prevalence of order and specific benefits deemed socially good. In myth, the ring had to be forged by a smith with supernatural powers. Nobody in Rhode Island yet had the craft.

❧ 3 ❧

Disintegration of the Communal Ideal in the Original Towns

The chronicle of changes and failures in the central government was loosely related to the towns. Much that happened in them went on independently. They observed or ignored colonial law as they chose. Their appeals to the colony to settle local disputes had few results, because the colony could not enforce its rulings. It served towns mainly by protecting them (after a fashion) against royal authority and neighboring colonies. Though it had sought a connection with England to give legitimacy to town government, basic laws, and a judiciary by derivation from the Crown, the results were meager. The original scope of self-government in the earliest towns could not be restored by the newly created colony government. Rather, town authority proceeded toward disintegration. People's primary loyalty devolved to the family, a church, or an economic enterprise.

Land, of course, was the basic resource for nearly everyone, but its relation to a community had changed already in the four original towns. At first, the founders had formed agreements to live together and had acquired land on which to do so. After a decade or two, however, instead of the human association coming first and governing the allocation of land, joint ownership of land itself had become the foundation for the community.

This reversal occurred as the inhabitants shucked their Old World assumptions about size. In England a rural village ordinarily had a small territory with fixed bounds. Villagers had small lots. Rhode Island settlers had founded towns on a similar scale but soon began to enlarge their ambitions. In New England vast expansion was possible. First-settlers wanted bigger and bigger landholdings for themselves. They might connect this desire to a social goal, as in Portsmouth and Newport, or make it an attack on one, as in Providence, but the result was the same. Some got much; those who got little objected. Either way, unification around social goals suffered. Contests among communities over land inspired attempts to strengthen each community by redefining it as an economic association which wanted to keep a sizable tract, enlarge it if possible, and divide it into shares in a way that the beneficiaries would regard as equitable without regard for a social purpose.

What followed depended on local circumstances. The island towns of Portsmouth and Newport had divided most of their land quickly, so they deliberated over how to divide the rest while the citizens sought additional land beyond Aquidneck's shores. The mainland towns of Providence and Warwick, however, had no such limit. They wanted land and sought to get it as enlargements of their jurisdictions. The result was decades of conflict. Avarice by itself would have accomplished little if the nearby Indians had not become willing to sell after 1650.

In the original towns, though with qualifications on the island, the ironic result of making collective ownership of land the foundation of the community and the ensuing rush to grab more land was to separate control of land from town government. Everywhere, as explained in chapter 1, those who could do so won a definition of rights to shares in undivided land that would benefit themselves. The rights were derived in a pseudotraditional way from priority of settlement, though formulas differed. The incongruity of graded rights to shares and equal votes in town meeting resulted in a division of town concerns into three parts. Except in Portsmouth, a syndicate of proprietors began to manage undivided land, also assuming some of the original functions of the towns, such as planning use of land, generating individual titles, and laying out roads. The town governments' role in land policy was reduced to record keeping and some slight regulation of use. The towns did, however, turn to using certain resources in land to promote trade and commerce. That is, they shifted from serving communal needs to promoting economic enterprises that presumably would radiate prosperity from the immediate beneficiaries to everybody else.

These results came about from the interaction of countless strivings without any of the persons concerned seeing a goal beyond individual advantage. In the process, however, they began to make a new category of town government, as distinct from comprehensive communal self-regulation, with certain kinds of social action consigned to other agencies and certain kinds to unregulated private choice. Thus, these developments produced the fact, if not the concept, of a private realm distinct from public authority but protected by it and subject to public law. The organizations of proprietors of undivided lands were historically understandable but legally anomalous, and they caused trouble for decades.

The Mechanisms of Town Government

The forms of town government changed slowly in the second half of the seventeenth century. The alterations showed a subtle revision of the town's place in the control of life, from a comprehensive management of the public affairs of families to a limited regulation bearing mainly on individuals. The basic pattern of institutions remained nearly the same. The only major change came with the end of town courts as a result of the new charter. Otherwise, the towns merely added a few specialized officers as they saw fit.[1]

The flourshing island towns found use for the most officials. The rosters reflected life. Portsmouth increased the number of constables, added three overseers of the poor, dropped the surveyors of land, added five surveyors of cattle, and chose assorted ad hoc committees, such as those to audit the outgoing treasurer's account or to lay out a road. Newport created even more, including such distinctive ones as a corder of wood, a bellman, and a viewer of ladders who was to make sure the residents had proper equipment for fighting fires. The lists of regular officers began to reflect the economic character of the communities, if not a profound redesign of the town government.[2]

In some measure the towns turned from the easygoing procedures of a community taking care of itself toward punctilio and administrative routine. Significantly, several towns reduced their individual forms of the "engagement" of office to a simple promise to a duly authorized official to act according to the law—no more exchange of promises between the elected man and his community. The smaller towns went on relying on neighborly generosity to help the needy, but Portsmouth and Newport transferred such business to overseers of the poor. Town meetings themselves, at first frequent and at irregular intervals, settled into a fixed calendar, partly determined by the time for choosing jurors and other officers for the colonial government.[3] All towns began to create standard methods to apportion and collect taxes.[4]

Greater reliance on regular officers and less on general meetings led to more systematic records and other safeguards against official misconduct. The point must not be exaggerated, however. Most obviously in the mainland towns, the town meeting kept a potentially total power over town business, often called itself a court (in the old sense that included administrative as well as judicial functions), and indeed tried to dole out justice. Yet the towns began appointing auditors to inspect the treasurer's books and committees to supervise the transfer of records from one officer to his successor. The thousands of file papers kept by the Providence town clerk—and the surviving collection is by no means complete—testify to the growing attention to paperwork.[5]

Townsfolk, however, wanted more from public records than a report of governmental action. They wanted their officials to assume functions performed in England by parish registers and manor rolls. Records of marriages would help detect misbehavior such as desertion and bigamy. Records of births would provide knowledge of who had responsibility for children. Warwick said that the value of recording births was "so Orfanes may know when to Claime theiere Inharitances." Instead of an intent to patrol morality for the community's well-being, the towns avowed limited aims that were as much administrative good practice as service to social ends.[6]

Likewise, the town councils' increasing regularity in probate procedure by about 1680—better documentation, greater fidelity to legal rules rather than paternalistic improvisation, requirement of periodic accounting from guardians of orphans, and so on—served both to improve administration and to prevent pauperism by ensuring orderly transmission of property and preparation of minors for economic usefulness. In all these respects, the towns may have aimed for comprehensive control but veered to the goal of preventing expense for the indigent or the harboring of miscreants. Implicitly, people might do as they liked, provided they lived within the law, and the towns would facilitate orderly family conduct in limited ways and either screen out or punish ne'er-do-wells.

Recording documents on land rights began as a method of improving communal control over ownership by ensuring collective approval of each transfer of rights but gradually lost this function and became only a means to make conveyances open to public view. At least two towns for several years required town approval before deeds could be recorded: Providence by the town meeting and Portsmouth by a committee. Providence also devised a system to document individual divisions of the commons. If the grantee wanted one, the clerk would draft a deed to be signed by himself and one of the magistrates "in the behalfe of the Towne," which would be "as authentick to all intentes, and purposses . . . as [if] Every man of this Towne did perticularly sett unto [it] his hand and seale."[7] These practices faded away, however, by the 1680s. People often ignored them. Towns stopped trying to regulate conveyances, and most of them gave proprietary organizations the function of documenting commons divisions. The clerk recorded any document presented to him, provided it bore the marks or signatures, seals, and attestations required by law. Step by step, the law grew more exacting, and as land records became systematic, people began to use standard forms of deeds usually derived from English law.

Similarly, as roads and bridges increased in importance, towns began to make rules on the inhabitants' duties to make and repair them. Newport divided its highways into districts to clarify responsibility for their condition, a practice that ultimately became universal.[8] Everywhere, the routes had to be defined and marked, the widths specified, the fences kept up, and the encroachments by abutting landowners rolled back.

The increasing economic reliance on export of livestock or its products such as meat or butter, as well as the growth of population and the fixity of roads and property lines, made restraint of domestic animals vital. Towns improved methods to patrol fences and wrote more elaborate laws to resolve disputes over depredations by animals. Towns recorded earmarks and, on Aquidneck, established pounds and chose officers to prevent sale of livestock by persons who did not own the creatures.[9]

While the tenor of town action changed, the scope shrank. Taverns, initially communal facilities, became private concerns regulated under seldom-enforced colonial laws and licensed, if at all, by a town council. The inhabitants wanted taverns, and to get them, councils sometimes cut the license fee below the statutory level. At most, the town fathers insisted that the publicans curb unruliness under their roofs.[10]

Likewise with mills: the early plans to set up reciprocal obligations gradually became pointless. In the generic form, the town gave land and promised a road to a mill and a monopoly to the miller, while the miller promised to keep the mill operating, serve local customers before others, and abide by a maximum toll. Where the miller had a monopoly, the town had to keep a road to his mill and depend on him to abide by his terms. The promise of monopoly was no more than a declaration against granting land for another mill. Towns did nothing to thwart competitors, and when they appeared, the original agreement became worthless.

Only Warwick, with the smallest population, persisted in communal guidance until the end of the seventeenth century. Even there, the abandonment of town control in one case, the fulling mill at Apponaug, well illustrated the process that had been going on elsewhere. The town gave the site to John Micarter, set a ceiling on what he might charge, and gave him ample land rights, and permission to keep ten cattle on the town common. It promised not to authorize a competitor on the same river but reserved a right to allow another kind of mill there, providing Micarter be compensated for any inconvenience. Then the agreement broke down. The town abandoned its control, and Micarter, without getting the town's permission, sold out to a man who did not know the trade. After several years, the town proprietors released the site from all restrictions in exchange for the owner's relinquishing the mill's rights to pasturage and woodcutting on the common.[11] Everywhere, mills became private enterprises, and control over them shifted from the terms of town grants of privilege to agreements among the persons who owned the sites and operated the installations, agreements often woven into deeds or wills.[12]

By the late seventeenth century, governmental action shifted from promotion of mills for the communal welfare to determination of owners' liabilities. Waterpower sites rarely could be developed without inundating arable land to create mill ponds. One pond damaged a bridge in Portsmouth. The General Court of Trials indicted the town, which foisted the burden of repairing the bridge onto the mill owner.[13] Before long, the General Assembly and the courts, rather than the towns, had to define millers' obligations in law.

Neither towns nor any other institutions in Rhode Island had attempted collective control of apprenticeship and bound servitude. These kinds of unfreedom were regarded, like the family, as requiring no institutional or legal setting, as arrangements of concern only to the parties immediately involved. The contractual basis for servitude was not entered in a public record. Even when town councils bound out orphans or poor children, the terms of the contract seldom were written down in the minutes. And of course, there were no guilds to supervise apprenticeship. Without a highly patterned society to patrol them, servitude and apprenticeship became flexible devices to serve many nontraditional purposes, the most striking of which was the binding out of Indian captives in several towns at the end of King Philip's War. What probably began as a vengeful makeshift turned into something like hereditary peonage.

More important, the Old World view of village commons as a vital resource for the community, a necessary part of the balanced agricultural household, all but vanished. It remained alive longest in Warwick, where most of the Four Mile Common was reserved for collective use until the early eighteenth century.[14] Even there it dwindled. In fact, the traditional relation of village to commons in all the original towns had been unhinged from the start by the nontraditional geographical and social conditions. There was no lord of the manor to enforce observance of the village rules; there was no tradition. On the mainland, even when townsfolk kept the divisions of land within a medieval scale, the commons deviated from the norm by having a potentially vast extent of land and a lack of clear limits. On the island, Newport and Portsmouth gave the favored men large blocks of territory intended to include the pasture that commons in much of England would have provided, little was reserved for collective use.

Rhode Islanders were torn between antithetical impulses. Everywhere, the inhabitants as individuals began to look on the commons as free pickings for commercial rather than household use, so inhabitants as a corporate group at town meetings began regulating what might be done on the commons. Providence and Portsmouth, for instance, penalized those who cut wood to ship out rather than use at home. Towns restricted the livestock their inhabitants might turn loose on the commons. Periodically, towns declared that certain expanses of commons should be perpetual and that the vote might not be rescinded except by unanimous voice of all interested parties—and then went back to parcelling out the territory into individual holdings as before.[15]

If commons declined as communal resources in the old sense, they remained so in another. Towns continued to allocate land for favored occupations. The main object changed, however, from fostering local services to promoting external trade. Newport created its first subdivision of lots to be granted for nominal fees to men who would promise to build houses and practice trades on them, with tenure conditional until the stipulations had been met. This plan succeeded; Portsmouth's imitation failed. Newport also made more specific allocations for urban amenities, such as land for school-houses and endowments for the masters. More directly related to commerce, Newport planned a public market, granted use of Goat Island to a group of men who wanted to cure fish there and to a man who proposed to set up a shipyard. Newport gave a syndicate of citizens use of harborfront property to build a major wharf and then in 1685 transferred the rights to another organization to replace it. Providence merely gave small lots for wharves and warehouses.[16]

Commons and Proprietors on the Island

When the island towns decided against keeping most of the small commons they had, they followed similar policies in divisions; but Newport consigned the bulk of the land to an organization of proprietors, while Portsmouth kept control in the town meeting.[17] Yet in both, equity appeared to call for a division to holders of early allocations rather than all inhabitants or all landowners. The result was to intensify the original pattern of distribution, though not much.

Newport, as already mentioned, created an organization of proprietors of common land quite early, perhaps around 1644. The scanty evidence suggests that before 1702 this institution cooperated closely with the town meeting government and did not consider itself a completely independent entity. The proprietors initiated the plan in 1667 to create a subdivision near the harbor for tradesmen, but a town committee was also envisioned. Moreover, the town meeting granted tradesmen's lots at least until 1695 and assigned parts of the commons, especially in the commercial zone, for public purposes.[18]

The proprietor's independence from the town increased in 1702, however, after a series of disputes over pasturing cattle on the common. People without clear rights had been turning livestock out to graze, which in 1692 became a grievance to inhabitants who observed the law when the town levied a tax on the animals they pastured on the common. The town had to repeal the tax and instead decided to fine the violators. Discontent simmered until March 1702, when, with the town's acquiescence, the proprietors set out to end the friction by dividing the common land.[19] They acted as though they had full control of the business, although the town continued to make decisions (which the proprietors contested) on the territory they regarded as theirs. Also, the town kept control of school land and a few other common resources.

When they planned the work, the proprietors made a revealing classification of Newport's population into five parts and looked on the first two as their members. The five were (1) those who held land that had been granted to original settlers and who had "built Large Buildings and . . . made greate Improvments on said Land and are Persons that are and may be very servisable" to the town; (2) those with the same kind of land who either had not improved it or were "not Deemed to be servisable to the publique"; (3) possessors of lots granted by the town subsequent to the original allocations, who had built large buildings and were considered serviceable; (4) possessors of town lots who had made less improvement or were less serviceable; and (5) those with unimproved town lots. In practice, the categories overlapped (men with original allocations also might have acquired other lots), and original allocations had been subdivided.[20] So clarity of proprietary rights and proportions among them were far from unmistakable. Besides, the classifications rested on two bases. On one side they recognized a formal and heritable right, while on the other they made a paternalistic judgment of who had been useful to the community.

Portsmouth never spawned a proprietors' organization but otherwise treated its commons much as Newport did. The town meeting voted to give neither land nor freeman's rights to any more newcomers. Ambiguously, the town drew no distinction between "free inhabetants" and the assemblage to regulate or parcel out the common lands.[21]

In the early 1680s, Portsmouth began to fear royal action against land titles generated by the towns acting as corporate entities to give common land to individuals. English officials were alleging that such allocations in Massachusetts were an abuse of that colony's charter. In hope of heading off trouble, the colonial government of Rhode Island, in May 1684, followed Connecticut's example and wrote a clumsy endorsement of titles. The law first confirmed all those held by "the first freemen of the . . . towns, their associates and derivatives, and their heires, and assignes." This endorsement of the freemen's control over the commons superficially met the immediate danger and also provided a motive for restricting the franchise.[22]

To imply a policy, this formula had to be elaborated. Did it mean equality of shares? Of votes? Without writing down rulings on such points, Portsmouth in 1686 planned to subdivide the commons completely. Collective assignment of lots in the town might be considered doubtful in law but unlikely to be disturbed in practice, because English law normally protected individual titles, however derived. Before the plan was carried out, Rhode Island submitted to the Dominion of New England, so Portsmouth tried dickering with the governor of the new jurisdiction, Sir Edmund Andros, for confirmation of its land rights. Again the plan came to nothing, this time because Andros was overthrown.[23]

In deliberations on a division approved in 1694, all of Porstmouth's freemen who were landholders (including nonresidents) had equal voices in town meeting, which allowed equal shares to the freeholders and nonresident landholders, subject to adjustment of quantity for quality. The town also set aside a tract to be divided into small lots to be offered on special terms as bait for tradesmen, people the town wanted to lure into a compact settlement.[24]

Providence

Providence had an especially acrimonious debate over land policy considering that the community was first settled on the principles of natural law and shared land rights. Step by step, the town retreated from its early ideas and went from considering land a collective concern to considering it a matter of individual right, though the opposing values were not cleanly arrayed against each other so much as mingled in the thoughts of both sides.

The transition, furthermore, was vexed by interlocking disputes and personal animosities that dwarfed the altercations in Portsmouth and resulted in subdivision of the town lands into segments under different sets of joint owners. The disputes inspired frequent and invariably ineffective appeals to the colonial government and then to the imperial power and so advanced the subordination of communal autonomy to jurisdictions of a different sort. At the center of the conflicts stood William Harris, who tried to get a vast estate by magnifying the Pawtuxet reservation, in which he had several of the thirteen shares, at the expense of the rest of Providence and the northern part of Warwick. The strife at times convulsed the town of Providence, threw the colonial government into turmoil, provoked Warwick and Providence to oppose any colonial taxes, and inspired Harris, later still, to plot for extension of Connecticut's jurisdiction to Narragansett Bay. In the end, Harris won far less than he sought, and Providence surrendered allocation of land to proprietors' organizations that proliferated beyond its control.

The battles over the Harris claims have been recounted many times with more or less accuracy and need not be rehearsed in full.[25] The focus here will be on the implications of arguments and the consequences for the town of Providence.

The controversy was touched off when Providence, with the permission of the colonial government, set out to acquire more land. William Harris began in 1657 to get what he thought were confirmations of the full extent of the original purchase, which by his reading of certain documents extended twenty miles westward from Fox Point at the head of Narragansett Bay, up the Pawtuxet River without limits, and on a similar scale to the Blackstone. Roger Williams believed that these documents merely conveyed grazing rights by the rivers and that the town lands fanned out only three to five miles west and north from the original settlement by the Providence River.

Williams negotiated what he thought were augmentations of the original purchase or preemptive rights to augmentation.[26] From a distance, the two men appeared to be pursuing roughly the same end, but their interpretations had an explosive difference.

Harris held his for self-serving reasons, as his enemies pointed out repeatedly. Pawtuxet was about a quarter of the original Providence purchase, bordering on Warwick and extending westward from Narragansett Bay and northward to halfway between the Pawtuxet and Woonasquatucket Rivers. The farther the original Providence purchase went, the larger Pawtuxet became. Harris's determination to define the purchase as extending south to the southernmost main tributary of the Pawtuxet created major conflicts with Warwick. By contrast, if the new concessions from the Indians were enlargements of the original purchase, the Pawtuxet reservation would not be extended.

Williams and Harris both claimed to be serving good purposes. Williams objected to defrauding the Narragansetts by artful readings of their generous donation and wanted to expand the town to make room for more victims of religious persecution. Harris worried about the ambitions of Massachusetts men and others to gain control of the lands of the Narragansetts. Plans astir in 1656 led to results that posed the greatest danger six years later, when a syndicate from outside Rhode Island, called the Narragansett Proprietors, foreclosed on a mortgage they held from the Indians. The mortgage had been obtained by force and chicanery, but the United Colonies endorsed it. It transferred all the Narragansetts' land to the proprietors. So Harris could present himself as establishing that a large part of what appeared to be included in those lands actually had been given to Providence long before anybody dreamed of the mortgage.[27]

More interesting, if harder to fathom, were the arguments that the contestants tirelessly spun against each other. Their reasonings reflect the partisan battle as well as differing beliefs over the foundations of society. Usually, Williams's side upheld communal values, while Harris's ostensibly stood for English authority and land law but did so to defend limited rights to divisions of the commons. Harris scoured old law books to find definitions of terms and interpretations of conveyances that would sustain his purposes, even though the conveyances had been drafted without a desire to conform to English law. Running through all of his jumbled arguments was a persistent theme that denounced communal control of land for collective purposes.[28]

The strange struggle between the opposing sides began in 1660 and continued, bitter and indecisive, until both leaders had died, over two decades later. For years at a stretch, the town government divided into opposing regimes claiming legitimacy and making antithetical decisions. Along the way, they reached only a few compromises, notably to clarify part of the northern limit of Pawtuxet near the salt water. Often, they appealed to the General

Assembly to adjudicate their differences; the Assembly called for harmony or reluctantly ruled on which side's representatives should be seated, or rejected both, but brought no peace.[29] Central authority in the colony could accomplish nothing and grew weaker as a consequence of the quarrel, in fact to the point of being unable to impose taxes on the mainland.

During the contest, Providence—the Williams wing, mostly—for a time tried to persist with communal purposes in the control of land but could not maintain a consistent approach. Irresolutely, it established a large permanent commons of the traditional kind. It also began to require that deeds be recorded. It agreed to make new divisions only in meetings of men with rights in the Providence Grand Purchase, a step toward a separate proprietary organization, but for the time being continued to treat allocations of land to individuals as exercises of the town's collective authority. The town also voted to admit no more people to share rights. New propriators would have undoubtedly endorsed Williams's side of the dispute. Still, the town went on granting land for purposes deemed beneficial for the community.[30]

The transition to a separation of town and proprietors could not be completed, however, until after Harris had made his most dramatic appeals to outside authority and died in the attempt. First he went to England to appeal to the king. He won the appointment of a royal commission to hear his suits for Pawtuxet as he defined it. These suits pitted him not only against the prevailing camp in Providence but also against the colony of Rhode Island and the town of Warwick, which frantically resisted his assertions about the southern border of Providence. Harris seemed unmindful of the consequences of making so many enemies.

The commission met in 1677, just after the devastations of King Philip's War, but the old sides resumed their fight with unimpaired vigor. Both struggled partly in vain to translate a dispute over claims founded on communal will into the terms of English land law. As a result, both made murky arguments. In the end, Harris seemed to get more out of the judgment, but both parties planned an appeal to the king.[31] Harris joined forces with the Narragansett Proprietors in his appeal; both hoped to get their claims by an extension of Connecticut's jurisdiction to Narragansett Bay. On behalf of himself and his new allies, Harris set out to argue the appeal personally before the king but was captured by Algerine pirates and sold as a slave. His wife and the government of Connecticut eventually ransomed him, but he died three days after reaching London in the fall of 1681. Within two years, Williams too went to the grave.[32] Near the end of his life, however, Williams lamented the bitter land dispute and his own role in it.

By then the old dispute was approaching settlement, and the parties began to separate town and proprietary concerns, a process that took about twenty years. In one important move, in 1686, the town meeting voted to give up its authority to decide on claims to purchase rights. Gradually, it conceded allocation of land to the proprietors and repudiated control over common land in 1704. The proprietors began to keep their own records about that time, and the two institutions were finally set apart. This result came about through negotiations between the Providence interests, weary of political strife and anxious to avoid subjection to rulings by external tribunals.[33]

Beleaguered Warwick

Warwick, too, began to separate town government from control of common land in the 1670s but for reasons somewhat different from those in Providence. No internal disputes raged; no litigation forced precision on share rights and the vote on allotments. From the start, the purchasers had made reasonably clear distinctions between managing their part of the Shawomet purchase by themselves and joining with the other freemen who held rights in the Four Mile Common to manage that territory. Rather, Warwick separated town and land to improve security for holding the land. Perhaps the strong community cohesion did not seem at stake. Unfortunately, amid the profusion of documents on the disputes, there is little to explain the underlying values in Warwick unless the overwhelming record of solidarity in the face of danger is testimony enough. Communal cohesion fell apart, however, after the common lands were subdivided among various groups of proprietors and after outside rivals seemed to be vanquished. The dissension began to appear in 1676, when elimination of the Indian population made the land accessible to occupation by White people.

The contests were partly of Warwick's making, partly the product of ambitious outsiders. The townsfolk felt the same land lust that other people in Rhode Island did and sought more before somebody else got it. On the north, the town fought over its border with Providence and with the supporters of William Harris's position on the Pawtuxet purchase. In the south, Warwick faced even more danger; the Narragansett Proprietors claimed the entire territory and wanted a jurisdiction other than Rhode Island's. In the west, Warwick courted more trouble in 1654 by acquiring land across Greenwich Bay, known as Potowomut. There Warwick met a few rivals acting under Rhode Island's authority as well as the Narragansett Proprietors. In all, the town had enemies on every side except the east.

Warwick's contests with William Harris followed roughly the same chronology as Providence's and involved many of the same issues, but the effects were quite different on the Gortonian community. Warwick men drew together instead of quarreling among themselves. They faced Harris in the colony's Court of Trials rather than in town meeting. They, rather than he, began appeals to the throne. They took their case to the General Assembly oftener than he did, for they desperately needed to preserve Rhode Island's jurisdiction. And they always had regarded their collective existence as a function of a central government under an English grant of authority. The intricate record of litigation and maneuvers need not be discussed here; it is enough to report that Warwick held its own resourcefully until the Pawtuxet claimants lost their last appeal to the king in the early eighteenth century.[34]

Throughout its adventures to keep rights to land and gain more, Warwick often found occasions to clarify share rights to the different parts of the territory and to complicate the patterns. Presumably, defining rights looked like a way to safeguard claims, both by creating the next thing to individual ownership and by stimulating improvement. The process, however, divided what had been remarkably solid communal interests until the local Indians were eliminated in King Philip's War.

Separating the business of the town from deployment of land had begun earlier, to be sure, with creation of the Four Mile Common. Though that segment and the rest of the Shawomet purchase were managed by different sets of proprietors, they acted jointly to buy Indian rights to Toskeunk in 1654 and oppose Harris. The townsfolk ran the western line of the common across Toskeunk and began allocating individual tracts on the east side while the Shawomet purchasers did likewise on the west.[35]

Still, the town meeting managed the Four Mile Common and continued to do so until the expense of defending the land against Harris built up and drove the townsfolk to expedients that undermined the ability to act together. In 1677 the town began mortgaging small portions to raise money. Some of the lenders formed partnerships to develop their property in independent systems of share rights. These arrangements inspired other men to petition for special tracts, several successfully, until an opposition arose and forced most takers to surrender their awards. In reaction to this squabble, the town meeting separated voting rights on civic matters from voting rights on common land, the latter to be arranged so as to give each share one vote, regardless of how the rights or fractions of rights were owned. It also ruled that no more shares should be created without unanimous consent of the freemen and, because of a different series of conflicts, devised a distinct proprietary system to manage Potowomut. Thus, voting on common land lost its identity with voting on other town business. At the same time, the town abandoned its old rules requiring holders of shares to improve their property, notably the one requiring them to build a house within a short time. That separated ownership from communal obligations. Thereafter, the proprietors of the Four Mile Common met as a distinct body. Township rights became units of property rather than connections between land and men that bound them into a community.[36]

Other parts of Warwick also broke into separate proprietary blocks. For a time, Meshanticut was treated as part of the business of the town, almost like the Four Mile Common, but ended as a separately organized entity after

Harris's death.[37] The Shawomet purchasers subdivided their territory into six main segments, each with a proprietary organization.

The purchasers tried to promote a second town center west of Greenwich Bay, with disappointing results. The influx of population into Warwick went slowly, and Indian villages inhibited the spread of European settlement until after King Philip's War. Still, in 1672 the purchasers planned a system of small lots near Greenwich Bay at Cowesett, with sizable farms behind them to the west. They looked forward to sixty-eight shares ultimately, four to each purchase right.[38] If the planners intended to live at Cowesett rather than merely sell real estate there, they would have detached themselves from the original community. The new village, however, never materialized. The purchasers subdivided the rest of the western expanse of their lands into four more blocks. Soon, their heirs began disputing their borders.

The purchasers as such went on managing their lands in Warwick Neck but with progressively less success in serving communal ends, especially as the last of the founding generation died and an entirely new set of leaders emerged.[39] On the whole, the tendency of their decisions was to give up cooperative pasture and to divide the land.

Throughout Warwick, guarding land rights subverted social solidarity based on shared use of them. Attendance fell off at town meetings; the inhabitants made grabs for parts of the Four Mile Common; the town clerk grew careless in keeping records. The confusions resulting from the Dominion of New England and its overthrow only made things worse. Various Warwick interests sought safety by any means they could imagine. At times, the town government, so far as documents reveal, ceased to function.

The Proprietary Organizations on the Mainland

The dynamics of divorcing control of land from other town affairs left a new sort of town and a new sort of landholding institution. While no two were exactly alike, the proprietary syndicates shared a few fundamental traits. They had a public character as well as a private one. They took over much of what had been the communal self-government in the original towns. They allocated land for mills, planned commons, and tried to sponsor new villages. Their decisions generated individual titles and laid out roads. So their records, though held as private property, functioned as adjuncts to the land evidence volumes kept by town clerks.

Furthermore, they conducted their affairs in ways that differed from those of strictly political institutions, ways that nearly assured a process of change that the organizers presumably did not anticipate. The proprietary groups began with fixed numbers of shares, determined by men who bought the land from Indians, from the town, or both. The proprietors refused to increase the shares, but they did not limit sale or partition or acquisition of more than one. Accordingly, their voting rights could become proportional to holdings rather than based on the simple fact of membership, and they exerted no control over who might join their ranks. Thus, the proprietary syndicates differed from governmental institutions, where equality of votes prevailed. The clerks dodged all controversies over succession by keeping books in the names of the first holders of shares, though the organizations at times tried to resolve quarrels. The evidence is sketchy but suggests that subdivided shares usually cast one vote and that a share owned by a woman or a minor was represented by a man. These traits proved a source of both strength and weakness—strength by exempting the proprietors from the kinds of quarrels that wracked Providence during the controversy with Harris, and weakness by preventing a socially coherent group from maintaining control.

In addition, the proprietary organizations either had no long-range plans or almost always abandoned them in the midst of dispute and controversy. They quickly made subdivisions into individual tracts. This had a developmental function that influenced a social result and would end the collective arrangement sooner or later. For years, disputes over property lines and other products of collective action kept the organizations in existence with ever feebler abilities to act collectively.

Proprietary organizations used variants of a fairly simple pattern of self-government. In addition to a moderator for their meetings, they normally chose a clerk and treasurer (often the same man), surveyors, and a committee either to conduct all routine business or merely to review the plats prepared by the surveyors, both as to the availability of the land and the foundation of claims on share rights. An approved plat would be entered in the books.

These institutions often began with a collective purpose. It might be as limited as united action to sustain their rights against either rival proprietors or trespassers, as traditional as arranging to use pastures in common, or as extensive as planning a new village. At the outset, strong feelings persisted that society could and should be shaped by deployment of land and that shared rights naturally created a social unit. A few examples will illustrate the spectrum of possibilities.

The Providence purchasers who controlled territory east of the Seven Mile Line tried limited projects beyond dividing their acres. When they organized apart from the town, they made a few rulings between claimants on shares but generally let contestants settle matters between themselves or go to court. The organization collectively pursued little more than development of harbor properties to enhance Providence's commercial prospects and tried unsuccessfully to manage the town commons. Mostly, they let recipients of dividend rights locate them wherever they pleased. Still, they met for many years and chose a treasurer-clerk, surveyors, a committee on surveying, and a few special committees. To summon a meeting, an officer or some of the shareholders obtained a warrant from a magistrate—sometimes the treasurer-clerk under a different hat—to the town sergeant to notify those who should attend. To that extent, they put themselves under the comprehensive framework of colonial law.[40]

The Pawtuxet proprietors laid their plans fairly soon after the death of William Harris. They agreed with the town to abandon all claims to land west of the Seven Mile Line and beyond a northerly limit. Then they split into two organizations. The one controlling territory east of the Pocasset River quickly settled old conflicts and planned to divide nearly all of the land— much was occupied already. They kept an organization for a long time. It had a highway laid out through their territory in 1701 and maintained control over a small tract, which they leased to bring in rents to be divided among the shares for many years. They also developed a village at the falls of the Pawtuxet and even intervened in a controversy over land titles between members.[41] Those with rights west of the Pocasset had to go on contending for Meshanticut and Toskeunk (in the end to no avail), so they needed an organization to do this work before extensive allocations were feasible.

The Cowesett offshoot of the Shawomet purchasers introduced a technique that already was common among proprietors in the southern part of the colony, that of putting their business into the hands of an executive committee called trustees. The proprietors signed a document by which they pledged "the whole plantation . . . for security to . . . [the four] trustees." They anticipated expenses for buying Indian rights or for litigation, which were to be met by proportional payments according to shares. If any members failed to pay, "then his or their shares shall bee at the dispose of the said trustees to answer the charges about the premises." With the scattering of members, collection became difficult. (The Shawomet purchasers decided in 1682 to apply this agreement to their whole territory to raise money to oppose Harris. The trustees created the subdivisions of the rest of the territory west of the Four Mile Common and Toskeunk.) The Cowesett trustees failed in their main task, creating a new village. In fact, the intended site was subject to a long controversy over its northern limit.[42]

These diverse examples both sketch the possible courses for the new proprietary institutions and mask their importance. The visible evidence suggests a prevalent fecklessness, but a misleading one. The new organizations, after all, took charge of a major part of what had been town business, a part that had seemed, for a few decades in the middle of the seventeenth century, to give a foundation to the towns. The proprietors began to manage most of the common lands, which meant not only efforts to supervise areas that towns had set aside for collective resources but also the immense reserves for future settlement by Europeans. While Narragansett Indians occupied most of these reserves, the practical effect of proprietary control remained only potential; but when it became actual after King Philip's War, the proprietors saw prospects for tangible benefits and began to squabble over how to get them. The desired influx of newcomers and the spread of White settlement posed new challenges to the proprietary groups in the eighteenth century. It remained to be seen whether these institutions could guide the social development of their territories.

Conclusion

By the end of the seventeenth century, the recourse to basing the towns' collective existence on control of land and the votes of the freemen produced a split. The two legs of the body politic, as thus conceived, had different joints and gates. The basic organization of society had to change. The towns put most of the undivided land into the hands of proprietors, except in Portsmouth and with imperfect clarity in the others. The towns, in spite of disruption by war and politics or occasional paralysis due to apathy, kept their other functions and moved toward formalizing procedures and assigning duties to a slowly growing roster of regular officers. This amounted to a change from treating town government as collective management of a community toward treating it as a limited administrative device to regulate the lives of individuals residing within its jurisdiction. As a by-product, many undertakings originally seen as parts of communal self-regulation drifted into a de facto realm of the private.

The separation of proprietary from civic business produced new needs for change later. The land-controlling organizations were often intricate and also had a dangerous potential to wield social and political power. The danger remained to be remedied in the eighteenth century. The town government, bereft of management of land, had no purpose or defining element to fall back on for the time being except inertia. In Warwick and Providence, internal conflicts easily gave way to apathy.

The tranformation of the towns came from no simple conviction on how to conduct public business. The incandescence of ideas in the period of foundings had come to an end along with clashes among them. Rather, a combination of practical considerations, debates on the wisdom of specific choices, free-swinging vituperation, arguments of all sorts to sustain private interests, and the tactics of appeal to higher jurisdictions provided the medium in which towns made decisions. If the decisions tended in the same direction, probably this happened because circumstances nudged the process, circumstances for which nobody had clear concepts.

Was there an undertow beneath the ripples on the surface? Clearly, the White newcomers around Narragansett Bay made an assumption that defied Old World experience: they could have land without limit. No neighboring

(White) villages blocked the way in most directions. Quarrels broke out over the two lines of contact between White communities. Consistency and clarity of ideas broke down in the absence of limits and in the absence of firm higher authority. A crass logic of greed raged, yet also a defensive logic of protecting oneself and one's community from competitive greed.

Realities of life around Narragansett Bay undercut the connections of land to government that had seemed likely to provide a solid foundation for society. The old belief that an endowment in land would sustain and define an association of people, whether in village or market, mill or family, turned out to be a half-truth where available acres existed. Equality of political rights for the freemen would not square with fixed inequalities in land and the absence of a religious or social ethos that preached or counselled the propriety of distinct social gradations. Ambition could either use or defy the land-based polity. Gaining security in unequal rights called for segregating them from the realm of equality. Orderly town government could best develop when detached from the commons.

❧ 4 ❧

Land Promotions and New Towns

While the original towns were disentangling themselves from the management of traditional commons and reserve lands, new colonization ventures got under way. Unlike the original towns, most of these undertakings began with a basis in shared ownership of land rather than an agreement to live together in a community. As in the original towns, the shares were unequal, and absentee and resident interests diverged; so the landowning organization began to split away from the simply political. By the terms of the charters, the new ventures should have been under the direction of the colonial government, but in fact the colonial government had too little power to shape the new settlements into a pattern. Instead, they developed in diverse ways amid conflicts and so prevented rather than furthered a strong colonial structure.

The promoters came from two sources: inside the original towns (chiefly Aquidneck towns) and Massachusetts. Within each category, some important rivalries sprang up, but the main contention was between the two major groups. They sought all the land in Rhode Island still occupied by Indians, the big prize being the Narragansett country south of Warwick. It was thought to share the attractions of Aquidneck for husbandry, but the smaller islands, too, looked valuable as safe pastures.

The major purchasers formed proprietary institutions to buy land and decide on how to put it to use. Most of these combinations were founded by men who wanted a fairly firm organization by which the many investors would entrust the business to a few leaders. These institutions followed no uniform pattern, yet they had marked similarities. They all had to quantify share rights from the start, usually allowing unequal shares to investors. They also had to levy assessments and impose penalties on noncompliant members, without any grounding in law for doing so and probably without any thought that such a grounding was needed. Most of them learned to rely on a basic core of officials yet had to keep the general meeting vital for one reason or another, especially when it provided the foundation of a town meeting. Regardless of organization, nearly all these institutions complicated the public affairs of the colony for many years. Ironically, the only one that did not, the one on Block Island, was founded by men who thought the place belonged to Massachusetts and proceeded to create a town along the lines of those in the Bay Colony.

The purchasers had a great variety of plans for using their control of land to shape society. The intentions ranged from firm to none. The Massachusetts men ordinarily had the firmest goals. They set out to create towns as they knew them at home, with carefully screened settlers and public support of a Puritan minister. The Rhode Island men thought of forming communities, if at all, only by simple measures of reserving land for lots in a central village. The one exception was the design of East Greenwich, the only town Rhode Island's colonial government ever launched.

The relations between organizations that obtained large blocks of territory and the residents on them differed greatly. In some places, the aims of the proprietors of undivided land eventually came into conflict with the local government. The settlers wanted to deploy common land for their own ends, not for the profit of absentee proprietors. The resulting disputes weakened the institutional fabric. During the seventeenth century no effective rules existed to resolve them. Indeed, such rules were all but impossible to devise while the proprietary organizations remained self-created entities without regard to, if not in open defiance of, the framework of law and distribution of authority prescribed by the charter.

Rhode Island's colonial government usually did little to control the acquisition and occupation of the land it claimed. It exercised no authority to speak of in the founding of the two new island towns. It tried to forbid all purchases from Indians without its blessing but repeatedly had to condone what it could not prevent. It tried to create a system under which its inhabitants would gain ownership of the Narragansett country but kept backing off from projects it initially sponsored. It moved assertively only in planning East Greenwich, but even there it had to retreat to placate some rival claimants. Yet it never lost its largest contest, the one over the bulk of the Narragansett country. What the government could not do on its own its inhabitants made possible by seeking its backing for their titles after they had occupied most of the territory.

The fact of pell-mell acquisition of Indian rights, mostly within a few years after 1656, testifies to the land hunger gnawing at New England colonials but hardly explains why the Indians fed it. Natives on Conanicut were few and weak and easily overborne. Those on Block Island and the Pequot country east of the Pawcatuck River had been cowed by Massachusetts already. But why did the seemingly strong Narragansetts suddenly sell both willingly and under compulsion? After the deaths of Miantonomi and Canonicus, principal sachems were as likely to make deals as village chiefs. They often had to.

The Narragansetts were disintegrating, the process hastened by Massachusetts and Connecticut, usually acting through the United Colonies. The Narragansetts pursued their conflicts with other Indians and thereby either alarmed the Puritan colonies or threatened the relations among Indians that they wanted to impose. The United Colonies sent punitive expeditions to the region and declared that the Narragansetts must pay reparations or fines, often in land. The sachems' appetites for White men's indulgences kept feeding other obligations that also could be satisfied in land. Among the heirs of the departed sachems, none could halt the dissolution of central authority. Village chiefs acted on their own. They put their marks on deeds for tracts large and small. King Philip's War finished in a rampage by fire and sword what had begun by subtle corrosion. In the aftermath, the nearly deserted Narragansett lands invited Europeans all the more irresistibly.[1]

Conanicut and Block Island

Radically different ventures resulted in the towns of Jamestown on the island of Conanicut and New Shoreham on Block Island. Though the two islands had town governments with the same legal principles and had small populations that raised livestock for export, the contrasts reveal much more. The Conanicut promotion was in the Rhode Island style, with few plans for a community; the promoters of New Shoreham, in the Massachusetts style, had more plans than they could implement. The one was organized by men who mostly remained absentees, the other by men who mostly became residents. Accordingly, in Jamestown a proprietary organization diverged from the town, while on Block Island no such separation took place.

The Conanicut company began as an enlargement of the ambitions of Portsmouth and Newport settlers. By the original deed to Aquidneck they had received rights to cut grass on Conanicut, but by 1654 they wanted the island as pasture. When their efforts to work through the town governments led to paralyzing disputes, William Coddington and Benedict Arnold, who was then rising from obscurity in Pawtuxet to wealth and power in Newport, organized an entirely voluntary association in March 1657. They had no official sponsorship and had to weather a political storm raised by opponents within the colony.[2]

At an early meeting, the founders organized what they called a company and drew up a slate of thirteen articles of agreement. Ultimately, approximately a hundred men signed them. The lineup kept changing. Arnold and Coddington each took a twentieth share of the whole island; others took as little as one nine-hundredth (rights to about six acres). The articles specified that the business of the company would be carried on by a committee of seven major shareholders, called the trustees, who might act by majority vote. They might call on other partners for assistance or summon a general meeting. The trustees were nominated by a Perpetual Council of sixteen major shareholders and approved by the membership at large. Although the members empowered the council to coopt men to fill its ranks as needed, it did nothing after selecting the first trustees.[3]

The trustees, however, exercised extensive powers. They might spend money on behalf of the shareholders and recoup it by proportional assessments on pain of forfeiture of shares, sell forfeited shares, select a secretary to make copies of company documents and issue deeds, survey and divide Conanicut, lay out highways, and manage the adjoining Dutch Island as a collective pasture for the shareholders to use proportionally. This system, by creating a coercive power outside the laws, began the series of organizations that flagrantly violated an orderly derivation of authority supposedly assured by the first charter.[4]

The trustees promptly bought Indian rights to the islands and decided what to do with the land. Their surveyor mapped Conanicut and proposed to reserve a portion of the land for a town center, including twenty acres for roads, burial ground, a military training field, prison, and whatever else might prove desirable. The shares being so unequal, "there Could be no drawing of Lotts among them," so the company let each member (in order, beginning with the largest shares) choose what he wanted. The surveyor took notes, and from them he prepared a plat, which the shareholders approved and located property lines.

A resident population slowly accumulated, and in 1678 the colonial government recognized Jamestown. As organized the next year, the town's body politic included absentee owners, mostly Newport men, some of whom held high office. For years, the town meetings were called meetings of proprietors and freemen. Though Jamestown made the usual rule that no one might become an inhabitant without the consent of the majority of freemen there, it could not enforce this rule against proprietors. They might take up residence or send a tenant at pleasure, provided they gave security to the town against his becoming a public charge. The act creating the new jurisdiction provided for two elected magistrates, a warden and a deputy warden, just as Portsmouth had had from 1648 until reorganization of the colonial government under the charter of 1663. The colony also required election of four other men to complete the town council. The town government gradually took shape more or less on its own as population increased and the proprietors lapsed into inactivity.[5]

The planting of an English community on Block Island in 1661 or 1662 resembled the beginnings of Providence and to some extent followed the same course to a stratified body of inhabitants. John Alcock, a physician in Roxbury, Massachusetts, took the lead in organizing the pioneers in 1660. He believed the island could support sixteen families in addition to the Indian population of several hundred, so he sought fifteen partners to put in equal shares of £25 with him to buy the land from four prominent Massachusetts men who had obtained title from their colony.[6] Unless he wanted an isolated retreat into egalitarian simplicity and neighborly virtue, his goals are hard to imagine.

If he had any such vision, reality fell short of the ideal. He could not find all the desired partners; some took more or less than a whole share. Some shares changed hands; owners of others may have sent tenants to tend flocks on the island. Nevertheless, the group did add a share for a minister.[7] The heads of families who went to Block Island probably managed the initial allocation of land and the small amount of day-to-day collective business, much as in early Providence. Eventually, they began to admit inhabitants without proprietary rights.

Rhode Island claimed jurisdiction over them under the charter of 1663 a year after its promulgation, making island men freemen of the colony and planning something short of a town government for them. The General Assembly prescribed a town meeting, a clerk, a constable, and three selectmen, mainly to perform judicial functions on the island. The Assembly gave the selectmen powers rather like justices of the peace. It also allowed the islanders to send two deputies to represent the island at the provincial level, although they seldom availed themselves of the opportunity. In most ways, Block Island was left to do nearly as it pleased.[8]

Even the simple concerns of the small settlement, however, soon gave rise to secondary groupings. In this outpost as elsewhere, the shared rights to land ineluctably defined a collectivity. The proprietors occasionally conducted their own business. Then, when Alcock died in 1668, it turned out that some of the partners had not paid for their shares. So another secondary organization came into existence for a time, "the Overseers and Guardians to the Will and Estate of the lat mr. John Alcock Deceased." This group, consisting of a few islanders and some Massachusetts men, had to collect the debts to the estate and issue deeds to the partners in the purchase when they had paid in full. The estate was not entirely disposed of until 1679. In the process, Alcock's original plan of a combination of sixteen families and a minister necessarily suffered.[9]

Moreover, population was increasing, leading the freemen on the island to aske the colony for a full-scale town government in 1672. They requested privileges similar to those in other towns, an imprecise request in view of the existing variety. The Block Islanders wanted better means to keep the peace, by which they meant local judges with wider competence. The General Assembly gave them the English name of New Shoreham and granted "Towne-shipp Authority and Liberties" in what amounted to the model of

Portsmouth before the royal charter. The central feature was authorization to elect a warden and deputy warden, each with the powers of a justice of the peace and together the bench of the town court. As in the original towns, the key element in local government was the magistracy. The town distinguished itself mainly by informality. For instance, the town meeting sometimes admitted freemen, sometimes the council did. Until the eighteenth century, the town had about thirty freemen.[10]

New Shoreham had among its few major concerns the control of livestock, to prevent damage to crops and the export of animals not owned by the exporter. It used traditional methods, like those of Portsmouth. As elsewhere, simple community self-regulation failed and had to be replaced by more elaborate methods, with requirements on fences and limits on turning animals loose to graze.[11]

As in the original towns, New Shoreham controlled the distribution and transfer of land to shape a community, though the means it used are not always clear. The freemen were classified into two categories: proprietors, who had at least a quarter of an original share, and mere householders. The town meeting retained control over several resources, such as beach, meadow, and clay pits. It gave the use of land to men, sometimes in collaboration with the proprietors, as an inducement to them to pursue crafts. It planned a compact settlement by arranging a cluster of five-acre lots. It leased out the ministerial land for the benefit of the town treasury, except for a few years after 1700, when the profits went to a resident pastor. The records also hint at actions by the proprietors alone.[12]

If the community's management of land provoked no assertive institution of proprietors, its efforts to create a harbor produced a succession of three similar ones. All were conceived in the fashion of an Old Regime privilege, a combination of duties and rights bordering on private authority, intended to bring private investment to produce a public benefit while rewarding the holders. Under the first arrangement, approved by the inhabitants in 1680, John Sands, John Williams, and their associates agreed to build a harbor by digging a channel from the ocean to Great Pond. They would get from the town any land drained as a result plus "the Whole priviled[ge] of the Harbor," which probably was expected to profit from fees charged to users. The townsmen for their part promised to supply two workdays apiece each year to maintain the harbor and also to give for that purpose "the Worke of the Indians," who owed it as a result of defeat in war. The undertakers dug a narrow channel but made no profit. They gave up their rights in 1694. The town tried two similar arrangements in later years, but storms did more damage than profits from wharfage could undo, even when the town supplied free labor and subsidies. So no durable organization of privileged masters of the crucial public facility could gain power. Later, the town's direct control came to grief, and the island had no harbor for years.[13]

The two new island towns showed how dissimilar such developments could be. The isolation of Block Island gave it a special self-contained quality and created distinctive needs. By contrast, Conanicut lay within sight of Newport and Portsmouth, whose inhabitants saw it as a splendid pasture. This outlook shaped the purchase of Conanicut and the assignment of shares in it. Finely varied fractions let people of widely different means invest, usually as absentee owners. The Conanicut company more or less accomplished the promoters' purposes but left a potential for discord between proprietors and town. By contrast, the scheme of equal shares in Block Island, though short of success, embodied a different goal. The Block Island settlers, however, failed to preserve equality and so had to maintain a distinction between proprietors and householders among the freemen. Yet they retained their confidence in energetic collective action and continued to devise new organizational techniques to achieve their most urgent collective need, a harbor.

The Narragansett Proprietors

While contrasting intentions went their separate ways in the new island towns, they collided in the Narragansett country. On one side was a swarm of uncoordinated and often ill-defined schemes promoted by separate organizations more or less under Rhode Island's aegis. On the other was a much clearer plan promoted by a single organization based in Boston and willing to accept the jurisdiction of any colonial government, though it usually set its hopes on Connecticut. In broad terms, the question was how the territory was to be settled, whether in a rather incoherent or improvisatory fashion by the Rhode Island interests or by a system of towns with publicly supported churches in the manner of Massachusetts. The ultimate victory of Rhode Island, which often seemed unlikely in the seventeenth century, has been regarded in retrospect as predestined, so the aims of the opposing side have been almost unexamined.

The Boston organization went by the name of the Narragansett Proprietors, though now it often is called the Atherton syndicate in honor of its most conspicuous figure, Major Humphrey Atherton. It began to take shape in 1658. The partners included several passive investors as well as three Bostonians who really led the group; prominent men from Connecticut and Plymouth; and two part-time Rhode Islanders, the Richard Smiths, father and son, who kept a trading post north of what the proprietors named Wickford.[14]

The proprietors acquired claims to land in two ways. The first was by the usual sort of purchase from Indians. In this manner they bought two sizable tracts in 1659, one called Quidnesset or Aquidnesset, lying north of Wickford, the other to the south, extending to the tip of Boston Neck. The second means was a mortgage, which they obtained in 1660, on the entire territory of the Narrgansett Indians. After a punitive expedition against the Indians and the capture of three principal sachems, the Commissioners of the United Colonies levied a huge fine on them, which they could not pay, and instead gave a mortgage on their territory. The Narragansett Proprietors agreed to pay the fine in exchange for the mortgage. When the Narragansett Indians could not redeem the mortgage, the proprietors foreclosed on it in 1662, and shortly thereafter they procured a royal endorsement of their claims. The government of Rhode Island regarded the transactions concerning the mortgage as fraud piled upon extortion.[15]

The proprietors could scarcely hope for Rhode Island's blessing and preferred a strong Puritan government anyway. When making plans for a town in 1663, they took advantage of a clause in the agreement between Dr. John Clarke and John Winthrop Jr. that was intended to resolve contradictions between the new Connecticut and Rhode Island charters. The clause allowed colonists in the Narragansett country to choose between the two jurisdictions. About a dozen of the proprietors and their settlers met near Smith's trading post and chose Connecticut, which responded by appointing officials for the locale. Neither the proprietors nor Connecticut accepted any adverse ruling on their jurisdiction, certainly not the decision of the royal commission of 1664 and 1665 to settle disputes over colony lines by making the Narragansett country the King's Province and putting it, at least temporarily, under the government of Rhode Island. The Rhode Island officials endorsed this decision as the best they could get.[16]

The Narragansett Proprietors acted energetically for a few years. At first they developed the two initial purchases apart from claims under the mortgage and proceeded with slight regard to colonial jurisdiction. The partners concerned in Quidnesset decided to form "a Plantation" there with sixty shares, which would be granted to men who would pay a shilling per acre and agree to support "an able goodly orthodox minister." They put the business in the hands of a committee composed of the four Boston partners, who drew in a number of Rhode Island men from all four towns. The committee, together with ten of these associates, might decided by majority vote to admit settlers and in conjunction with the share owners might "act in all things which concernes thie setling of the said plantation." The original proprietors, however, disliked the arrangement and negotiated a revision to take back control of the project. The proprietors made simpler plans for Boston Neck but changed them, too. Ultimately, the partners divided most of the land among themselves and sold the rest. They won Rhode Island's sanction for their titles in these two tracts in 1672.[17]

For the next forty years, most of the business of the Narragansett Proprietors involved the campaign to gain governmental backing for claims under the mortgage. The convoluted story need not be explained here. Briefly, the proprietors tried many tactics, including an adventure in Rhode

As authorized by the General Assembly in 1677, the East Greenwich grant had five thousand acres, less than half of what the town ultimately included. The grant overlapped the vague "Potowomut" tract obtained in 1660 by purchasers encouraged by the General Court of Commissioners; the Fones or Devil's Foot Purchase, acquired in 1762, which the claims of the Narragansett Proprietors made under the mortgage; and perhaps also the Mascackuak (or Maskachusett, or Mascuchusick) purchase. Beginning in 1678 and 1679, the East Greenwich grantees combined with some of the partners in the Fones purchase and all those in the rather mysterious Maskachusett purchase, the later probably included in compensation for what they lost when Rhode Island accepted the Quidnesset cession. Thus, the town extended southward to approximately the present line. The Narragansett Proprietors, however, sold the territory in the extension to a group of French settlers, who stayed there until driven out after the fall of the Dominion of New England in 1689. By 1716 the town boundaries were nearly the same as today, though subsequently the eastern bounds of the extension were revised, mainly to follow Hunt River. Unfortunately, not even approximate boundaries can be shown for the "Potowomut" Purchase or the Mascackuak (or Maskachusett, or Mascuchusick) purchase.

Location of Smith lands and Quidnesset purchase, maps by M. S. Greene, made in 1880 and published in James N. Arnold, *A Statement of the Case of the Narraganett Tribe of Indians* (Newport, 1896), after p. 70; Fones or Devil's Foot purchase, the same map as emended by description in William Davis Miller, *Notes and Queries Concerning the Early Bounds and Divisions of the Township of East Greenwich as Set Forth in William Hall's Plat, 1716*, (Providence, 1937), 11; and a nineteenth-century copy of a plat said to be by Peter Sanform and to date from 1679, Rhode Island Historical Society; East Greenwich lines in same plat and as explained in Miller, *Notes and Queries*; Potowomut purchase (shown as ultimately limited), according to deed in Howard M. Chapin, ed., *Early Records of the Town of Warwick* (Providence, 1926), 444–45; miscellaneous emendments according to plats at the Rhode Island Historical Society. The extent of the "Potowomut" Purchase of 1660 and the Mascacknuk (or Maskachusett, or Mascuchusick) Purchase may only be surmised.

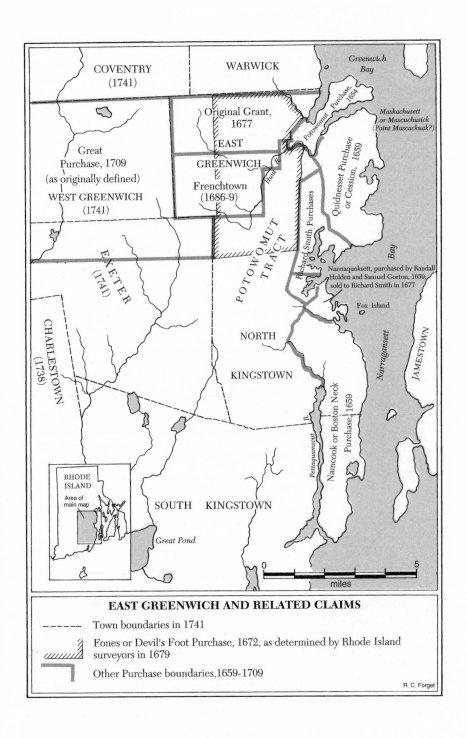

COVENTRY
(1741)

WARWICK

*Greenwich
Bay*

Original Grant,
1677

EAST

GREENWICH

*Potowomut Purchase,
1654*

*Maskachusett
or Mascuchusick
(Point Mascackuak?)*

Great
Purchase, 1709
(as originally defined)

WEST GREENWICH
(1741)

Frenchtown
(1686-9)

Hunt R.

*Quidnesset Purchase
or Cession, 1659*

Richard Smith Purchases

Bay

Nannaquoksett, purchased by Randall
Holden and Samuel Gorton, 1659;
sold to Richard Smith in 1677

Fox Island

EXETER
(1741)

POTOWOMUT
TRACT

NORTH

KINGSTOWN

Narragansett

JAMESTOWN

CHARLESTOWN
(1738)

Pettaquamscut R.

Namcook or Boston Neck
Purchase, 1659

RHODE
ISLAND

Area of
main map

SOUTH   KINGSTOWN

Great Pond

0   5

miles

EAST GREENWICH AND RELATED CLAIMS

Town boundaries in 1741

Fones or Devil's Foot Purchase, 1672, as determined by Rhode Island
surveyors in 1679

Other Purchase boundaries,1659-1709

R. C. Forget

Island politics that nearly succeeded in 1672, but usually looked to Hartford for support while angling for a new imperial endorsement. But they never could undo the decision of the royal commission of 1664 and 1665, nor could they sponsor settlements on the land as quickly as several Rhode Island interests did.[18]

King Philip's War seemed to give the Narragansett Proprietors a glorious opportunity by killing or expelling most of the Indians from the area and leaving the troops of Massachusetts, Plymouth, and Connecticut militarily in control of the land. The proprietors reorganized in March 1677, levied an assessment on the shareholders, and reestablished cooperation with Connecticut. That colony, however, wanted to assume more control of the territory than the Narragansett proprietors would tolerate. Worse, it proposed to buy up the mortgage. When that threat receded, the proprietors looked ahead hopefully. Rhode Island successfully founded East Greenwich, and the proprietors had to concede land to some Rhode Island rivals, the Pettaquamscut purchasers. A few years later, the proprietors won a favorable ruling from a new royal commission and soon saw several of their backers gain key offices in the Dominion of New England. The syndicate expected to have all their claims upheld in law and by force.[19]

Strange to say, the only tangible result of their efforts was a short-lived settlement of French Protestants, who bought land northwest of Wickford. They organized a village that suited the plans of the proprietors quite well. It was to be a Massachusetts town translated into French. The settlers laid out house lots, farm lots, and streets. They built dwellings and a meetinghouse, set out orchards and vineyards, organized a church, and honored their pastor. To their shock, the English in East Greenwich disputed their title. Governor Andros of the Dominion refused to uphold the proprietors' claims to the exclusion of all others. Instead, he imposed a compromise between the French town and its hostile neighbors. He then reviewed the mortgage and found it was insubstantial because the debt that lay behind it was a product of extortion practiced outside the borders of any of the United Colonies. Moreover, the Narragansett Proprietors had not paid the debt. Nevertheless, Andros referred the dispute to the king. The proprietors won an order in England for grants of Narragansett territory, only one of which was made before the Dominion fell.[20]

The contest soon heated up again. The East Greenwich men drove out the French, actual settlement progressed in disregard of the mortgage, and the proprietors and their opponents resumed maneuvers against each other. In 1699, Rhode Island cautiously moved toward a compromise that undermined the proprietors. The colony proposed in rather misty language that settlers actually on the land, relying on titles derived from the Narragansett Proprietors or any other source previously disapproved by the colony, might put themselves on the right side of the law by coming to terms with persons holding an adverse claim that Rhode Island recognized. The proprietors virtually lost Connecticut's backing a few years later. That colony ceased to care about land ownership and sought only jurisdiction in the Narragansett country. The proprietors tried working through Rhode Island politics again, then carried futile appeals to Connecticut and the throne. The efforts collapsed soon after 1708.[21] So the Narragansett Proprietors engendered little settlement except at Boston Neck and Quidnesset and no proper town.

Rhode Island and the Southern Narragansett Country

Instead of the Narragansett Proprietors, several groups of men, sooner or later with Rhode Island's approval, promoted most of the land settlement south of Shawomet. The five combinations that acted on a large scale call for consideration. The first to form was the Pettaquamscut purchasers, who obtained their basic Indian deeds in January and March 1658, before the colonial government had a firm law forbidding such purchases without its prior consent.[22] The Pettaquamscut men tied their prospects to Rhode Island's jurisdiction. They claimed a huge but vaguely described block of territory, roughly seven miles square, on the mainland west of Newport. Ultimately, it was scaled down to modern South Kingstown and Narragansett minus Boston Neck. The purchasers defined a simple organization in brief articles of agreement. The five founders, four Portsmouth men and John Hull, the mintmaster of Massachusetts, added only two partners, both men of means and political strength in Newport.[23] They held equal shares and generally acted harmoniously. The purchasers or their agents met at irregular intervals, at the outset in Newport but later on their land.

Their plans remained fluid for years, as well they might, considering the dense Indian population on the territory and the rivalry with the Narragansett Proprietors. The Pettaquamscut men sold large tracts and made no effort to shape the pattern of settlement, apart from granting a mill site and reserving land to provide income for "an orthodox person" to preach the gospel to the settlers, until they futilely set aside land for a town center in 1689. They kept most of the territory for themselves, and at least one partner went to live there.[24]

The Rhode Island government rather than the purchasers tried to set up town government at Pettaquamscut, lumping it with the territory occupied by people who had bought land from the Narragansett Proprietors. The object was to assert jurisdiction against Connecticut rather than to foster communal life. The two colonies dueled, each appointing local officials and organizing towns from 1663 to 1696. Rhode Island, to little effect, in 1674 tried to erect the town of Kingstown, "with liberty as hath bee[n] granted to New-Shorrum."[25]

The contest remained inconclusive, and the White residents in the Narragansett country got along without government—or taxes—most of the time. No colony could protect them during King Philip's War. Little changed even while the Dominion of New England held sway over the territory. In 1696, Kingstown finally accepted Rhode Island jurisdiction. The populace held an election, chose officials in the pattern then used in the original towns, and sent deputies to the General Assembly. Soon, the town conducted business roughly in the way of others in Rhode Island.[26]

Kingstown never could grant land, so it escaped entanglement with a proprietary organization. It would not take sides with contenders for valid title. It even declined to record deeds until 1699, probably to stay out of the essentially judicial business of deciding whether a title had legal derivation. It left basic disputes to the colonial government.

While the Pettaquamscut purchasers held the southeast corner of the Narragansett country against outsiders, some Newport men, led by William Vaughan, formed a much more elaborate enterprise, the Misquamicut company, to buy the southwest corner, technically in Pequot rather than Narragansett or Niantic territory. The government of Rhode Island prompted this purchase in 1659 but, probably because of internal politics, withdrew overt involvement while maintaining tacit sponsorship. Massachusetts claimed the territory as spoils of the Pequot War and authorized the town of Southertown there. All the same, Vaughan and his partners gained claims over a tract along the ocean between the Pawcatuck and Weekapaug on the south and stretching north for several miles. Other deeds extended the claim north and east.[27]

In March 1661, the Newport men organized a company rather like the Conanicut one. The articles of agreement required that the shareholders make decisions in general session by majority vote, that any share should be forfeit for nonpayment of assessments, and that assessment be apportioned to size of share. Several dozen men took shares, ranging from one-sixteenth of a whole share to one and three-quarters, held by Vaughan.[28]

After some experiments, the Misquamicut company worked out its procedures. Though it chose a clerk and treasurer and tried to put its business in the hands of trustees, it had to rely on frequent general meetings to admit members and conduct other business.[29] The company needed general participation to carry on the costly and time-consuming work of holding Misquamicut against Massachusetts and Connecticut. To begin with, the partners agreed to go there a few at a time and camp out. Later, they paid men to live there as residents, usually by giving them land. When Massachusetts opposed their efforts, they raised money to finance their own legal defense. The general meetings served, as nothing else would have, to give effect to the long series of assessments.[30]

Quite early, the company clarified its plans, which included designing a settlement. It created a cluster of seventy six-acre house lots and then confronted the puzzle of dividing them among men with grossly unequal shares. Here was a point where the system of investment collided with the business of shaping a community. The partners solved the problem by letting each person who held at least a one-eighth share have a house lot, provided he accepted an equitable diminution of his other allocations. The company also gave a share to one settler who promised to operate a mill and provided him with a suitable site. With these preparations made, the company held a meeting at Misquamicut in September 1661, at which it agreed on the location of a town center and the division of house lots.[31]

The anticipated countermoves by Massachusetts soon began, leading the promoters to seek help from Rhode Island, which they did not get for a few years. Rhode Island publicly took the company's side only after Connecticut, under its royal charter, replaced Massachusetts as the rival. Then Rhode Island won a favorable ruling on the Misquamicut purchase from the royal commission of 1664 and 1665, appointed conservators of the peace for the district, admitted a few freemen, and in 1669 authorized the town of Westerly. The General Assembly simply granted Westerly "all such previlidges" and allowed it to use all "methods and formes for the well ordering their Towne afaires as any other Towne in this collony may now use and Exercise." Unlike other new towns, however, Westerly received no permission to elect wardens. Instead, the Assembly intended to continue appointing conservators of the peace, who might "[e]rect courts for Triall of such small matters as other perticelerr courts in this collony may doe in that respect."[32]

Lack of further specification scarcely mattered. The freemen seldom conducted town government for several years while Rhode Island and Connecticut contested jurisdiction. Connecticut regarded the town as part of Stonington, which granted land there. Probably quite a few Westerly residents accepted the opposing jurisdiction at times, while at other times they contested it. Even such routine functions as regulating admissions of newcomers or rules on harboring strangers, registering brands and earmarks, or working on roads could be carried out that way. The act on entertaining strangers, for instance, was used against a partisan of Connecticut. The rules on maintaining highways were applied to keep Westerly's roads open through Stonington's allotments.[33]

During these troubled years, the Westerly freemen began to gain control of the undivided land of the Misquamicut company and even to acquire more. Among their tactics, they respected the Rhode Island government only when it was expedient to do so. Their opposition to outside authority was the most extreme of any town or company of proprietors in the Narragansett region. In defiance of Rhode Island policy, the company asked for and won an endorsement of its land claims from the royal commission of 1683 and in 1685 persuaded the General Assembly to endorse extending its jurisdiction to the Pettaquamscut line. Under the Dominion of New England, it went on resisting land grants made under Connecticut until some compromises seemed prudent, and it carried on more self-government than the Dominion allowed until it obtained Governor Andros's permission for even more. When the Dominion toppled, the town avoided submission to any colonial authority.[34]

In the next few years, the townsfolk undertook no serious public business except to give themselves more land. Probably by design, they left crucial details unrecorded and adopted a misty resolve "to settle the propr[ietor]s land within their township." Perhaps the verb was deliberately ambiguous. They meant the undivided territory of the Misquamicut shareholders but also some land to be taken from Joseph Stanton, who had been using an extensive tract under a Connecticut-derived title. Ingeniously, they pitted against him some other claimants they previously had refused to recognize. Then they agreed to divide among themselves some five thousand acres of land within the new eastern extension of the township, allowing shares to some former Connecticut adherents.[35]

Subsequently, they sought colonial endorsement of these machinations as the price of rejoining Rhode Island. Westerly resumed a Rhode Island form of town government, sent deputies to the General Assembly, and got the Assembly's consent to the eastern division. As wrapped and tied, the package made security of titles in most of the township dependent on its falling within Rhode Island.[36] It also gave the town control of the undivided Misquamicut lands. In a sense, town and colony had combined against the proprietors. The strategic purpose of the Misquamicut purchase had been served, but the absentee proprietors were in great danger of losing their rights. In time, they fought back.

Rhode Island and the Northern Narragansett Country

Until after King Philip's War, Rhode Island men and their government did little to oppose the Narragansett Proprietors in the northern part of their claims, but the proprietors did less there to assert their interests. Just after 1658 the colonial government encouraged purchases in the northern part of the threatened territory but soon dropped its backing. The Court of Commissioners appointed a committee composed of four men, one from each town, to negotiate purchases. They bought rights south of Shawomet and promised to regard the land as in Rhode Island.[37] This purchase became known as Potowomut, though it was different from Warwick's overlapping Potowomut purchase. So it will be designated here as "Potowomut." It probably overlapped also and more extensively the Quidnesset purchase of the Narragansett Proprietors as well as the East Greenwich grant.

The committee wanted to increase the political benefits by bringing as many men as possible from Providence and Warwick into the proprietary partnership. The Court of Commissioners repudiated the project, but the committee persisted, winning support in both mainland towns. Then somehow the plan collapsed. The colonial government obtained custody of the "Potowomut" Indian deed and left the purchasers to improve their land as best they could. Few did anything with their claims, and the rights generated by the promotion merely hovered, waiting to bedevil other purchasers.[38]

For the time being, even less came of the purchase of the northwest corner of the Narragansett country, thought to be west of Providence. Without official sponsorship, William Vaughan, the Misquamicut leader, organized a new group. Composed mainly of Newport men, many of them old Misquamicut hands, the group made a purchase in 1662 that became known as Westconnaug. The anticipated relation between proprietors and community never developed, however, let alone one between the proprietors and a town government. Yet the claim lay waiting to be resuscitated when the possibility of settlers materialized.[39]

The land promotion that got the quickest results was the second one in the northeast corner of the Narragansett country, the East Greenwich grant made in 1677. For the only time in its history, Rhode Island directly sponsored a town. King Philip's War had just removed most of the Indians from the region, so the colonial government hurried to get ahead of the Narragansett Proprietors by putting settlers on the land. It promised protection from Connecticut to refugees who would move back to the mainland and offered up to ten thousand acres in the Narragansett country in parcels of one hundred acres to additional settlers who would go there and promise to remain loyal to Rhode Island. A dozen men in Warwick and parts adjacent mobilized to take advantage of this offer. They intended to draw in additional partners and to avoid the contradictions of equal political rights and unequal proprietary rights. Each partner would have one vote regardless of the number of shares he owned. The company would conduct its business by majority vote of those attending any meeting.[40]

Probably to please the organizers, the Assembly laid down more confining stipulations on land rights and authorized them to form the town of East Greenwich. The plan called for a real community, one without absentee ownership and speculation in shares. In October 1677, the colony granted five thousand acres at the head of Greenwich Bay, to be divided among fifty persons in parcels consisting of a ten-acre house lot and a ninety-acre lot of arable land. The Assembly required grantees to build on their house lots within one year or to forfeit all the land and forbade them to sell or otherwise alienate the land to anyone else in the plantation for twenty-one years without permission from the colony. All the grantees would be freemen, and their town would have "all Rights, Libertys and previledges whatever unto a Town appertaininge." The settlers duly met and organized a town government.[41]

In a further effort to use East Greenwich for political ends, the General

Assembly allowed for the possibility of absentee ownership and created a proprietary organization distinct from the town government. Absenteeism materialized; the distinct proprietary organization existed only in an innocuous way. In response to objections against the early actions of the new town, the colony engineered a revision of the basic grant to placate persons with conflicting claims based on three prior purchases of parts of the same territory—one of them the "Potowomut" purchase. Using terms that were sufficiently imprecise to generate trouble later, the Assembly blended most of these claims into the share system of the new town, let some of the owners become freemen there, doubled the territory under the new jurisdiction, and watered down the restrictions on the original tenure. These changes brought a number of absentee proprietors into the town's land system and thus broke the initial strict connection of unitary shares to membership in the community.[42] Hence, the potential for dividing the town from the land syndicate.

Yet the town meeting exerted firm control over the undivided lands while honoring all the rights to shares that it knew about. It put tracts into individual ownership, reserved some as a communal resource, set aside plots for a burial ground and other public uses, granted a mill site, and kept a strip along Greenwich Bay to be developed in the future as the commercial center. Like Westerly, East Greenwich remained aloof from Rhode Island after the fall of the Dominion of New England and used that interval for actions of dubious legality, in this case hounding out the French settlers. By 1695, however, the town government was officially back in operation, reorganized in rough accord with Rhode Island practice, and resumed treating undivided land as its own to bestow.

In the founding of East Greenwich, the colonial government reached its high point in directing settlement. It was, however, less than masterful. The General Assembly energetically set out to promote the settlement but kept weakening the initial plan to please petitioners or win over people who had disregarded the colony's authority in the past. The town itself took up local government and control of land more smoothly than had its predecessors, in spite of the Assembly's changes of course and the shifts and uncertainties of colonial jurisdiction.

Conclusion

The scramble for land and the resulting new settlements in the second half of the seventeenth century led to variety rather than uniformity, local self-control or near anarchy rather than orderly delegation of power. The chief partisans of uniformity and a disciplined society, the Narragansett Proprietors, never shaped a community and sponsored only an ephemeral one. Still, they remained a force to be taken seriously. Their political strength in two New England colonies and the imperial government almost allowed them to triumph on a number of occasions. Besides, by being the one great enemy, they gave such coherence as there was to the groups arrayed against them. The colonial government in Rhode Island, even if it fashioned a comprehensive policy, could never implement it. Instead, it went along with plans laid by some of its inhabitants or took the initiative feebly, often to retreat or change its plans in the face of any opposition.

The organizations of proprietors manifested with special clarity the salient traits of institutional development in the later seventeenth century. They reflected the expectation that institutional solidarity would flow from shared property rights, the vagueness of the distinction between property and power, the corresponding tendency to make political functions an attribute of ownership, and the lack of central authority within the colony. The purchasers' organizations formed their own plans and inner structures. They endowed themselves with capacities to act by majority rule, entrust their affairs to executive committees, grant deeds to individual allotments through an elected official, levy assessments on the members, and declare members' rights to shares forfeit—in short, they assumed quasi-governmental capacities.

The proprietary organizations used similar arrangements that they probably drew from antecedent institutions. They may have imitated the share systems of joint-stock companies or age-old methods of subdividing ownership in commercial voyages. They may have derived the format of a few basic officers and an executive committee from town government. Unlike the towns, they had no commitment to equal votes for all members. Still, they had difficulty in arranging voting rights for holders of unequal shares. Necessarily, the inequality of rights pertained to assessments, whether in money or work, and above all to land dividends. Elaborate quantification interfered with easy transition of a company into a community, so the syndicates that sponsored towns created potentially antagonistic institutions.

Though they designed firm quasi-political structures, the founders of proprietary organizations began quite early to retreat from strong collective action. They never governed transfers of shares and seldom penalized members. They lost their initial zeal to regulate admissions. Before long, the organizations treated share rights almost as real estate in fee simple. Perhaps lack of a secure connection to the colonial government made the proprietors cautious. The solidarity of members, so obvious at the start as to suggest a social foundation, tended to shatter when some of the partners took up residence on the land or sold their rights. The proprietary organizations conspicuously did not become developers of income-yielding property, like markets in the Old World fashion. Neither the pace of settlement nor the ambitions of the settlers would allow such collective economic functions for the proprietors. Instead, the members merely used their shares by taking land dividends. Yet the potential remained for building a group for united action, at least in political efforts.

Rather than land syndicates, the towns, for all their frailty, usually gained importance. Westerly and East Greenwich made the best of turmoil to gain territory and probably a social solidarity as well. Kingstown, by contrast, lacked control over its own undivided land and drifted virtually unorganized from affiliation with Connecticut to Rhode Island to the Dominion of New England to practical autonomy. In the end, it benefited from not playing a part in disputes over land. New Shoreham lived much to itself in a manner that retained a strong communal approach to local affairs. Gradually, Jamestown residents took control over their public concerns, and the proprietors' importance diminished. In time, some order had to be brought out of the random striving and tendencies to subdivision in institutions. The proprietary organizations still could act for themselves, and in time they stirred up a new round of conflicts.

❧ 5 ❧

Religious Association Replacing Secular

In the realm of religious institutions, developments in the late seventeenth century went counter to the disintegration of the political realm. New churches, in effect, created means to govern life for many in Rhode Island, both to connect them to a wider world and to regulate their daily affairs. Quakers nearly separated themselves from the secular society. In the early years, religion in the colony had produced institutions quite as unstable as secular ones. After 1657 the existing churches continued much as before, but new ones introduced stronger and more comprehensive organizations. The founders of the original towns had insisted that a church be a fellowship of active believers, and thus, except in Warwick, they had produced small coteries detached from communities. The resulting diversity of convictions and practices dashed hopes that Christ's church in freedom would enjoy concord and uniformity. Soul liberty, moreover, allowed quite a few to drift away from Christian discipline altogether. If many serious Rhode Island Christians prized the freedom that let them depart so radically from the practice of the immediate past, some aspired to churches with ties beyond the immediate fellowship.

In the later seventeenth century, four novelties entered the scene. All conceived their religious practice in a cosmopolitan framework rather than a merely congregational one. Two of them proved durable: the Seventh Day Baptists and the Quakers. Both of these new persuasions created more elaborate ecclesiastical structures than others in New England, but Quakers outdid all the rest by far. Their organization grew in complexity and effectiveness most rapidly in times when government was weakest. The other two, a French Protestant congregation and a colony of Jews, scattered after a few years. Yet the French, too, brought a new concern for discipline and formality. Their church, like the Quakers, assumed many of the functions of secular government and did so when political association was especially disorganized. The Jews carried on many traditional observances, if not the full scale of religious ceremony, and maintained ties to Jews elsewhere.

The new religions shared propensities for multidimensional solidarity within the fellowship and, except for the Jews, for highly developed organization. These traits had been weak or missing in the original churches. The examples may seem few, yet the magnitude of the Quaker structure and its immediate appeal to a large part of the population show that they were significant. The new churches, however, had their limits. They could define communities with impressive success, but they could not entirely supplant an orderly secular society, and the governments needed to make one.

Old and New Baptists

The older fellowships remained indifferent to keeping records, so little can be known about them. The people who thought the laying on of hands was mandatory also were apt to frown on ecclesiastical formalities and to believe in direct inspiration and general redemption—that is, that any one could achieve salvation. Conversely, those who reserved the laying on of hands for ordination usually doubted direct inspiration and believed in predestination. They, however, began to take a small interest in ecclesiastical machinery. They were, for instance, the first to appoint deacons.[1]

The schism that produced the Seventh Day Baptists showed that the ferment and fractiousness of the first decade persisted, although Baptists of different sorts did have some sense of belonging in one classification. The Rhode Island churches lived in a little world of disputes and customs nearly their own, having few neighbors who agreed with them and infrequent correspondence with like-minded people in England. The New England Baptists, however, settled into the ways of Massachusetts orthodoxy, having an inner core of members in full communion surrounded by a larger and as yet unorganized number of people who accepted the doctrines taught in a church and brought up their children with some undefinable relation to it yet never felt able to claim full membership. Tightly restricted communion surely led to this end. In these years the outer circle had nothing like its later importance in supporting the institutions financially, because the churches neither had meetinghouses nor paid their pastors.

The Seventh Day Baptists withdrew or were excommunicated from the first Baptist church in Newport. The events began with the arrival of Stephen Mumford toward the end of 1664. An obscure man, he had been associated with an English congregation that believed God had appointed the seventh day (Saturday) as the Sabbath. He soon found converts. They remained in the first Baptist church for several years, probably meeting by themselves on Saturdays "to pray and edify each other." When four of them abandoned this innovation, the others refused to take Communion with them any longer.[2] This disturbance to the original flock finally brought on a controversy over the Sabbath. Samuel Hubbard and William Hiscox defended the seventh day, referring to the relationship between Jewish and Christian law. They were willing to abandon the strictly ceremonial and dietary laws of the ancient Hebrews but nothing in the Ten Commandments. It was not long before the elders of the church began to preach against seventh-day observance. At church meetings, disputations over the meaning of the Ten Commandments for Christians remained unresolved. The sticklers for the Saturday Sabbath, often called Sabbatarians, insisted that dropping any rule in the Commandments meant dropping all and with them the definition of sin and the need for a savior. The controversy expanded to cover the scope of God's covenant with humans under the old dispensation and the alleged desecrations of the Sabbath by leading figures on the opposing sides.[3]

At length, the futility of further debate became clear, and the Sabbatarians formed their own church. Hubbard reported, "We Entred into Covenant with the lord and with one another and gave up our Selves to god and Each other to Walk together in all gods Holy Commandments and the Ordinances according to What the Lord had Discovered and should Discover to us, to be his Mind for us to be Obedient unto; with Sence upon our Hearts of great need to be watchfull over one another, Did promise So to do in building and Edifying Each other in our Most Holy faith." They believed in predestination and yet practiced the laying on of hands for all believers. Also, they expected continuing inspiration from the Holy Spirit, spoke in tongues, and encouraged the brethren to exercise "gifts" of preaching or prophecy. For all the doggedness of their stands on several points, however, they regarded themselves as having affinities with all other Baptists, a view that some others shared.[4]

The Sabbatarians began a distinctive process of developing institutional formality when some of the Newport members moved to Westerly and tried to remain in the original fellowship. After several years, the church in Rhode Island began to hold general meetings every eight weeks, alternately at the two locations. On such occasions, participants took Communion and conducted church business, including baptisms, receiving new members, hearing disputes between brethren, and disciplining wrongdoers. The church had adopted the usual Baptist procedure on discipline, derived from Matthew 18:15–17, customarily known as gospel order. When it heard a rumor of sin in a member of the flock, it would send a messenger, equipped with pertinent biblical texts, to speak to the errant one. If the wayward member proved obstinate, the church might vote an admonition against further ill conduct and obstinacy or proceed to excommunication. The church had officers besides its pastors, including a deacon, a baptizer, and perhaps others to keep records and hold funds. An intriguing entry of 1698 alluded to the church's decision to choose officers by lot out of a group of nominees. Further elaboration of the institution took place only in the eighteenth century.[5]

Quite early, Newport Sabbatarians began to communicate with like-minded souls elsewhere. They corresponded with brethren in London and tried to hold the small number of Americans in a denominational form. They found other adherents scattered from Boston to Long Island and even received a visit from some Virginians who sought baptism. These sojourners objected to public lectures on Sundays and also to psalm-singing, and thus, the Newport Sabbatarians gave up singing. This event dramatized the lack of orderly procedure in the congregation, and Hubbard recommended a general meeting to frame regulations for a church. Such a meeting was held at Newport in May 1684; unfortunately, the conclusions do not survive.[6]

Paradoxically, due to its weakness in numbers and its dispersed membership, the Seventh Day Baptist fellowship broke out of the pattern of militantly independent congregations set earlier in the seventeenth century. It pleaded for unity among Baptists of all kinds to preserve religious freedom. The Sabbatarians carried biblicism to new and more divisive extremes, but the widespread hostility they aroused gave them an incentive to join a coalition whenever possible. Their dispersed geographical situation gave rise to the novelty of keeping in one church, members who lived in several places. The Sabbatarians had to make their own world even if they needed connections to a larger one. In these respects, they resembled the Quakers, who won a far larger number of adherents.

Quakers

Quakerism in Rhode Island began as the most thoroughgoing religion of direct inspiration and so of anti-institutional tendencies, yet it adopted an ecclesiastical system that became ever more intricate as it bound together and regulated the entire denomination. It was quite the opposite of the Baptist style of organization. The Friends used New Testament precedents, to be sure, but went well beyond them. The system was devised in England to enable members to withstand active hostility from their more numerous neighbors; persecution by the officials of the realm, and the perils of existence as a minority sect where the church had a partnership with the state. In Rhode Island, none of these conditions obtained, yet the organization proved quite as valuable where society was loosely knit, the secular government weak, religious liberty assured, and where popular opposition amounted to little more than disparagement. In both situations, the Quaker system enabled the members to be almost entirely self-governing. That may well have been one of Quakerism's foremost gifts to its adherents around Narragansett Bay.

Quaker missionaries found converts all over eastern New England in the 1650s, nowhere more than in Rhode Island, especially on Aquidneck. The beliefs of the Hutchinsonians and Gortonians prepared the way. Quickly, the island became the center of the new religion in North America, to be relegated to second place only with the founding of Philadelphia.

At first, befitting a religion based on the workings of the divine Inner Light, ecclesiastical concerns sat lightly on Rhode Island Quakers. Though the new Friends held regular meetings, they were almost exclusively for worship. In addition to weekly gatherings, they held monthly meetings on Aquidneck, perhaps as early as 1658, and yearly ones at Newport beginning a few years later. Gradually, the monthly meetings turned into occasions for regulating religious fellowship to prevent members from drifting into eccentric opinions or sin.

In these years the Quakers, according to an opponent, went further than they would ever go again in detaching themselves from the surrounding society. They shunned public office and refused to present for public records accounts of births, deaths, and marriages.[7] Although they abandoned such extremes after 1671—they grew so numerous in Portsmouth that conducting town government without them would have been nearly impossible—they remained resolute in maintaining good order among themselves according to their own standards. Obviously, this required a strong organization. At least by the 1670s, church structure began to grow quite elaborate. The oldest surviving records reveal a system in routine operation in 1676, so it must have taken shape earlier, probably after the first visit of George Fox in 1672.[8]

If George Fox in many respects founded Quakerism, he also preserved it by devising an ecclesiastical system. He balanced mysticism with a passion for record keeping and procedural formality. Firm organization kept reliance on the Inner Light from having its individualistic and centrifugal effects. Most New England Friends accepted his organizational plans.

By the end of the seventeenth century, this meant a double pyramid of assemblies for church business—all called meetings—distinguished by their periodicity, location, and sex of membership. (Later, there was another set of meetings for cultivation of the ministry and restraint of heterodoxy.) At the bottom in many places were preparative meetings held every week or once before each monthly meeting. As with the more inclusive meetings, these came to be separated by sex. Each preparative meeting included the people who met for worship regularly at a certain place. A few of these meetings combined, comprising a monthly meeting which was the basic unit for disciplinary actions. Several monthly meetings joined in a quarterly meeting, several quarterly meetings in a yearly meeting. New England had a yearly meeting, held at Newport, but it gave final authority on matters of belief and discipline to the London Yearly Meeting.

The completed structure was barely in view during the 1670s, and as in England, its creation stirred up opposition in Rhode Island. As first revealed in the records, there was only the monthly meeting composed of both men and women, which assembled at Joshua Coggeshall's house in Newport before a meetinghouse was built. No ceremony was used to induct members. Surely, they observed no rite like baptism or confirmation, which Friends militantly rejected along with the traditional eucharist. Accordingly, there was no clearly marked core of members, such as Baptists had, and the number participating in ecclesiastical deliberations could be fairly large. The guidelines for procedure and the categories of business began with transcriptions of Fox's advice, to which were added other exhortations and local precedents.[9]

The monthly meeting probably devoted time to worship, but nothing was said on this subject in the minutes, which reported only church business. The entries mentioned many essentials in the operation of the fellowship: travelling Quaker ministers who visited Rhode Island, the time and place of meetings for worship or business, acquisition of property, repair of meetinghouses, approval of marriages within the fold, issuance of certificates to Friends who planned to visit other meetings, efforts to resolve disputes between members, care of the poor, disciplinary actions, raising and spending money, appointing ad hoc committees and standing officers (notably the trustees of real estate and the clerk and treasurer), and recognition of members' spiritual gifts as they became visible for preaching. Contrary to common belief, Friends had ministers, though their only function was to speak as the spirit prompted them. The clerk kept vital records for the members in addition to recording the meeting's decisions and carrying on its correspondence. The meeting disseminated Quaker views by distributing publications and holding quarterly sessions where suitable material might be read to children as well as their parents. From the start, the range of business was extensive and voluminous beyond anything found in other church records at any time during the colonial period. The systematic use of committees and the number of people serving the church were truly remarkable.

Friends carefully watched the conduct of members and tried to guard the reputation of their religion against accusations that it led to immorality. They used their version of gospel order not only to deal with sinners of the usual kind but also to discipline people who transgressed a wide range of sectarian rules on good behavior.[10] The meeting also adopted the policy of publicizing its repudiation of sinful conduct. A repentant wrongdoer had to condemn his actions before the monthly meeting. Ultimately, that meant a written statement including assertions that failure to follow the Inner Light and neglect of his religion, not obedience to it, brought about the dereliction. If misdeeds were widely known, the self-condemnation had to be publicized just as widely. In one case, the meeting required a slanderer to tell all who might have heard him that he had spoken falsely "or Ells freinds must publish the paper [of self-condemnation] that he signed."[11] If the sinner remained obdurate, the meeting publicized its decision to cut him off from membership. Again, nothing so systematic was used in other religious organizations in the colony.

The monthly meeting, once more in contrast to the Baptists, aborted a schism, albeit at the cost of losing a few members. The disagreement probably began in 1676, when George Fox decided that Henry Bull should not have shot some horses that had been pastured on his land without his permission but should have tried arbitration or an action at law against the owners. Though Bull and others who sided with him acknowledged their fault and were shortly reconciled to the flock, they appeared at the center of the schism a few years later.[12] By then, the dissident opinions of Robert Hodgson and Joseph Nicholson (or Nickelson) further complicated events. They had opposed Fox's system of organization when, in 1679, after some altercations with the meeting, they temporarily renounced their heterodoxical views. They gave up their determination to "[c]onfess to god and not to the Church" and their belief "that after a man is Inlitened and have Tasted of the good word of god and the power of the world to Come [he] Cann never more fall a waye." These views were incompatible with the increasingly assertive ecclesiastical government and smacked of antinomian perfectionism.[13] The schism soon revived. The dissidents briefly held their own meetings for worship, but the monthly meeting persuaded most of them to rejoin it. By 1687 the separation had come to an end, even though a few people may have drifted away permanently.[14]

One means of subduing schism was the organization of a yearly meeting. The monthly meeting in Newport decided in May 1682 to call a "generall mans meeting," presumably a gathering from all nearby colonies, and the first recorded session of New England Yearly Meeting convened the following month.[15] In addition, well before that time and long afterward, annual meetings for worship were held at several places in New England. Even when they conducted no formal business, they brought together multitudes and surely provided occasions for informal confabulations. After 1682 a yearly meeting at Newport made official decisions on discipline and practice and became the institutional bulwark for the defense of Quakerism in New England.

Other complexities in organizations followed. Quarterly meetings, to be held every three or four months, were created as an intermediate step between the monthly and annual ones. The quarterly meetings were given an educational function for a time. Part of the session was reserved "for the Reeding of friends Epistles" and other edifying literature, but this became the provenance of a gathering exclusively for that purpose beginning in 1693.[16]

By the mid-1690s the monthly meeting began to separate into men's and women's branches, a common practice in both the Puritan and Baptist churches. The change was probably facilitated by construction of meeting-houses where segregated sessions were possible.[17] The division began in 1693, though sometimes men and women met together later. By the end of the century, Friends held separate monthly meetings on Aquidneck and on the mainland to the west, as well as separate quarterly and yearly meetings. In addition, they had begun to create a similar hierarchy of meetings for ministers for men and women together. During the elaboration of an ecclesiastical pyramid, most Rhode Island meetings extended their business over more of the details of everyday life.[18]

The Aquidneck Friends also began to look for safe ways to own real estate. They were the first ecclesiastical organization in the colony to acquire land and always had by far the most. They went further in securing legal control over their property than non-Quakers did for some time. They started by creating committees to take title on condition of trust. Gradually, they made the terms stricter. In 1692, when the meeting bought land for a meeting-house in Portsmouth, it added a clause allowing the monthly meeting to designate replacements for any of the trustees who might "by any wise Refuse or neglect or by any wise [become] Disabled by death or other-wise, to performe the Trust comited to them."[19]

Surely, the most extraordinary feature of the Rhode Island monthly meeting was its endowment in land. Ironically, acquiring it began in a mad tea party of confusion over titles and the terms of a will, which lasted fifteen years. The executors of the will, which contained a large bequest to the meeting, tried to cooperate with a committee of the meeting but quarreled over the use of the money; then they spent it to buy Easton's Point in Newport in 1698, receiving the land both as executors and as trustees of the meeting.[20] There were many further complications in the transaction, aside from the unworkable double role assumed by the purchasers. After various conveyances had been passed back and forth and after a number of false hopes of a solution were dashed, by 1710 the meeting finally managed to get its assets concentrated in land, most of it at Easton's Point, securely held by trustees and beginning to produce income.[21] The complex series of events demonstrated how important it was to have a legal means to own real estate once the land of an ecclesiastical organization had some value.

Unfortunately, very little evidence survives to shed light on the human dynamics of the Quaker structure—the methods for conducting business, the beliefs about why it was as it was, or the currents of prestige and influence that flowed among the members. Consequently, some features of church government stand out clearly, and others remain mysterious. The rough parallel in development of institutions between English and Rhode Island Friends makes it tempting to interpolate Old World experience and ideas into the New World. For example, Rhode Island Quakers may have shared with their English counterparts the uncertainty in thinking about the ecclesiastical structure as it took shape. A tendency to think that chuch government, like worship, was to be controlled by the Holy Spirit in every detail jostled with a supposition that mundane needs controlled some decisions. Also, a belief in spiritual equality of members coexisted uneasily with a nontheorized reliance on a core of proven leaders and a theorized distribution of "gifts" by God. But it is impossible to know. Rhode Islanders probably adopted the "sense of the meeting" procedure and the justifications for it. The records are silent on these subjects and many others. At best, the absence of surprise or objections by traveling Friends affords evidence of similarities on the two sides of the Atlantic, and a few declarations and precepts on conduct framed in the early eighteenth century convey a basic and rather standard Quaker point of view.[22]

Similarities between Friends' ways in Rhode Island and England, however great they may have been, need not vitiate the main argument here, that the Quaker organization met the needs of many Rhode Island people in the late seventeenth century. Beginning with the discipline over individual behavior, which was stricter than any other church imposed, the monthly meeting expanded its services to include resolving disputes between members, providing for the poor, regulating marriage, and helping parents rear their children. The meeting set standards of conduct and provided a routine of life, a society. It kept up intercourse with the outside world, largely through epistles and traveling Friends, even before the elaboration of the pyramid of meetings, which created institutional devices to hold together Friends from Maine to New York. Quite clearly, this organization could do much that Rhode Island's secular associations could not in the late seventeenth century.

Ephemeral Religions

The Jews and Huguenots passed quickly across the scene. Yet they had traits in common with the Seventh Day Baptists and the Quakers, notably a strong emphasis on enforcing their distinctive standards in worship and daily life and also a sense of themselves as existing in a transatlantic framework rather than in isolated congregations. Granted, the case is conjectural with regard to the Jews. Several lived in the colony during the 1680s. Some may have arrived earlier, and others may have stayed later. While there is no record of a religious organization in Rhode Island, these people could pursue a traditional routine of religious observances in many respects. They had their standards of conduct. They were accustomed to living outside an established church, outside if not in fear of a predominant nationality. What several Jews asked the General Assembly in 1684 does not survive, but the Assembly assured them only that "they may Expect as good Protection here, as any Strainger being not of Our Nation residing amongst us in this his Majesties Collony Ought to have, being Obedient to his Majesties laws."[23]

The French congregation introduced by the Narragansett Proprietors in 1686 brought a mode of religious organization that allowed it to take shape quickly. The group quickly decided to set aside land to support the minister, Ezekiel Carré to require future settlers to pledge to contribute to his salary as a condition of obtaining land; and to build a "Temple." The edifice was ready for use in three months, and a routine of services began there at once.[24]

The congregation arrived with the blueprint of an ecclesiastical organization, "the discipline of france," which it resolved to observe. Thus, it chose a consistory composed of the minister, the secretary, the syndic, and one other elder. This group assessed each member's financial obligation toward the minister's stipend by assigning pews and fixing the rent on them. It also exercised church discipline by reprimanding wrongdoers, hearing accusations, imposing penalties of suspension from communion, and arbitrating disputes.[25] The first meeting of the consistory welcomed heads of families; together they resolved "to regulate all our ecclesiastical affairs by public assemblies." At those gatherings, decisions were by majority vote. Presumably, there was no boundary between a small number of members in full communion and others of the congregation, as there was in New England custom. After the first major decisions had been made, however, the general meetings had little business.[26]

This highly organized congregation, comparable only to the Quakers in strength of ecclesiastical discipline and like them in following a system of European origin, lasted for about four years. Just as it seemed to be gaining strength by forging connections with two other French churches, it encountered two setbacks that ended its existence. The first was M. Carr's decision to accept a pulpit in Boston after the congregation found it could not support him. The second was the collapse of the Dominion of New England, which allowed hostile neighbors to harass the French settlers. They began to move away, in spite of efforts by the church meeting to convince them of their duty to stay. The church collapsed in 1690 when the neighbors demolished the temple.[27]

The French colony, during its brief life, illustrated again to what extent religious bonds could replace temporal ones. The community governed itself, largely through its church. Of course, because it was a foreign enclave, the French colony gained an added solidarity. Still, it managed to create as tightly knit a society as any early Massachusetts town.

Conclusion

The French settlement also suggested the limits to the power of ecclesiastical organizations to supplant all other associations. The French could no longer live a life of their own when they lost the Dominion's protection of their land rights. Quakers were not being quirkish when they continued to search for ways to keep title to their properties. For a religious group seeking to guide every facet of its members' lives, it was essential, after all, to forge an effective relation to civil authority, weak as government was in Rhode Island. Besides, submission to church discipline remained voluntary, so it could be rejected at any time; and the relations between insiders and outsiders normally fell beyond the church's control and so had to be regulated by civil laws and courts. Religious affiliation could not wholly replace political obligations. Security in land did indeed reinforce institutions, even those that profited from the disarray of civil society.

The French also displayed another salient feature of life in the late seventeenth century. They sought connections beyond their immediate congregation. They brought with them not only a plan for operating a congregation but also methods to associate with congregations elsewhere. If they innovated less than the Seventh Day Baptists, they resembled the Quakers. Yet all three of these religious newcomers tried to create institutional structures to counteract the fragmentation of secular society.

The Quakers were by far the most important. Their ecclesiastical structure was the most tightly organized and complex and by far the most inventive. Their church discipline and their ability to control doctrine were the most effective. Befitting their beliefs and circumstances, they found a way to reconcile a continuous leadership with general participation. They managed to hold together a religion explicitly based on belief in universal individual access to divine inspiration and an ecclesiastical form implicitly based on the supposition that the Holy Spirit ruled through the church collectively. Achieving this amalgam made Quakerism uniquely successful in Rhode Island when social fragmentation and political chaos were driving people to find solidarity with each other on any available basis.

Lessons for the future lay at least implicit in the ecclesiastical trends of the late seventeenth century. Perhaps it was only accidental that the French began to bring traditional forms of Christianity to Rhode Island. In the aftermath of their tragedy, however, other such churches arrived, and surviving Huguenots gravitated to them. The Sabbatarians, beginning as a variety of the already familiar Baptist propensity to schism, in their weakness followed the lead of the Quakers toward novel structures to hold people together beyond the immediate circle of worshippers. Other Baptists soon would take cautious steps in the same direction and would make some reconciliation with the Christian past. And beyond the implications for religious association lay comparable ones for political organization.

❧ 6 ❧

The Rise of the Colonial Government and a New Direction for Institutional Development

Rhode Island escaped from the near anarchy of the late seventeenth century through a profound reordering of its collective concerns in most branches of the institutional configuration. The process took place unevenly, over a forty-year period. Its ramifications continued in the late colonial period. On the basis of what had been created in the first part of the eighteenth century, it was possible to build the rudiments of a new sort of relation between government and a widening variety of other institutions. By 1740, however, the people of the colony began to agree on how to fit institutions together, how to settle conflicts, how to treat the aspirations of individuals and small groups in relation to the whole, how to define and limit coercive authority, how to keep internal conflicts from destroying their society or subjecting it to unacceptable rule from outside, and how to form ties to external institutional frameworks.

The colonial government was the star performer. It recovered after 1695 and soon raced ahead, far beyond its effectiveness at any earlier time. It truly began to exercise the powers assigned to it by the charter, and it won the long struggle for the Narragansett country. It devised and implemented consistent policies to foster Newport's commerce. It put Rhode Island securely into the British empire, partly by tacit surrender of some of its autonomy but without surrendering its essential charter privileges. Within its jurisdiction, the colonial government advanced toward legal supremacy as the regulator of the terms of association of other kinds—at least as far as its inhabitants wanted regulation.

The other conspicuous forms of association played their parts. Town governments became less autonomous and more standardized. Their business fell increasingly under regulation by colonial law, they stressed procedural formality more than before, and they began to act more like administrative arms of the central government and less like agencies of communities. Syndicates of proprietors of undivided lands also fell under regulation and abandoned plans for highly disciplined organizations to advance the collective interests of the shareholders. Most of the churches became more formal. The new faiths, Anglican and Congregational, adapted organizational rules from England and Massachusetts, respectively, to their own circumstances. Their ties to the churches in those places were analogous to the colonial government's ties to the empire. And all the churches began to seek a relation to the civil legal order, if only to assure their control of their land. Typical of the smaller forms of association, the family was largely autonomous but regulated by law in a few ways, especially ones that required procedural uniformity, such as reporting births and deaths or observing the rules on publishing intentions to wed.

Dramatic as the changes were, they had limits. Orderly relations among the collectivities in Rhode Island could be achieved to a degree by a rather hierarchical arrangement and precise formulations of the points of contact, yet ruthless central control was impossible. Resistance to the colonial government had been common in the seventeenth century; it persisted in the eighteenth. The whole system depended so heavily on consent that all institutions had to respect the procedural rules and limits, and they could do only what the members wanted. Presumably, what institutions did was perceived as beneficial to the members or they were thwarted. Attempts by the colonial government to impose unwanted coercion, as in taxes, had to be given up, while other rulings secured obedience.

The emphasis on procedure, of course, was only a revised version of the legalism that had been common in the colony from the founding, but now it flourished. It had two important by-products, however. The first was a paradoxical combination of enhancing institutional effectiveness and limiting institutional authority. The second was the beginning of what later would be called constitutionalism, whether the charter or the Bible or the Quaker Discipline, to be implemented by changeable statutes.

Limits became important in another sense, too. The scope of coercive power narrowed to what has since become regarded as government. Churches never had been coercive in Rhode Island, of course, nor did they have a partnership with civil authority. But civil authority in the founding years had recognized no boundaries in mundane affairs. The comprehensive management by towns had failed or withered steadily, yet some of its manifestations persisted into the eighteenth century. Moreover, when population grew and trade began to prosper, people in the colony often borrowed practices from English models. To be sure, nobody tried to create traditional guilds, autonomous schools, or the privileges held by owners of regulated markets. No one ever attained coercive or monopolistic control exercised by self-governing sets of member-owners. Instead, intermediary institutions became voluntary and nonmonopolistic. Coercive authority remained distinct and affected intermediary institutions through regulation, which usually meant restraint, expressed in terms that applied to whole categories, such as owners of milldams, rather rather than specific persons or organizations. As a result, government became a clear category with clear functions.

Rhode Island underwent an astonishing metamorphosis in the early eighteenth century, and this phenomenal change needs explanation. The explanation comes from the conjunction of two sets of intentions, those from inside the colony and those from the imperial government. Between 1660 and 1686, people in the colony had either pursued their own ends atomistically, as William Harris did, or, like the pioneers of Newport commerce, had been able to survive with a weak institutional structure.

Internal conditions put matters in a different light by 1695. The Dominion of New England and the near anarchy to which it led exhibited evils to be escaped by effective internal order and implied the value of some sacrifice of private ambition or local autonomy. The appeals to the Crown, from the petition for the second charter to the request for the charter's reconfirmation thirty years later and all the appeals of disputes over land in between, were so many steps toward acquiescence to imperial authority. By 1695 basic acceptance existed, though terms that would be compatible with extensive local self-government remained to be worked out. The prosperity of Aquidneck and nearby towns had been growing, for all the turbulence, and had brought Newport to the point where it could begin a major commercial expansion. The town had acted in partnership with the colonial government all along, so it harbored no hostility to central authority. On the contrary, it wanted the colonial government to serve it on a wider scale to enlarge the port's hinterland. Dogged localism had to be overcome chiefly on the mainland. Even the Quaker organization had played a part by introducing an elaborate hierarchical network that prefigured the governmental one. And probably some weight should be put on the cycle of generations. The immigrant leadership had died, mostly in the decade before the Dominion, and so removed from the scene their preoccupations with the implementation of Puritan reform, their sense of place in the world, and their characteristic hostility to compromise. No comparable figures, no coherent policy, followed for several years. Opportunity lay open to men with a new outlook on what could be done.[1]

To an extent, the experience of the two decades before 1695 pointed toward what should be done. The governmental system would have to be subordinate to the empire. Workable internal arrangements would require compromises and horse trading as well as generally acceptable definitions of powers and duties for the elements in the system. The concentration of trade at Newport implied that all might gain by the expansion of production elsewhere, whether on fields and pastures or forests and fisheries, to feed exports to the capital—and further, that governmental measures might facilitate this process. Preservation of religious freedom would require equal protection for churches. The profusion of private interests needed predictable relations to government. Too many undertakings that once had been functions of a community had drifted into private control but still required some regulation. Too many proprietary syndicates quarreled interminably with each other or assumed governmental functions; they could not be left to themselves.

Probably no one understood these lessons in such a way as to map out the grand reordering of Rhode Island that took place; no doubt many people ignored them entirely. Those who designed or futilely advocated changes did so usually with intentions that appear to have been short-range, improvisatory, or self-seeking. Hence, the irregular record and the shifts of action from one topic to another, the second thoughts and maneuvers.

Most of those who built the rather different institutional edifice that took shape manifestly sought personal profit and glory. They met emergencies and seldom changed much between them, which suggests no pursuit of an ideal. The only man who may have been an exception was Governor Samuel Cranston, who held office from 1698 to his death in 1727. He profited occasionally from his high position, yet the record suggests someone devoted to public service and ingenious in finding ways to solve old problems not one out for gain. Surviving evidence shows him firm on a few points, notably the preservation of the colony's charter privileges, the creation of a strong and centralized military system, scrupulous adherence to legal formalities, and, once he understood the need for it, the acknowledgment of obligations to the imperial government. Indeed, to him these probably were parts of a whole.

Moreover, though Newport leaders may have managed public business to benefit their town, they could do so only with the backing or acquiescence of others. Evidence of balkiness in other towns is abundant but pertains to a short list of topics: taxes, town boundaries, dependence of the militia on local wishes, paper money, the routes of roads, and land rights. These were not parts of a coherent opposition but rather discrete subjects. Most likely, the non-Newport men found the reordering of the colony attractive in several unrelated ways. At some cost, it preserved the essentials of colonial autonomy and advanced the prosperity of most people by stimulating internal trade and ending some old disputes that had paralyzed development. For the time being, the interests of Newport and hinterland coincided to allow cooperative action on what amounted to a comprehensive program, punctuated by occasional disputes. Though few men, if any, had a coherent goal, many could agree on most of the steps taken.

Rhode Island's progress toward an institutional overhaul was helped by more than internal concerns. The colony was pushed. After 1689 the central government had reverted to its old ways, only to find them less effective than ever. Imperial officials sent commissions to accuse Rhode Islanders of malfeasance and to gather evidence to support abolishing the charter, to assume military command or impose a royally commissioned admiralty court, to resolve disputes on land, and in general to put Rhode Island under the direction of men who would take their orders from Whitehall.

The imperial pressure in effect set much of the agenda for those who would resist it. They tried, in particular, to demonstrate that the colony could support the monarchs in international wars on its own initiative, an effort which required a wholesale change in the colony's military and fiscal organization. In a sense, nothing that Rhode Island itself could do would alter imperial intentions. The colony was only part of a large-scale American resistance to domineering imperial officers, and British politics more than American countermeasures ended imperial assertiveness.[2]

The political contests that naturally swirled around the capital in Newport grew out of the process of change that was already under way. The resurrection of the charter in 1689 began a long campaign pitting advocates against opponents. The charter's opponents, who may be called the Newport Tories, favored a royal government similar to the Dominion of New England. Eagerly submissive to London's direction, they formed a continuous, identifiable opposition to the colony government during the period of strident assertiveness from Whitehall—that is, until around 1708, when their cause became hopeless. They relied on intrigue, primarily in London, along with intermittent public advocacy in New England. They obtained royal investigations of their charges against the charter government. They rarely worked to gain power in it.

After this opposition to the basic terms of government failed, some of its members joined with a few military heroes, the Wanton brothers, and some of Cranston's associates to create a new opposition. It was genuinely successful by 1714. It accepted the charter and worked to gain support from the voters. It won assorted private benefits of public power, issued paper money, and in the now familiar fashion demonstrated that it could run the government better than the other side could. This opposition forced the remains of the coalition around Cranston to organize in its turn and perhaps even outdo the other side in securing alliances outside Newport.

Rhode Island thus gained a distinctive political life. The opposing forces that polarized the colony in the early eighteenth century exhibited a few traits of later American political parties and gained more as time passed. The sides often underwent some realignment but on the whole remained constant for the rest of the colonial period and continued to invent new methods. Election of all main officials and a nearly omnicompetent governing board in the General Assembly went far to determine political techniques and goals. Rhode Island escaped most of the entanglement with backstairs British politics so familiar in other colonies during the eighteenth century. It had, however, its own place in the imperial structure; it came to accept the jurisdiction of a few royal officials and, like other colonies, needed an agent in London.

Formal Changes

Building up the power of the colonial government required few changes in its form except for the inauguration of a military organization outside the militia, the development of the judiciary, and the creation of a fiscal apparatus. Though not strictly necessary, the General Assembly adopted a bicameral form in 1696. The disarray of public institutions makes the reasons for the innovation unclear, but it occured about the time when imperial pressure on the colony became intense.[3] Though bicameral organization was an imitation of English and Massachusetts practice, it also was part of the effort to impose a property tax. The Assembly adopted the two-house form just after designating the "Representatives or Deputies, or the major part present" a committee to draft a tax law.[4] The deputies wanted bicameral organization, presumably, to raise their importance. If so, they succeeded. The division of houses seemingly added little to the decision of 1672 to require a majority vote of the deputies to pass any weighty measure and to give them the exclusive right to initiate tax laws. In fact, however, the deputies rose rapidly to legislative leadership.

By the 1720s the Assembly had developed enduring organizational procedures. The two houses met jointly for several purposes. Together, they heard judicial appeals and occasional messages from the Governor. Together, they ascertained the results of elections in May when the freemen at large voted for Governor, Deputy Governor, assistants, General Treasurer, Secretary, and General Attorney, after which the Assembly appointed a lengthening list of other officials, such as justices of the peace, sheriffs, and militia officers.

From the beginning of its existence as a separate body, the House of Deputies elected a speaker. Soon, it elected a clerk, as well. By 1729, it had a slate of procedural regulations, including items clearly derived from the British House of Commons, such as the requirement that each bill be read three times and the prohibition against any member's speaking twice on a subject until all others had had an opportunity to do so. Other rules governed such matters as fees for hearing petitions and procedures for nominating committees.[5]

Ordinarily, all ad hoc committees were joint creations of the two houses, each one choosing members. They might select persons outside both houses as well as those inside. Surprisingly, neither house ever won exclusive right to rule on the qualifications of its own members or to punish contempt of its authority. The two decided on those issues by concurrent votes.

The upper house, commonly called the House of Magistrates until the 1740s, was less formal than the House of Deputies. Although the charter prescribed no geographical distribution of seats, law and custom did so. By the early eighteenth century, the older distribution was revised to give one assistantship to the Narragansett region. The magistrates devised no written rules of procedure, though surely they had some.

The General Assembly gained power to create special military forces for the service of the Crown during Queen Anne's War and later contended against localism with some success for control of the train bands. The charter granted the colony authority to organize its own military forces, but at first this was merely a paper power. Change became unavoidable when, in effect, part of the price of reaffirmation of the charter was acquiescence to the Crown's requirement that the colony send a quota of forty-eight men to the empire's wars under the command of a royal governor of a nearby colony.[6] For Rhode Island, this acquiescence served a valuable function, for it enabled the Assembly to assert power over its militia, organize local defense, and create coastal fortifications.

The Assembly took the initiative in 1702. Partly with gold confiscated from a pirate, it had a fort built to guard Newport harbor and then employed a small garrison there. The Assembly also hired men to be used as scouts in the mainland, impressed men from the train bands if too few volunteered, and sent men to guard Block Island. The climax of wartime actions came between 1709 and 1711, when expeditionary forces joined attacks on the French in Nova Scotia and Quebec. Rhode Island provided a few vessels, mainly transports, and over two hundred men—deliberately more than required—in two of the years. The Assembly authorized enlistment of Indians to supply as much as as a third of the force in 1710. It also set town quotas and allowed impressment. Rhode Island finally fielded a small army and sent a small fleet of its own to sea.[7] At the end of the war, the Assembly made permanent the Governor's authority to float a naval force. It gave him power to commission officers and enlist men, or even impress seamen for service against pirates or privateers.[8]

Also, during these years the Assembly created a hierarchical table of command. It authorized two councils of war—island and mainland—combining civilian and military officials, a system continued with modifications when the mainland was split into counties. Simultaneously, the Assembly grouped the train bands under each council of war into a regiment and appointed officers for it. It was led by a major under the Governor serving as colonel of the whole. Later, the legislators elevated the majors to colonels and the Governor to Captain General. In theory, a rational order had been created.[9]

Other aspects of central control over military organization, however, especially the choice of officers for the train bands, remained subject to political contests. For once, the aims of Governor Cranston are clear. He favored actual selection by the Assembly as stipulated in the charter, rather than endorsement of the officers the companies wanted. He also favored nearly universal militia service. After 1713, the Governor's opposition championed exemption for pacifists and election of officers in the train bands. The colonial government finally assumed the function of choosing the officers in 1741.[10]

The Assembly's decisions, were not automatically obeyed. In the past, inhabitants had often ignored them. The heated political controversies, however, hint that the laws were being implemented. So did some lesser controversies and actions by towns to support the military system, whether to arrange for training fields, procure ammunition, or lend dignity to the swearing-in of officers.[11]

Yet glimpses into the train bands suggest that only a few men felt genuine military fervor. Petitions to divide companies complained of inconvenient places of muster. In 1737 the Assembly declared that it was "common for Persons to take offices in the Militia and keep them for a short time and then lay them down for no other Reason but to be Excused from Training thereafter." Pacifists, allegedly, attended muster to jeer at the militiamen and join them later at taverns.[12] In sum, efforts to centralize control of the militia had some effect but probably left most of the train bands relatively autonomous.

Similar to Rhode Island's revision of the military system were the changes in law and the judicial apparatus. Again, the Assembly made changes to meet the challenges by men favoring royal control. Again, localism succeeded in softening an inherently centralized and hierarchical design. Though Rhode Island had adopted and improved a code of laws beginning in 1647, it had not covered all necessary topics. Consequently, the towns and the colony had used English law, as on land ownership or judicial procedure, and had developed local usages as well.

Discrepencies between colonial behavior and English standards rarely drew attention before the 1690s. Then the colonial government had to answer the complaints made by the Newport Tories and the royal officials who investigated them between 1696 and 1704. The Board of Trade continued the pressure. The complaints covered a wide spectrum from the well-founded, such as assertions that the colony's laws were not readily known or were incomplete; to the problematical, such as allegations of bias in the courts or leniency to pirates; to the absurd, such as condemning the colony for exercising the full scope of criminal justice. Colonial officials kept denying everything and promising to support their claims with a copy of the laws. While it stalled, the General Assembly sporadically gathered, improved the laws, and elaborated the judiciary.[13]

The Assembly began the process of compiling laws in 1698 but produced no publishable text for over twenty years. The first result, sent to the Board of Trade in 1699, elicited scorn. The Assembly went back to work and as a stopgap took the rash step of deciding "that where the laws of this Collony or custom shall not reach or comprehend any matter, cause or causes, . . . it shall be lawfull to put in execution the laws of England, etc."[14] Nobody could determine what this meant in specific cases. A new draft of laws finished around 1706 was not published, and with pressure from London easing, the Assembly deferred further efforts until after Queen Anne's War.[15]

This time the Assembly called on Nathaniel Newdigate, one of the two attorneys practicing in the colony, who helped compose a presentable document, published in 1719.[16] It set the model of putting the charter first, with its own title page and pagination, followed by a new title page for the laws in chronological order. This form distinguished constitutional law, which the colony wanted to present as fixed, from statutes that might be changed. The charter came from the king, the laws from elected officials.[17]

The effect of the published laws is hard to gauge. Quite likely, the justices relied as before, though no longer exclusively, on a combination of knowledge about scraps of colonial law, English law as found in books like Dalton's *Country Justice*, and a sense of fairness. Certainly, they made occasional allusions to English laws.[18] Between the new law book, hectoring by the attorneys, and awareness that judgments might be appealed to the king's privy council, magistrates began to take care to act within laws and procedures that would be comprehensible and respectable to English judges.

While Rhode Island reduced the laws to something like a system and tinctured the conduct of litigation with English professionalism, the Assembly made further changes. It organized a surprisingly complex pyramid of tribunals and began to separate adjudication from other official powers. The separation proceeded only part of the way before 1747, however, and for long after that remained incomplete because the legislature maintained judicial functions and often chose its own members for the benches below the Superior Court.

At the start of this process in 1696, Rhode Island had four kinds of tribunals, all held by men with other duties attached to their offices. About two dozen men enjoyed powers of justices of the peace.[19] These men had peacekeeping functions of a fairly elastic nature in addition to judicial ones, which they performed either individually or in small groups. They also served as members of town councils, the second variety of tribunal, which had probate jurisdiction as well as civil administrative responsibilities, military capacities, vague duties to oversee local welfare, and quasi-judicial obligations to act against migrant paupers and violators of the economic regulations that were administered by towns. The Governor and Council, in addition to serving as the bench of a provisional admiralty court and the one court of record in the colony, the General Court of Trials, doubled as an administrative council, the upper house of the Assembly, and part of the council of war. And the General Assembly had some functions as a high court; indeed, it was later described by the Governor and Council as "the Supream Court of this Colony."[20] The judicial part of public business hardly could be distinct from the rest.

Changes took place at the lowest level, though they were not so extensive as to slice up the undifferentiated powers of the justice of the peace. The Assembly increased the number of justices for specific towns. It continually added to their responsibilities by legislation stipulating their duties to enforce various laws. The importance of justices grew.[21]

Beginning in 1690, the Assembly authorized another sort of tribunal, justices' courts, to be held in the several towns by any two magistrates who resided there. They had limited criminal competence and civil jurisdiction subject to appeal to the Court of Trials.[22]

As before, the town councils had judicial competence, one that had an oddly defined place in the system. A council was "the ordinary" for its town— that is, the probate court with jurisdiction over movable estate—so its other judicial functions also became classified as belonging to the ordinary in Rhode Island. Accordingly, an appeal against a council's decision on a liquor license followed the same route as an appeal from a decision on probate, to the Governor and Council as the "Supream Ordinary."[23] The councils could behave like magistrates in emergencies, notably quarantine, when they could restrict individual freedom and confiscate property ruthlessly.[24]

As early as 1703, the Assembly debated creating counties; yet it did nothing until 1729, when it created three, one for the islands and two on the mainland. Each one would have a criminal court, competent to try all but capital offenses, and a civil court with original jurisdiction over actions concerning more than forty shillings' value and appelate jurisdiction over actions concerning less. Both courts would meet regularly twice a year, though they might be called into special sessions at other times.[25]

After tentative plans for separate benches, the Assembly gave the two courts, General Sessions of the Peace and Inferior Court of Common Pleas, the same judges, and appointed them annually. Appeals from both civil and criminal proceedings lay to the old General Court of Trials, renamed the Superior Court of Judicature Court of Assize and General Goal [*sic*] Delivery.[26]

Under strong English pressure the high court surrendered admiralty jurisdiction to royally appointed judges. The Governor had assumed admiralty functions in granting authorization to privateers ever since the middle of the seventeenth century, and in 1694 the General Assembly authorized the Governor and Council to act as a provisional admiralty court. Then and later, the colonial officials assumed they had this power under the charter. Royal officials challenged this belief, particularly in connection with condemning prize vessels and suppressing piracy, through a series of altercations that continued until the early eighteenth century, when Governor Cranston acquiesced in the installation of royally appointed judges of vice-admiralty and ceased asserting the colony's claims.[27]

Equity, another branch of adjudication outside common law, also came under challenge, though the colony managed to retain it. Equity was the branch of English law developed in the king's chancellor's court, based on Roman law principles and procedures, to provide substantive justice where the common law's formalities seemed to require injustice. After the privy council objected to its conduct in one case, the Assembly foreswore its equity jurisdiction, promised to create a special court for that function, and then resumed it.[28] The Assembly also had an informal place in the hierarchy of tribunals. Litigants dissatisfied with rulings of the inferior or superior courts could present their complaints to it by petition.

Ultimately, the privy council came to serve as the final point in the judicial chain of appeal. This was no trifling power. Proportionally to population, people in Rhode Island carried appeals to the king in council at least as often as in any other colony. The General Assembly decided in 1719 that these appeals should not be allowed unless the amount in controversy came to at least £300 in Rhode Island money, or about £150 sterling.[29]

The elaboration of machinery and jurisdictions surely conduced to an orderly and predictable system of adjudication. The Assembly's intrusion in the process did most to render procedure subject to manipulation. Though the pyramid of courts had been well defined by 1738, the adjudicators remained mired in responsibilities, governed in part by concepts of undifferentiated magisterial authority—ironically, the type of authority that the original towns had struggled to create in their early years.

Finance

The need to obtain funds for the revived colonial government revealed both its weakness and its ingenuity. The inhabitants might accept the need for a stronger central government, but they avoided paying for it. Thus, they made the process of change difficult until the colony resorted to the printing press. Taxation succeeded in a few cases but commonly failed to overcome mainland town resistance on the mainland to a levy on property. War needs drove the colony to imitate Massachusetts in issuing paper currency; then postwar depressions led to more of such issues. Income from interest, along with more treasury emissions, eliminated the need for property taxes for three decades.

When the colonial government reorganized in 1695, it resumed trying to impose rates on property and again met the refusal of most towns to obey the tax laws. Towns objected to the apportionment of the total tax, complained that their boundaries were improperly drawn or simply nonexistent, and refused to collect the money for the central treasury. Apportionment disputes recurred throughout the colonial period, and the Assembly made headway only to the extent of enforcing boundaries before giving up the levy. Without much effect it tried to impose a standard procedure for tax collections in the towns. Failing to secure compliance, it tried to gain power to create its own agents. These measures had indifferent success. Only some of the taxes were collected. Only a few towns appointed the required assessors before 1704, and some did so only sporadically thereafter. Nevertheless, the Assembly kept authorizing new rates and variations on the methods to assess and collect them. Even the Aquidneck towns fell behind in payments toward the end of Queen Anne's War.[30]

Presumably, the rapid succession of rates resulted in enough money to foot most of the bills for military actions and defense of the charter in London. The expeditions against the French, beginning in 1709, required greater outlays than could be met. Consequently, Rhode Island began to issue treasury bills in anticipation of taxes that in fact it never managed to collect, especially after peace led to economic stagnation.[31]

Then the colony gave up the property tax. The political coalition behind John and William Wanton, which gained many seats in the Assembly in 1714 and 1715, enacted a policy of expanding rather than contracting the currency as a means to ameliorate hard times. The policy had economic ends, as well as fiscal. On the fiscal side, it meant financing the colonial government by intermittent issues of more bills of credit, especially by following the new Massachusetts practice of lending bills to inhabitants in exchange for mortgages on land—the system commonly known as land banks. Payments of interest on the mortgages were intended to provide a regular income for the colony, whereas payments of principal would retire the bills. In time, the General Assembly extended the benefits of the bills to town governments by giving them part of the interest money, so often they too could stop taxation. Before 1740, currency finance was an almost unqualified success. In six land banks, from 1715 to 1738, Rhode Island lent £384,000 face value. It also issued a substantial amount in treasury bills.

The new fiscal methods required an increase in administrative machinery and required continued adjustments to that machinery for years. The new officialdom showed the growing importance of the colonial government and its ability to affect directly the lives of individual inhabitants.

To begin with, in 1715 the Assembly planned to lend £40,000 at 5 percent interest for ten years (though repayable after five) on security of land of at least twice the value of the loan. A panel of six trustees, also known as the Grand Committee and composed entirely of Newport merchants, was to oversee the business. They signed the bills, transmited them to town committees, inspected mortgages from outside Newport, and negotiated them inside. Committees of two men chosen by the Assembly for each town except Newport, negotiated individual loans. They also had the responsibility to transmit mortgages and other papers to the trustees. All these men were rewarded by commissions on money passing through their hands.[32] The General Treasurer received interest payments and sued for arrears. By implication, all the officials had to keep detailed records, invent a system for verifying the many transfers and payments and obligations, and secure faithful observance of the law. These tasks implied a need for a few clerks.

Early modifications usually scattered responsibility with doleful effects. For instance, in 1720 the Assembly authorized the town committees rather than the trustees to extend loans from five years to ten, to receive repayments of principal, and to relend these payments on new mortgages for five years. This dangerous decentralization was probably enhanced by the trustees' practice of conducting their business by turns as individuals and as a panel.[33]

By 1728 concentration of responsibility improved. The trustees allowed one of their number, Jahleel Brenton, to keep all their documents. This man, later called the Keeper of the Grand Committee's Office and so designated by the Assembly, assumed control of the committee's business and presumably had a clerk or two for such paperwork as was done. Brenton had this role for almost twenty years, thus providing more stability than the Assembly actually envisioned.[34]

In some ways the forms of administration had little connection with their use. The General Treasurer barely tried to attain the statutory goal of using interest money to retire wartime bills of credit. He ordinarily treated interest payments as all-purpose revenue. The Assembly did not even write rules on payment of principal into issuance of the first two banks. Its statute of 1715 mentioned loans for ten years, but it wrote the plan for repayment at the last minute, in 1724, and a few years later changed it to more lenient terms.[35]

For years the Assembly emphasized the importance of putting paper money into circulation rather than taking it out, and the administrators acted accordingly. The records fell into some confusion, and the officials neglected to dun people who owed money to the colony in spite of clauses in several statutes that empowered the General Treasurer to sue for overdue interest and the trustees to sue for overdue installments of principal. Audits for the General Assembly paid little attention to the loans and mainly chronicled the slow retirement of wartime issues of fiat money. Ordinarily, the treasury had adequate resources, including interest payments, misuse of special funds, excises, and further authorizations to emit unsecured bills.[36] The officials had nothing to gain by hauling the voters into court except political hostility. And the law had no provisions on how the Grand Committee might assume title to land by foreclosure.

The need for care began to appear in the 1730s and stimulated a mild response. The once-satisfactory rate of voluntary payment of interest fell off. The General Treasurer successfully sued for most of the arrears, thereby managing to retire nearly all of the bills of credit issued directly by the treasury. Repayments of principal diminished at a much faster rate. The rate of voluntary payment dropped from over 60 percent of what was due in 1734 to little more than 30 percent by 1738. The Grand Committee, despite instructions from the Assembly, allowed a long period of grace.[37]

Poor administration of the paper money loans should not obscure the effectiveness of the fiat currency system in building the power of the colony's central government. Though officials mainly wanted to float money rather than retire it, the central government not only created its most elaborate civilian subsidiary but also deeply affected the towns by giving them shares of the interest money; it established, almost for the first time, direct connections with hundreds of individual inhabitants. The colony made its business a matter of concern as never before, except occasionally during wartime. And in the simplest terms, the creation of currency gave the colonial government a power of the purse for the first time.[38]

Economic Development

The paper money system also served to foster Newport's commerce, which was an essential component of the reordering of the colony. Using the colonial government for this purpose began early but increased markedly in the late seventeenth century and then expanded into a profusion of measures to serve nearly all interests. The central regime went far toward replacing the town as the agency of economic development and therefore the focus of the inhabitants' loyalty. The General Assembly tried direct regulation of trade and promotion of transportation facilities before resorting to paper money loans to eliminate taxation, facilitate business, and finance bounties and public works.

Rhode Island followed Massachusetts in the main features of its fiscal devices. For many years both governments allowed or condoned free interchange among their currencies. Rhode Island's participation in a regional monetary system obviously simplified commerce with neighboring colonies and with Boston. Rhode Island's decision to reject the policy of currency contraction, adopted by Massachusetts and Connecticut in the 1730s, gave its inhabitants great advantages through access to ready money when commercial stagnation depressed Boston.[39]

From the start, advocates of paper money argued that it would stimulate trade and so give markets and higher prices to farmers, thereby raising the value of land while encouraging local handicrafts and nonagricultural manufacturing for export. All of this more or less came to pass, although with un-evenly distributed benefits. The key was commerce, so the effectiveness of paper money had to be measured by its effects on trade. While Newport merchants bought imports mainly through Boston and the suppliers there accepted Rhode Island pounds, the bills certainly appeared to fulfill the prophecy and also to flow inexorably to Boston. This situation persisted until the 1740s, contributing to Rhode Island's lassitude in collecting principal and interest on its loans.[40]

If the paper money system was the most conspicuous component of the economic development policy, it was not the only one. The colonial govern-ment began a few traditional measures to regulate buying and selling. The laws usually called for observance in all towns, but compliance was voluntary, so their effects centered on Newport and often were lackadaisical even there. The first device was actually a revival of a failed earlier policy to set standards of weights and measurement, unquestionablely a governmental function. When it finally succeeded, the Assembly could regulate cooperage; the packing of meat, fish, and liquids offered for sale; and the quality of leather, bread, shingles, and clapboards. If these devices changed little, they marked out a formal legal place for traditional regulations and made the col-ony a little more like the parent country. Perhaps the most effective resort to an old technique was a statute that authorized Newport to elect a vendue master (auctioneer).[41]

Clumsily, Rhode Island tried to restrict access of outsiders to trade within its borders and then adopted a more viable policy of promoting the capital's port evenhandedly. After trying to exclude peddlars and impose discrimina-tory terms on outsiders using the port, the General Assembly set general fees for using the facilities, to be collected by the naval officer. Port fees would re-ward him, help pay for fortifications, and aid disabled seamen, a benefit that was intended less as benevolent than as a magnet to the seafaring population. The legislators also lowered and standardized the fees charged by the impe-rial collector of customs.[42]

In more important ways, too, the colony assisted trade by providing facil-ities open to all rather than giving preferential treatment to insiders. The courts, as before, enforced the agreements—on shares in voyages, seamen's wages, freight charges, and the like—that took standard forms in the British commercial world. The courts supervised the rapidly spreading use of bonds to strengthen such agreements. The General Recorder provided a notarial service for the recording of documents pertaining to maritime affairs.[43]

Important, too, were the efforts to improve transportation within the col-ony and related measures to facilitate travel and funnel products of the inter-ior to Newport. These actions showed how the interests of the capital and the hinterland could harmonize, how central authority could increase by virtue of its ability to override the towns—that is, to create a hierarchy of law and administration. The Assembly began to exert regulation over the ferries, which had been supervised by towns before asserting authority over licensing and in some cases promising to protect monopolies in return for free passage to the post, for persons on official business, and for maintaining adequate facilities for passengers. The only strong opposition to central supervision of the ferries came from Portsmouth. After a long controversy, the town surrendered in 1727.[44]

The colonial government also started backing creation of roads, though it left them mainly to town action. At the behest of the royal postmaster general in New England, the colony persuaded the towns to act together to lay out the post road from Providence to Westerly. At the request of Portsmouth and Kingstown, the General Assembly prescribed a procedure whereby town councils might have roads opened. The two towns wanted authority from above to overcome resistance to the policy among their residents. In 1715, after one false start, the legislators devised a durable plan, under which the town councils appointed juries to devise routes and determine the recompense to owners of land taken. The procedures usually worked, but the Assembly had to intervene directly in several quarrels and make or tolerate special variations on the basic law for Newport and other towns. And it oiled the system by using proceeds from paper money to grant subsidies for bridges.[45]

In composite, the Assembly's actions on ferries, bridges, and roads had two sorts of effects and fairly well symbolized the colony's new circumstances. First, the Assembly imposed a colony-wide network of transportation against local interests. The network served Newport and Newport's customers but was designed in some respects to fit into an imperial web. In the second place, the General Assembly gave towns new abilities to act, backed them against recalcitrant minorities, and overruled them when they would not cooperate with colonial intentions.

The General Assembly took over the regulation of mills from the towns. If its new measures fit the English pattern, the reasons for initiating them were local and had the effect of halting the drift of mills into unregulated autonomy. New laws revealed an approach toward what later would be a concept of a public utility, though movement in that direction plainly was a response to complaints rather than a pursuit of a well-defined social goal. Indeed, as economic policy, the Assembly's actions did not add up to a consistent whole.

Mills, once functions of communal self-development, had gone into private control, with less and less subjection to town government. Local regulation lost a sense of direction. Towns continued to authorize mills, but the meaning of their decisions became unclear. Were they grants of monopolies? Did a would-be miller need town authorization? John Whipple Jr. posed these questions to Providence when he asked whether "rivers belonging to the Towne are Comon and ffree to sett up any mill or mills, or Contrary to law so to doe"?[46] The answer, based on the record of events, could have been

that mills might be established under any combination of town and proprietary permission or without any permission at all. The General Assembly
hardly clarified the issue when, in 1707, it ruled that towns might determine
the use of rivers, coves, and the like for their greatest benefit, provided they
avoided impairing property rights.[47]

In the end, the Assembly developed a policy on mills that became unworkable after a few years, and it modified arrangements that had become
obsolete on a case-by-case basis. On occasion it even overruled the courts,
especially when the public's interest conflicted with private benefit.[48] In such
instances, the concept of public utility can be dimly perceived.

This concept was developed in some respects a few years later, when the
Assembly enacted a general statute pertaining to such disputes. It provided
that when owners of a mill had legally acquired the land they might create a
millpond. Those aggrieved as a result might appeal to the inferior court of
general sessions for the county, which would obtain an impartial appraisal of
the loss and order suitable compensation, such as an annual payment for land
inundated by the pond. Other provisions prescribed a similar method to resolve disputes between quarreling partners operating a mill. The object of
the law was to provide ways to keep mills running. By this time, that was the
only public good recognized by the legislature, by contrast with its earlier
interest in limiting the tolls of millers or requiring them to serve their customers impartially. Still, the Assembly could not devise a formula to resolve a
dispute over water rights between two mills on the same stream.[49]

The difficulties of reconciling private and public interests in mills became
entangled with fishing interests. At first, the conflict was between people
who caught a few fish for their own use and those who used weirs, with an intention to sell the catch. Towns granted privileges to set out weirs, sometimes
imposing restrictions on the terms of selling the fish, sometimes with requirements to let migratory fish proceed at their accustomed seasons. In
1719 the Assembly endorsed the power of town councils to regulate weirs.
The councils, however, failed to reconcile the competing interests, so in 1735
the Assembly enacted a general law protecting migratory fish and leaving enforcement of the law to the freeholders if the council failed to act. Any inhabitant might take a complaint to a magistrate. Still the statute did not satisfy
everybody, nor did the councils enforce the law. Thus, the Assembly was
often forced to intervene.[50]

By then the interests of milling and migratory fish had collided. Disputes
went to justices' courts or town councils. In Warwick, for example, the council sent men to see that a passage for fish be made through dams annually
from March 20 to June 1 and again in September for infant fish to swim
downstream to the sea.[51] This policy was modified and made colony-wide in
the law of 1735. Officials were determined to put fishing for private con-
sumption before milling or commercial fishing. The policies—or appearance

of policies—on fish and mills were hopelessly opposed. For the time being, the contradiction may have seemed insignificant. Laws on opening dams imposed expenses on mill owners, to be sure, but laws to keep them in business balanced the account. Yet if such was the thinking of the Assembly, it was wishful. Growth of the size of mills, with resulting vast expense to accomodate the fish, was not far in the future. Furthermore, the seemingly clear tenor of the laws, favoring the average voter who wanted to catch his alewives and herring and have his corn ground at the local mill, contradicted colonial policy to encourage production of exports. The resulting economic anomalies were probably politically astute. The members of the Assembly, after all, faced the voters once or twice a year in elections; hence, the machinery for resolving conflicts that might otherwise stop mills.

Regulation of Town Governments

The colonial government began to regulate town government in several other ways, too. The changes conduced to uniformity in operations and conversion of towns into agencies of central authority; but just as important, they hastened the drift of town government away from communal expression toward a mechanism bound by procedural rules that protected individual rights. Change in these directions was limited but decisive, because the General Assembly began to enforce its rulings. On the few occasions when the Assembly defined a town government in general terms, it described an agency in a hierarchy, with powers and duties prescribed from above, rather than a largely self-governing body with authority delegated from a higher level with a virtual blank check.

Quite reasonably, the colony could establish methods for electing its own officers,which it used to intrude on town autonomy. For instance, in 1695 the Assembly declared that town rules on quorums should have no force at meetings for electing jurors or deputies. It ruled that any number of freemen present at noon at a meeting properly summoned might proceed to elect such officers and transact business. It regulated some procedures in elections of colonial officers chosen at large but proceeded cautiously in the 1730s, in spite of partisan rivalries that made the contestants' claim to want to prevent fraud. A plan to synchronize election meetings in the towns, advocated in 1732, came to nothing for ten years, partly because some legislators feared violating privileges already granted to individual towns. Although the right to vote continued to be a matter of town discretion, a colonial law in 1724 began requiring a property qualification for all candidates except eldest sons of freemen.[52] The laws on voting and qualification for freemanship remained nearly constant in later years except for the addition of procedural rules and adjustments to the property requirement as the Rhode

Island pound declined in value. The towns were being made cogs in the electoral machinery operated by the colony.

The Assembly even invaded what had always been fundamental to town autonomy, admitting inhabitants. A law of 1718 required a town to allow anyone to reside in it who owned £50 worth of land there.[53] Minor though this decision may have been in practice, it breached a right previously considered absolute.

Colonial law gradually shaped town officialdoms. In addition to putting a description of required officers into the statute books, the Assembly added rules for town meetings. For example, it declared that "all Controversies . . . relating [to] Town Affairs ought to be decided by a Majority of Voices" and stipulated that a moderator must put to a vote any proposal advanced by seven freemen. An obstinate moderator was subject to suspension and a fine. The Assembly also confined the agenda by ruling "that no Vote be past in any Town Meeting concerning Money in the Treasury, Disposing of Land, or making a Rate unless it be mentioned in the [customary] Warrant given out to warn in the ffreemen to said Meeting."[54]

The colonial government made greater changes in the town councils than in the town meetings, but the councils had been established at its behest in the first place. The Assembly gave them increasing administrative and judicial burdens, often seeing them as arms of the colonial government as much as of the towns. For instance, the legislature gave them duties to protect paupers and migratory fish and to take the initative in laying out roads. It changed and standardized their composition. Old laws specifying six members never had been universally observed, until a new one in 1719 stipulated six men to be elected and to sit with the resident magistrates. Objections, primarily from Newport, where the magistrates sitting ex officio outnumbered the elected members, resulted in a law to reduce the council to six elected men. This time the towns complied.[55]

Throughout the early eighteenth century, laws concerning town government kept giving more attention to procedures, and the procedures were used more and more often. There were rules for punishing fraudulent voting. The sealers and packers had methods prescribed for them by which they could certify compliance with colonial law and invoke judicial power to impose fines or forfeitures on those who did not comply. Town clerks had procedures for use on high-handed moderators. Men who refused certain offices were subject to penalties to be imposed and collected by fixed methods.[56] Increasingly elaborate procedures governed the handling of migrant paupers. Possibly, the drifting poor were becoming more numerous proportionally, but even if they were not, the sheer growth in numbers and the increased emphasis on due process required more systematic administration than before. Procedural correctness both limited and expanded official power; with it, officials could exert more control than when they had no method for enforcing a law. At the same time, town government was losing the quality of being the expression of an autonomous community and often simply made local applications of a higher authority.

The shifting relationship between the colonial government and the towns was more complicated than a slow imposition of centralized authority might suggest. In the first place, central control had serious limits before 1738. It acted sometimes more in form than in substance. Laws might specify fines for towns that failed to elect certain officers, for instance, but towns ignored the requirements with impunity. The colony's power to tax property might be established in law, but the colony stopped trying to exercise that authority after Queen Anne's War. The General Assembly won the decisive voice in determining town boundaries but only demanded what the towns would obey. Centralized authority rested on consent rather than force.

In the second place, enlargement of central authority kept meeting resistance based on claims to rights of one sort or another until the rights were interpreted as creations of central authority itself. The Assembly could set forth its views of the relationship between colony and town in a charter for Newport but could not keep the grant within limits. It gave Newport a document quite different from those granted in the seventeenth century, neither like the extensive powers it gave to the other three original towns in 1648 and 1649, nor like the offhand grants to other towns later. Instead, the Assembly recited its own charter authority to create town governments and set their boundaries and then gave "the freemen of Newport, legally called together, . . . [authority] to consider and act on . . . prudential affairs in passing acts and orders for the duly governing the affairs only properly needfull and necessary for said town, and proper and allowable for said town; . . . . And such acts so made shall be good, allowable and in power, force and strength for them to act by, and see executed."[57] Vague though this language was, it gave Newport only a power to make acts and orders in town meeting. Nothing pertained to a judiciary or control over land. The charter merely defined the town government in a hierarchy of authority flowing down from the Crown. Portsmouth soon obtained a document in nearly the same terms.[58]

But towns began to assert that whatever the Assembly gave in a charter could not be infringed upon except by legal proceedings to justify annulling them. This concept of privilege, while a product of views about a hierarchy of authority, served as a barrier to unfettered central power. Respect for town privileges, for instance, could inhibit colonial action to synchronize elections of colonial officials. Moreover, as will appear, this sense of privileges arose in several places, especially in the 1730s. It was a fitting accompaniment to the stress on procedures, which appeared on all sides, not only in laws on town government. In the long run, procedural nicety and privilege had to be divorced.

Defining a Place in the British Empire

The towns' interpretation of their governments as corporative privileges granted by the colony and therefore guarantees of extensive exemptions from central control echoed the colonial government's official interpretation of its charter vis-à-vis the empire. Unlike the towns, however, the colony got nearly all of what it claimed. Only in a few respects did it have to obey the imperial government against its own will. By submitting with the least possible acknowledgment that it did so, it retained the sanctity of the charter. Eventually, British officials accepted the colony's view as well as the practical concessions that it made to imperial control during a stormy series of controversies around the turn of the century.

Rhode Island, of course, could do little by itself to reach the ultimate favorable conclusion. The colony did not even appear on all British maps in those years. Newport officials could only make carefully chosen concessions to royal demands, balk at others, argue, secure skillful agents in London, and count on their jurisdiction's being too small to rouse Whitehall to take strenuous action. But because Rhode Island was only one target in a campaign to reduce all colonial governments to subordination and eliminate any barriers posed by charters, it benefited from much more powerful interests using roughly the same arguments and tactics for parallel ends. And it benefited even more when the general resistance and unrelated political changes in the parent country brought a change in policy.[59]

Ironically, the onset of pressure from Whitehall began almost masked behind royal acknowledgement in 1693 and 1694 that the charter remained unimpaired. Queen Mary in council added an order that Rhode Island, when called upon, must supply a quota of forty-eight men to serve in the royal wars under a royally appointed commander in chief.[60]

Colonial officials rejoiced in the charter's endorsement but not in the accompanying command. In fact, it was the beginning of only one of two kinds of pressure from Whitehall. This kind took the form of acknowledging the charter while insisting that the Crown might nevertheless override it to a great extent. The other kind was carried by a parade of commissions of inquiry to investigate charges of misuse of the charter's privileges, more or less overtly with a view to making a legal case for its revocation. The Rhode Island Tories rushed to aid those commissions and usually gained the backing of the Narragansett Proprietors. The visitations thus brought together a combination of threats to the charter regime. In these inquiries the inspectors professed a belief that the charter gave powers as limited as those of an English municipality. The two approaches sprang from divergent ideas in Whitehall. No consistent policy appeared until after 1707, when efforts were abandoned to reduce old colonial privileges. Then the advisory commission in London, the Board of Trade, settled into extending the royal officialdom in America, demanding colonial cooperation in imperial wars and conformity to the trade laws and policies, insisting that colonial courts allow appeals to the privy council and otherwise advancing imperial control by administrative techniques rather than constitutional changes in government.

Rhode Island officials at first tried total resistance to London, then began conceding the substance of English demands. Governor Walter Clarke insisted on the fullest interpretation of the charter against royal admiralty jurisdiction and against military requirements so long as neighboring colonies refused to respect the boundaries. After Governor Cranston took office, the government shifted to a policy of accomodation. Cranston accepted royally commissioned admiralty judges, customs officers, and a military commander in chief. He promised enforcement of the trade laws and suppression of piracy. He presided over efforts to bring system and English form to the colonial laws. Probably more important, in Cranston's administration the colonial government had the support (apart from taxation) of the towns and was able to govern; its courts probably began to observe the procedure of English law more closely than before. When the Board of Trade gave up thoughts of ending the charter privileges and began gathering information and advocating British commercial objectives, Cranston conscientiously responded.[61]

Rhode Island already had seen the need for a new kind of representation in Whitehall. Instead of emissaries chosen for specific missions, as before, the colony began to rely on English agents with connections in high places. The first was especially well chosen. William Wharton was a son of one of the leading Narragansett Proprietors and also a lawyer who had served William Penn and William Blathwayt, the dominant figure in the Board of Trade.[62] He personified the new relation of colony to empire.

The new agent's value was demonstrated by Wharton's handling of charges brought by the investigative commissions, notably those led by Richard Coote, earl of Bellomont (and governor of New York, Massachusetts, and New Hampshire), and Joseph Dudley, later a governor of Massachusetts. Among many other accusations, they alleged that Rhode Island had misused its charter by prescribing the death penalty and setting up courts that inflicted it—that is, that the colony exercised high justice. This charge was based on the idea that a colonial government had the same place in the legal and institutional structure as an English municipal corporation, an idea seemingly validated by a clause in the charter itself.[63] Other clauses and the whole record of practice in English overseas colonies supported a different idea. Rather than argue statecraft or political theory, Wharton showed that the City of London afforded an example of something close to the colonial assumption of high justice; the difference was no more than could be ironed out by a trifling procedural change in Newport rather than anything so drastic as revoking the charter. In like manner he reduced other inflamatory charges to fairly technical legal points.[64] Perhaps Wharton's nimble mind only delayed official action. As it turned out, that was sufficient. A political change in England brought an end to efforts to abolish charters.[65]

Thereafter, relations between Rhode Island and the empire settled into routine. If the board expected the General Recorder to send copies of all new laws passed by the Assembly, and he did not, or complained about paper money without deflecting the colony from its policy of issuing more, or suspected that Rhode Island indulged in trade that drew complaints somewhere under the British flag, the officials in Whitehall did nothing to disturb the status quo.

In fact, the Board of Trade was conspicuously passive in 1731 when it had an opportunity to resume efforts to exert more control over Rhode Island. Governor Joseph Jenckes opposed an act to float more bills of credit and refused to sign it. He hoped to veto it and received strong support from some men in Newport, including the royal customs collector. Their letters to the board inspired great alarm in the colony. The Governor asked the board for a ruling on his veto power. The question was put before the king's attorney and solicitor general, who said that the charter gave neither the Governor nor the Crown any negative voice on laws passed by the General Assembly. The board let it go at that.[66] After the tense contests of 1696 to 1705, Rhode Island had found a place in the imperial system, had allowed the authority of certain royal officials within its borders, had admitted appeals from its courts to the privy council, had even tolerated nullification of one of its laws by the Crown, and in the end won the first effective ruling on its boundaries and endorsement of the core of its autonomy under the charter.

Conclusion

The complex of changes that transformed the colonial government between 1696 and 1738, with far-reaching effects for other institutions, took place in a swirl of interacting events. Any one episode or line of development may seem comprehensible in itself but actually depended for its outcome on propitious circumstances. The colonial government's laws on standard weights, on laying out highways, on the composition of town councils, or on an expeditionary force in Queen Anne's War had their effects in a context including both local conditions and royal policy. These two in turn were related. The Crown tended to accept the charter government as it made its authority effective, and vice versa.

The colonial government, however, gained its effectiveness partly by proceeding in ways that differed from what the imperial government—and the local Tories—favored. The elected officials could not operate an overbearing regime dominated by the rich. In effect, they had to buy compliance with what London regarded as essential by nondomineering conduct wherever possible. For them, the happiest measures were those that cost nothing to anybody and offered only benefits. Colonial leaders might create a hierarchical arrangement of authority, but they had to use commanding central government with caution.

The practical limits on central authority were evident in many ways. The colonial government could elaborate a code of laws and create a comprehensive judiciary. It could not impose taxes heavy enough to support itself, however, and so resorted to paper currency that relied on voluntary borrowing for much of its initial circulation. The General Assembly could not impose complete uniformity in colonial elections but could make effective laws on admission of inhabitants or freemen by the towns. It could overcome stubborn local interests to see that roads and ferries facilitated travel, but it could not create lucrative monopolies or other privileges. It could back town probate courts and confine their discretion through general laws, and it could reinforce their powers to repel paupers or provide for the poor among the inhabitants, but it could not impose a moral code on private conduct beyond the restraint of criminal law. The colony could enact laws on mills and inland fishing, but it could not frame them to effect a systematic subordination of some interests to others.

Rhode Island, then, produced no all-powerful central authority. The colony rationalized the lines of authority in one respect after another. It worked toward a system in which its law stipulated how various forms of association should be conducted. It reduced the de facto autonomy enjoyed by towns and other associations in the seventeenth century. It did so, however, within limits built into the support for all forms of authority. Virtually all of them depended on voluntary participation, on elections and other active choices, rather than on passive acquiescence. Thus, central law had to be tailored to the willingness of those who were to obey it; it had to be responsive to their interests and convictions. The colonists preferred limited government. They achieved it most readily by accepting the rationalization of authority and the function of central law rather than by a swarm of drifting autonomous associations or submission to the dictates of a ruling class.

The organization that took shape in the early eighteenth century emphasized order and self-government within the colonial unit while making use of new ties to London. Economically, they encouraged a hinterland for Newport and protected Newport's economic existence from subordination to Boston's, with promises of benefits for everybody. The internal hierarchical arrangements—the ladder of courts, the military chain, the subordination of towns to centrally written law, and so on—kept emphasizing procedure, often in a judicial style even in administrative matters; the elaboration of law; and preservation of self-control for units below the top. In fact, the preservation occasionally led to treating the powers of the lower units as privileges.

The colony, for its part, insisted on the charter as a grant of privilege that would stand as a barrier against intrusion by royal authority. If the Newport merchant leaders allowed some intrusion while putting their house in order, so as to keep control in their jurisdiction, they acted prudently. They may not have attained the status of a ruling class in any strict sense, but they came as close to doing so as their world permitted. Their role as intermediary between internal and external affairs resembled that of the other colonial elites coming to dominance in the era.

❧ 7 ❧

Subduing the Conflicts over Land

The Newport leadership could employ an institutional framework that put towns under central control only to a limited extent, that granted wide free-dom to small private organizations and sustained individual rights adjusted by law—indeed, it had to—but it could achieve no easy accommodation with the major proprietors of undivided lands. Most troublesome were those con-flicts that stalled rapid improvement of the soil and ended in disputes that were appealed to royal officials. These ongoing disorders gave rise to plans to annul the charter, not unreasonably so as long as the government in Newport had no ability to control the contending organizations. It could not settle conflicts between those proprietary groups it recognized. In a very loose analogy, at the end of the seventeenth century the land syndicates were like feudal principalities that rarely honored their king. They existed outside a ra-tional system of law radiating from the central government. Moreover, they remained fixated on land rights held by collectivities that ill comported with development of land use for commercial benefits.

These organizations had been particularly corrosive to public life in the late seventeenth century. Some of them had conspicuously undermined governmental authority. Contending groups had resorted to any tactic that offered a chance of success—force, litigation, bribes, appeals to the king, po-litical intrigue in Rhode Island, manipulation of town governments, or alle-giance to other colonies. Even when they were not in conflict, they tended to act autonomously, often at cross-purposes to the towns.

The proprietary organizations had to be made compatible with Newport's ambitions, but there was no single way to do that. Consequently, the General Assembly improvised, often inconsistently, as it attempted to subject the proprietors to central legal control. Ironically, the processes included both the revival of some dormant syndicates and the creation of new ones, as well as the defeat of the Narragansett Proprietors. From the vantage point of Newport, the cases fell roughly into four categories.

Where towns or proprietors already intended to do nothing but divide land while retaining a few small tracts for collective ends, they were left to themselves, as in Portsmouth, Pettaquamscut, New Shoreham, East Greenwich, and Newport itself. When baffled by bits and pieces of their business, these proprietors readily turned to governmental authority in the town or the colonial court. They sought rather than shunned adjustment to a legal framework. Where Newport men saw fit, they revived old syndicates to finish dividing the land and make money in the process. In Conanicut, Misquamicut, and Westconnaug, they freely resorted to governmental authority, even to the point of advocating legislation to strengthen (and so regulate) the corporative nature of the proprietors.

In the region of Providence and Warwick, Newport interests, apart from resuscitating the Westconnaug claims, had no object other than to bring an end to old debilitating quarrels in order to foster improvement. The colony intervened to thwart the Pawtuxet proprietors' last efforts to revive the Harris claims. By doing that and trying to get colonial boundaries set to please the two northern towns, the political leaders made central authority vital to the proprietors there, forced recognition of Westconnaug, and created long roads through the territory to hasten its use and value.

The Narragansett Proprietors constituted a special case but one of central importance to Rhode Island, because dealings with them led to the most vigorous and successful assertion of the General Assembly's authority. To survive in imperial politics, the colonial government had to render this combination powerless. To expand agricultural development of Newport's immediate hinterland west of Narragansett Bay, the colony had to resolve the old conflicts over land and jurisdiction. The Assembly put this territory into private hands, under clear titles derived from its own authority, and thereby mobilized a swarm of owners to defend Rhode Island's jurisdiction against Connecticut's claims and also discouraged further machinations by the defeated claimants. In this striking demonstration of its powers, Rhode Island illustrated most clearly the value of central authority to replace one plan of development with another. This cluster of developments produced nearly uniform results but followed from no consistent thinking about proprietary institutions. Even prominent Newport men could pursue one approach when they conducted the affairs of a proprietary syndicate and another when they sat as judges of the General Court of Trials. The organizational practices they used, including assessments on shares, confiscation of shares for nonpayment, and delegation of nearly all business to an executive committee, implied continuing collective use of the land.

This view won a vague authorization by a statute that probably was enacted or at least planned in 1715. If used fully, it would have given the proprietary organizations a place in the colony's rationalized framework of institutions. The General Court of Trials, however, doubted the corporative powers of the syndicates and rendered the statute toothless. The law allowed an organization of proprietors at a meeting "convened by a Warrant" given by a justice of the peace—that is, only under the authority of the central government—to choose "a Clerk, and a Surveyor or Surveyors, and such and so many other Officers, as they shall Judge needful and convenient, for the orderly carrying on and management of the whole Affairs of such Community."[1]

The notes by Nathaniel Newdigate, a lawyer concerned in several major disputes over proprietary shares, reveal a little of the difficulty for the legal mind. Plainly, he was trying to develop ideas about what kinds of collectivities could exist and what they might do. Naturally, he turned to English law, presumably to find precedents for the Rhode Island statute. Unfortunately, his notes did not include the conclusions he drew. All the same, the framework of thought is important.

Newdigate described the traditional distinction between corporations "for publick Government" and "for private charity"—that is, governmental and eleemosynary. The first was "Governable by the Law of the Land—The second by the particular Government of them that Erect them etc." Presumably, this distinction pertained to matters emanating from the establishment of corporate existence by sovereign authority, although the distinction seems overdrawn in that both kinds of corporation made ordinances or bylaws in fields where they were authorized to act and observed national laws in others. Perhaps he was looking for the bearing of common or statute law on the two varieties.

Newdigate also commented on several other points: whether a corporation (the colony?) could grant to other bodies what the monarch had granted to it (did he mean land? corporate standing?) and what powers might be exercised by "companys of men not Corporate." He jotted down one point, of indeterminable relevance, that a corporation can make bylaws and "inflict a penalty to be Levyed by distress—or recovered by action of Debt—but they cannot imprison for the same." More to the point, he wrote "that the Major part of the corporacion or body corporate—have power to bag [enlarge? set aside?] the Common law—to lease out the lands of the corporation—non obstanti the dissent of the minor part—and that any act or order of the corporacion to the contrary shall be voyd."[2]

No clear colonial policy on proprietary organizations ever came into existence in Rhode Island. The Assembly acted without regard for consistency but with confidence in its powers. Even the aims of the Newport leadership, if they may be deduced from the sum of the changes actually wrought, were probably expedient rather than based on a comprehensive policy for the colony. And of course, the results may well have had a consistency in spite of the wishes of their authors. Lurking in the careers of several proprietary organizations were two phenomena that may be revealing: the members had no cohesion as a group, in contrast to the early years of the Misquamicut or East Greenwich promotions, and they often backed away from using the organizations they designed for themselves. These syndicates could agree on dividing land for individual exploitation, but beyond that they had only minor goals of laying out roads or setting aside special resources for collective use. There was no question any longer of associating a collectively managed block of territory with a community. The commercial-mindedness of Newport was becoming pervasive.

The Narragansett Proprietors and the "Vacant Lands"

Above all, Rhode Island had to end the threat posed by the Narragansett Proprietors. Conceivably, the colony could have forged a compromise with them, even after they had supported Connecticut's claims to the disputed territory or sought intervention by the Crown. Governor Cranston may have tried to achieve such an outcome, but if so, his effort was doomed. Sides had been taken, feelings deeply ingrained. In too many ways, restoration of the charter government rested on a unified stance against the Narragansett Proprietors. On a small scale, many people simply acquired use of land without respect for the claims under the old mortgage. Moreover, the leading Tories, who were Narragansett Proprietors or their friends, had such scorn for the charter government as to make compromise with them repugnant or risky. Furthermore, Rhode Island leaders wanted profits from the lands for themselves.

For a dozen years after the revival of the charter, the Narragansett Proprietors pinned their hopes on a change in government that would put some of them in power. With high hopes but without success, they looked to imperial officials to help them or gathered evidence to support abolishing the charter. They got less support than before from Connecticut, which already had begun to see its jurisdictional claims as separate from their territorial ones. They needed royal backing and were unlikely to secure it while Whitehall concentrated on other issues, such as military coordination of the northern colonies or suppressing piracy.

One vital topic continued to be ignored in official statements: what was happening on the land in dispute. Governor John Easton in 1691 launched what became Rhode Island's official opinion, that the contest was preventing settlement of the Narragansett country while Rhode Island people moved to other colonies in search of good land. The territory remained uninhabited when it could have been supplying wealth for the English commercial world. This idea was encapsulated in the repeatedly used term "vacant Lands." Yet it was deceitful to some extent. As a result of squatting by settlers, Rhode

Island's piecemeal acceptance of a few irregular purchases or Connecticut grants, and sales or leases by the Narragansett sachems, great tracts of land passed into the control of White colonials between King Philip's War and the beginning of the eighteenth century.[3] Still, people may have hesitated to invest much time or capital in land on which they lacked clear title. Unregulated settlement by itself could not thwart the Narragansett Proprietors, though it could erode or qualify the land rights they might obtain under a favorable ruling in Whitehall and frustrate their old aim of establishing orderly towns. They abandoned that goal in 1701, when they futilely announced their willingness to sell to anybody.[4] In effect, they reconciled themselves to the unregulated settlement patterns in Rhode Island.

They probably tried to reach an accomodation with the colonial government in the years between 1696 and 1704 but failed in the end. The Assembly hinted at willingness to compromise. In 1703 their prospects appeared to brighten after Rhode Island came to an agreement with Connecticut on the border, promising to honor grants under Connecticut's authority east of the line. But the mortgage had been negotiated before the Connecticut charter and foreclosed upon without that colony's endorsement. Only politics could decide what the concession to Connecticut would mean. The proprietors appealed to the General Court of Trials, probably encouraged by the election of two of their friends to the bench. They won a judgment; the defendant asked for a rehearing, which never was held. They tried twice more and lost. The Proprietors wanted to appeal at once to the queen in council but were told they must first exhaust all legal remedies in the colony, which meant asking for rehearings. They declined to do so.[5] The Narragansett Proprietors finally gave up trying to get their way under Rhode Island jurisdiction.

The General Assembly ultimately resolved the long dispute by creating titles, under its own authority, to most of the territory. In 1708 it adopted a plan recommended by Westerly, which had been horrified by the signs of compromise with the proprietors in 1703. That town proposed that the colonial government set up the Niantic sachem, Ninigret, as prince of the Narragansetts so that he could have the right to all land outside colonial hands. He had a claim, though not an unquestionable one, to succeed the old Narragansett sachems.

The Assembly began by making a survey of the so-called vacant lands. Then it appointed trustees for Ninigret and a committee to hear all claims. The committee approved roughly what the colony had approved before—the Quidnesset and Boston Neck purchases of the proprietors, plus assorted acquisitions by others. The Assembly accepted the report, recognized Ninigret as legitimate heir to Canonicus and Miantonomi, and created a new committee to purchase most of his land from the trustees. The sachem promised that the land he kept never would be alienated without the consent of colonial authorities.[6]

The Assembly then created another committee to sell what it had just bought. Within three years, it sold at least sixty square miles in Westerly, all of what later became West Greenwich, and large parts of Kingstown.[7] The money was designated to pay for expenses of the expedition against Canada in 1709, but the committee allowed payment partly in bonds, which turned out to be longer-term than intended. The General Attorney was suing for payment as late as 1729 and probably never collected all the money.[8]

The sales accomplished several purposes. They killed the chances of the Narragansett Proprietors' obtaining anything from the mortgage, first by setting up rival claims to every disputed acre and second by putting many of these claims into the hands of actual users, whom the courts ordinarily would protect. Furthermore, the purchasers would have to back Rhode Island's jurisdiction against Connecticut. Perhaps most important, the colonial government had proved that it could confer benefits on its supporters.

Rhode Island also legitimized the White occupation of the Narragansett country that was already under way and to a small extent guided it. The Assembly's committee sold most of the land in blocks to clusters of buyers rather than to individuals. In some cases all members had been using the land previously. One sale included the site of an operating sawmill. If the buyers thought they nevertheless already had a right to their land, they had to pay for a new one. More often, the group consisted of some men already using part of the land, as well as outsiders, commonly colonial officials from Newport. Only rarely did large blocks go to men with no prior interest in the territory. The most ambitious of such purchasers was John Mumford, the surveyor of the "vacant Lands," who obtained at least ten thousand acres.[9]

The clusters of purchasers differed radically from the proprietary groups of the seventeenth century. Only one, which purchased land farthest from the coast and therefore was the least suitable for rapid development, conducted collective business for more than a few years. Some organized to divide their purchase and did no more. One group had a plat made, designated roads, reserved three acres for common use, and then divided the rest. A few groups undertook more complex dealings, including sale of tracts to outsiders or reservation of special resources for use in common.[10] No obvious model exists for the procedure commonly followed. Whatever the inspiration, most of the takers of the "vacant Lands" formed no organizations that aspired to power.

In the exceptional case, the Great Purchase that became West Greenwich and some territory to the south of it, the buyers talked of a complete division within three months but maintained an active organization for nearly thirty years. They began in the usual way. Thirteen men, most of them prominent in public life, gave bonds for £1100 to pay for thirty-five thousand acres between East Greenwich and the Connecticut line. They then added forty-six more partners, with Governor Cranston at the head of a list that included several men who were also trustees of Ninigret, surveyor Mumford, the entire committee to sell the "vacant Lands," and a few other officials. The thirteen original purchasers also resolved to confirm title to men already improving parts of the tract. They wanted these men as partners to share in divisions but were willing to sell them the acres they used. Quite likely they did so.[11]

Although things turned out differently, the buyers envisioned a disciplined organization, a temporary body politic. It would act by majority vote and admit new members. Each full share would have a single vote, no matter how many parts it had been divided into, but a person holding more than one share also would have only one vote. The general meeting elected a clerk and treasurer (normally, the same man) and an executive committee. That group would act for the whole by majority vote, hire a surveyor, assess costs on the partners proportionally, and even replace its own members as needed. In practice, the committee referred important questions to a general meeting. Moreover, the plan for assessing costs proved unsatisfactory, so the partners decided to impose a fee on themselves.[12]

The proprietary organization began to do more than parcel out land when it decided to manage commons. In 1711, when the shareholders learned of illegal timber-cutting on their land, they appointed a committee to sell felled trees that had been seized by some members and to seize any more that it might discover. At one stage, they authorized their committee "to take all Lawfull meanes to Recover the mony" from interlopers and if necessary "to sue and Implead in as full and Ample manner as if the whole Proprietors were Present"—a voice of confidence that the organization had a corporative nature under the law. But the effort was futile; the organization could not control its commons. Boundary controversies kept the institution alive until 1735, when it disposed of its few remaining assets.[13] Surprisingly, it neither built a lasting political organization nor shaped a community.

The committee to sell the "vacant Lands" did not fully resolve uncertainties in earlier dealings or safeguard a permanent reservation for the Narragansetts. The sachems kept parting with their land by unauthorized sales and leases. Even when the Assembly, at Ninigret's request, appointed trustees to conserve the tribal territory, some of these men served themselves instead.[14] More important for the interests of Newport, the sales of land in the Narragansett country encouraged production there and furthered the development of great landowning families, which had begun already in Pettaquamscut and the territories north and south of Wickford. These families often had branches in Newport and also filled important colonial offices. Thus, they created a strong political and economic partnership with the capital.

Pettaquamscut, East Greenwich, and Aquidneck

Except in Conanicut, control of undivided lands on the islands and at Pettaquamscut and East Greenwich had no potential for preventing orderly conduct of public business or spawning loyalties at cross-purposes with the political framework. To the contrary, most of the proprietors had to rely on governmental authority. They chose to divide their holdings quickly, whether by town or proprietors or both. Moreover, the aims of all the proprietary organizations in this group harmonized with commercial development.

The Pettaquamscut purchasers had never aspired to a quasi-governmental role. They had planned commercially oriented agriculture from the start and did nothing more than enforce the value of the land by setting aside the rights-of-way for roads. They divided nearly all of their holdings by 1704. The purchasers consistently conducted business as a group of tenants in common and made no effort to adopt political practices of majority rule or collective determination of who held shares.[15]

In East Greenwich, the town retained control of undivided land, although it scrupulously allowed absentee owners of shares in the land system to vote on divisions. The absentees, surprisingly, produced no fully autonomous proprietary organization. The proprietors in 1711 designed a commercial center and continued to manage it, but four years later they decided on a complete division of the rest, reserving only eight acres to support schools, and then let the town carry out the plan.[16]

Portsmouth followed approximately the same course, though less smoothly. The town parcelled out nearly all of its small commons, using one formula or another. The Newport proprietors voted in 1702 to divide most of the commons. A committee headed by Governor Cranston decided to add a few provisions for public resources, reminiscent of the seventeenth century. It selected a site for a fort on Goat Island and reserved land for schools. It settled a few controversies quickly. Then the proprietors approved of its work, authorizing a form by which it could certify individual allotments.[17]

When the proprietors tried to dispose of their other lands, they met frustration repeatedly and finally returned their rights to town control. Thus, the town regained Goat Island and Coasters Harbor Island and later Easton's Beach, where the proprietors had been unable to subdue contrary claims. Likewise, they resigned to Middletown—a new town carved out of land between Newport and Portsmouth—a beach next to Sachuest Point.[18] The towns struggled for decades to get control of these beaches.

Conanicut, Misquamicut, and Westconnaug

The complexities of ending the vestigial commons on Aquidneck were minor compared to what awaited the leading Newport men who revived the old proprietary organizations of Conanicut, Misquamicut, and Westconnaug. They freely used the governmental hierarchy—the General Assembly, and in Jamestown the town as well—to attain their ends. They turned to a legally defined central authority when an autonomous proprietary syndicate failed to accomplish what they wanted. In these adventures, only a few Newport men sought vast estates for themselves, on the scale of the former Narragansett Proprietors. Most of the speculators wanted a tidy profit. Their actions amounted to a shakedown rather than a land grab. The cumulative effect of their actions, however, was to end old quarrels and deploy land for individual use.

A year after the Newport proprietors resolved to divide the common land, Samuel Cranston took the lead in advocating a similar project in Jamestown. He and a few others revived the Conanicut proprietors to dispose of the tract reserved for a commercial center or "township" and to end disputes over roads, disputes related to old disagreements about property lines. The proprietors formed a committee to make a new survey and, probably in anticipation of claims that it would violate law, got the General Assembly's blessing for the project.[19] Sure enough, it encountered frenzied opposition from proprietors who expected to lose by the resurvey. The routes of highways and the boundaries of the township had to be decided, however, if the town was to conduct its own affairs. So the town meeting backed the proprietors.[20]

After two years, probably spent in futile efforts to find an amicable solution, John Mumford concluded the new survey. When the objectors challenged the result in court, the committee went to the General Assembly and got approval of the plat and the roads it provided. More lawsuits sputtered over the outcome for three decades, but the main work had been accomplished, conspicuously with the backing of the General Assembly.[21]

The squabbles over property lines in Jamestown led to comments on a few points that normally went without saying and also dramatized the changing position of a syndicate of proprietors in the institutional pattern. Francis Brinley, a prominent enemy of the resurvey, objected to the political character of the organization. He complained that the shareholders had equal votes in meetings rather than ones proportional to their shares. He opposed a quasi-judicial authority whereby the proprietors' committee heard and resolved claims to share rights. And he resented the informality of the hearings. The political character had been uncontroversial when common land was the collective resource to be used at the pleasure of the community. Brinley, representing an absentee owner, saw the share system simply as an entitlement to a portion of real estate and therefore to be treated according to what he understood as English land law. Any change from the property lines of the original plat amounted to illegal confiscation of specific tracts and dissolution of the foundation on which all claims rested.[22] What most infuriated Brinley was Cranston's use of the General Assembly to impose the revised plan of highways and property lines.

Cranston left no record of his views. Obviously, he thought it justifiable to resurrect a proprietary organization that acted by majority rule and to secure the backing of a town meeting and the General Assembly. Maybe he wanted to bring a proprietors' institution into a legal framework by giving it a place in a hierarchy of authority. Or he may have been merely expedient. His actions in the Misquamicut and Westconnaug organizations suggest both possibilities.

The events in Westerly cannot be reconstructed fully because evidence is missing on important points, but some things are clear. After the 1660s, the organization of the Misquamicut proprietors went dormant. Newport members revived it in 1706, and Governor Cranston asked the town of Westerly "by what authority or power" it had assigned undivided land to individuals. He said only the proprietors could do that.[23] Receiving no satisfactory reply, Cranston and the speculators organized busily.

Plans formed at general meetings suddenly disappeared by 1708. The surviving proprietors' records left a six-year gap and resumed as the predominance of membership passed from Aquidneck to Westerly men. During these years, the Assembly's committee on vacant lands was selling thousands of acres of Westerly. In addition, Westerly records reveal many sales of Misquamicut rights, usually by outsiders to local men, often with allusions to the town surveyor laying out the land to the purchasers.[24] Quite likely, the Aquidneck men with Misquamicut shares were playing on the fears of local settlers that they might lose land they had already improved. Bolstered by provincial power, one Misquamicut proprietor made money from this thinly veiled extortion.

Nor did the Misquamicut company end its new life content with these small profits. Its members asked the General Assembly for a land grant to compensate them for what they claimed they had lost in the compromise on the Connecticut boundary and planned a division on the Rhode Island side of the line. They then scrapped most of these plans to seek their ends through the colony's sale of "vacant Lands."[25] The object was not to operate a proprietary organization but to manipulate land rights, and in the tangle of Westerly affairs the colonial government was the best agency to help them attain their lands. The Newport insiders surely profited, but people in Westerly benefited from the end of old quarrels and the creation of clearly defined titles.

The revival of the Westconnaug organization produced more extensive results—in fact, far more than pertained directly to its claims—and showed how much the colonial government could accomplish. Flimsy as these claims were, the proprietors converted them into a sizable tract. In the process, the proprietary organization, rebuilt by Aquidneck men as a body politic with strong internal discipline, was transmuted into a loose partnership in landowning dominated by Providence and Warwick men. In the process, conflicting claims were settled between several interests in and around Providence.

Cranston and other prominent Aquidneck men initiated the process in 1706 after a preliminary move. Four years earlier, "sundry persons" secured the General Assembly's approval to make a township out of Westconnaug so long as it infringed on no other town.[26] Nothing came of of that decision. Later, the Westconnaug shareholders reorganized and asserted a claim to land stretching north from the Showomet purchase and lying between Quinebaug River (in Connecticut) and the Pawtuxet and its tributary flowing out of Ponaganset Pond. Thus, they wanted what others thought was either Providence west of the Seven Mile Line or Pawtuxet west of the Pocasset River. The dispute between those two interests was then before the queen's privy council.

The Westconnaug men began to use political strength to advance their cause. They admitted a few important Warwick and Pawtuxet men, probably to undermine their opposition but also to bring into their ranks a few more high colonial officials. Three of the new northern members were chosen at once to hold office in the proprietary organization—all as members of the executive committee called the trustees and one as clerk and one as treasurer. The other three trustees included Governor Cranston and the colony's General Recorder, or secretary.[27]

The Westconnaug organization hired a surveyor, which led to open conflict with Providence interests. Two local magistrates, Joseph Williams and Thomas Fenner, authorized the arrest of two Westconnaug trustees, one of them being an assistant and the other the General Attorney. The dispute went before the General Assembly just as events combined to bring the opponents to a settlement—and to precipitate other events. Recently, news had arrived of the failure of the Pawtuxet appeal to the queen, and the Providence proprietors and the Pawtuxet claimants finally began running a line for Pawtuxet west of the Pocasset River, which in the end was to extend only to the Seven Mile Line. At about the same time, Governor Cranston soothed the Providence proprietors by intervening in their dispute with Mendon and began negotiations with Massachusetts to settle the colonial border. So the Assembly dropped proceedings against Williams and Fenner and referred the basic issues to negotiation between the Westconnaug and Providence interests.[28] Representatives of the two sides soon reached an agreement. The erstwhile opponents then began to work together as two sets of speculators who could make more through cooperation than rivalry.[29]

The Westconnaug organization changed fundamentally when Providence men joined it. As reassembled in 1706, it acted through virtually all-powerful trustees and levied assessments successfully on pain of forfeit of share rights. Further, it had enforced its old rule that any member would forfeit his share by selling it without the organization's consent. When Providence men took the lead, however, they decided to pay surveyors by using a fee on recipients of dividends, so a new assessment would be unnecessary. They gave up trying to declare forfeit the rights of those who sold land without the organization's approval. By 1718 they stopped trying to determine who owned shares.

Faced by competing claims, they decided to let the claimants settle who got the dividends as they saw fit.[30]

In the events touched off by reviving the Westconnaug organization, the colonial government pushed the conflicts to a resolution, but it did so in ways that differed from the experience in Conanicut and Misquamicut. In Westconnaug, the General Assembly created a pretext for proprietary action, and the colonial officials who held shares used their authority to help the organization. Moreover, they used conflicts over land to stimulate action on other disputes, such as the one over the boundary with Massachusetts. In the end, the Westconnaug shares, unlike the other two cases, were converted into extensive land rights.

Whatever their motives, the Newport men who resuscitated these proprietary organizations hastened some of the major institutional developments of the time. They helped put an end to conflicts over land that had slowed or paralyzed improvement in the area and so contributed to the advance of Newport's trade, which in turn helped rationalize authority in the colony. In addition, probably unintentionally, they helped to destroy the operation of proprietary organizations in the style of a body politic. In Misquamicut and Westerly, the strict organization failed when the Newport leaders had to share control with local men or sell out to them. What had been conceived as a body politic, a company of shareholders acting as one, became an association of partners with a common interest in keeping a tract of land until they could each have a slice. Their vital officers became the clerk and the surveyor, not the trustees and the treasurer.

Providence and Warwick

Disputes over undivided lands in Providence and Warwick had plagued Rhode Island for decades in the seventeenth century and, in addition to weakening the governmental framework, had led to the divorce of town from proprietary concerns and had factionalized the proprietary syndicates. The old contests continued in the early eighteenth century and new ones broke out, so the contending organizations had incentives to act vigorously as collectivities. Some tried to do so, and they bedeviled town government more than proprietors did elsewhere in the colony. By one route or another, however, the syndicates disentangled themselves from town business, abandoned vigorous collective action, and either resolved their quarrels or let individual members rather than the corporative organization carry on the fight.[31]

Strong self-government, where it was attempted by a proprietary organization, crumbled as its main purposes were stymied. In most cases, the social weakness of the organization hastened this process. Solidarity was undermined by absentee shareholders, ownership of fractional and multiple shares, old animosities, and in some cases the compromises that ended old conflicts by exchanges of share rights. The resulting rosters of people could not work together. They could not determine who held shares. All they could agree on was dividing the property. Lingering desires to manage a traditional commons collided with propensities to use available resources for individual profit in commercial channels. Neither towns nor proprietary syndicates, even with help from the magistrates, could patrol the commons. The commons had to be divided.

Even though they derived considerable support from well-placed friends at the colony level, the proprietors in most communities could not escape the power of their government. The towns made rules for use of the commons and also used the colonial judiciary to enforce laws concerning land usage. The government authorized exchanges of land that already had been laid out for parts of remaining common land. It assumed the function of creating roads on the proprietors' territory. It deliberated on granting wharf lots along the waterfront in the center of Providence, even after 1704, when at the proprietors' demand it officially left disposal of all the commons to them.[32] By 1710 the proprietors were exerting control over the waterfront. Next they took charge of the thatch beds in the cove at the center of town but, after despairing of keeping them as a common resource, divided them into individual lots.[33]

The proprietors continued to dismantle the old system of commons in even more striking ways. Although in 1700 they gave the town a site for a wharf, a burial ground, and a military training field, they parceled out the rest among themselves. They quietly divided the "stated common" that had been declared perpetual for the town's use earlier.[34] By 1724 they had parceled out almost all their valuable land. Thereafter, they continued granting piecemeal what was left. Soon they could no longer claim to be acting with the community's purposes in view. If they had no land, they had no power—or reason to exist.

Proprietary organization gradually separated from the town government, as already described to some extent in chapter 3. Though the proprietors in the 1690s began choosing surveyors and soon a treasurer, they relied on the town's moderator and clerk at least until 1707, when their decisions ceased to be recorded among the town meeting minutes. By 1718 they were appointing a treasurer, clerk, and committee to pass on allotments.[35]

After 1720 they lost their assertiveness They stopped trying to adjudicate disputes over share rights, realizing that such quarrels would go to court anyway. They met frustration in their efforts to maintain control of their particularly valuable land, even against the town. The town backed one claimant;

the proprietors created another, and he lost in court.[36] Even before then, they had confined themselves to carrying out the process of dividing land into individual holdings.

Events in Warwick resembled those to the north. Partitions of the Shaw-omet purchase during the seventeenth century led to each subdivision having its distinctive set of members and difficulties in acting together. Commercial aspirations intruded further than ever into the community, as elsewhere producing fears that common land would be exploited unscrupulously to provide commodities for export. The consequences were timid proprietary organizations that became content to divide their territories and let the town or the courts or arbitrators resolve internal conflicts.

The proprietors of the Four Mile Common offered a particularly good illustration of utter failure to keep common land for collective purposes. Facing the impossibility of maintaining common pastures, mostly along Greenwich Bay, the proprietors planned to divide them into individual lots and decided to promote one of them as a site for a commercial center. Efforts to secure contributions for building a wharf came to little, and the commercial center failed to materialize.[37]

They tried to maintain control of the vast timberlands reserved earlier. After the town futilely imposed fines in 1706, payable to the proprietors on persons taking trees or bark without authorization, the proprietors wrote their own rules, aimed chiefly at people who took trees "to make merchandise." They told their treasurer to sue perpetrators in actions of trespass, but they allowed anybody to carry a complaint before any two justices, who could issue a warrant to take the penalty by distraint. Then they relaxed their rules to give each other limited rights to cut trees or strip bark for commercial purposes. Probably these slight restraints, too, had little effect. The proprietors tried raising fines and hiring someone to keep watch for offenders, but soon gave up and decided to divide the timber reserve into individual holdings.[38] This decision touched off a controversy. Opponents feared it would lead to dividing the rest of the commons, as some of its supporters indeed wished. The proprietors adopted a reassuring ordinance but soon sought cumbersome compromises, such as setting aside three common fields in the western part of the township and letting their holders decide on cooperative fencing or allow some of their number to take individual portions.

By 1723 such temporizing gave way to a complete division. Three years later they began to divide the commons, and nearly finished the work within a decade.[39] Probably they were spurred on by litigation similar in some respects to the Pawtuxet cases, that undermined the proprietors' collective capacity.[40] The lawyers could find no way to argue private claims without treating proprietary rights as nothing more than tenancy in common. So it behooved the proprietors to avoid trouble by dividing their holdings quickly.

Conclusion

By one route or another the surviving proprietors of common lands came to regard themselves as doing nothing more than holding land as tenants in common until they could divide it up completely. They acted as collectivities to reach this end. Their surveyors and clerks created documents to transfer acres into individual ownership. The syndicates dedicated a little land to public uses. Yet even when they created roads, they did so to provide access to the intended individual tracts. The organizations lost both the power and the desire to shape communities. Their capacity to arouse important loyalties blazed up and then went dim. Clearly, they could not generate an internal solidarity to make majority rule effective. They tried to make their own decisions and then found ways to remain aloof from disputes between people claiming shares. Proprietary rights, which once had defined a status in town life, became simply land rights. The proliferation of categories of status collapsed.

Conspicuously, the proprietary syndicates lost what little ambition they had to exploit land rights collectively. In effect, they dismissed a baggage train of European devices to draw profit out of shared ownership of land. To be sure, many Old World practices were impractical. Rhode Island had few sites for mills or fairs that could be lucrative in the early eighteenth century and had a small attraction for renters, whether urban or rural. Yet neither geography nor demography prevented the proprietary organizations from acting like corporations. Rather, the members refused to wait for population to raise the value of specific sites and instead behaved as though individual exploitation was inevitable, and thus made it so.

The consistency of the outcome stands in sharp contrast to the diversity of roads to it. Contests of several kinds led to the colonial government's deciding among conflicting claims. Centralized hierarchical authority smashed the Narragansett Proprietors, nearly obliterated the Misquamicut syndicate, and imposed a system of land transfers that gave rise to many tenancies in common that were generally soon dissolved. The Newport men who led their town's proprietorial organization and revived others wanted disciplined self-governing institutions but consistently failed to make their self-control effective. In some cases the colonial government became so important to their success as to impose its ends in place of theirs. In other cases their efforts were frustrated, and they found it expedient to sell their claims to those residing near the land.

In the northern part of the colony, few men desired to make proprietary syndicates into corporative entities, yet those who did came to grief as they collided with contrary expectations. Whether among the Newport interests using old practices or northerners attempting to use the law of 1715, the men who tried to create a corporative character kept running into beliefs that English law did not recognize their pretensions. So on one level a real or supposed conflict between English and colonial law reinforced what on another level was implicit in the values manifested in actions to dissolve collective interests by dividing them. Although the colonial legislation of 1715 fell into impotence in this process, except for sketching a procedure for divisions, colonial authority became supreme in most respects. The central government manipulated several important conflicts to ends it found satisfactory; its courts became the unquestioned interpreters of law. Ancient ways and local custom receded before a centralized system.

❧ 8 ❧

Town Ambitions and Town Government

Between the end of the seventeenth century and the middle of the eighteenth, institutional developments at the town level had two distinct aspects. In their efforts to promote commercial zones, towns acted autonomously, by flexible and improvisatory means. In other business, towns became subordinate to colonial law, put new emphasis on procedural niceties, and so increased the importance of the town council as opposed to the meeting. In both lines of development, towns adapted English practices to serve the colony's needs in ways that had been less important earlier, but they still managed to deviate from the English model.

These two lines of change were contradictory on the formal level but compatible on another. Both were consistent with the reordering of Rhode Island as depicted so far. Toward the end of the seventeenth century, Newport's progress in trade had been sufficient to foster commerce there and to inspire imitation elsewhere. The capital for the time being had no significant rival within the colony and in fact could benefit from a set of secondary commercial nodes. At the same time, however, the colony needed a stronger central government than it had ever had and needed the town governments to serve as its agents. So commercial ambition fostered both the flexible and improvisatory measures to build up ports and the spread of system and regulation by colonial law in other parts of town business. The devices to attract trade, moreover, led toward the corporations and quasi-corporations of the late colonial period. These institutions reconciled, at least to some extent, daring and urban boosterism with systematic subordination to law. Corporative associations based on land weakened; they were followed by organizations useful to a growing urban sector.

Commercial Centers

While town governments and proprietary organizations were usually shrinking from control of land for social ends, they acted either separately or in combination to foster commercial centers. All towns began to look for ways to magnify their roles in trade by attracting crafts and the flow of commodities. Many schemes took shape, at least one in each town, though only five came to much. Sometimes these efforts meant creating new centers of population; sometimes, promoting old centers of agricultural villages or, in Newport, building on the start made in the first half century. The sponsors freely innovated to achieve their ends. The incidence of success reflected more the potential of particular locations than the cleverness of the planners, except in East Greenwich.

Of eight of these undertakings, too little is known to merit analysis; of the other four, Portsmouth's was revealing though a failure, while those at Newport, East Greenwich, and Providence exhibited a range of feasible institutional devices.

Much more than any other town, Newport stimulated its mercantile heart and did so by methods that consciously included resort to the ways of English market towns but never so far as to include monopolies or attempts to extract revenue from valuable land. The proprietors took a much smaller part in this—none at all after 1699—than did the town and the colonial government. The exclusion of the proprietors was a striking instance of a deliberate decision to avoid allowing a privileged syndicate to exploit land from which it might have drawn a steady income. Rather, the town continued the policy it had adopted before the proprietors became a distinct organization. The town had begun subdividing part of its territory for tradesmen's lots as early as 1667 and continued to do so. They were granted on easy terms to those who would improve them and thereby qualify for outright ownership in time.[1]

At some point the town entrusted promotion of the commercial zone to a committee, once called "the Commite Chosen to regalate the Town Consernes." Although the town meeting often tinkered with the arrangement and even occasionally awarded land, most of the time the committee supervised the business, taking on a variety of tasks besides managing the small lots.[2] This committee, too, was prevented from becoming an entrenched and quasi-privileged institution.

The town meeting never hesitated to act on its own. With help from the colonial government, it developed land by the cove north of the Long Wharf. In 1707, it offered water frontage lots to those who would build wharves there for four years. First it wanted the General Assembly's approval, presumably to anticipate objections that the wharves would extend into space under the jurisdction of the colony. The Assembly, citing the prospective benefits to queen and commerce, promptly complied giving the freeholders of each town "full Power and Authority" to award land along rivers and coves for the purpose of building wharves or making any other improvements, providing these actions did not impair existing property rights. Soon the town created a special committee to carry out a fairly detailed plan presented by some of the inhabitants.[3]

The town only briefly allowed the old committee to supervise public markets. The committee supervised construction of a market house in the 1730s but was not given responsibility for patroling it. Instead, the town appointed clerks of the several market houses and empowered them to make rules and present violators to a justice of the peace, who might impose fines up to forty shillings. Once again, the town drew upon the example of English market towns for their practices but with a significant emendation. The clerks were traditional officers but they were not given traditional judicial authority; instead, the hierarchy of colonial tribunals had yet another function.[4]

Perhaps before creating the committee, the town set a pattern for development of a wharf for general use. As early as 1685 "the new Long wharfe" existed. The town had allowed some inhabitants to build it but without any promise of monopoly. In that year the town authorized a new construction on the same terms. It gave both land and rights to extend the facility into salt water—no finickiness in the seventeenth century about infringing on the colonial government's sphere! The resulting structure fell into disrepair by 1702, when a new association of residents, a self-styled company, formed to take it over and restore its usefulness. By unanimous vote the town transferred the rights to the company for as long as it kept the wharf in repair and authorized it to choose a wharfinger "and take the usuall custom of wharfedge" for anything landed there. The custom presumably came from England.[5]

The members of the wharf company behaved as though it were a legal corporation, though the town had no clear right to make it one. They sold shares and, in the fashion of proprietors of undivided land, appointed essential officers, a wharfinger, and an executive committee. They established rules for use of the wharf and reward of the wharfinger, as well as distribution of dividends.[6] The striking feature of the table of fees was that it applied to members as well as nonmembers. The wharf truly was to be a public convenience. Yet it was not kept in repair, and it failed to meet the port's needs. In 1739 the town once again put it under a new organization.

In creating other attributes of a market city, Newport flexibly relied on its committee on small lots or on special officers, and it made its decisions either in the town meeting or through the General Assembly. The committee, for instance, generally saw to the maintenance of streets until surveyors of highways or other officers assumed the responsibility. It kept open thoroughfares that residents wanted to put to other uses.[7] It also persuaded the town to adopt regulations requiring uniformity in height and width of those roads and the removal of such nuisances as deposits of combustibles next to the streets or privies emptying onto them. At first the town appointed surveyors of the highways to implement this code and, appealing to "the Custom of England," asked the justices of the peace to aid them in compelling compliance with the rules. Yet this system was not completely successful, so the town in 1715 created an equally unsuccessful special committee on streets.[8]

The town meeting, often helped by the General Assembly, attended to many other issues. A long series of measures, beginning in 1698, dealt with the prevention and quenching of fire, both to put obligations on the inhabitants at large and to provide fire engines and companies of men under quasi-military disicipline to operate them.[9] The town adopted the English customs of setting a night watch and appointing a crier to advertise wares for sale during the daylight. Most of the colonial statutes on selling goods primarily served Newport, such as those requiring towns to choose a corder of wood or establish the assize of bread, though Newport often added to the Assembly's stipulations. Likewise, it went on its own in to restrain entry of outsiders.[10] The Governor and Council called upon the town meeting in 1712 to consider building a combined hospital and workhouse, after which the town toyed with a plan for a combined poorhouse and prison but settled on a simple almshouse.[11] Shortly thereafter, the town induced the colony to collect a tax on seamen's wages to provide support for them and their families in case of disability.[12]

By these and many other methods, Newport created a salubrious climate for trade. Its eclecticism is conspicuous. By turns innovative and traditional, experimental and respectful of privilege, casual about procedure and increasingly preoccupied with it, the town pursued its ambitions. It drew freely on English practices yet was never hypnotized by the Old World model.

No other town could achieve Newport's success or complexity until Providence approached it in the late eighteenth century, but most tried to imitate its methods. Portsmouth left on the record not only the plans for a commercial center, which never came into being, but also a unique statement of the town's motive in devising them. According to the town meeting in 1694, the intent was to enlarge the population and secure "the great benefit, and Profit, that may arise to Every freeholder . . . by Setling Tradesmen and Propagating a Manufactury, which way hath been the only Means and Motive of Enriching most Rich Places in the world."[13] To let the residents share in the wealth, the town offered them first pick of the small lots laid out on what was called the South Side, near the Sakonnet River south of the original settlement.

The town gave the management of the project to a committee that was to operate within certain prescribed rules. Because these rules probably were modeled after the ones in Newport, they give a clue to the now-lost terms under which the capital deployed its lots for tradesmen. Everybody who bought a lot had to sign a set of stipulations and pay 20 shillings to the town.

The recipient then had to build a house on the land at least sixteen by eighteen feet, within two years, promise not to sell to anyone but a resident of the town, and renounce claims to rights of commonage based on ownership of the lot. The town offset these requirements by promising to exempt the owner from town taxation for four years. Nothing the committee could do, however, would make a success of the scheme, so the town divided up the remaining lots as it had the rest of the commons.[14]

Although the committee conducted the town's affairs, responsibility for the land ultimately flowed back to the town. For instance, the town paid for the surveyor's plat and granted concessions to people who moved in to occupy the lots. In the 1750s the town, proprietors, and dissident freemen wrangled over use of the waterfront for wharves; they finally reached a patchwork of compromises. In the aftermath, the proprietors gave the town responsibility for enforcing the building requirement.[15]

Indeed their policy was rather like those in other towns. The proprietors sponsored a plan that did more than distribute land to themselves, and yet they made no effort to generate recurring income from outsiders who took lots. Evidently, the proprietors had no hope of creating something along the lines of English market towns, where owners of the land merely leased it to users or kept rights over commercial life there. The proprietors could profit, of course, from their lots and their prospective increase of value as trade swirled around them. Yet the basic aim was to attract trade by giving land to people at no more than the price of fees to administer the allocation.

In contrast to East Greenwich, Providence promoted its commercial center in a haphazard manner. Both the town and the proprietors took a hand in the business, but the leading inhabitants there probably acted without much regard for institutional niceties. The town tried the traditional device of obtaining permission from the General Assembly to hold an annual fair and choose a clerk of the market to supervise it. Nothing much came of those efforts. The town and the proprietors tried to provide some civic facilities. A group of residents began contributing toward a new bridge over the Providence River. After a controversy, the proprietors gained nearly complete control over allocating waterfront property.[16]

The proprietors, as in East Greenwich, made no plans to reap a durable collective income for themselves. They also stopped imposing the town's requirement that takers of waterfront lots abide by conditions designed to assure economic development. Presumably, there was no need to assure use of the land for commercial ends.[17] The arrangement of land use was taking care of itself.

Behind all the plans to foster trading centers probably lay Portsmouth's belief that trade was the way to wealth. Yet making headway required adapting traditional methods to realities around Narragansett Bay. The promoters never tried to assure a regular income to their organizations. Monopolistic institutions and even most privileges were unwise where a swarm of competitors tried to attract business to their locations. Promoters seldom followed the seventeenth-century method of granting land to support a specific economic function. They did more to support civic services, such as schools. People borrowed from English town ways but sparingly. Altogether, their behavior was expedient, with success in commerce the prime consideration rather than fidelity to consistent procedures, even when those prcedures had obvious traditional precedents.

The Routines of Town Government, Membership in the Community

By contrast with the improvisation in efforts to lure trade, towns cultivated system and uniformity in other business and accepted their subordination to the colonial government. They were well aware of the growing importance of their relation to central authority, as illustrated by Portsmouth's description of itself as "[a] branch or Limb" of the colony.[18] In their formalities towns became increasingly alike. They adapted English usages when suitable, notably in their reliance on the authority of justices of the peace, and developed local institutions in the spirit of English practice, yet inevitably they had to find their own paths. While similar to other New England towns, they all differed in some ways from practices of neighboring colonies. The most obvious differences were the functions of town councils, which were greater than those of boards of selectmen, and the gravitation of power toward the councils and away from the town meetings instead of the other way around.[19]

The trends in town government were all the more striking after the quarrels of the previous century, the collapse or near collapse of most towns after the Dominion of New England, and the resistance to the central power to tax and define boundaries in the early eighteenth century. For convenience, the evidence may be organized by a few simple categories: membership in the towns' population and the forms and actions of organs of town government, chiefly the town meeting and council.

Subtle but fundamental changes took place in what mattered in analyzing a town's population and the ways in which people joined it. Quietly, the intricate classifications built up in the seventeenth century lost significance. Instead, among the men, legal differentiation made four distinctions important: free and unfree, White and non-White, freeman and inhabitant without political rights, and requirement of or exemption from service in a train band.

General law, rather than local choice, regulated all four. The color lines, as in all of Anglo-America, began to mark sharp barriers while class lines softened. In most respects, freemen and free inhabitants had the same rights, as in power to buy and sell or freedom of religion. And the rights were clearly individual; the old interest in the household as the basic cell in the body politic vanished from public deliberations. To some extent the new property qualification for freemanship put into abstract form the old concept of a member of the body politic as the captain of a viable economic unit, yet the implication was limited. Single women and women with absent husbands often shared the rights of free inhabitants, though little in law or its application spelled out a status for such persons.

At first, special rules for the non-Whites were linked with servitude; towns had made no regulations for unfree Whites. After King Philip's War, the Indian population spread out of the Narragansett lands, at first as refugees from military campaigns but later as paupers. The White townsfolk forced the fugitives into servitude. Indians were gradually controlled by various towns, and their descendants became in effect hereditary paupers. It became normal for magistrates to ask an unfamiliar Indian where she or he had served a term of servitude or apprenticeship. Even after such formal unfreedom had ended, these people seldom could rise above the status of laborers.[20]

Slavery, whether of Blacks or Indians, gradually became common in the decades before 1720. A status reserved for people brought into the White settlements of the colony from outside, this form of bondage clearly was confined to non-Whites. Seventeenth-century laws against it, like the religious principles behind them, faded away without being formally repudiated. After 1720, Rhode Island merchants entered the slave trade with mounting avidity and, while carrying most of their wares to the Caribbean, inevitably took some of their cargo home to sell.[21] From the start, most slaves were owned in the towns around the mouth of Narragansett Bay.

Various towns enacted laws regulating non-Whites. Quite early, Portsmouth and Jamestown treated the local Indians as town wards, and the latter created a special obligation for the men among them to work on mending the roads and to perform other civic tasks. Warwick imposed a curfew on all Indians and Blacks, with violators to be "[p]unished at the Discretion of the Justices." Newport forbade sale of anything to unfree non-Whites after sundown and, like South Kingstown, forbade slaves to own domestic animals, especially swine. South Kingstown vainly tried to stop a special local festival, a little saturnalia held by local Indians and Blacks in "the Third Weak in June Annually" and other "[s]candalous meetings."[22] The old notions of important elements and dangers within the population were being supplanted by new ones.

Changes were afoot, too, in granting membership in the body politic at the town level. Town meetings retained the power to admit new men to voting rights, even though the charter clearly gave it to the colonial government. The General Assembly only ratified town votes, but it began to restrict town discretion by enacting a property qualification in 1724 and later developed procedures to enforce it. Although these measures aroused some resistance, they usually were observed.[23]

Similarly, colonial law increasingly restricted the towns' ability to screen potential inhabitants. On the whole, the town council gained power in this field. By the end of the seventeenth century, councils rather than town meetings might admit newcomers. The councils could also require potential residents to post bond against becoming town charges. Authorized by colonial law in 1682, this practice was not adopted at once in all places but ultimately became universal. In 1718, a colonial law forbade a town to refuse admission as an inhabitant to anybody with property worth £50 within the borders.[24]

By 1718 the towns were using a version of the English system of admitting persons who had certificates from the place where they had a "right of settlement," which meant that the place honoring this right would support them if they became destitute. Presumably, everyone had a legal place of inhabitation under English law. The colonial assembly wrote the concept into a statute only in 1727, and then so imperfectly that towns could ignore it. While it had to be clarified later, the concept itself was never challenged. Towns and courts continued to adopt procedural niceties from English ways with or without colonial statutes. The councils proceeded with vigor and appealed to the judiciary to support them.[25] Instead of being autonomous communities, the towns were particles of the British Empire.

The Town Meeting and Its Executive Officers

As town government accepted the role of local units in a colonial jurisdiction, the schedule of town meetings, the routine of business, the assortment of executive officers, and procedures used in official actions all changed. Approaches to urban conditions in Newport and Providence and to a much lesser extent in East Greenwich, rather than local tradition, came to make the content of action conspicuously different in those places. Everywhere, much of the old particularity in such areas as managing commons gradually disappeared.

Colonial measures conduced to standardized times and procedures for town meetings. For many years, the older towns had held at least four meetings, called quarter meetings or courts, and had convened other sessions as well. The new towns adopted this practice.[26] Once a year the town had to choose officers, and eventually, all of them settled on the spring meeting. Further, the routine of colonial government required choice of officials at least twice a year, which led most towns to adjust their schedules to the colony's calendar.[27]

Business other than elections at town meetings also responded to colonial requirements or prompting, and colonial law increasingly stipulated procedure. New statutes from the General Assembly prescribed the quorum when colonial officers were chosen, required that moderators put any proposal to a vote when asked to do so by seven men, or stipulated that certain types of business might be on the agenda only when announced in a warrant (duly publicized) summoning the meeting.[28]

In response to regulations of this kind and to the general rise in formality, town decisions tended to be classified. With increasing frequency, town meetings segregated major pieces of legislation, often passed pursuant to a colonial enabling act, as town laws, to distinguish them from orders or grants. Clerks clearly set these laws apart on the books.

With the detachment of the town meeting from an actual community came fraud. This was especially the case in South Kingstown, where corruption flourished. Early on, the town had to pass a law against casting more than one vote for an officer or a town law, on pain of a fine of up to twenty shillings or sitting in the stocks for up to two hours.[29]

Town meetings became more and more routinized, sometimes to the point of rendering their decisions nearly idle rituals. Generally, these assemblies had the final say on expenditures, for instance, but lost much of the real control over funds. Town councils or overseers of the poor, pursuant to general laws, decided on support of the paupers and left the town meeting to approve their disbursements after the fact. Roads and bridges inevitably deteriorated and required more than the unpaid labor of the townsmen to fix them. Sometimes town meetings pursued projects, such as building a pound, and learned the price only when they were finished. Commonly, bills piled up, and towns let them be examined periodically by a committee of auditors to recommend which to approve and how to pay them. Usually, the town endorsed the report, but in Providence in 1713 the town referred the business back to the auditors "to act in the matter as their judgements shall direct them and what they determine shall be Authentick." In East Greenwich in 1739 the town meeting found the finances so confusing that it let the council authorize disbursements from the treasury.[30] Surely, the willingness to let elected officials control expenditures stemmed partly from the towns' drawing part or all of their funds from payments of interest money on the colony's land banks.

As towns stopped granting rural land, gave up efforts to manage commons, and were more densely populated, the freemen devoted more and more attention to a cluster of regulations on country life. The objectives were often traditional, but the style of town action changed. In the seventeenth century, town meetings had declared the duties of residents positively. Provisions on enforcement were rudimentary until the 1680s. Towns also had ruled on highly specific points to confer benefits or impose restraints, sometimes even on individuals. By the eighteenth century, the regulations were framed in general terms, sketched standards of conduct only by implication, were negative in that they prescribed circumstances when people would face penalties for neglect of obligations, and with increasing intricacy spelled out the procedures by which the penalties would be imposed. Instead of the old declarations requiring the inhabitants to yoke and ring all their swine, for example, towns passed ordinances on who should capture hogs turned loose without yokes and rings, what should be done with the animals, how the owners might reclaim them, and what penalties and fees the owners would face.[31]

Towns often wrote measures within terms set by colonial statutes and required a flock of new officials to enforce them. In these, as in all other branches of regulation, the voice of the magistrate became necessary to give force to the actions instigated by town officials or aggrieved inhabitants.

Town meetings found it increasingly necessary to regulate roads. Although the councils, under general laws and specific orders from the General Assembly, had responsibility for getting roads laid out and owners compensated for confiscated land, town meetings tried to determine their width, maintenance, and routes. These topics were all subjects of controversy. The meeting's vote on a route, for instance, might call for a road to a mill or from the center of town to the edge or for opening and even paving city streets.[32] Then the council got the task of translating general decisions into specific thoroughfares and confronting persons whose lands were affected or whose preference had been voted down.

Part of the difficulty came from a change in the sense of what a road was. When it had been no more than a designated route from a central village to patches of agricultural land, only the villagers had to know where it lay and they seldom used it. Though in legal description it was merely a stripe across the landscape, in practice it was not. It could be used by abutting property owners in ways compatible with infrequent traffic, such as pasture. So the road was marked not by barriers on its edges but by gates and bars across it. Denser population and more intertown travel made a clearly visible route necessary. Town documents began to refer to roads as ways for the king's subjects to pass and repass. That is, a road suddenly had zoomed into a vast frame of reference as a result of the practical immersion of the colony in the British Empire.[33]

So towns as local agents of imperial coordination had to carry out their responsibilities. Often this meant requiring abutting landowners, much against their will, to build fencing along the right-of-way and take down the tranverse fences with their gates and bars. In other cases, this also meant narrowing a road. Some original rights-of-way had been ample to allow food for livestock on the way to market and most of the time to allow untaxed pasture for abutting landowners. Greater traffic and population made wide and unmarked roads so many invitations to rural chaos. Portsmouth and South Kingstown "stinted" their roads to leave a simple route for travel. North Kingstown kept Ten Rod Road wide to funnel traffic into Wickford.[34]

The new sense of what roads were required a new approach to maintaining them. If they had any regular traffic, they needed upkeep. Seventeenth-century methods, adapted from English precedents, set the standard. The original towns had declared the obligations of inhabitants to devote time annually to mending roads and had appointed surveyors of highways to organize the work. Beginning in 1700, most towns amplified their regulations on the duties of townsmen and surveyors. The duties could be specified minutely, designated who must report for work, what the crews must do, where they must do it, how the surveyors were to notify the men, what fines the men were to pay for absence, and how the surveyors were to invoke the power of a magistrate to compel payment.[35] Some ordinances allowed surveyors to buy materials at town expense or arrange swaps of land so that roads could be straightened.[36]

Irksome though traditional methods probably were, towns no longer could devise others. Westerly twice authorized the council to hire men to mend roads, only to be overruled by colonial law. Some towns could use paid labor for special purposes, such as repairing bridges. Providence (in vain) bravely proposed to be more English than anybody by turning over upkeep of roads to local justices of the peace, who would "[p]roceede according to the statute of the 22d of Henry the 8th Cap[i]t[ulum] the 5th." At most, the colonial government would condone departures from reliance on the unpaid labor of the inhabitants only to the extent of subsidizing repair of bridges and allowing several methods to hasten pavement and maintenance of streets in Newport.[37]

Practices developed for rural areas sometimes failed to serve the needs of urbanizing ones. As in other parts of promoting commercial zones, towns such as Newport and occasionally Providence and East Greenwich disregarded efforts to standardize and instead improvised or turned to English models when they sought to provide government for urban sections.

Newport, for instance, with support from the General Assembly, established regulations for controlling fires in the area where buildings were close together. Inhabitants there had to possess buckets and ladders, submit to inspection of chimneys, and remove combustibles from the streets. The town acquired fire engines and gave special privileges to men in a fire company.[38] These and other measures did not pertain to the rural part of the town. By 1730, Newport was a town of two contrasting elements.

The difference produced tensions that led to a split. In 1733 the General Assembly authorized the commercial zone to hold its own town meetings and levy taxes on itself. Unfortunately, the Assembly did not immediately determine a boundary, and the consequent uncertainty aggravated ill will from the rural section. After a long controversy, it won separation as Middletown.[39] By then, Providence was moving toward a similar subdivision.

Town government employed a growing number of specialized officers, and the obligations of existing ones expanded. By the late seventeenth century, the clerk's duties, for instance, began to swell prodigiously. Though he no longer served a town court with broad competence, he was still clerk to the town council, the probate court. His work in keeping town records grew with the tendency toward formality. Not only did deeds increase in number, but their recording began to be verbatim in all cases, which probably had not been true before, and they grew longer as people took care to observe the cumbersome forms in English models. Town records previously had been kept somewhat haphazardly. Several towns had entered everything in one volume until it was filled. Even that much system was abandoned in a few places during the troubled years after 1689. Early in the next century all towns began a much more elaborate routine, segregating records into several series: town meeting deliberations, town council records, commonly separated into a series for probate records and another for other business, land evidence records, and maybe a set of vital records, a book for earmarks and brands, and occasionally special records for miscellaneous entries. And in addition, clerks kept a file of loose papers, containing wills, petitions to the town, documents on award of land, drafts of town laws, and so forth. In similar ways, the treasurer's obligations mounted.

The list of officers of the seventeenth century had included a small number of special functionaries of the sort that became so numerous later—a constable or two, the sergeant, and perhaps a surveyor or a few fence viewers or surveyors of highways. Rhode Island towns may well have swelled the total beyond what was common elsewhere in New England. By the 1730s, depending on the local economy, a town might elect swarms of fence viewers, field drivers, or surveyors of the highways, perhaps a large number of constables, overseers of the poor, pound keepers, viewers of hemp and flax, corders of wood, cullers of clapboards and shingles, and an assortment of others, such as a sealer of weights and measures, a packer, a sealer of leather, a vendue master, an attorney, and so on. The onset of taxation had given rise to a new set of fiscal officials, notably the ratemakers or assessors and the auditors. In 1736, Warwick had forty-two officials; Westerly, forty-three. In 1738, Portsmouth had fifty; Newport, at least eighty-six. Most of these posts had been prescribed in colonial law by 1719.[40]

The men filling the various slots were chosen on different grounds. Moderator, clerk, treasurer, councilmen, auditors, and ratemakers were usually prominent members of the community. By contrast, constables and sergeants were not; indeed, towns sometimes had to look hard to find men willing to take these offices. As early as 1694, Providence was baffled and let the magistrates pick a sergeant and pay him out of the fines extracted from a man who had refused election.[41] Some officials, such as surveyors of highways and fence viewers, had to reside in their districts. Men with the relevant skills, if available, had to fill positions like sealer of leather, corder of wood, or auditor.

Town Councils

As with the town meetings, town councils also changed focus and acquired new traits without entirely abandoning old ones. The councils, however, gained in relative importance. They kept their original character of conclaves of village elders, to which had adhered the duties of a probate court. They expanded their functions as administrative boards for the town and agency for the colonial government. If anything, the administrative flavor grew most pronounced, but the judicial remained strong, even outside of probate; and the old quality of village fathers continued to lurk behind the new facade of statutory specification in such powers as those to repel undesirable newcomers or prevent the spread of smallpox.

As mentioned already, membership in the councils began to grow at the end of the seventeenth century with the Assembly's appointment of justices of the peace, only to be reduced in 1733 to the old statutory six, excluding all but the men elected by the town. This alteration probably led to a shift away from a judicial approach in some parts of the councils' business. In several areas, the remaining members in effect consigned to the excluded magistrates the duty of giving judicial starch to administrative rulings. Perhaps if one had to write a recipe, it would start: take one part old all-purpose paternalistic authority, three parts judicial, and four parts administrative (half and half for town and colony); mix until the paternalistic moistens the judicial and administrative.

The part played by the council in town government slowly became the same everywhere. At the beginning of the eighteenth century, councils did such eccentric things as send justices of the peace from house to house to assess property for a rate, summon proprietors' meetings, and lease town land. Surely, the oddest situation was in Westerly, where things occasionally seemed upside down. The town meeting granted tavern licenses, even though the Assembly returned that function to the councils in 1698, while the council sometimes chose the deputies to the Assembly. The council also had other functions unthinkable elsewhere, some trifling but some of considerable magnitude, such as auditing town accounts, levying taxes for the town and colony, hiring men to repair roads and bridges, and giving conveyances of land on behalf of the town.[42] By about 1710 most of such deviations from the norm were eliminated; by 1740, virtually all.

Even before their functions multiplied, town councils standardized and ritualized their own behavior. Some decided on regular monthly meetings in addition to special ones to act on probate business. Some got their own seals. The members began to receive rewards for their service, whether compensation for their time or merely dinner. In some places one member rejoiced in the title of president.[43]

In probate business the councils increased fidelity to law and correct procedure but in some ways painted themselves into a corner. They began to sue on the bonds of executors and administrators who misused their powers, for instance, or appealed to the Assembly to appoint a substitute for someone who refused to serve as executor. They grew cautious in acting in the paternalistic ways of the founding years until the Assembly put a legal floor under these actions. New laws specified what a council should do when an executor refused to serve, how it should divide the property of intestates, and how it might depart from the normal distribution (as councils often had done) to avoid subdividing real estate into parcels smaller than sufficient to support a family.[44]

Nevertheless, councils had difficulty with land. They (and colonial authorities) described their probate jurisdiction as that of the ordinary, an ecclesiastical court in England. But the ordinary court had jurisdiction over movable property, not freehold land. Councils kept much fuller records on dealings with movable estate than with land. They granted and recorded letters of administration on movable estate and referred to the recipients as administrators, but they did nothing quite parallel concerning land. Presumably, the councils could regard a will as sufficient authorization for an executor, once the will had been admitted to probate, but did nothing to authorize anyone to distribute the land of intestates. Nor did they preserve documents to show exactly what an executor for an intestate did to parcel out land. The effect suggests evasiveness.

And so does the absence of a statute to remedy a result of avowing probate jurisdiction on movables and remaining nearly silent on realty. Administrators had the responsibility to pay charges against the estate—final illness and burial of the deceased, satisfaction of debts, support of widows and children—and in some cases either could not raise the money by selling the movables or thought it imprudent to do so. Yet they could not touch the land, and the councils had no power to authorize its sale. So administrators or executors had to petition the Assembly for permission. When granted, the permission usually had the proviso of selling only with the advice of the council.[45]

Probate jurisdiction almost by implication extended the councils' responsibilities into care for all sorts of people. Quite directly, a probate court had to see to orphans, a category that often included children with a living mother, and might have them brought up by relatives, bound out, or put in the hands of guardians.[46] Responsibilities for orphans merged with those for the poor. Although town meetings continued to regulate paupers and in form kept the final say on providing money for their relief, the councils were much better able to handle such matters and increasingly did so, both in judicial and administrative ways. The councils met often, had few members, and had judicial powers. They could require people who were unable to support themselves to turn over their assets, even land, and bind out their children. Colonial law finally authorized these practices in 1741.[47]

Slowly an administrative as well as a judicial approach to poverty emerged. Councils began to rely on auxiliary officials. Newport in 1693 began appointing officers to watch for new paupers arriving in the town and later for poverty among the inhabitants. Though colonial law, when finally written, directed all towns to select these officers, by then called overseers of the poor, and described their tasks as merely to keep their eyes open and report what they observed to their town council, councils sometimes asked the overseers to provide aid for the poor. The Newport council put the overseers in charge of the almshouse until the town meeting began electing managers for it.[48] In Jamestown and South Kingstown the councils had the task of binding out children of nonslave Indians and the power to commandeer the labor of Indian men for repairing roads and the like.[49] From orphans and paupers the councils easily extended their purview to unwed mothers, bastard children, aged and infirm parents, and sometimes apprentices.[50]

As already mentioned, colonial law gave councils extensive authority to have roads laid out. The procedure using a jury had a judicial flavor and soon began to undergo alterations toward more administrative techniques. Providence persuaded the Assembly in 1725 to enact a law allowing the town council to use "[i]ndifferent Persons" rather than a jury to lay out roads.[51]

Councils obtained functions as executive committees for their towns, sometimes as a result of colonial laws. Newport town meeting, after deciding on appointment of a bellman, let the council hire men and give them detailed instructions. There the council also carried out such tasks as choosing a burial ground for Blacks and specifying the relations between prices of wheat and bread. Elsewhere, towns assigned a variety of duties, including fiscal, to their councils, a procedure sometimes graced after the fact by colonial law.[52]

In the long run, colonial statutes conferred on the councils their most sweeping powers in quarantine laws. Governmental cognizance of disease began in the early eighteenth century. At first, the Assembly assigned duties to restrain contagion, which always meant smallpox, to magistrates and a few specially appointed officers. The councils exercised only moderate powers until 1738, when the Assembly gave them full responsibility. Under this legislation, councils could post an officer on board any vessel arriving with an infected person or from a port where smallpox was active, to see that nobody on board came into contact with people on shore. They could put infected persons arriving in the colony in quarantine and charge them for their expenses there, and if they recovered and could not pay, put "them to Service In order to satisfy and pay such Charges" as they had incurred. Additional legislation appropriated money for improvement of the pesthouse already in existence on Coasters Harbor Island off Newport, forbade healthy people to visit sick ones without official permission, and authorized the death penalty for "evil minded Persons" who deliberately spread smallpox. Councils took the implications of quarantine to great lengths and at great expense. In this field, paternalistic, judicial, and administrative authority came together.[53]

Custom and law combined to create Rhode Island's most distinctive organ of local government. At once town fathers and colonial administrators, court and executive committee, public prosecutor and legislative body, the councils fit no simple concept. They resembled elements in some English boroughs but followed no pattern. They were clearly local products.

Conclusion

Town government settled into a routine during the early eighteenth century. No longer the expression of a community and yet not merely an administrative apparatus in an arbitrary geographical unit, it served both to carry out a shortened list of traditional duties and shoulder new ones given by the colonial government. It adjusted to colonial law in carrying out old functions such as keeping track of property rights, providing essential services, and caring for the needy. It also accepted new obligations to regulate an increasingly commercialized life. It began to impose standards, for example, on the buying and selling of goods for export, and it provided roads for through traffic.

And it applied procedural rules to all its business. Whether the rules came from colonial statutes or officials' understanding of English law, the result generally was the same. Local officers no longer could declare the inhabitants' duties with hope of success. Towns had to adopt the use of rules for justices to enforce, rules mainly in the English style.

Communal use of a town's territory largely perished. Towns could not keep commons as regions where townsfolk supplied their own and future needs. Either people exploited these regions ruthlessly to get materials for export or their neighbors said they did. Quite likely, even the complainers did so as well and projected what they wanted to regard as the impropriety of this behavior onto vaguely defined others. In the circumstances, the only reasonable thing for a town was to turn from attempting communal management of individuals, to adjusting property relations to behavior. As a consequence, towns lost the role of guiding village life and took to imposing abstract rules of restraint or civic chores such as road mending on their people.

Only where new forms of life were coming into existence, in urban zones, did collective action still seem likely to be effective. In this sphere, the old particularity nearly reappeared. Ambitious towns took courses that looked good to them and used a few general rules given by central authority. Exploratory and individualistic as these towns were, they took guidance from the manifold possibilities in English local government, using those that seemed suitable and rejecting many others. The total could be confusing. The appeals to ways of the parent country, though genuine enough, never added up to true imitation. Nowhere did towns try traditional monopolies, strictly regulated fairs or markets, or valuable facilities owned by the municipality or a privileged corporation of citizens. The closest approximation came in Newport's Long Wharf, but even there the owners were as subject to their own fees as anybody else was. Rhode Island never could be England.

Still, calculation of what suited the colonial condition came to a sort of reconciliation with imperial loyalties. The town, in both rural and urban concerns, tied local government to the past, even to rituals of the past, and also to reasoning about the future; it tied little clusters of population to an empire, acting in ways that were unimaginable before 1685.

❧ 9 ☙

Sacred Fellowship in Relation to Time and Space

Between 1695 and the Great Awakening, religious institutions took striking new directions and often did so in ways that were analogous to secular organization. Both new denominations and old sought to fit themselves into large frameworks of time and space. They cultivated institutional and intellectual connections with coreligionists elsewhere. They defined and elaborated their ecclesiastical polities. They sought new means to rear their children in the faith. They tried to place themselves within colonial and English law, with success coming mainly in their relation to property. The result was the beginning of finding a way to give churches legal protection without establishment. All of this made quite a contrast to the inward and local focus, the preoccupations with living faith in the present, prevalent in the seventeenth century.

The churches displayed, perhaps more fully than governmental institutions, what possibilities were open and what needs had to be met. They could follow different paths; government was becoming unified and systematic along one pattern.

Congregationalists

Almost simultaneously with reorganization of the colonial government in the 1690s, two kinds of Christianity appeared for the first time in Rhode Island: Congregationalism and the Church of England. In an uncanny parallel with the maneuvers to situate the colony in a political framework embracing both New England and the British Empire, these new churches were launched by missionaries from Massachusetts and England. Both also introduced what most Rhode Islanders previously had cast aside, the ecclesiastical structures and intellectual life of traditional Christianity. The newcomers arrived with links to solid organizations elsewhere and relied on these connections for many years. They forced the discussion of ties between church and state because they were accustomed to some form of legal backing and wanted it wherever they went. They provoked the colonial government to elaborate in a statute the charter guarantee of religious liberty but nevertheless found adequate protection for themselves under the law. Ultimately, they adjusted their ecclesiastical polities to conditions in Rhode Island and the challenges the colony posed to ministerial authority. In these respects they were like the ephemeral French community before them, but they came to stay.

Congregationalism dramatized most of these developments in its first foray into Rhode Island. The mission began in May 1695, when John Danforth, the first of "neare a score of ministers, coming one after another, one weake after another," journeyed to Newport to preach the gospel. They were sent by an informal association of Standing Order clergymen based in Boston. Danforth tried to attach himself to the colonial government by obtaining the use of the Colony House and preaching to newly elected colonial officials.[1] Local opposition to this conduct resulted in a vote by the General Assembly to forbid use of the Colony House for any but secular purposes. Still, the missionaries managed to gather a flock of local people inclined to the Congregational way under a young Harvard graduate named Nathaniel Clap. It barely struggled along for many years.[2]

One trouble was Clap's interpretation of traditional doctrines. In Newport, an ecclesiastical polity originating from outside was just as subject to dispute as one created on the spot based on the Bible. Clap clung to old Massachusetts standards that required the formation of a church of the putative elect followed by ordination of a pastor before he could administer the sacraments to anyone. And he was reluctant to credit anybody's putative election. Visiting evangelists baptized some people and unavailingly tried to persuade him to follow their example and defer only Communion to the formation of a church.[3]

Finally, in 1720, he accepted the likelihood of election of thirteen men, accepted atheir written confession of faith, and joined them in subscribing to a church covenant. The covenant set down the terms of church fellowship: members must own the true God and lead a Christian life; the pastor would administer baptism to those or the children of those who professed the faith and led a blameless life, were willing to submit to church discipline, and would try to attain worthiness to take Communion. With these constitutional foundations laid, the church formed and proceeded to an ordination of Mr. Clap in the Massachusetts fashion.[4]

Still, Clap had doubts about the result, which led to a series of difficulties and finally a schism. He continued to question the fitness of church members for the Eucharist and stopped giving Communion for long periods of time. He was prevailed upon to accept assistants who were less exacting. When one, John Adams, served the disgruntled members who wanted Adams ordained as a co-pastor, the discontent came to a boil.[5] At the members' request, a conference of lay and clerical delegates from nearby churches was convened, a well-established practice in Massachusetts, which found Clap guilty of irregular proceedings, including his refusal to assent to Adams's ordination. The council recommended a division of the congregation. As the flock somehow had acquired a meetinghouse, ceremonial vessels, and a school, the council suggested that both congregations share them.[6]

The second church formed by nearly the same procedures as the first and soon chose a deacon and added bylaws to prevent repetition of some of Clap's behavior. Laying down rules, however, failed to prevent friction between Adams and his flock. He tried to assert ministerial rank, always a risky move in Rhode Island, failed, and resigned. The church devised even more confining bylaws for his successor. Soon, the two churches resolved their quarrels over the property and school.[7]

When the Second Church decided to build a new meetinghouse in 1733, it brought into the open two developments in the adjustment of Congregationalism to conditions in Rhode Island, the mode of transacting business for the temporalities and the relations to civil government. The religious body had imitated the characteristic forms of its Massachusetts antecedents. The church proper consisted of the men and women who accepted the likelihood of each other's election. They all might receive Communion, but only the men had an active voice in church deliberations. They decided, probably under pastoral guidance, on admission of new members and disciplinary measures. Around this core was the congregation, composed of all adherents, and somewhat informally the children of both church and congregation, for whom the school existed. These arrangements served the spiritual needs of the fellowship and were instrumnetal in bringing in the upcoming generation.

So far, apart from establishing a school, the Congregationalists followed the same pattern as the earlier Baptist flocks and for the same reason: their desire for restricted full membership. But the Congregationalists went further, forming a distinct institution, called the society, composed of the men of both church and congregation. For temporal affairs and even the calling of a minister, the men of the church needed the concurrence of the men of the congregation. The latter had to be given a voice because they supplied most of the money for the pastor's salary and other routine expenses as well as purchases of property and buildings.[8]

The society appointed a committee to have the new meetinghouse erected. It bought land and secured recognition by inserting into the deed clauses alluding to the organization that acquired the property. The committee assumed ownership as trustees rather in the way that Quakers did. When any member of the committee died, his successor would be "chosen by the Majority of the

Male Members both of the Church and Congregation conjunctively met at a Meeting for such a Choice."[9] Thus, a private agreement that required use of a distinctive organization took a form that could be enforced by the courts, giving an ecclesiastical polity derived from Massachusetts some claim to governmental protection where law upheld religious liberty.

Congregationalism struck roots elsewhere in Rhode Island less rapidly or successfully than in Newport, but the type of ecclesiastical organization usually was the same and reliance on Massachusetts precedent and support was generally greater. Block Island tried feebly to reintroduce the ways of the founders. It hired a local son who had graduated from Harvard to be the town minister and later obtained Joseph Mayhew, paid by the Society for Promoting the Gospel in New England, but both left after a year or so for more attractive situations. Missionaries from Massachusetts labored in Providence before 1700 but promoted no church there until a local zealot raised money and bought land for a meetinghouse in 1721, to be owned by trustees in Massachusetts and Connecticut. Even then, seven years passed before Boston funds helped secure a minister, Josiah Cotton. Congregationalists in Kingstown had a large endowment donated by the Pettaquamscut proprietors but attracted a minister only briefly. Moreover, the donations of land had been phrased so as to allow conflicting claims; the grantors naively gave the site of the meetinghouse "for the Use of the Inhabitance of . . . Kingstown." The town plausibly claimed the building, and the Anglicans wanted the whole property. In Westerly, a man named Joseph Park, sent by the society based in Boston, ministered to some Narragansetts and White people beginning in 1733.[10]

Altogether, Congregationalist forays into Rhode Island enjoyed fair success. To be sure, only Newport could survive without financial support from Boston. The new denomination institutionalized ways to rear children in the faith and until 1740 insisted on a learned ministry. The churches had to forgo governmental backing but contrived to get a token of statutory recognition by a law allowing their clergymen to solemnize marriages.[11] And more important, they obtained a roundabout legal support by ingenious use of land conveyances and testamentary bequests, which they knew would be upheld in the courts even though a church or religious society had no standing in law. With less success, the ministers struggled to reconcile their convictions about pastoral duties and authority with the realities of a population in which religious affiliation was strictly voluntary.

Church of England

Anglican missionary work began in 1694 with the arrival of John Lockyer, who founded Trinity Church in Newport. Later, Anglicans set up churches in

Providence and Kingstown and held occasional services in several other places. The beginnings in Newport were inspired by appeals from local Tories. For many years the project continued to have loud political overtones, though they soon ceased to be associated with the campaign to replace the charter with a royal government.[12] Anglicanism in Rhode Island was a part of imperial efforts to extend English influence in America. On the simplest level, the Church of England spoke for imperial loyalty and in theory placed its adherents in a hierarchy of authority under the throne. Church of England ministers made gestures of respect to colonial officials, especially the governors, and attracted the small but growing number of Crown appointees and men of means whose ambitions pointed to imperial connections as a way to get ahead.

To a great extent, the Church of England came with its practices prescribed, whether in ecclesiastical polity or liturgy. There was no question of doing without a learned clergy or deviating from the *Book of Common Prayer*. Yet the episcopal hierarchy did not extend clearly to America, so there was no canonical confirmation, and parish ministers enjoyed a new discretion over admitting people to the Communion table. Furthermore, the church brought none of the baggage of tradition in the operation of parish government, no rights of advowson outside the parish officials, no independent endowment, no legal position secured by English common law. The church had no courts in the colony and no prospect of getting them, let alone the functions of the ordinary exercised by ecclesiastical courts in England. Thus, at least in some respects, Rhode Island Anglicans had to adapt traditional modes of organization to new conditions.

As with the Congregationalists, most of the important aspects of the Anglican arrival appeared in Newport. The Narragansett church, however, waged a revealing struggle to obtain the land intended to endow Congregationalism there and explained the adjustment of the vestry to Rhode Island circumstances. Like the Congregationalists, the Anglicans depended on subsidies from outside—in their case, England. They benefited from various kinds of generosity—donations, a Communion service from Queen Anne, and so forth—but relied primarily on the Society for the Propagation of the Gospel in Foreign Parts (the S.P.G.). Technically outside the episcopal hierarchy, this royally chartered corporation depended on voluntary contributions and began with a zeal to foster the Church of England in the outer reaches of the empire by enticement and persuasion rather than legal coercion. It was an aggressive organization and was active in both Massachusetts and Connecticut, where it raised the hackles of the establishment in both colonies. The S.P.G. had the backing of the hierarchy—the Archbishop of Canterbury was president ex officio—and came to be an organization that could foster demands for legal privileges for Anglicans in the colonies and the appointment of an American bishop. The Rhode Island

ministers, who depended on the society for all or part of their salaries, duti-
fully clamored for a bishop. They also tried to achieve financial security by
claiming legal benefits on the local scene. Moreover, Rhode Island
churches, for all their possession of the right of advowson and lack of episcopal supervision, needed the S.P.G. to supply them with clergymen. In practice, they took what they could get.

From the beginning, Rhode Island Anglicans adapted traditional organization to nontraditional circumstances. Under colonial law, Newport Anglicans might organize a voluntary association as they saw fit. They created an
abstract form of the basic plan of an English parish by securing two church
wardens and a number of other vestrymen to join the minister. These laymen
were replaced by cooptation until the congregation began to elect them in
1742. The wardens served as executive assistants to the minister.[13]

The church worked out this plan under its second clergyman, James
Honyman. He agreed in 1709 "that Nothing Relating to this Church shall be
transacted . . . but by the Joynt Consent of the Minister Churchwardens and
Vestry." The vestry became a panel to declare policy and make decisions for
the wardens to carry out. Once the vestry was elected, it became in form
what it had been said to be in substance all along, a body "representing the
congregation."[14]

A similar but clearer development took place in St. Paul's, the Narragansett church, founded at least by 1718, when the first known church officers
were elected by the congregation. To satisfy the Anglican desire for a connection to government, a member of the Governor's Council swore the two
wardens and four of the seven vestrymen into office. Thereafter for several
years, the vestry became cooptative. Then under a plan adopted in 1729, the
minister appointed the first warden and the clerk, while the congregation
elected the other officers. Further, the vestry was declared "the Representative of the whole congregation" so that "theire acts and decrees shall at all
times bind every particular member of the congregation in all matters relating to the peace good order and management of the affairs of the church,
and all nonsubmission to their orders shall be Deemed contumacious," although any parishioner might request a change in a rule.[15] This arrangement
created a suitable distribution of power between ministerial and congregational authority, one quite congenial to Rhode Island and quite antithetical to
usual Anglican practice. To be sure, the minister at the time and for many
years afterward, James MacSparran, exerted greater influence than the plan
seemed to envision.

The Anglican churches had to be made financially sound. Efforts to attain
public support came to nothing, so S.P.G. subsidies generally remained vital.
Voluntary contributions on an irregular basis proved inadequate, so the
churches turned to the sale of pews to finance themselves. In 1719, officers
of Trinity Church devised a plan to do just that. The buyer would hold a pew

with a right of inheritance, provided he remained a member of the congregation, attended services, and paid regular rent. Anyone absent for seven years would lose a claim. No owner might sell a pew without consent of the vestry. St. Paul's adopted similar regulations a few years later. Yet the pews failed to provide sufficient income, and the vestry supplemented them with a subscription list.[16]

In both Newport and the Kingstowns, the Anglicans tried to provide schooling for their children. To do this, they needed annual subsidies from the S.P.G. Though Trinity could support itself otherwise, it steadily asked for help in finding and paying a schoolmaster. Sometimes St. Paul's did likewise.[17]

This blend of dependency and independency, prescribed practices and improvisation, roughly reconciled the Church of England to realities in Rhode Island, yet the Anglicans kept trying to attain standing as an official church. Quite early, the Newport church joined S.P.G. efforts to obtain the appointment of American bishops. Anglicans favored bishops not only to perform their historic functions of settling churches, confirming the young, and ordaining men to holy orders but also because they could "by their presence . . . [influence] the Several Governments into the faithful discharge of that part of their office, the Restraining of vice, and encouraging virtue, awing the multitude into an observance of Religious duties, and Giving a Check to . . . licentious practices."[18] When the Newporters wrote to the S.P.G., they put the case in more pointed fashion: "Since our Church receives no Countenance or encouragement from the Civil Government in this place, it's in vain to expect that it will arrive at its Wished for Happiness without the Superintendancy of a bishop in these parts."[19] Perhaps wisely, they remained vague about what a bishop could do for them. Everywhere in colonial America, the specter of an Anglican bishop provoked fear of arbitrary power, but no other colony could match Rhode Island's historic commitment to religious liberty.

The S.P.G. agitation inspired approximately the opposite of the ends the Anglicans sought: the act of the General Assembly elaborating on the implications of the charter's promise of religious liberty. After a preamble echoing the colonial charter, the legislature asserted that religious liberty had been "an outward means of continuing a good and amicable agreement amongst the inhabitants of this colony." It declared that "for the timely preventing of any and every church, congregation and society of people now inhabiting, or which shall hereafter inhabit within any part of the jurisdiction of this colony, their endeavoring for pre-eminence or superiority of one over the other, by making use of the civil power for the enforcing of a maintenance for their respective ministers," the support for ministers had to be "raised by a free contribution, and no other ways."[20] The Assembly thus wrote the only ecclesiastical law it ever put on the books, standing in direct opposition to Anglicans' wishes.

More serious than calling for bishops, though just as quixotic, was MacSparran's effort to get the endowments to Kingston's Congregationalists donated by the Pettaquamscut purchasers. The possibility had been under consideration at least since 1714. The Congregationalists first stopped the town of Kingstown's efforts to obtain the meetinghouse site and then, quickly aware of Anglican designs on the land, undertook to protect their rights with an intricate web of possessory acts, leases, and litigation, waging a war that went on until 1752. The details of the struggle need not be laid out here. The S.P.G. advised early and futilely that St. Paul's Church buy out the claims for £150, if possible, presumably to allow the implications of the result to ripen as best they might, but the parish went to court.[21]

The contest pitted a claim based on the intent of the donors against an interpretation of the legal meaning of their words. The Pettaquamscut purchasers had given the land for the support of "an orthodox Person" who would preach the Gospel. Most of the donors surely had in mind something like the Massachusetts Standing Order churches. In the first suit, which MacSparran ultimately lost, the Anglicans, using highly suspect testimony, maintained that most of the donors favored the Church of England and then went on to argue that in any case the land should go to Anglicans because MacSparran was the orthodox minister in North Kingstown, as "Lawfully Settled . . . in . . . Narragansett as a Minister of the Gospell for the same as allowed Qualified and approved as the Laws of the Realm provide."[22] English law, he argued, recognized only the Church of England as orthodox. Counsel for the Congregationalists argued not only on the terms of the donation but also from the colonial statute of 1716 and the English Act of Toleration.[23] When MacSparran appealed his case to the privy council, S.P.G. officials decided that his case was hopeless. He won a second suit, however, in the new Kings County Inferior Court and was upheld by a majority of the bench at the Superior Court over strenuous protest by the minority. Once again, however, the privy council ruled for the Congregationalists.[24]

In a third case over a small part of the land, MacSparran won in the colonial court, which allowed no appeal, and he went on to yet a fourth. This time, the Congregationalists won in the Superior Court, only to face a new appeal to the privy council, which allowed MacSparran to begin the suit again. He lost again and appealed again to the king in council.[25] Then he faced surprising opposition. Both sides had enlarged the stakes beyond the scope of Rhode Island issues, to include consideration of the legal rights of dissenters throughout the British Empire. Thus expanded, the case became too controversial for the officials of the Church of England. The archbishop of Canterbury himself opposed MacSparran. After several delays, the privy council ruled against him again in 1752. In the end, the intent of the donors remained decisive, and British officials refused to support an assertion that English law establishing a national church must flow unimpeded into the colonies.[26] Like the other Anglican congregations founded in Rhode Island, the Narragansett church reconciled itself to living under local conditions, while relying on aid from the S.P.G.

Baptists

While the incoming denominations were being naturalized, those already on the scene, especially some Baptists, came to resemble more mainline churches in ways unthinkable a few decades earlier. The urban Baptists converged in many respects with the Congregationalists. They began to make explicit ecclesiastical rules, build meetinghouses, keep records, and seek a relation to law. Some revived the doctrine of predestination, which connected them to the Puritan heritage. Out of these developments came the doctrinal controversies of the early eighteenth century, which focused primarily on ministerial authority. In rural areas, much of the new remained alien.

The most obvious harbinger of change was the building of meetinghouses, perhaps only as a convenience for growing flocks but representing a new commitment to time and land ownership nevertheless. Baptists had previously disdained them on scriptural precedent and changed their minds without recording their reasons. The Providence congregation built a meetinghouse just after 1700. The three Newport churches and even some rural flocks erected their own about the same time.[27]

With the movement toward meetinghouses, the Baptist flocks had to own land and secure it for their uses. The rural churches used the most casual means, such as outdoor locations and private homes, without suffering any consequences.[28] Urban Baptists, however, slowly explored more elaborate forms. The Six Principle Church in Newport led the way, introducing a trust agreement that went beyond the Congregationalist version in weaving religious principles into a legal framework. The trustees proclaimed their right to determine use of the land "to future generations forever" and declared that their successors would be persons "in the same faith and Practice" with themselves. They then spelled out certain essentials, including devotion to "[l]aying on of hands," that referred to a digest approved by seventy-three Baptists and printed in England in 1691. These clauses were emphatic but contained no procedure for succession to trusteeship and left ambiguous whether the trustees were to be church members (they probably were) or merely contributors to the meetinghouse maintainance.[29] The Seventh Day Baptists and the First Church used similar arrangements.[30]

While Baptists were building meetinghouses and devising legally enforceable trust agreements to safeguard ownership, at least the First Church in Newport resorted more directly to governmental power, when the church tried to gain its expected benefits from Dr. John Clarke's estate and required a new colonial law. Executors named in Clarke's will abused the trust placed in them and defrauded several beneficiaries, including the first church. The Baptists hired a lawyer, who helped them bring the scandalous executors to account. The lawyer and First Church also lobbied for help from both the town meeting of Newport and the General Assembly and used governmental power to redress their grievances in ways that would have horrified Roger Williams and earlier generations of Baptists.

Along with meetinghouses and forging of ties to the legal system, the Newport and Providence Baptists returned to a professional learned, even salaried, ministry and the enhanced authority that education implied. The First Church of Newport took the plunge in 1725 by choosing John Comer as an assistant pastor. He attended Yale but had not graduated. Still, he passed in Baptist circles as an educated man.[31] After brief service, he joined the Six Principle Church and then left the colony altogether. At the First Church he was replaced with Harvard graduate John Callender; at the Second Church, by Nicholas Eyres, a learned man if not college-bred. In Providence, a project to ordain Yale graduate John Walton was defeated after an acrimonious dispute. The Sabbatarians had no college men under ordination, but two of their elders had education beyond the basics.[32]

These pastors and others brought to the fore questions of ministerial authority and dectrine and the formalities of ecclesiastical government. The Newport Six Principle Church had rehearsed the controversy over ministerial authority a few years earlier. Comer found himself at odds with two churches over his belief in predestination, which one preferred to ignore and the other simply rejected. Walton, by contrast, aroused opposition partly by opening a catalog of doctrinal points on which Baptists differed and urging mutual forbearance.[33]

Surprisingly uncontroversial was the performance of marriage ceremonies by elders. Like the old Puritans, Baptists had long and vehemently insisted that marriage was only a civil contract. In the early eighteenth century, they relented silently, without admitting any sacramental quality in the ceremony.[34] For the Baptists, who could not adopt infant baptism, the prime symbol of the linkage of generations in the church, the admission of weddings into ecclesiastical routine probably was as great a step as they could take toward acknowledging and encouraging such continuity. Perhaps not incidentally, the new function boosted ministerial importance.

Baptists also began to show a concern for keeping church records, in itself a way of setting the church in time. Records served to preserve precise lists of members and also to commemorate and thus to increase the importance of rules and precedents. Baptists also turned toward ecclesiastical counterparts of constitutions and procedural formulas. Elder Daniel Wightman of the Newport Six Principle flock defined a church as "a Companie of Believers,

Combined togather by Covenant for the worship of god" and concluded that they "must have a visible Political union among themselves," which to him implied written records. For Baptists, surely, stress on the letter of church regulations was but a step from the old biblicism, because they saw their regulations as distillations of Scripture. Soon they began to appoint clerks and require written testaments on the character of people who transferred in from other churches.[35]

As they had from the start, the Seventh Day Baptists developed more complex organizations than the rest, and they went beyond biblical precepts. In the early eighteenth century they continued to revise the arrangements to hold the Westerly and Newport members in one church and then in 1708 split into two churches while holding two general meetings a year. The Newport half established a plan of monthly meetings and Communion services. Later, they made provisions for a quorum and doctrinal requirements for membership. They kept accounts, membership lists, and minutes.[36] In keeping with the widening gap between urban and rural ways, the Westerly church kept unsystematic records.

Less than precise in church records but implicit all the same was the crystallization of the structure of religious fellowship among Baptists, like the one found in Congregational flocks. Around the inner core of church members existed a larger congregation, with male members of both generally managing the temporalities.

Also less than clear was the approach to denominational ties with other churches. The Seventh Day Baptists maintained both a sense of unity with other flocks of their stripe and with Baptists in general. They corresponded with congregations at a distance and sent them "Evangelists or messengers in gods service" or "Travelling Ministers" to them who were empowered "to administer the ordanances of the gospell as they shall be occasionally Called."[37] The First Church in Newport had no neighbor of like principles except the one in Swansea; hence, the frequent resort thither for aid in ordination and church business. These people participated in an annual general meeting of Baptist churches, a shadowy institution that had existed since the end of the seventeenth century, but they toyed with a project to form an association of particular (i.e., predestinarian) Baptists in 1734. The Six Principle churches made up the bulk of the Rhode Island flocks and while taking part in the annual meeting also, as occasion arose, held church councils on vexing questions.[38]

Much remains unknowable about early-eighteenth-century Baptists, because of their historic antipathy to record keeping. What stands out from the evidence, however, is the drift to respecting tradition, increased formality in the conduct of churches, the beginnings of denominational organization, and occasional hostile outbursts against these developments. Normally silent or unrecorded, the opposition was strong and could prevail on specific points.

Quakers

Quaker developments between 1696 and 1738 on the whole were parallel to those among the other denominations but with variations. Friends had for years kept up a denominational consciousness that reached over great distances. They had been zealous in keeping records and careful in owning property.[39] They already had a remarkably elaborate ecclesiastical structure and went on to make it more elaborate still and gave it increasingly formal rules. In the eighteenth century they began to use it to bind past to future. They invented a provisional hereditary membership and devised new methods to steer the young into the fellowship. Although they never resorted to an educated or paid clergy and had a modest intellectual life among the flock at large, they revived interest in their own brand of Christian learning and created an institution to keep the ministry faithful to it. Curiously, these trends comported with a near demise of evangelical outreach at a time when the colony's population was burgeoning and Congregationalists and Anglicans were seeking adherents.

The most striking novelty in controlling land occurred when the Rhode Island Monthly Meeting finally had a firm title to Easton's Point. The tract was held by trustees and an advisory committee. Together, the two panels, who were often called the proprietors, decided to subdivide the land. On advice from Philadelphia, the group sold lots on fee farm, something closely resembling quitrent tenure. The proprietors carried out most of the details, but the meeting continued to give them instructions and even appointed an officer to collect the rents and gave him orders on spending the money.[40] The endowment from the subdivision gave the monthly meeting a handsome income, which it used for many purposes, including subsidizing the yearly meeting.

Quakers elaborated their ecclesiastical structure, either to accommodate the changing distribution of members or to institutionalize important functions of the fellowship. Naturally, as Quaker settlement proceeded, two new monthly meetings were necessary on the mainland and were set off from Rhode Island Monthly Meeting.[41] Subdivision of the monthly meeting reduced the weekly meetings. After 1705 they did their important work once a month, in time to send a report on their spiritual and moral condition to the monthly meeting. Later, some preparative meetings were discontinued.[42]

The monthly meetings created a new system to keep watch over the membership. In 1701 they began appointing officers to visit all the families to discover "of their life and conversation whether it be According to truth and the good order of it."[43] The visitors were to admonish the wayward and report obstinate ones to the monthly meeting. The yearly meeting provided a table of "queries," covering the main points of distinctively Quaker behavior, to use as a standard. The visits, which for a while came four times a year, fell to two in 1720. This method too tended to decline, until revived in 1736. All the while, meetings continued to use—even to elaborate—their version of gospel order to impose discipline on the members.[44]

To make the monthly meetings more effective, from aiding the distressed to managing property, Friends divided them finally into men's and women's groups. The women performed their distinctive duties: discipline and charity for their own members, cleaning meetinghouses, providing hospitality for visiting Friends, and vouching for the freedom of their members to marry or travel. They kept their own treasuries but in Newport relied less on donations than on disbursements from the proprietors of Easton's Point. In both men's and women's meetings, unofficially designated "waightey ffriends" had the real responsibility, though all members in good standing were encouraged to attend.[45]

In the conduct of business, the clerk had the most obvious influence, framing the minutes and choosing the committees. The clerk's appraisal of the sense of the meeting, probably conditioned by a reckoning of which members had superior wisdom, was subject to reappraisal at the instigation of dissatisfied participants but carried a presumption of authority that was likely to be decisive. In the early eighteenth century, clerks, like representatives from subordinate meetings, tended to hold office for many years.[46]

Once the Rhode Island Monthly Meeting set off Greenwich, the largely hypothetical Rhode Island Quarterly Meeting gradually became a genuinely separate assembly, divided into men's and women's parts. In each case, the core was composed of persons designated by the constituent monthly meetings to speak for them, and the quarterly meetings in turn chose persons to attend the men's and women's yearly meetings. In time, the quarterly meetings began to compose epistles of advice to the monthly meetings to call their attention to spiritual needs or dangerous tendencies in behavior. The quarterly meetings also became a first appellate tribunal in disciplinary cases.

The yearly meetings, which convened in Newport every June, capped the twin pyramids of meetings for general ecclesiastical business. The men's meeting decreed a representational system for ecclesiastical business in 1692 but changed it seven years later to one more in keeping with Quaker practice: encouraging all members of experience and proven devotion to attend but placing responsibility on representatives from the constituent meetings. Actually, the lower meetings observed more or less than the letter of these plans.[47]

Somewhat loose at first, the hierarchical scheme of meetings tightened with time. Eventually, the yearly meetings spoke for the whole organization, on both internal and external subjects.[48] The men's meeting asserted exclusive control over publication of manuscripts by members. And of course, though lower meetings might lay down rules for their members on fairly narrow points, the yearly meetings alone promulgated the queries.[49]

To the two pyramids of meetings for general church business, Friends added a third to supervise the ministry. Sometimes called select meetings, these were attended by ministers, later by elders as well. At first this pyramid had only the top layers. The quarterly meeting began in 1701; the yearly, in 1707. These meetings were operated mainly by men, though women ministers existed. In 1708 they began to appoint overseers or elders (at first men only) for each meeting; they reported to the Quarterly Meeting for Ministers. The elders watched over ministers, guiding the young ones and keeping them all from heterodoxy.[50]

The founding of select meetings accompanied a decline in efforts to reach outsiders and a rise in attention to Friends' children and lukewarm or ignorant Quakers. Beginning in the early eighteenth century, most of the yearly meetings for worship in New England were dropped. Instead, a few occasions were created for small groups of Friends, such as those in Warwick, and for the young in places where Quakers were numerous.[51] This shift accompanied a new zeal to preserve the faithful and clarify membership. As before, the meetings expected parents to rear their young in the faith, and the visitors encouraged this process. Meetings for discipline stressed the importance of marriage within the fold. The yearly meeting in 1707 gave the first reasonably clear definition of a member, someone under the care of a monthly meeting, and created a place for children of members. Soon a stronger note of hereditary status appeared to underline the responsibility of parents to prepare their children to succeed them.[52]

Friends recognized the importance of sectarian schools. Quaker schoolmasters would prevent the young from being taught "the Corrupt ways ma[nn]urs fashons and Language of the world."[53] Further, Friends' children would be kept from the "hurtful Conversation of Other Youth."[54] Yet purely Quaker schools were impossibly expensive in most places. The Greenwich Monthly Meeting could do no better than order copies of George Fox's primer and hope that parents would resort to an approved schoolmaster. Only on Aquidneck were Quaker schools practical. Portsmouth Friends eagerly made arrangements with a proper master. Newport Friends accomplished more. They actively sought masters, sometimes with disappointing results, but by the 1730s managed to maintain a schoolhouse with two or three classes in it.[55]

Although Quakers, like Baptists, became gradually more traditional, they did so without resort to a learned clergy and the questions of authority that it raised. Yet both a revival of learning and an assertion of authority took place. The select meetings stressed fidelity to the message of the Quaker past and created a spiritual elite partly independent of the meetings for discipline. The men's yearly meeting fostered knowledge of Quaker doctrine by distributing or publishing works it regarded as timely. The titles included everything from Fox's writings to recent imports from Britain. The outstanding project, however, was the edition of Robert Barclay's *An Apology for the True Christian Divinity*, the standard Quaker theological work, undertaken in 1727. Rhode Island meetings spoke for three-quarters of the copies to be printed.[56] Inclined to keep contact with the past, these Friends showed little sign of innovative thinking, though they engaged in important discussions of slavery and the possibility of universal salvation.[57]

Even if the assertion of authority in the ecclesiastical structure often was incremental and intangible, conservative and practical, the church never resorted to full-scale pastors. The functions of the traditional clergy were distributed. Yet as the ecclesiastical structure grew more intricate, the roster of officers lengthened, so functions separated steadily from collective action. Clerks, ministers, elders, visitors, ad hoc committees on disciplinary cases and many other assignments, treasurers, trustees, even a schoolmaster in Newport added up to a far more effective pastoral care than existed in other churches. By being distributed, it created no focus for an opposition. All in all, the direction taken by the Quakers in the early eighteenth century was comparable to the paths of other denominations, although with a few deviations. If the order within the Quaker fold no longer offered a haven from a disorganized world, the fold became a rather self-absorbed part of an increasingly orderly colony. Its members included men of wealth and high office, but the group had no propensity to infuse their beliefs into society at large.

Conclusion

Religious developments in the first part of the eighteenth century had two conspicuous features and several less visible but equally important ones. Obviously, two new denominations came to stay, Anglican and Congregationalist, bringing traits similar to those of the French in the 1680s but becoming permanent additions to the Rhode Island scene. Also obvious was the growing distance between urban and rural religion, especially for Baptists. In addition to these changes, several others were clear. They included increased links to people and institutions outside the colony, the beginning of church ownership of real estate, introduction of the professional clergy, controversies over its implications, the elaboration of ecclesiastical regulations and procedures, and the adjustment of ecclesiastical institutions to the legal framework provided by Rhode Island. Less tangible were the renewed respect for Christian tradition, the diminishing insistence on utter purity in the fellowship in order to prevent discord from driving away members, and the turn from regarding religion as purely a relationship between the present and eternity toward a greater concern for linking past to future, even to making the church an institution to help rear the young and marry them off within the faith.

The changes brought a reconciliation with time and society and the world of the British Empire. Meetinghouses, schools, rules, professions of faith on paper, and the like were meant to make the religious fellowship part of a larger civil community. And the linkage would pull in both directions. The human setting might bend the church. Custom might harden into immutable rule, even for a Baptist. Pastors eager to attract and keep large flocks would argue for tolerance of differing opinions on what had been essential to many people in the past. Harmony and inclusiveness sometimes became more important than purity.

The churches had to find ways to fit into the colony's legal framework. Congregationalists arrived with thoughts of obtaining official favor, only to be stonily rebuffed by the General Assembly. Later, in Kingstown, they fancied themselves acting rather like a Massachusetts town church, only to have the town try to take over their meetinghouse. The Anglicans wanted official standing and entertained futile hopes of calling in a bishop or getting English law extended into the colony. Instead, they got the statute of 1716 and, along with the Congregationalists, the indifference of the local courts to their notions of what they ought to be. The Baptists learned early what the Quakers already knew, that the judiciary gave them safety in a narrow scope. Property for ecclesiastical ends would be secure. The limited support of government, accordingly, required astute use of deeds and wills.

Out of these institutional modifications and adjustments to colonial conditions there persistently kept emerging a structure of action and an implicit design of authority rather like those arising in the governmental sphere at the same time. The churches tended to run through oligarchies—the weighty Friends and select meetings of the Quakers, the minister and vestry of the Anglicans, the male members of the flock, led by the foremost contributors and the pastor among the Baptists and Congregationalists. Yet they all needed the passive support of the others. Authority could not be wielded from above where adherence was voluntary, where solidarity of the flock might be a matter of habit, not legal coercion.

❧ 10 ❧

The Framework of Government
after 1738

The years from 1738 to the Revolution brought changes in Rhode Island's institutional configuration that were less conspicuous than those in the colony's first century but just as important. By then, dramatic events took place more outside than inside the governmental framework, which was less reshaped than augmented in the late colonial period. The changes that did take place, however, seriously modified the General Assembly's role. While it remained supreme within the colony, it relied more and more on other organs.

Both colonial and town governments reduced the overlapping functions of officials and created new subsidiaries. On the edges of what was indubitably in the governmental purview, the colony and the towns established organizations that began in new ways to serve some of the functions of intermediary institutions. In this category fell associations to own and use schoolhouses, fire engines, or wharves, as well as an array of chartered corporations to operate a benevolent society, library, college, church, or waterworks. The governmental framework as designed in the early eighteenth century clearly contrasted coercive authority with private associations but set the latter so adrift as to leave many social needs unserved or at least unregulated.

Particular circumstances prompted innovation. They included the grand events of the times as well as fundamental changes in the colony resulting from the very success of the reorganization just accomplished. International wars and British attempts to modify imperial government produced effects in patterns of institutions, often by putting heavy demands on the fiscal resources of the colony and forcing it to abandon free use of paper money. As a consequence, the colonial treasury could no longer pay for central government without taxation and could no longer help the towns and subsidize the old developmental projects. Because taxes were almost as firmly resisted as before, colonial and town governments had to devise cheap measures that would meet the inescapable responsibilities of government. Abruptly, the colonial treasury stopped being a fountain of paper pounds that could pay for public business without pain to the inhabitants.

This shift occurred almost at the same time as the development of Newport's trade, which early inspired emulation and had put Providence on the track to equal competition with the capital and encouraged hopes of doing the same elsewhere. The policies of the Cranston years could no longer promise a coherent program for government, just when fiscal stringency exacerbated political discord and gave leverage to the contestants. Moreover, increasing density of population and acquisition of new territory in 1747 diluted the political power of Newport and its old partners in the other island towns and the Narragansett country. Growing poverty and the Great Awakening had their effects, too.

Under the surface, a profound political change occurred. Previously, Newport leaders argued among themselves over means to attain goals on which they all agreed. Because of the distribution of power determined by the charter, they enlisted support elsewhere by promising something to everybody. Gradually, the reliance on this support grew; outsiders made the best of the quarrels in Newport. The old concepts of what was good for Rhode Island no longer sufficed. The concentration of political power that had brought order to the governmental structure in the Cranston years broke down, and the ensuing diffusion brought ramifications in the pattern of institutions that sketched a new plan. So many aspirants clamored in the political arena that no preponderant voice was possible, no steady course could be held. To take advanatage of this situation and incidentally to eliminate the possibility of chaos, the political leaders formed something close to parties.

The General Assembly

In many outward respects, the presiding organ of the colonial government, the General Assembly, continued unchanged through the storms of the late colonial period. It struggled with the procedures for election of members but found ways to enforce rather than modify the existing plan.[1] Even the division of old towns and annexation of new ones, which necessarily changed the distribution of seats in the lower house and inspired a reapportionment of the upper, served to maintain the proportion of voters to representatives.[2]

As before, the Assembly ordinarily used ad hoc joint committees rather than standing committees of the usual sort. Two entities that in form were standing committees—the Grand Committee to manage the colony's land

banks, and the Committee of War—were actually more in the nature of executive departments. The Assembly experimented with a few standing committees on routine business—to review petitions or hear pleas for subsidies
for bridges—but soon abandoned them. Briefly, it created a committee to
operate ferries on the west side of Jamestown and later a committee of correspondence.[3] Sometimes, the House of Deputies could not even form its own
committee for what was indubitably its responsibility to initiate a money bill
but had to bow to the demand of the other house for a joint committee.[4]
Nevertheless, because the deputies initiated nearly all action when the
houses met separately, in effect they set the agenda for the upper house as
well.

The work of the General Assembly changed, however, in important ways
because the nature of public business changed. The Assembly relied more
than before on four administrative arms. It divested the upper house of most
of its judicial character by appointing a distinct bench for the Superior Court.
And it responded to the loss of Newport's hegemony with a political system
that mediated between a swirl of interests and official decisions.

Administrative Arms of the Colonial Government

Three of the administrative arms had been on the scene for years and underwent changes that were prompted by external events. They were the Grand
Committee and the offices of the General Treasurer and Attorney General.
Like the fourth, the Committee of War, they grew in importance because of
wars and other demands resulting from the imperial connection. Because
they all were deeply concerned in fiscal matters, their concerns often intertwined. They too had to adjust to Newport's decline.

The Grand Committee to supervise the land banks had begun as a group
of Newport merchants with town committees as its local agents. Even when
its work consisted mainly of floating loans, it had realized the usefulness of
centralizing its business by selecting one member, at first called the secretary, to provide its office and manage its papers.

Then in 1739 and 1740, four changes, two emanating from inside the colony and two from outside, forced a new set of conditions on the Grand Committee. The payments of interest and principal on the first paper money
loans were falling behind, probably even more than the officials realized. The
mounting burden of repayment very likely contributed in 1740 to the political victory of those who opposed lavish issues of paper pounds. Yet the beginning of the War of Jenkins' Ear in 1739 meant new expenditures while imperial officials, under pressure from West Indian interests, began a campaign
(at first only half sincere) against colonial paper currency. In the resulting
circumstances, the Rhode Island government had to do several things at

once. It had to issue more paper by loans and fiat, repair the system for retiring the old money, defend itself and its freedom to resort to the press, placate voters, and mollify politicians who had attained office by opposing paper money.

Circumstances changed little after the first round of war. Another followed, and imperial policy firmly opposed most issues of colonial paper. In colonial politics, the arguments shifted away from simple support of or opposition to paper money and instead clashed over increasingly subtle alternatives. Public resistance to retiring the bills continued. The administration by colonial officials remained slipshod or worse.

The whole fiscal story need not be told here, but a capsule summary will be helpful. Rhode Island floated three more land banks, then ceased in obedience to a parliamentary law aimed at New England. Ultimately, the colony officially adopted the specie-based standard originated in Massachusetts, called Lawful Money of New England, which was approximately a return to the seventeenth-century standard of four pounds equalling three pounds sterling, with the difference pegged to silver. In practice, the new standard deviated somewhat from its legal value, and the colonial treasury as well as private parties often went on using old tenor, so the conversion was not abrupt.[5]

The Grand Committee continued to supervise loans but increasingly aimed at retiring them. The need for increased care began to appear in the 1730s, as the first in a long procession of audit committees appointed by the Assembly uncovered the confusion in the accounts of the secretary, Jahleel Brenton, and the extent of dereliction by the town committees and by the residents in paying interest and principal.

These discoveries inspired various reform measures, which gradually ended in revising the Grand Committee's operations. The Assembly endorsed its plan to have one member assume primary responsibility for its activity and gave the old secretary the title of Keeper of the Grand Committee's Office. It also gave him firm instructions and insisted that he post bond.[6] The burden of the committee's work shifted from arranging loans to compelling repayment. In this effort the old town committees were considered useless, so they were abandoned after the last bank had been floated. Instead, the Assembly added non-Newport men to the Grand Committee and withdrew much of its original autonomy.[7]

The Grand Committee as a whole had rather vague duties, and the Keeper carried on its increasingly narrowly focused business. He managed the small office and presumably hired a few clerks to process paper and keep the records straight. Thus began the first clearly bureaucratic element in the Rhode Island system. For years, the efforts of Keeper and clerks were insufficient, whether due to their carelessness, the sheer impossibility of keeping track of sales of mortgaged land, the disappearance of mortgagers, the committee's favoritism toward some delinquent borrowers, or the need to release documents from the office for various purposes, such as litigation. Failures in this system gave rise to a curious distribution of responsibilities in a pattern that was repeated in several other cases.

Instead of having the committee take legal action to get loans repaid, the Assembly required the committee to transmit the papers on delinquent loans to the Attorney General (or for a time the county attorneys) to be put in suit for immediate payment.[8] For several years, the attories won some judgments but could neither account for the money nor keep the papers in order.[9] Rumors of these shortcomings led to investigations by audit committees appointed by the Assembly.

They found not only the muddled affairs of the attornies but also those of the Grand Committee's office. As a result, the Assembly created a succession of committees to take over much of what originally had been the Grand Committee's work—to inspect the records, review the conduct of the Keeper, receive and burn paper money due for retirement, and keep the Assembly informed. Necessarily, these committees had to keep tabs on the attornies, too. When the Assembly eventually found effective keepers in Benjamin Nichols and Edward Thurston, the functions of the ad hoc committees and the attornies settled into routine. The serious campaign to finish retirement of the loans, begun in 1763 when Rhode Island resolved to hasten the transition to Lawful Money of New England, occasioned a new dispersion of the Keeper's tasks. This time, the work did not get loaded onto the Attorney General. Instead, first Thurston and then the Assembly chose his deputies and agents.[10] The usual slipshod work by these subordinates led to a renewed campaign by the Assembly to compel efficiency and to a renewed resort to the Attorney General.[11] Though loose ends remained for years, the Grand Committee had finished most of its business by the time of the Revolution.

The General Treasurer's office underwent a similar transformation, mainly to bring order and vigor to the handling of paper currency but also because the Treasurer's duties kept expanding. Though committees of the Assembly supervised or took over much of his work, his discretion widened somewhat during the war years. He was largely on his own in borrowing for the colony, exchanging forms of currency in the markets, and creating notes and bonds with which to retire expiring paper pounds when specie was unavailable. At times he selected his own agents, sometimes the same men as the Grand Committee's. By statute, the town officials responsible for taxation were his subordinates, though they did not always act that way. He probably had a small staff to assist him.

Regardless of the conspicuous makeshift changes that remained part of the Treasurer's life, his role in Rhode Island's fiscal business acquired a routine seasonal cycle after the harrowing crises early in the French and Indian War. The officials planned the wartime expenditures in the spring, and in the summer the Assembly thrashed out the tax measures and issues of short-term paper money in the form of bills of public credit. The Treasurer borrowed what was necessary, retired bills of credit as they expired, saw to the creation of new ones, pestered the officials responsible for assessing and collecting taxes, and carried on the usual business of receiving, converting, and disbursing funds. Committees of the Assembly assisted or inspected his efforts.[12] Peace only revised the system in several ways, notably by replacing expenditures for war with expenditures to pay war debts and by encouraging resistance to taxes.

Similarly, the Attorney General fell into a routine, in his case determined by the cycle of court sessions and meetings of the Assembly. He was largely responsible for suing people who owed principal and interest on paper currency loans; he advised the Assembly on legal matters, especially the language of statutes; and he prosecuted criminal suspects. He also chose his own.

The fourth important administrative arm of the colonial government, the Committee of War, had great powers during wartime and endured a continual revision of its duties. Like the Grand Committee, it began as a group of Newport merchants and later obtained a geographically scattered membership. Indeed, local members acted as independent agencies. This committee was intended to be an improvement over the earlier makeshift efforts. In Queen Anne's War, the Assembly had left most matters to Governor Cranston, with various ad hoc committees to advise him; most, but not all, were chosen from Newport and vicinity. It assigned other duties to the Commissary-General, who was the General Treasurer wearing a different hat, and used several methods to appoint officers for the expeditionary forces.[13] This improvisatory style was resuscitated at the resumption of war in 1739. Then the Assembly entrusted several tasks to a couple of existing institutions, such as the Governor and Council, but most to a spate of committees composed mainly of its own members and nearly always composed of Newport merchants. Because committee membership overlapped extensively, the work of the several groups could be coordinated informally.[14]

The political changes that began in 1745, just after the war had revived with the entry of France, inspired change in military administration. Political turbulence made it wise to give most responsibilities to a single, long-standing committee. The result was the Committee of War in 1746. Composed entirely of Newport merchants, it had wide authority in procurement and finance as well as power to supervise military preparation and displace or replace officers in the expeditionary force. The Assembly still used ad hoc committees but mainly to bring the business to a close in 1748 and to attest to the colony's claims for royal reimbursement. Alas, rational administration did not lead to success at arms or at the fiscal accounting before the Treasury Board in London—or in the Assembly in Rhode Island.[15]

When the next war began, the colony resorted to the military administration roughly as it had been operating in 1747; it created a new Committee of War and for a time added to its powers, beginning with those formerly falling on the Commissary. The revived Committee of War was to see to procurement of ammunition and supplies, transportation of troops, and payment of enlistment bounties with funds it could draw from the treasury. During the recesses of the Assembly, it could also appoint recruiting officers. Central direction soon began to break down. Political realities—both partisan conflicts and local jealousies—required that the committee be expanded from a coterie of Newport merchants to include mainland men—first from Providence, then from elsewhere.[16]

From 1755 to 1757, as the war expanded, the Assembly built the Committee of War into something verging on collective dictatorship. By May 1755 it could buy and deploy all of the colony's military supplies, draw funds from the treasury, raise money by mercantile dealings "upon the Colony's Account," and between sessions of the Assembly do all that the Assembly could do if it were sitting. It could stop commerce out of Newport and search for deserters. It obtained authority to raise men by any means it could devise, including imposing quotas to be impressed from the militia companies; to commandeer supplies for the men; to appoint officers; and to act with or independently of the General Treasurer on the colony's behalf.[17]

A political reaction set in. Though the colony increased its contributions to the war, the Assembly took back parts of the administration and decentralized the rest. It prescribed a series of methods to extract manpower from the militia companies. It limited the committee's powers to raise money and draw funds from the treasury, and it ended the committee's powers to select officers and organize recruitment.[18] It broadened the committee's composition to include members from all the counties and treated them in audits as separate entities; they were made subject to annual reappointment.[19]

Interpreting the record in military administration poses a few difficult problems. The change from ad hoc committees, vaguely coordinated by overlapping membership, to a Committee of War has the air of progression from improvisation to system. But did the result improve? Probably it did, but the evidence is far from revealing. Likewise with the ascent and decline of the Committee of War. The highly centralized powers in the early years of the French and Indian Wars may have had an effect, but if so it was submerged in the failure of the imperial force that the Rhode Island men joined. What seems most clear when the Committee of War had its wings clipped and its membership scattered was the search for methods to enlist the energies of many inhabitants. The experimentation with methods of recruiting and drafting troops also suggests an effort to disperse responsibilities as well as to restore the power of the Assembly over officers. Conceivably, patronage power figured in the revisions of plans, but again this is a consideration beyond measurement.[20]

Another possibility to consider is that centralization was only a response to an emergency, that subdivision of responsibility was always preferable for political or instrumental reasons. Surely, the centralization suggests bureaucratic rationalization, and the retreat from it looks like inelegant experimentation amid shifting political winds. At the beginning of the Revolution, Rhode Island returned to the methods of 1755. Whatever the case, the retreat from what looked like orderly administration may also be seen as a move to restore the General Assembly's supervision of military affairs in keeping with the terms of the charter.

The Judiciary

As the General Assembly changed its role in administration, it shed part of its judicial functions and decentralized the courts more than before. In sheer numbers, the judiciary grew—more justices of the peace, more towns and so more town councils, more counties and so more county courts, and even more colonial courts when the Assembly experimented for a few years with a Court of Equity. The Assembly extended the list of officials who were purely judicial both by appointing more justices and by making the bench of the Superior Court different from the Governor and Council. To be sure, these judicial offices were often filled by men elected to positions in town councils and the Assembly. The division of government into functional components was more legal form than political substance. Still, the formal change clarified the kinds of authority to be exercised on different occasions.

Nonetheless, the Assembly continued to intervene in judicial matters. It routinely heard appeals of cases on personal (as contrasted to real) actions and conducted hearings on petitions. It even intruded into probate jurisdiction, a field where the legal course of appeal lay to the Governor and Council as "the Supream Ordinary," and it heard appeals from town decisions to remove prospective paupers, although by law an appeal in this case lay to the local inferior court.[21]

The Assembly made the greatest change in the judiciary when it redesigned the Superior Court. For years, non-Newport men had demanded sessions of this court (or its predecessor, the General Court of Trials) outside the capital. They clamored louder in 1734 and proposed to separate the bench from the Governor and Council, but they were not successful until 1747, when Rhode Island's acquisition of territory from Massachusetts required an amendment of the laws on courts. At that time, the Assembly adopted both proposals. It agreed to five justices for the Superior Court annually, who would hold sessions twice a year in each county. Statutes defined their powers and included in the list authority to grant divorces and award alimony to ex-wives.[22]

Subdividing the Superior Court into county branches surely gave a population of around thirty-two thousand access to adjudication. Yet the legislators continually devised circumstances whereby the populace might obtain a special session of a county inferior or superior court. It all began in 1719, when vendue masters were allowed special sessions of the General Court of Trials to sue their debtors. Likewise, the previous owners of the goods obtained special sessions to sue vendue masters who refused to pay them. Once the precedent was established, the demands for special sessions expanded until, eventually, any freeholder might demand a special court.[23]

As before, two parts of the judiciary lay beyond the colony's power to regulate. The Assembly could not limit appeals to the privy council, except to make a few technical rules and determine the amount of damages warranting an appeal.[24]

The Assembly could do a little more about the vice-admiralty court, even though for many years it was based in Boston. By the middle of the eighteenth century, increasing burdens on the court led to the appointment of ostensibly temporary officers residing in Rhode Island. In this case, temporary merely meant that they lacked regular commissions. Recommended by the colonial government, these officers were Rhode Island men who remained in their positions for years. By 1758 the colony had secured a permanent judge, whose jurisdiction was separate from Boston. One way or another, the court became geared to Rhode Island interests. The Assembly also regulated its fees and provided a procedure to challenge its jurisdiction.[25]

Altogether, the development of the judiciary by the end of the colonial period approached a system. The colony created a distinct judicial hierarchy and extended its influence over functions it could not control completely. Yet persistence of the Assembly's elastic functions requires some comment. Explanations have stressed a lack of legal knowledge or scruples, offering some extreme examples as proof of ignorant or intentional highhandedness by the Rhode Island government.[26] As a rule, however, the legislators unsnarled procedural tangles in the judicial process or insisted on substantive justice when the courts clung to legal forms that seemed to produce injustice. So the Assembly, even when adding tribunals or specifying rational relations between them, deliberately kept its character as an omnicompetent governing board of the colony-corporation.

Town Government

For all the variety among the towns, their conduct of government had obvious parallels to that of the colonial government: increasing concern for orderly procedure, specialization of function, emphasis on administrative action and the separation of executive from judicial concerns, creation of subsidiary arms of public authority, and respect for a system of law. And towns more than ever acted as local units linked to a colonial system. The experienced eye can date a town or colonial decision with fair accuracy by its position on a steadily increasing scale of precision in wording, intricacy of procedure, and even the length. In formal respects, the towns were alike.

Developments that had begun before 1738 continued. Town meetings took on ever more standardized behavior, often retaining only a shell of their former control over community affairs but assuming authority over prominent public questions. Town councils continued to gain in importance, though less as courts than as administrative boards. Both, in rather inconsistent ways, continued to seek legitimacy in statutes from the General Assembly or analogy to English local practices. Towns elaborated their rosters of officials according to local circumstances and created subordinate institutions to operate such institutions as workhouses and schools. They continued to promote commerce but no longer developed large-scale plans based on allocations of land. Rather, they sought the Assembly's aid for such projects as public buildings, bridges, pavement, or laws against rambling livestock. Towns had changed considerably since they were shaped by the ideals of their settlers.

The changes were dramatized in the organization of new towns. Obviously, they began as creations of the central government rather than as communities designed by their first White male settlers. Rhode Island, too, had its representative Middletown. It had been a part of Newport until 1743, when internal tensions finally led to the separation of as much of the rural section as geography allowed. The goal was to disentangle areas with contrasting economies. Instead of relying on an Indian deed or a covenant among the first heads of households or an initial spate of allocations from common lands, Middletown opened its town books with a statute of the General Assembly that set it off from Newport. This law specified the town's boundary, promised it the same status as other towns, and directed the freemen to observe Rhode Island law.[27]

Middletown complied. Its officers both respected the essentials of colonial law—all towns had to elect certain essential officials—and reflected the nature of Middletown by such flexible elements as the number of fence viewers and the assortment of economic functionaries such as viewers of flax and hemp. The list changed in accordance with local need or colonial law. Almost every official existed under the regulation of colonial statute. The chief exception was the school committee, to which Middletown gave uncommon importance, though Rhode Island law said nothing about it. Most of the town meeting's business in its early years focused on the implementation of colonial statutes, maintaining a pound, keeping records, gearing town meetings to colonial elections, granting liquor licenses, arranging a share of interest money from the paper money loans, requiring inhabitants to maintain fences, restraining livestock, and on and on. When it began to tax its inhabitants, the town used procedures required by colonial law.[28]

Although Middletown affords a fair example of how a newly organized town conducted its affairs in the late colonial period, other towns better exhibited changes from earlier times. A few topics may illustrate the direction of the change. The councils continued to create roads, on the whole in accord with established methods, but they moved toward an administrative and away from a judicial deportment. In theory, a colonial statute of 1741 gave all town councils the authority to use a three-man committee to lay out roads rather than requiring the old jury of twelve or more. Yet difficulties persisted; townsfolk disagreed over routes and whether a town meeting or the old jury should decide between opposing interests. Local aspirations, such as the commercial ambitions of East Greenwich, aroused complex antagonisms as the council sought to extend the web of roads leading to the port. When South Kingstown set out to narrow its roads, it had to make basic policy in town meeting, which appointed a committee to carry it out. Even so, uncertainty over legal procedure led the interested towns to obtain a colonial statute prescribing ways for the councils to sell land from unused former highways.[29]

The councils' authority, as before, reached its zenith in measures to restrain the spread of highly feared diseases, which ironically prompted efforts to take much of the responsibility off the councils' backs by creating pesthouses. The East Greenwich town fathers decreed a ruthless destruction of mad dogs on one occasion. Though most towns continued the old procedures of quarantine under increasingly elaborate statutes, Westerly's council delegated virtually all of its powers to a prominent inhabitant, a practice that became common in outbreaks of smallpox. Still, the councils themselves took the most drastic measures. Newport even stopped the royal post in an effort to contain infection from Boston. South Kingstown seized an abandoned sloop after smallpox victims had been removed, extracting the expenses of quarantine from the owners in exchange for relinquishing forfeiture rights to the vessel and its cargo.[30]

If the councils' burdens lightened in some ways, they grew heavier in more. Workhouses and pesthouses might free the councils from supervision of the poor and dangerously sick, but laws and decisions on convenience more than compensated by adding supervision of surveyors of highways, review of expenditures, drafting laws for the town meeting, enacting laws on subjects specified by statutes, keeping out paupers, and a host of miscellany. Broadly, the administrative role grew. The judiciary, licensing taverns and serving as a probate court, remained vital but did not spread into other business as it once had done.

Town meetings, too, were boiling down to a few salient functions, even though these institutions acted on a profusion of subjects. What in retrospect might seem their weightiest concerns—legislating in several important fields, controlling town fiscal business,supporting education, authorizing taxes—attracted surprisingly small attendance by the freemen. Whatever orders and legislation went on the books, the town meeting was no longer the primary expression of communal cohesiveness.

Colonial elections aroused the hottest sentiments and the most careful attention to procedure at town meeting—both signs of how far the town had turned into a local unit in the colony. Colonial law against fraudulent voting provided a steadily growing set of rules for assessing the qualifications of freemen.

The town government could be dragged back into control of the management of common lands, especially when a threat arose against private titles. In Providence, Westerly, and East Greenwich, litigation emerged that was appealed to the king's privy council. Westerly may serve as an example. The challenge came from Daniel Stanton, a Philadelphia Quaker minister and heir to an original Misquamicut share. He sued for a fifth of an undivided cedar swamp of almost a square mile in extent. Because it had become a common resource for the town, the townsfolk had a strong interest in defending the other successors to the old Misquamicut proprietors. The town meeting instructed the council to appoint a committee to support the defendants—ultimately, only Elias Thompson after others backed out. The council did so doggedly. It supplied documents, sent an agent to assist the barrister when Stanton appealed to the privy council, paid court costs, and agreed to pay for Thompson's attorneys. After years of litigation, the town prevailed.[31]

Westerly's conduct was quite different from the seventeenth-century style, as illustrated by the resistance to William Harris in Warwick. In Westerly, the meeting decided on general goals and left the council to handle the business. The meeting, practically speaking, gave the council a blank check while technically reserving the ultimate decision on footing the bill. Furthermore, when the victory had been won and a few freemen objected to the expense, instead of thrashing the matter out in town meeting, the dissidents presented a petition to the town; failing there, they appealed to the General Assembly, which rejected the plea.[32] The town government had an orderly place in colonial jurisdiction, and the Assembly's decision was final.

Towns' Subsidiaries

If promotion of new commercial centers characterized the first part of the eighteenth century, invention of adjunct institutions characterized the years after 1738. In this, towns resembled the colonial government's resort to administrative agencies or to nongovernmental corporations, which will be considered below. But the parallels cannot be drawn closely. To be sure, towns like the colony used adjuncts to assume responsibilities that previously had been classified as fit if not necessary subjects of government. Also, towns to some extent developed a counterpart of the General Assembly's participation in the work of its administrative arms. They used their subsidiaries more flexibly, however, and often left them on their own after giving them an extensive slate of rules for the operation of a civic property—workhouse, almshouse, pesthouse, schoolhouse, market, or fire engine.

The Newport workhouse affords a good example. The town turned to it when traditional methods of coping with the poor failed to keep costs down. It was operated by a board of five elected town officers, designated first as overseers of the poor and later as managers of the workhouse. The town laid down the basic stipulations. The managers and the person directly in charge of the workhouse—Master or Mistress or later Keeper—should provide food and cleaning for the inmates, guard against fire, and impose a disciplinary code forbidding a catalog of mischief, such as malingering and "lascivious behaviour." And of course, the inmates were to be kept at work on drudgery such as picking oakum. The rules spelled out the keeper's authority but also instructed the managers to examine the conduct of the inmates.[33] The town meeting appointed both keeper and managers, so the line of responsibility was muddled.

The town corrected that anomaly but complicated the arrangements in ways similar to the Assembly's dealings with the Grand Committee. The town had its audit committee watch the expenses, while it gave the managers of the workhouse authority to appoint the Keeper and send people to the workhouse. Thus, the main lines of authority became clear. Apparently pleased by the result of bureaucratizing the institution, the freemen then added to its functions by making it "a house of Correction for people to send their servants to be corrected."[34] This decision in theory introduced a new purpose for the institution, but quite likely the prevailing view of the poor had already been tinctured with punitive attitudes.

Other towns looked hopefully to workhouses to reduce the expense of supporting the poor. Providence and its neighbors planned one in 1753. East Greenwich did so on its own, as did Warwick. The basic approach was like Newport's.[35]

Management of schoolhouses led to subordinate institutions rather like the workhouses. School committees in several towns amounted to more than regular officers of the town meeting. They were responsible for keeping publicly owned schoolhouses in repair, renting them when not in use for educational purposes, keeping teachers, and managing any endowment lands. After some fumbling, Middletown set up two committees, one for each schoolhouse. The record was similar in East Greenwich and Newport.[36] As with workhouses, so with schools: the foremost concerns were with providing the building and a slate of rules for the administrator and inmates—in this case, the master and pupils—covering everything from admission to deportment to the price of diet or tuition.

In Newport and Providence, the towns made subsidiary institutions of markets, though the buildings themselves were usually paid for with voluntary contributions. In fact, Providence twice rejected pleas for a subsidy. It merely provided a site. The town's regulatory function was a pallid version of traditional English practice. In Newport, the town meeting decided on who might erect a market house, named a clerk, and laid down rules for the conduct of business there. The clerk was to keep a set of weights and measures and also to see to sweeping out the market and enforcing the rules.[37] Yet he did not have the traditional clerk's judicial functions beyond his powers to dispose of substandard goods. This made him much more an administrative officer than his medieval counterpart.

Both Providence and Newport developed organizations to prevent fire. Newport's first fire company began in 1726 as a club of prominent residents, who bought their own buckets and engine. The town meeting soon began to weave this little institution into the operations of public authority. The members devised some basic policies but left detailed guidance to the town council. Soon the town bought a new engine, and a wealthy man donated another, prompting the creation of a second fire company. The town meeting appointed directors and members for the fire squads, stipulated their basic responsibilities, exempted firefighters from several civic duties, and left the companies to frame such additional rules as they saw fit. At least as fast as the population, the number of companies grew and eventually reached five. By 1747, the town made a few modifications in the basic system and obtained a colonial law that authorized firefighters to demolish buildings to prevent flames from spreading and gave various powers to the town firewards to curb looting and other misbehavior. Providence followed the same path.[38]

With the new kinds of subsidiary institutions, the towns that used them achieved a supple style of action resembling the colonial government's. Granted, the results could be disappointing, but a remedy always seemed to be available. The new modes also had the virtue of harnessing private investment, as in the market houses, to civic purposes. And the town meeting's legislative function remained unmistakable, while it put primary administrative responsibilities in the hands of people who were independent of annual elections. Yet the responsibilities were not simply delegated; they were subject to review and surveillance by town officers such as auditors or the council. As in the General Assembly, the various officials had duties suitable to their positions, in such a fashion as to make them both control and collaborate with each other. This was not a system of rational delegation but rather of administration through distributed functions that worked like checks and balances.

Policies and Political Organization

The changes in form and operations of the governmental structure fairly well reflected changes in purpose, and they in turn stimulated the development of associations that may be called political parties. Bringing order to Rhode Island, chiefly to boost Newport, had been the main focus in previous decades, and Newport merchants had held key offices and been the political leaders of the colony. During their ascendancy they centralized authority and developed a coherent policy for the colonial government and went far toward reshaping town government to play its part in the system. For them, procedural nicety and an elaboration of law had ordinarily been useful rather than ends in themselves. On many occasions they disregarded formalities and treated government openly as an agency to accomplish their purposes. These purposes, especially in view of the unavoidable diffusion of political rights, had called for policies that could benefit people throughout the colony. The capital's gain was not the hinterland's loss—or not visibly so. Central to this happy state of affairs was paper money. The capital found it could not tax the provincials and cleverly substituted a device that was touted as a stimulant to their prosperity by the delightful means of putting cash in their hands. After some initial suspicion, most of them were beguiled.[39] So the Newport leadership could lead.

Fundamentals changed before the middle of the eighteenth century. Economic development worked so well that the capital's interests ceased to overpower the others. Imperial demands stopped the expansion of paper money while piling up military expenditures. The spread of wealth and population diffused power. When taxation had to be resumed, when the glory and profits of war were to be distributed, when the terms were written for conversion to a silver-based currency, to name a few salient issues, Newport's old preponderance was severely curtailed.

The condition of the colony had its counterpart in the towns. Zeal to promote commercial centers had translated colonial into town policy: arrange the use of land and the pattern of transportation to serve trade and handicrafts; reshape rural areas to support urban needs; and promise the country folk that they would profit, too, from nearby markets, eager customers, higher prices for land, and lower prices for nonfarm goods. Where such visions were dispelled or never held sway, towns had fairly serious choices to make. By the middle of the century, the desired commercial zones either were making headway or were abandoned. Most common lands were divided.

What, then, could guide policy? In some respects, procedural tidiness and fully elaborated law shifted from means to ends. They became some of the enduring methods to keep government effective and restrained—in this regard, to inhibit its capacity to have much of a policy, to prevent it from tuning policy to a pitch set in Newport or anywhere else. Consequently, the aimlessness that had appeared earlier in governmental action on interests in mills and inland fishing appeared in countless other places.

After 1738, for instance, there was no longer a comprehensive goal for the colony's transportation. The Assembly usually insisted that main roads, especially those used by the post, remain open and even be straightened regardless of local objections. The colony tried to operate ferries on the west side of Jamestown for a couple of years.[40] It also built a lighthouse at the south tip of Jamestown and used money from port fees to keep it operating.[41] The Assembly continued to subsidize bridges. In fact, it did so promiscuously. It no longer required an argument that a given project had significance beyond its immediate neighborhood. The profligacy was the more astonishing as it advanced while the colony suffered fiscal famine and people balked at paying taxes.[42] This was simple pork-barrel politics.

Rather than promote a plan of transportation, the colonial government revised general laws on mending roads. A statute of 1745 spelled out the obligations of householders and surveyors of highways more fully than ever. Refinements followed. In 1773, the Assembly began to allow a few towns to hire workmen to mend roads, a rational practice forbidden to Westerly at the beginning of the century.[43]

A hundred years of intimacy between the colonial government and Newport continued, but the old political monogamy could not go on. The Assembly was first seduced into bigamy and then had to favor a harem. If Newport wanted special laws, as of yore, a right to tax to finance urban services or authorization to set up a workhouse, pave streets, maintain a watch, build a market house, or pass town laws to control fires or firearms, the Assembly obliged. But it had to do the same for Providence, then Bristol and East Greenwich. The Assembly distributed favors lavishly as long as they cost the colonial treasury nothing. Enabling acts, permission for special local taxes or statutes on stray livestock, could be had for the asking. The Assembly finally drew the line at subsidizing creation of ports in Westerly and New Shoreham.[44] Fiscal stringency or party politics, not economic objectives, guided decisions after 1740.

The colony was able to act consistently to disentangle land from old laws, to guard it as an endowment for families, and to make it a freely transferable commodity. The point should not be unduly stressed; law changed more to reflect than to shape general practice. Although the Assembly did nothing to give executors power to sell land to satisfy an estate's creditors, for instance, a statute of 1745, later amplified, made land accessible to creditors after a fashion.[45] Another law in 1770, appealing to "Reason and Equity," prescribed equal partition of intestates' land, except for a double share to the eldest son and so replaced the older law that had let town councils divide land only into as many parcels as would be large enough to be freehold units.[46]

The Assembly, however, could not firmly set policy on two topics that were important to a society where commerce was pervasive: bankruptcy and usury. A series of measures tried to balance the claims of creditors against the social goal of enabling a bankrupt to regain solvency.[47] Probably no one was satisfied. Usury laws had many friends but could not be passed or obeyed while the old paper currency prevailed and lost value daily. Conversion to a silver-backed money let the Assembly set a 6 percent ceiling on what a lawful contract might require.[48]

At the town level, freemen were less and less interested in framing plans for their whole communities. As already described, town business fell into routines in which the town meeting and the council had their distinct segments. Debate over the promotion of commercial centers still enlivened a few places, but colonial elections rather than town business brought the largest attendance at meetings. Newport freemen may have been peculiarly apathetic. On one occasion, two turned out. On another, the town had to defer action on a local tax until fifteen attended. The only question to draw large numbers was whether to authorize inoculation of smallpox, a topic remarkably peripheral to basic town functions. Around two hundred freemen appeared at stormy meetings for four successive days until the proposal was defeated.[49] Even then, the attendance was lower than for colonial elections. In Newport and probably in other towns as well, local government had become largely a unit at the bottom of a hierarchy.

The colonial government transacted important public business, and in the late colonial period the imperial authorities often set the agenda. In the internal affairs of Rhode Island, confusion or absence of policy could be illustrated by many examples but to misleading effect. The colony could evade many choices that before had been controlled by the Newport elite, but some decisions had to be made, above all on fiscal policy. Political parties provided the medium for decisions on these and several other issues. Parties could mobilize majorities out of the swirl of local interests.[50]

Two party-like organizations existed in the late colonial period, continuing with fair clarity as the result of disagreements that began in 1715. Their origins and much of their early operations are all but untraceable. Glimpses of their inner workings during the years after 1756 reveal the expectable similarities to the colonial government itself. An acknowledged leader—Stephen Hopkins on one side, Samuel Ward on the other—had a circle of immediate assistants reminiscent of the Governor and Council. One or more of these men assumed executive roles for such ends as raising and dispensing money or conducting the communications with town chieftains, who were reminiscent of the deputies.

The political organizations had two overlapping functions, fighting to win elections and directing their partisans in the General Assembly. They were concerned with elections at both the town and central levels. In the towns, the local captains had to recruit members, whether to run for office, vote for the party candidates at town meeting, contribute money, or help in the organization. A meeting of stalwarts deliberated on the ticket. The captain's forces then used bribes, cajolery, and small favors such as credit, employment, treats, and arguments to get freemen to vote for the right candidates or not vote at all. At a colonial election in Newport in May, the party chiefs guided the process of counting the proxies (as the ballots were called) and rounding up additional backers to vote by hand. This phase of the political process featured challenges to qualifications of voters and ingenious parliamentary maneuvers. Then the leaders steered the new General Assembly through a long list of civil and military officers, after which they settled down to the routine of controlling legislation.

Obviously, communication was vital throughout this business. The party leaders had to know who their friends were, who could get elected, and what their friends wanted. They had to get their backers qualified to vote, even if this meant granting spurious deeds to land. They also had to make sure that the men in the rank and file knew whom to vote for and why. Much of this aspect of political action never touched paper, but broadside appeals were published fairly often, pamphlets less so. The two sides eventually had newspapers. Hopkins and his friends launched the Providence *Gazette* in 1762, at a time when the Newport *Mercury* was generally impartial. Later it became the organ of the Ward faction. In the Assembly, the members had to be kept aware of their side's aims, but now and then they lost touch. On one occasion, the Hopkins forces turned down some of their own candidates by mistake.[51]

Partisan control of public offices obviously had consequences, though some of them were trifling. Partisan choice of justices of the peace and militia officers, for instance, probably had little effect on the level of competence or use of power. Nor did changes in office lead to great economic benefits. Neither salaries nor fees in Rhode Island nor even extralegal profits made anybody rich. Power for its own sake exerted its usual appeal. Yet even at such simple levels, partisan politics brought a kind of regularity to public life. The leaders chose candidates who would attract as many votes as possible. Balancing the ticket by geography and religion offered all the freemen hope of gaining a voice. Whichever side won, its officials would have a predisposition to work together.

A working majority had to serve many interests. Although the Hopkins party might predominate in the northern half of the colony and the Ward party in the south, both sought support everywhere and garnered at least a third of their votes in the other side's territory. To compete for every freeman, the opposing sides had to share many traits. Still, like offices, other rewards of power lay to be fought over. Hopkins and his friends wanted privileges useful to their planned iron foundry. Ward's Warwick allies wanted similar benefits for their complex of mills.

Though the parties fought over several rewards, the big contest was over fiscal policy and had three foci: colonial taxes, the ratio of conversion between old tenor and Lawful Money, and the method of retiring the old bills. The furor over taxation revealed two concerns: the assessment policies and the apportionment of the total tax among the towns. Both were major political issues, but potentially they divided the colony differently, because the apportionment controversy touched off battles between coalitions of towns, and assessment policy pitted economic interests against each other.[52]

The issue of evaluating old tenor also put interests rather than regions at odds. The conversion rate between paper and specie had immense importance, not because of the small volume of currency outstanding, but because of the volume of pounds in the old-tenor currency that were expressed in notes, bonds, bequests, balances in accounts, and the like. The Hopkins forces championed rates that changed as market conditions further devalued the old-tenor pound against Lawful Money. Ward's backers in Newport wanted to reverse the devaluation, at least to a small extent. Quite likely, much of the rural wing of Ward's party opposed such a scheme. Obviously, it benefited creditors of all kinds, and it was said to be essential to preserving commercial capital that had been eroded by the slide of old tenor. The Hopkins plan, which sounded fair, if anything, benefited debtors.[53]

Further, Hopkins favored—and ultimately got—a simple retirement of the old bills of credit, treasurer's notes, and other governmental paper created in connection with replacing the old paper money with Lawful Money. This his party achieved by stiff taxes. The Ward side, by contrast, kept scaling down or postponing the taxes necessary to complete the conversion. Instead, it created short-term interest-bearing securities to replace what had been scheduled for retirement. Whether this was merely yielding to popular resistance to taxes or was the beginning of a permanent funded debt cannot be determined.[54] Perhaps the prospect of a durable burden of interest on treasury bonds was an element in the breakdown of party discipline on fiscal policy in the Ward administration of 1766. In any case, the Ward side lost, and the Hopkins side won decisively in 1770.

The implications of the partisan conflict over fiscal policy are not altogether clear but luckily are tangential to the point at hand. Political organizations mobilized the votes to get one policy adopted and held steady. In this, the central issue of the day, the opposing parties most plainly exhibited their constructive potential.

Conclusion

In the last four decades of the colonial period, the central government of Rhode Island changed in many ways, but the main ones were clear. The advance of technicality and elaborate machinery, already begun, became increasingly pronounced, not only in the operations of the central government itself but also in what it prescribed for the towns and in what they did on their own. Still, there was little experiment in bureaucracy, strictly defined, apart from the Grand Committee. In addition, the government moved toward a division of responsibility along procedural lines. For example, the operation of the treasury, which once had included initiating lawsuits against its debtors, was confined to the technical management of funds, while the Attorney General organized any necessary litigation. As a result, the various subsidiary organs increasingly collaborated in the operation of government. Yet the General Assembly remained unwilling to delegate authority completely. Between its audit or inspection committees, its part in the judiciary, and its choice of most of the military officers, it kept a hand in all branches of business.

Therefore, the change toward elaborate machinery and procedure could not shield the functions of government from political rivalries. Moreover, the diffusion of wealth and population that subverted Newport's commanding position made the Assembly's intrusion potentially disruptive, because the legislators usually had no fundamental aims.

Where other colonies might have a staple crop around which policy formed, Rhode Island had its commerce, but that entailed only the broadest guidelines. Trade was profitable and needed exports as well as facilities for transportation. So almost any plan to increase these objectives might win favor. But so might any plan to resolve a local squabble or keep a gristmill operating. The Assembly had few general goals aside from political expediency to guide its decisions and had little inclination to develop strong connections with institutions other than strictly governmental ones to improve the functions of the society within its jurisdiction. It even considered marriages and apprenticeships as private contracts beyond public control unless the parties appealed to the courts. Where once the family had appeared to be the building block of society, it finally had been reduced to a par with agreements to staff a ship or build a house. Paternalism disappeared from the operations of the Rhode Island government even faster than the dominance of Newport merchants. Power by status was never secure and was giving way to individual rights. Limited government was a by-product of these changes.

Under these conditions, government achieved two qualities that are generally admirable, a marked responsiveness to its constituents and an inhibition on highhandedness. If Rhode Island lacked some of the restraints ordinarily implied by the term *limited government*, nevertheless its charter, its requirements to maintain basic harmony with English law, its dedication to religious liberty, and above all its susceptibility to the demands of its inhabitants kept it limited in fact. The danger of losing any sense of direction was curtailed at times by the flow of events, such as the imperial wars of 1739 to

1763, and more steadily by the development of organizations strongly resembling political parties. For all the disapproval they inspired, even among their leaders, these organizations made it possible for the General Assembly to have consistent working majorities and sometimes for major public questions to be approached by constructive proposals rather than palliative or temporizing measures.

❧ 11 ❧

Steps toward the Private Corporation

The development of administrative arms by the colony and subsidiaries by the towns showed only part of the colony's inventiveness in creating agencies for social purposes. People in Rhode Island created a new pattern of intermediary institutions to stand between the individual or the family and the entire body politic. The pattern included a great variety but recognized none of the old monopolistic or power-wielding groups. Instead, participation was voluntary. Associations of this sort had existed for years in the colony. The novelty after 1738 lay in the ways associations managed to gain legal standing to back their practices of internal self-government and control of property. The salient new forms were the nongovernmental corporation and similar entities. The variety allowed great flexibility for collective action, and the potential would be expanded for many years—without threatening individual rights.[1]

The traditional types of intermediary institutions in England often had restricted individual rights by providing governmental backing for monopolies or involuntary participation or control over nonmembers. Guilds, proprietors of markets or other essential real estate, or parishes either had been rejected from the start in Rhode Island or had failed.[2] The early town mills and taverns had ceased to be manifestations of communal authority and had become private associations based on ownership of property. Common fields and pastures had gone from town control into the hands of proprietary organizations and generally had been divided. Towns had shrunk to the role of administrative agencies of central government with limited capacities for independent action. Proprietors of undivided land had asserted corporative powers without success. They could not screen their own membership because they could not treat their land as owned collectively apart from the members' individual property rights. Promoters of urban centers consistently attempted to exert only a few controls over the persons who took lots and avoided attempts to keep vital land in collective ownership to generate income for the organization. Even Long Wharf in Newport, for all the irregularity of its institutional origins, never claimed monopoly rights.

The institutional array had polarized in the early eighteenth century, setting off a governmental hierarchy with monopolistic and coercive power over everything in its jurisdiction against a swirl of voluntary associations. Some of these associations had the support of the judiciary, which enforced contracts, standard commercial agreements, deeds to land, and the application of legal actions to shared property rights. Churches that acquired property sought to avail themselves of this advanatage even while governmental fidelity to religious liberty seemed to preclude them from seeking any public support from public authority. But no intermediary institutions could wield power beyond their members' consent.

Though government could use force and make law, it could not subsume all aspects of life in a single system. Creation of an effective hierarchy of public authority was accomplished by elaborating law and paying more attention to procedure. The charter required frequent elections, in which a majority of the White men could vote. The result was limited government. It offered some support to assorted private associations. It also restricted what they might do and guarded them from private interference. This limited control over what groups of inhabitants did served the dominant interests of Newport for several decades.

Many inhabitants wanted the government to do more than it could and demanded more protection for their pet projects than it gave to church properties or mercantile agreements. Such people needed various new institutions with powers to make their own rules, act by less than unanimity, screen their own membership, and manage collectively held property in a form that was legally separate from the individual property of the members. These powers would have to be conferred by government, but no one knew which layer of government to turn to. Despite the fact that the colony government technically could not issue an act of incorporation—after all, it *was* a corporation, and one corporation cannot create another—Rhode Island inhabitants never sought royal approval of new institutional forms. They approached the colonial government for a charter of incorporation or permission to hold a lottery; often they found town authority sufficient to buttress their activities. If neither colony nor town had an unquestionable power to confer rights on corporative organizations, no serious challenge to their existence appeared.

Some organizations required no governmental sanction. Especially in Newport, people created a variety of institutions—a Masonic lodge, a dancing school, an insurance firm—that needed no special rights. Nevertheless, there were some functions that had to use new forms created by public authority: the lottery and the chartered corporation. Rhode Island resorted to both in uncommon numbers.

These new forms shared one crucial attribute: a personality in law or existence as a body politic. That is, in Rhode Island the General Assembly made them capable of managing property and engaging in litigation in their own names and conducting their own affairs by some system of majority vote or delegated power. The managers or directors of a lottery had a collective standing for a limited time, whereas a corporation went on indefinitely and had a succession of officers and members. Still, the common trait sheds light on the experiments with corporations.

Both forms, of course, were familiar in England and hardly unknown in the English colonies. Ordinarily, in the parent country, both had been allowed only for public purposes, which in practical terms meant that they needed the endorsement of the men who set policy for the monarchy. The public purpose for a lottery, to be sure, was quite elastic. And in England, corporate charters generally went to members of the ruling class and so strengthened their connection with the Crown.[3] In Rhode Island, both lottery and corporation began with clear expressions of governmental approval of their plans, but in time that approval lost its importance. The absence of potential for harm to the public was enough. Further, though a charter might gain official favor while one party was in power, it protected the corporation from partisan reprisal when the political winds shifted. Rhode Island began to authorize lotteries and corporations when circumstances ruled out confining such favors to any one element.

Lotteries

The General Assembly started on the path to innovation in the use of incorporation with two preliminaries: the elite military company and the lottery. The lottery has often been treated as an ugly stepchild in the family of institutions. Little attention has been paid to its forms of organization. Rhode Island lotteries scarcely deviated from English prototypes either in purposes or form or mode of authorization. Parliament as well as the monarch in England had authorized lotteries, so a colonial legislature could readily do so.[4] As in the parent country, Rhode Island temporarily outlawed lotteries by statute and then authorized exceptions to its own rule on a case-by-case basis.[5] The ban came to an end with the plainest possible appeal to a British precedent of 1743 but no clear resort to a temporary body politic. The immediate occasion was the desire for an expensive bridge at a time when the colonial treasury could not afford lavish subsidies. Eleven inhabitants wanted a span across the Providence River and asked permission for a lottery. They called it euphemistically "a voluntary Contribution" according to a plan "formed very nearly upon the plan of the state Scheme in England for the building the Bridge at Westminster without any Expence to the Government." This language first echoed the colonial statute of 1716 on religious liberty and then hinted that the lottery was a governmental function, cleverly presenting it as something other than a game of chance. The promoters asked the Assembly to appoint three disinterested gentlemen under bond as directors to supervise the lottery, and the Assembly granted their request.[6] However, it kept changing the rules. Responsibility for conducting the lottery itself remained with the directors, though by turns the colonial and town governments took charge of applying the money collected to the bridge.[7]

The lottery's success inspired dozens of successors, whose purposes ranged from public to private. A few were to raise money to pave streets in Newport and Providence, one to rebuild the colony's fort, some to improve harbors, others to build or repair roads and bridges, still others to finance public buildings or religious edifices. But almost from the beginning, the Assembly, just as the authorities in England had done before, also allowed lotteries for individuals who had fallen into desperate straits. Eventually, it allowed them for private clubs, including a library in Providence and the Masonic lodge in Newport, and for rebuilding an ironworks that had gone up in flames. Beneficiaries might be individuals or institutions, and the institutions usually needed no previous explicit recognition by law.

The petitioners for the early lotteries based their pleas on public improvement, but later ones made such claims vaguely or not at all. Backers of the third lottery, the first designed for a distressed individual, described their effort as public charity, needed where the burden was too great to be shouldered by private means. Another debtor sweetened his plan to raise money to satisfy his creditors by promising to donate suplus proceeds to the colony to pay for roads and bridges. The library society in Providence wanted money to buy books to be housed in the local courthouse for the members' use but still described the plan as being "of a Public Nature, tending to promote Virtue, and the Good of Mankind."[8]

When churches began asking for the benefits of lotteries, they said little or nothing about the public good. Perhaps any religious purpose was simply assumed to exert a benign effect on the community. Or perhaps nobody wanted to ask the colony to back religion. The Johnston Baptists merely lamented that "the Circumstances of said Town are low." Likewise, the Cranston Baptists asked for a lottery to buy a meetinghouse "in Pity of Our Inabilities and for Incouragement of a Good Intent; whereby to Enable Us to Set a good Example for our Children." Providence Anglicans asked for a lottery to raise funds to repair a steeple and clock, on the grounds that they had already spent so much on repairs that they could afford no more. Congregationalists of the same town attached their plans to the general welfare by alleging that "Peace, Harmony, and Happiness in all Communities, are much in Proportion to their Growth in Virtue and Knowledge" and that the manse they wanted to finance would lead to these good results.[9]

The method of conducting a lottery soon fell into a routine.[10] In most cases, the directors appointed by the General Assembly (under bond to the General Treasurer for faithful performance) had full responsibility for the project. They sold tickets, supervised the drawing, paid the prizes, and spent the profits on the purpose for which the money was raised. They had to render accounts to the Assembly whenever asked and refund the price of tickets if the lottery was not drawn within the stipulated time, though the Assembly sometimes granted an extension. They usually earned a commission from the funds as their compensation. In effect, they were officers of the colonial government. The authorizing statute prescribed the financial dimensions of each scheme until after 1761. By the end of the colonial period, the Assembly allowed institutional beneficiaries of lotteries to replace directors in case of need.[11]

Nonecclesiastical institutions could get legal recognition as a by-product of their sponsorship of lotteries. When the Masons obtained one, they planned to put the proceeds in the hands of their treasurer. Because this office previously was unknown to law and therefore without a responsibility ex officio and because part of the money was to be spent to buy land, the act authorizing the lottery made the "Master, Wardens and Society of Free and Accepted Masons" in Newport a corporation with perpetual succession. The Providence library lottery allowed any buyer of sixty tickets to become a member and required the members to buy unsold tickets, which amounted to an assessment, in order to hold the drawing on time. Churches never used a lottery as a backdoor to obtain legal recognition. On the contrary, they described themselves in the briefest ways when approaching the General Assembly for authorization.[12]

The point of special interest here is that the lotteries gradually had taken on some of the attributes of corporations. Though the directors collectively were subordinate to the General Assembly, normally responsible financially to it rather than the recipient of the money, they could act by majority vote, could sue and be sued. Their collective existence was limited in time and created no perpetual succession. But in one essential point they had been similar to corporations all along, in that as artificial entities in law they had special powers given them by their creator. The lotteries had a species of monopoly right; they could do what actual persons could not.

Corporations outside the Framework of Territorial Government

In the 1740s, Rhode Island began to charter corporations of sorts new to the jurisdiction and divergent from English precedents. The departure from the past cannot be appreciated without a review of earlier actions. Previously,

the General Assembly had incorporated towns and had given some corporative attributes to proprietors of undivided lands.[13] Moreover, the town of
Newport had created a corporative body, the proprietors of Long Wharf.
These earlier creations had followed traditional lines. The towns, for all the
defects of their charters or equivalent authorizations, had been corporations
of some sort for local government. The original towns had been founded before they received their charters, but so had many in Europe. The statute extending corporative traits to proprietors of undivided lands likewise followed
traditional lines. If the proprietors had been able to use the advantages it
gave them, they would have resembled divers organizations in England or
Massachusetts formed to exploit property held in common.[14]

Long Wharf also had a traditional cast and significantly was never mentioned in connection with the late colonial charters. Yet it was too important
to be ignored, and it received governmental benefits, including a lottery, as
though it had been a corporation. Newport authorized Long Wharf before
1685, in an era when the town government was most closely wedded to the
province. The town granted privileges on unknown terms and revised them
in 1702 when it transferred control to a new organization to repair the structure.[15] The new proprieters would have the wharf and any profits from it only
as long as they kept it in good shape. They had the authority to appoint a
wharfinger to collect fees for use of the facility. This was essentially a joint
stock company.[16] It was also like other organizations of its era in that it was
based on shared control of land and never could escape the implications of
that fact.

The proprietary organization of 1702 allowed the wharf to decay and was
replaced by another in 1739, again by the decision of the town. Nobody
questioned the town's power to do this. The new arrangements made no
basic change in the conception of the institution. The new version, however,
went the way of the previous one. Management of the enterprise had become cyclical. A group of men would get the rights to the site by authority of
the town government, with the expectation of acting as a businessmen's civic
club to benefit themselves and the port alike.[17] They would take shares, pay
assessments on them to finance repair of construction, refuse to pay more,
fail to reap sufficient profits to pay for routine upkeep, part with their
shares, and thus leave quite a different kind of association, one with socially
diverse members holding unequal shares. This made an ineffectual organization, in which the members would not invest but would cling to share
rights as a species of property. Eventually, one optimist would begin buying
up all he could get and find himself stymied. Then governmental authority—the town in the colonial period, the state later—would replace the organization with a new one. But the new one would be like the old one. Nor
would the town break the cycle by subsidizing the enterprise or giving it
something like a monopoly.

The transfer in 1739 set off a new round in the cycle but with a few special curves and a display of ingenuity by the town to aid the enterprise when it faltered. When the proprietors found collective action ineffectual through officers and assessments and when the shares had scattered and become subject to quarrels within the ranks, the members abandoned much of the basic plan.[18] They parcelled out sections of the wharf and associated property to themselves. Perhaps this justified their investment in the end. They made a number of divisions and then, instead of trying to manage the remainder in common ownership, leased it in small and large parcels.[19] The property under collective management brought in too little revenue to pay for itself, let alone yield cash dividends, so individual exploitation became the substitute.

Although the traits of the organization that made it like the proprietors of common lands led to a similar dissolution, the members as a group often obtained unusual governmental favors. The General Assembly gave them a license to operate a ferry to Jamestown.[20] The town helped them immensely by tolerating their failure to meet the terms of their original grant and their division of the property. It also collaborated with them to build a new market house at the east end of the wharf, a project that the General Assembly helped with a lottery.[21]

Rhode Island after 1740 did not repudiate its inheritance of corporative institutions but neither did it build on it. The later corporations and similar institutions grew out of shared social goals rather than shared interests in real estate. In the last thirty years of the colonial period, the General Assembly chartered a library, a mutual aid society, a college, several churches, and three water supply companies and gave something short of full corporate rights to other institutions. In the nineteenth century, lawyers would call the towns public corporations (or quasi-corporations) and the library and waterworks private corporations—and would have serious difficulty with the proprietors of Long Wharf and the incomplete corporations. No such scheme of classification existed in the eighteenth century, and the realities on the scene did not imply it unambiguously. Yet the colony created what amounted to private corporations by any test except an explicit label.

The General Assembly's resort to granting corporate standing needs to be explained from three directions. One is the legal or constitutional rules in the British Empire. Another is the bearing of actions by other colonies. And the third is the internal development of Rhode Island that made the institutional novelties attractive.

If the General Assembly could appeal to the example of Parliament to justify authorizing lotteries, it could not do so when chartering corporations. Instead, it remained mute. The Bubble Act of 1720, supposedly extended to America in 1741, made it clear that English law forbade any group to assume corporate standing without authorization either from Parliament or the monarch. In England, lawyers whittled down the effect of this statute; in America it served to quash the Massachusetts Land Bank and was never invoked against any other organization, although many organizations feared it would be. Rather, after 1741 as before, British policy, frequently backed by legal opinion, allowed colonial governors in royal and proprietary colonies to erect corporations (often in the monarch's name) at the behest of their legislatures. A substantial number of institutions obtained charters. The governors exercised authority from the crown, and the legislatures acted as Parliament did on those occasions when it instructed the monarch to grant a charter.[22]

However, Rhode Island, as a charter colony, could not rely on this view of the realities. The colonial government was a corporation. A well-established rule in English law held that one corporation could not create another. Moreover, the charter explicitly required the governor and company to make laws in conformity to English practice. Because the governor was elected by the freemen, he could not be seen as having authority delegated from the Crown, like a royal governor. Connecticut, which had a corporate charter like Rhode Island's, saw the difficulty and for years avoided presuming power to incorporate Yale and refused to charter a trading company that proposed to operate a land bank. Rhode Island glimpsed the difficulty when Newport men began to organize the Redwood Library.[23]

Instead of inaction or construction of a rationale, the Rhode Island General Assembly tested British tolerance with two experiments: an elite military company and the first lotteries. The risk could be great. Because the Crown had reserved no power to disallow Rhode Island statutes, it might have to express displeasure by action against the colony's charter. These ventures drew no fire, however, nor did Connecticut's belated charter to Yale in 1745. The General Assembly then proceeded to erect corporations of a few sorts already known in other colonies. Finally, it pioneered in corporations for ecclesiastical purposes and waterworks.

The Assembly's first charter went to a group of prominent Newport men who wanted to found an artillery company outside the regular framework of the militia. They did not ask for incorporation but only authorization, such as had been given before, to form a special military unit and choose their own officers.[24] The Assembly not only awarded a charter but gave the petitioners more than they had asked. It justified its decision on the grounds of public purpose. The Newport Artillery Company would be "a Nursery of skilfull Officers," which would also "in Time of actual Invasion by their Superior Skill and Experience . . . render the whole Militia more Useful and Effectual."[25]

The charter laid down terms for the organization. It would have perpetual succession, choose its own officers annually (subject to approval by the Governor and Council), make its own rules, set fines for infractions of up to forty shillings, and recruit members. Its members would have to train at least four days per year but need not attend the training days of the regular companies of their districts unless they were officers, though the company would be subject to orders from the field officers of the Newport County militia regiment.[26]

Incorporating a military company served well as a prelude to civilian companies for three reasons. By its charter, the colonial government had the duty as well as the right to organize military forces, so presumably it could claim that an incorporated special unit was expedient for its undoubted responsibility and thus justify granting a charter to a citizens' organization. Further, the military corporation conveniently bridged the gap between a voluntary association and coercive powers wielded by a group outside the basic governmental framework, because the artillery company would be in the colony's military chain of command. If officers of the company could impose martial discipline on the other members, then a charter that would give the majority in a civilian organization the power to bind the minority would be a comparatively inoffensive curtailment of individual discretion. And finally, the new military company was certain to be pleasing to the proponents of strong royal government, the very people who might ordinarily oppose an expansion of the colony's power.

The founders of the new corps, surprisingly, postponed using the charter. Only after prodding by the Assembly did they organize in 1744, just as King George's War started. They appointed a clerk and four sergeants and adopted a set of rules. Any member might resign at pleasure. Finally, on September 17, 1744, "[t]he Artillery Company of the Town of Newport made their first Appearance compleatly Arm'd and Cloath'd According to the Rules and Orders of said Company." From then until the Revolution, most of the recorded actions were elections of officers. They also authorized expenditures for dinners or for the company's only property, drums and flags.[27] The artillery company was at least as much a gentlemen's club as a military organization. Its uniforms most clearly distinguished it from regular militia companies. If it intended to acquire expensive equipment, it failed to do so.

The Newport Artillery Company inspired imitations whenever wars began. A counterpart in Providence obtained a charter in 1744, then three others at the outset of the French and Indian Wars and several just before the Revolution.[28] The performance of these companies, which might reveal the motives for forming them, is mostly past recapture. Some probably did little or nothing while their members basked in exemption from regular militia duty. A few surely performed as they said they would, whether inspired by snobbery or martial ardor.

The record of the elite companies discloses no reason for their charters. Such units had been authorized without them. The charters gave them modest benefits in authority to make their own rules, choose their recruits, design their uniforms, set their own schedule of training, and choose their own officers. Maybe these benefits seemed important enough. But the record suggests a little more, because the gentlemen of Newport set the pattern and did so just after the onset of war and a major political contest that sapped the dominance of their town's interests. The charter to the artillery company bestowed a traditional sort of favor on members of the ruling element, enshrining its standing in a special niche, marking it out as the source of officers. A royal charter traditionally lent prestige; in England it showed royal favor. In Rhode Island, however, political realities required a fairly even hand in granting favors. Once it started, the Assembly could not confine charters to men of only one area or social level.

Broadly, this record of creating corporations as a favor to the elites characterized the other corporations and near-corporations, beginning with the Redwood Library. That organization obtained a charter in 1747 at the request of forty-six Newport men, including several organizers of the artillery company. From the outset, the library company intended to own property in books and real estate and sought legal recognition as well as power to govern itself. The organization had its roots in the Philosophical Society formed in 1730 when George Berkeley was in town. It consisted of ministers, lawyers, and a few well-educated laymen and officials, who gathered every Monday evening to discuss topics considered efficacious "for the promotion of Knowledge and Virtue."[29]

The club expanded its aims when Abraham Redwood returned from Philadelphia full of enthusiasm for the Library Company there, which recently had received a charter from the provincial proprietary. Redwood offered to donate £500 for books and probably suggested incorporation as a sure way to put them into ownership by the collectivity.

The petition for the charter used glowing and quite traditional terms. The petitioners reported Redwood's generosity and their own intention to raise money for a building to house the books. They said they wished "to promote Virtue Knowledge and useful Learning" and that Redwood had "nothing in View but the good of Mankind." They argued that because "the Smiles of Men in Power always aid and reflect a Lustre on such Things," the Assembly could lend its support by granting their request.[30]

The Assembly, now emboldened by years of unchallenged precedent, did as they asked, as though nobody might question its authority. It fully spelled out the powers of the corporation. It made the petitioners "a Body Politick and Corporate . . . by the Name of The Company of the Redwood Library," to have perpetual succession, power to admit new members, "and be Persons able and capable in Law To have hold receive and enjoy" property of all sorts, to sell or otherwise dispose of the property, to sue and be sued, have a seal, and to make bylaws and transact business at their meetings. The Assembly specified an annual meeting in September, a quorum, and a few essential officers. Beyond these specifications, the company could organize as it saw fit and make any decisions by majority vote that were not repugnant to the laws of the colony or England.[31]

The company organized quickly. It elected officers, chose titles for the initial collection, raised money for a building, and began construction.[32] By then Henry Collins had conveyed a site for the library by a peculiar indenture deed, which shimmered with uncertainty over the soundness of the charter. Though the document cited the incorporation of the library company, it conveyed the land to Redwood, his heirs and assigns, to be held for the use of the company. The terms fell short of the careful precautions in transfers of Quaker ecclesiastical properties of the day. Collins, however, promised to make any further conveyance thought necessary by Redwood or his heirs or assigns or by the company to make the transfer of rights more secure for the purpose in view. Moreover, the wording contained a superabundance of qualifications and the redundancies beloved of lawyers.[33] Collins's doubts were unfounded. The organization proceeded untroubled. It elaborated its bylaws and conducted its affairs successfully until the Revolution. It was even able to levy an assessment on its members, a sure sign that they accepted its corporate powers.[34]

As with the elite military corps, the Newport gentlemen could not have special privileges in a library all to themselves. Seven years later, ambitious men in Providence and vicinity, led by Ephraim Bowen and Stephen Hopkins, sought similar privileges. They did not seek a charter, probably because they lacked funds to erect a building, but obtained governmental favor that rendered them a self-governing institution anyway. The General Assembly let them store their books in the Providence County courthouse and gave them a vague authorization "to make such Acts and Orders as may be fit and Necessary for the proper regulating said Library," their decisions to be "good and valid for those Ends."[35] In this modest grant, the Assembly showed its flexibility in tailoring corporative rights to the occasion. There was no need to choose between a fully rigged corporation and nothing at all.

When fire destroyed the courthouse and books five years later, the Assembly revised the institution, authorizing a lottery to buy new volumes. Presumably, the members themselves designed the change. It let anyone who bought sixty tickets be a member. So the club of readers lost control over admissions. Besides, the Assembly reserved for itself a right to use the books, which made the library partly a public institution with less self-government than a true corporation.[36]

The third kind of charter graced a patently private club. The members were Newport sea captains who wanted a social organization that would serve as a mutual aid society. Such a club, The Marine Society, had opened in Boston in 1752. Later that same year, Newport Merchants decided to form the Friendship Club, which had "an Intent and Design to promote the Interest of each other the Members thereof and their Families." When they sought a charter in 1754, they professed to serve no public good except to ease the town's burdens in supporting the poor by raising "a fund to relieve such Members . . . who by Misfortune and Losses shall become proper Objects of the Help and Assistance of said Society." They already had drawn up some rules for the society, which they showed to the legislature, and asked for incorporation to enable them to choose officers, conduct their affairs under these regulations, and make additional ones "consistent and subordinate to the Laws of the Land." In fact, they already had been acting according to these rules, even to the point of gathering money that they lent at interest on "bonds taken In the Name of the Fellowship Club."[37] Presumably, the main purpose of the charter was to safeguard the fund as well as to reinforce the rules and give the luster of governmental approval.

The Assembly granted the petition, approved the rules, and called on the Governor to issue a charter. The text of this document was simple. It allowed the corporation, under the name of the Fellowship Club, to choose officers and admit new members. It included nothing about holding property, suing and being sued, using a seal, maintaining financial accountability, or the time of an annual meeting—all normal ingredients of such a document. Rather, the rules submitted to the Assembly were appended to the charter, giving them an ambiguous standing between it and the usual kinds of bylaws. Some of these regulations covered topics normally in a charter, such as the principal officers and the time of their election. Other rules, however, were like bylaws, such as those on dues and fines for absence, supplying aid to needy members and their dependents, sharing knowledge of soundings at sea or compass variations, and attending deceased members' funerals.[38]

No other organization attained legal privileges such as those of the Fellowship Club; only the Newport Masonic lodge came close. When the Masons planned a hall for their meetings, they obtained permission for a lottery to raise the money. The Assembly at the same time granted their wish for a peculiarly limited kind of incorporation. They might be a body politic under "the Name of The Master, Wardens, and Society of Free and Accepted Masons, in the Town of Newport." They might have perpetual succession, govern themselves by some sort of majority rule or delegation of power to officials, sue and be sued, and so forth. But these attributes applied only to affairs "touching the Building aforesaid."[39] Legal recognition in this case was tied strictly to management of real estate. It had nearly nothing to do with the public good nor the approval of Masonry as such. In any case, the plans remained ideas, as the lottery raised too little money.

Another kind of corporation favored education. Foremost was the charter to a college in 1764, which was followed by the plan for another in 1770 and for some near corporations to own schoolhouses. The college had obvious precedents in adjoining colonies, where degree-granting institutions had been created by legislative decision. Thus, the proposal to charter a college in Rhode Island called for no exploration of unmapped legal ground but required only adroitness in framing its terms to accomodate local circumstances.[40]

All colonial colleges had been shaped to survive in an environment devoid of the traditional underpinnings of such institutions in Europe. Without a large landed endowment and the patronage of a rich ruling class, American colleges depended on fees, donations, and occasional governmental aid for routine operation. Lacking connections with an extensive learned community, they relied on presidential administration under a board or boards of outsiders. The small and often transient faculty had the character of employees. Even when a college had a straightforward responsibility to an established church, it also had territorial responsibility and so imposed no religious test for degrees.[41]

The charter for the College of Rhode Island, later Brown University, faced complicated conditions, and in the end it failed to satisfy all interests. Inspiration for the project came from Baptists in the Middle Atlantic colonies, who correctly estimated that Rhode Island had the resources and will to support it. The Baptists in the colony, especially the urban ones who had been moving toward respect for higher learning, wanted the institution to train their ministers and demonstrate their persuasion's intellectual respectability. They wanted a clear denominational flavor. Other churches in Rhode Island, however, also wished to support learning and insisted on interdenominationalism. The Newport patriciate fancied the college as another manifestation of their leadership, whereas Providence wanted to hold its head up higher, which set off a quarrel over where the college should be built. Because the charter was to be the product of government, competing ambitions worked through partisan politics.

In any case, the college needed incorporation for a few fundamental purposes. If all went well, it would own extensive property and manage an endowment; so it needed a corporate standing to keep the property safely in its own control. It needed a treasurer to conduct the expected flow of income and expenditures. It needed power to make and enforce rules for its internal operations, rules including discipline over students. And it needed authority to confer degrees. After some nasty incidents, a charter was written and adopted by the Assembly—but not wholly observed. It distributed seats on two governing boards so as to give clear control to the several kinds of Baptists combined. One board, the fellows, was composed of the president, James Manning, and eleven other men, mostly ministers and mostly Baptists. This board had the power to confer degrees. The other, the trustees, had assigned places for Baptists (the majority), Congregationalists, Quakers, and Anglicans, and was staffed at first by thirty-six prominent men. Succession to these positions was to be "by separate election of both branches of this corporation, which shall at all times sit and act by separate and distinct powers," an opaque formulation suggesting that each branch should keep its ranks filled by cooptation. Beyond their special authority, the fellows had to initiate all decisions on regulations "for the successful instruction and government of the said college or university," though the trustees had to ratify the conclusions of the fellows in this field. The two governing boards were to share equally in the financial management of the college.[42]

When the corporation organized in 1764, it immediately began to deviate from the plan laid out in the charter. The two governing boards did not function separately. The fellows had no use for their special power before the college existed. Moreover, in the first major business, raising money, the ministers served at least as well as laymen. Together, the boards appointed officers, including Stephen Hopkins as chancellor, and assigned various duties to an interim committee.[43] They appointed Manning as president in 1765 and adopted the disciplinary rules he wanted. He gathered his students and a small staff in Warren. At first the corporation seemed content to leave the institution there.[44]

Then the controversy over a permanent location broke out, bringing with it contests over the organization of the two boards. After some complicated maneuvers, the choice boiled down, not surprisingly, to Providence or Newport, with the decision to be made on the basis of which town gave more money. In the early phases of this rivalry, members of the Ward party wanted the two boards to vote separately. Opponents from the Hopkins side objected that doing so would give the fellows more than coordinate power, because they had fewer members. The boards faced a deadlock and decided to continue unicameral proceedings. In 1770 the Providence advocates won the institution for their town.[45] As was true of other colonial colleges, Brown was neither a strictly private nor a public corporation. Its public attributes were clear. Its commencements became public celebrations; the Governor led the procession at the first one held in Providence. The public officials among the trustees and their prominence in the corporation's affairs manifested the governmental blessing.

Although the General Assembly appropriated nothing for the college, the colonial treasury managed its funds in a very generous way after 1768. The college treasurer took the notes given as pledges of donations and other obligations to the colonial treasurer, who exchanged them for a single interest-bearing note to the college. Thus, the college converted promises and receivables into an income-earning fund at the taxpayers' expense. Of course, the charter let the college own its property safely and sue for debts, assured the donors that their gifts would be used as intended, and let the college advertise its privileges as a magnet for gifts. Incorporation put the institution out of the Assembly's control.[46]

While the college was getting started, the Assembly gave something less than corporate privileges to two societies of men in Providence who had contributed to building schoolhouses. These projects were like earlier ones

there and elsewhere, yet the promoters sought legal endorsement of practices previously followed without it. They obtained power to act by majority
vote to make rules "Valid and Binding upon . . . the Society and each member
thereof," providing their rules were not repugnant to laws of the colony or
acts or orders of the town of Providence.[47] Quite likely, the intended rules
provided a code of discipline for the classes and fees for tuition as well as assessments for repairs and conditions on continued ownership of proportional
rights in the buildings. Without charters and their traditional trappings, these
societies got what was then the essence of corporate power.

The last type of corporation created by Rhode Island in the colonial period, the water company, had consequences as great as those of the next to
last, the religious society, which will be examined in the next chapter.[48] The
water companies took on characteristics of business corporations after the
Revolution, partly because of their frustrations as private clubs before and
during the war; but even in their earliest years, they met some of the difficulties of defining ownership of shares in law and using corporate power to restrict what the shareholders might do with their rights. These organizations
were conceived, however, as associations to distribute water to their members. They needed corporate standing not only to control their source of
water and the main conduits but also to have rights to lay conduits under
public thoroughfares. Similar organizations had existed in England and English America previously, not always with benefit of incorporation. The
Rhode Island promoters could have drawn on these precedents, but there is
no sign that they did. Three companies obtained charters.

The first two were in Providence, where a growing population had spread
to low-lying areas nearly surrounded by salt water. Unable to satisfy their
needs by digging wells, people there decided to bring water by wooden conduits. In 1772, two groups organized to acquire springs and distribute water
to themselves. One found its source on land owned by John Field and took
the name of Field's Fountain Society; the other, for a parallel reason, was
Rawson's Fountain Society. The two obtained charters and later merged. The
third company, Cooke's Fountain Society in East Greenwich, got its charter
in 1773. The three charters were nearly identical.[49]

Of the three, only the records of Rawson's Fountain Society survive, so it
must be taken as illustrative of the type. It began in September 1772 on the
basis of articles of agreement, declared to be effective once eighty shares had
been subscribed for, though the members began work before they reached
that goal. The articles contained plans for the main conduits and raising a
fund to pay for them and for future development. Members had to pay for
the branches to their own houses or shops.[50]

Clumsily, the articles defined the members' rights to water. The association could limit or end service (with compensation) to manufactories if the
flow fell short, but the rules allowed conversion of a right designed for a

manufactory to one for a house without stipulating whether conversion would nullify a curtailment of service. Other provisions called for preferring service to older before newer members when a choice had to be made. To complicate the subject further, the articles declared "[t]hat the Right or Rights taken by Each and Every Proprietor shall be his, his Heirs and Assigns absolute Property" and might be transferred freely upon "giving proper Notice and Evidence" of the transfer to the organization. If rights were property essentially like land, then the organization could hardly vote them out of existence, however good the reason or fair the compensation. The only justification for nullifying the rights was the acceptance of the articles of agreement by all takers.[51]

The articles also included some practical plans. A committee would seek the "Consent of the Town" to lay conduits under the streets, make "Contracts with Persons possessing the Lands that may be affected thereby, and with the workmen to be employed," and "direct and inspect the whole Proceedings" and report periodically to the other associates. The articles concluded with a declaration that other business would be transacted by the proprietors or their officers as they saw fit from time to time but stipulated no internal organization.[52]

The proprietors soon devised an organization. They chose a moderator, clerk, and two ad hoc committees, one to draw up a lease for Rawson's spring and one to petition the Assembly for a charter. Both finished their work in a short time.[53]

The committee with the petition also presented the draft of a charter to the Assembly, for adoption. The petition claimed that the waterworks would be detrimental to nobody and would promote "the public Utility" and went on to request the proposed terms of incorporation. The charter made the society "a Body Corporate and Politic with perpetual Succession" under the name of Rawson's Fountain Society; it was able to sue and be sued, admit new members, levy assessments on its members, pass bylaws, and choose such officers as they wished at an annual meeting. The document went into detail on the water business. The company had to appoint a committee to keep the system in repair. Each member might take water for one house through pipes, installed at his own expense, to the main conduit, subject to regulation by the committee. The company might dig up any street to lay pipes, provided it made no interference with those of Field's Fountain Society and left the thoroughfares in as good repair as before. One elastic but useful clause allowed the company "to do every Lawful Matter to complete the Execution" of its plans.[54]

The society did not rely on the charter to transact business in the corporate capacity or name. The chairman of the committee still signed leases for land on behalf of the other members, "severally and not Jointly."[55] The members had individual responsibility for the society's obligations, whether for rents or workmen's wages—a serious responsibility because the company had no assets beyond the leases. The organization used the charter to give a little strength to its internal government. Without approval from the Assembly, the society merged with Field's Fountain Society through an exchange of shares.[56]

Incorporation, however, could not impose discipline on the organization. The members wasted water and failed to report leaks. They conveyed rights without notifying the clerk. Unauthorized people somehow got connected to the system. When the rules were flouted, the society's officers would not turn off the water to the delinquents. In 1781, when the company needed money, some members did not pay the assessment, and the collector would not distrain the overdue amounts "in the same Manner as Town Taxes are collected," in spite of the society's vote. The company decided to sell the delinquent shares at auction, yet even this remedy was neglected.[57]

Matters grew worse instead of better after the Revolution, and the society gave up trying to restrict distribution of water to members. Instead, it began selling water to anybody who would buy it. Thus, it turned into a business corporation. Its shares became transferable rights to proportions of the profits and were bought and sold like land. Inadvertently, Rhode Island had created the first public utility in the United States.[58]

Conclusion

The immediate background provides some reasons why the General Assembly began to authorize lotteries and incorporate nongovernmental institutions in the 1740s, a good enough explanation. Plainly, the Newport patriciate wanted to create institutions, from a select military company to a college, that would flesh out its leadership in the colony. Also, some of those institutions had to guard against disruption by the operation of inheritance and bankruptcy laws as well as by internal disagreement and external partisan rivalry. A wide range of public and private projects could seek funds through lotteries when interest money from the colony's loans had ceased to provide subsidies from the public treasury. Partisan politics in Rhode Island, particularly the rivalry between Newport and Providence, prevented confinement of lotteries and corporate charters to the Newport leadership; so sooner or later, ship captains in the capital and ambitious businessmen in competing ports could get charters, and practically anyone could try a lottery. Newport could not even capture the college.

Furthermore, plans for some nongovernmental institutions made corporate standing valuable in ways demonstrated elsewhere and known to the organizers in Rhode Island. An undertaking on the scale of the Redwood Library had to rely on an organization capable of conducting its own affairs while the roster of members continually changed. The Newport Artillery Company needed a special place in the militia system. And so on. Charter privileges could serve a variety of purposes. The first experiments in granting them proved that the colonial officials could do so without bringing down British wrath. Yet the power of internal self-government, so vital to a corporation, and a collective entity in law, vital to both corporation and lottery, had in the past required no special approval from the General Assembly. Towns and proprietors of undivided land had formed themselves. Newport created the proprietors of Long Wharf. Smaller institutions like mills had regulated themselves by articles of agreement among the partners. The family had been considered a fact of nature, given outward form at the outset by a contractual agreement between husband and wife. These kinds of association had seemed to need no delegation of authority from a central sovereignty. They could be started by the participants or by local government.

Such expectations had been unrealistic. People had sought cures for shaky institutions and for social incoherence in general. Foundations in land had seemed likely to solidify some forms of association. Towns also wanted a derivation of authority from the English government. The colonial government had assumed an indispensible function of defining or regulating—or ignoring—certain kinds of collective action. It had tried unavailingly to confer a basic set of powers on proprietors of undivided land by statute. It had chartered towns and given marriage a public dimension. It had enforced with few qualifications the standard kinds of agreement by which commerce was conducted in the British orbit. It had restricted mills in a few ways. It had provided a judiciary. This modest rationalization at first left no place for certain kinds of collective endeavor because it confined collective action by majority rule. By compressing government into a rough hierarchy and giving it a place in the British Empire, the Newport leadership brought internal order and safety from intolerable external control. The colonial courts implemented what they found useful in English law and so made ownership of property and the conduct of commerce safer than it had been in the seventeenth century. In general, this meant treating rights as individual and associations between people as contractual. The General Assembly could regulate in a comprehensive legal system those operations of nongovernmental collectivities that, for purposes of public order, had to be put beyond purely voluntary action.

This polarization left no foundation outside government for collective action by which individual rights or claims could be modified by majority rule, so any new social undertaking that required such a capacity had to be given a new form of legal standing. The authorized lottery created temporary collectivities with legal capacities and responsibilities to be exercised by the directors or a majority of them according to what settled into a standard method. Corporate charters and kindred devices created enduring bodies with a few features prescribed and others left to the members' preference. Such organizations could manage extensive property held by large and changeable numbers of people.

The new kinds of legally authorized collectivities secured a place in Rhode Island, though without a formal derivation of power from the Crown or a colonial proprietor as in other colonies. These organizations greatly enlarged the range of possibilities for action by groups of inhabitants. They did so without creating coercive institutions outside government and so left unimpaired both the individual rights of inhabitants and the monopoly of coercion in the hands of government. The corporation solved the earlier puzzle of how to create a large effective organization without entanglement with individual rights to land. And more strikingly, as will appear below, the colony's corporate charters gave churches ways to reconcile satisfaction of some new ambitions with public determination to uphold soul liberty and religious principles against anything smacking of establishment.

✣ 12 ✣

Ecclesiastical Organization and Civil Incorporation

During the late colonial period, the Rhode Island churches improved their institutional clarity and found a method to secure a place in the legal structure without compromising their religious freedom. The method was to obtain a charter of incorporation for the congregation or its affiliate. In these respects, ecclesiastical developments were like secular practice.

Among the denominations, however, elaboration of church organization was likely to occur in inverse ratio to the congregation's interest in incorporation. At one end of the scale stood the Quakers, who shunned incorporation but as usual neatly translated changes in the spiritual association into changes in their organizational forms. At the other end stood the Anglicans, who saw no need to reorganize their parishes but led the way to incorporation. In between, the various kinds of Baptists did more to spell out their ecclesiastical forms than to seek incorporation, and the Congregationalists tilted the balance in the opposite direction. In the long run, civil incorporation for religious bodies had important consequences. Though used by only a few churches, the methods devised in Rhode Island, which had counterparts in other colonies, ultimately became routine in the United States.[1]

By contrast, the foremost spiritual ferment of the time, the Great Awakening, had minor institutional consequences in Rhode Island. The revival divided Baptists and Congregationalists, but like their ancestors, they either toned down their quarrels or collapsed into schism.[2] Religious liberty meant that there was no obstacle to forming a new church. Schisms spawned by the Awakening thus proceeded virtually the same way as before. The spiritual intensity, paradoxically, inspired both sides to more precise formulation of ecclesiastical rules. Much more among the Quakers, the rough counterpart of the Awakening—the spiritual revitalization, often called a moral reform movement—directly affected church organization.

Church Politics and Denominational Ties

After 1738, churches, like civil governments, gave increased emphasis to explicit and technically adequate law, to procedure in all actions, to proper verbal formula in written statements of all kinds, and to hierarchy or its equivalent in interchurch associations. If members of the Church of England did nothing in these respects—they had already adapted parish ways to Rhode Island and were stymied in any hopes they retained for clear connections to the episcopate—other denominations did, Congregationalists less than Baptists, Baptists less than Quakers.

The Congregationalists showed little propensity for institutional precision except for church quarrels, and those quarrels revealed that the rules were there to be used as weapons. Of course, the rules would have been dull swords if the disputants had not placed a high value on correct procedure. The clearest case was in the controversy over the revival that produced a schism in Providence. All sides accepted the Cambridge Platform, approved in Massachusetts in 1648; all said they would accept the determination of a church council chosen in the correct way. Such a concession to a denominational organ in effect acknowledged a hierarchical arrangement. But the two sides interpreted the Cambridge Platform differently and never could agree on the composition of a council. The partisans of revival deposed their minister in accord, they claimed, with denominational laws. Then they organized their own church and created their own version of the rules.[3]

For Baptists, too, the Awakening stimulated appeals to the rules. Even without this revival, untroubled flocks took greater care than before to keep written records and to proceed in an orderly way. They took unprecedented pains to determine membership and ensure formality in ordinations. In the process, all kinds of Baptists developed denominational networks just as Quakers and Anglicans had done before.

Gradually, the Six Principle churches moved from simple congregational autonomy to denominationalism when they formed a church and ordained officers. When one such church formed in East Greenwich in 1743, it carefully described its procedures in writing. Some pious people met together several times, they said, then decided that God had favored them "with a minister of his word," Daniel Fish. After making sure that they were satisfied with his preaching, they concluded, "Wee think it our duty to Choose him to take the wach Care over us." That is, they intended that he be their elder. Each decision was signed in a record book by a long list of participants.[4] To them, the essence of a church was a flock of believers with a pastor to administer the sacraments, preach, and lead their ecclesiastical discipline.

In later years the process became more complex, and the founders of new churches formally sought the approval of existing ones. When a remnant of a church in Richmond contemplated a fresh start just before the Revolution, the participants explained their intentions to a conference composed of delegates from other churches. The delegates examined the principles of the new organization and the spiritual qualifications of their members, resolving some of their doubts before a second conference approved embodiment of a church. An elder from a neighboring church occasionally administered the sacraments. Once this ecclesiastical routine had been established, the group drew up its articles of faith and practice, elected a clerk, and procured a Communion service. They built a meetinghouse in 1776 but only in 1781 elevated a man to the pastorate.[5] Ordination itself was likely to be a ceremony to express denominational concurrence in the choice of an elder rather than just the congregation's election.[6]

Urban churches led the way as Baptists codified their disciplinary procedure. By 1742 the Newport Six Principle flock began recording its use of the two-admonition rule for treating a wayward member. It also prescribed formal rules for treating disputes between members over "temporal interests in personal matters."[7] Rural churches recorded such systematic procedures only after the Revolution but clearly had been using the traditional Gospel Order all along.[8]

Baptists grew more formal in defining church membership. As always, each flock defined the terms of its fellowship and ruled on admission to communion. They also gave new importance to written testimonials from previous churches when somebody transferred, rather in Quaker or Congregationalist fashion.[9] The Awakening injected its own tone into affected flocks by inspiring stress on soul-wrenching conversion experiences that had to be reported to the church. Occasionally, a Baptist church reviewed the ranks to obtain accurate lists of members and weed out those who had drifted away.[10]

Religious ferment generated attention to ties between sister churches. The revival led the Baptists through a three-stage process, taking them from the pan-Baptist solidarity of the earlier colonial period through a time of polarization during the Awakening to stricter denominational subdivisions. A rather informal general association of Baptist churches in New England had existed since 1692, composed mainly of the most numerous Six Principle churches but including no Sabbatarians.[11] In their annual meetings, elders and lay messengers discussed matters of mutual concern, such as ecclesiastical taxes, but offered no more than advice on disagreements within constituent churches. For years, disagreements on a variety of doctrines divided many flocks haphazardly. To counteract this tendency, the association built on those beliefs that distinguished Baptists in general.

It shattered after 1743, leaving only antirevivalists. By 1764 it became the organization of Six Principle churches. The partisans of the Awakening at first associated with their counterparts in the Congregationalist tradition, commonly called "Separates" in Connecticut and Massachusetts, but then began to oppose open communion and to insist on adult believer baptism.

Efforts to form an association on open communion led to a split by 1754. For a time, a Six Principle Calvinistic Baptist Association straddled the fence between the old and new ways, but ultimately the predestinarians became such militant advocates of congregational autonomy that they only reluctantly formed even those institutions designed for them alone.[12] Revivalist Baptists clearly wanted to coalesce, but their attempts kept failing. Forming a church and ordaining its officers no longer was to be simply the business of the flock. Baptists went about as far as Congregationalists toward creating a church hierarchy.

Quakers, of course, already had devised a well-constructed pyramid of meetings to exercise collective authority in the church. The spiritual revitalization accompanying the Great Awakening, however, led to additions and revisions as the denomination exhibited new zeal in purifying the members' behavior, preserving unity in belief, and urging separation from the world, even to the point of shunning public office. At the basic level of the monthly meetings for discipline, little structural change took place. These meetings always had had the task of curbing sin. After prompting from the men's yearly meeting in 1755, they revived the neglected device of committees to visit families and began to send detailed written replies to the quarterly meeting's queries. Some meetings were reluctant to commit their replies to paper, so the yearly meeting resorted to a new device, a standing committee of its own, to put pressure on the heel-draggers. This committee, eschewing the usual hierarchical arrangement, dealt with two layers below it, monthly as well as quarterly meetings, instead of just one. The first such committee was succeeded by two slightly different ones, the second being concerned mainly with slavery; the third, a permanent new organ of the church called the Meeting for Sufferings.[13] Begun as an agency to distribute aid to Quaker victims of warfare and to act for the church in any emergency between sessions of the yearly meeting, the Meeting for Sufferings settled into the role of all-purpose interim committee quite soon. It made provisional rulings on ethical questions, arranged publication of denomination literature, corresponded with counterparts in other yearly meetings, and in general did all that a newly centralized church needed.

The first committee looked beyond the accustomed ways of the meetings for discipline. It found a disturbing incidence of non-Quaker conduct and ignorance of Quaker standards and proposed new methods to stimulate reform. It began to encourage new strictness in educating children, the goal being to put pupils into Quaker-taught segregated schools sponsored by monthly meetings. Newport had sponsored such schools before but never managed to maintain them for long. Elsewhere they were impractical. Ultimately, the yearly meeting set a new goal of bringing the children together in a denominational boarding school, but that plan, too, was impractical for many years.[14]

With ignorance, even illiteracy, disturbingly common and those most ignorant also apt to be least able to afford a Quaker schooling for their children, zealots for reform had to think of educating adults. At least every household should have a Bible. Monthly meetings should have libraries of denominational books. But nothing in print would help those who could not read. So the reformers fell back on encouraging the leadership to read the staples of Quaker literature and persuading the yearly meeting to sponsor republication of such items as the main writings of Robert Barclay.[15]

The second of the yearly meetings's succession of standing committees had the special goal of bringing conformity to the new standards of conduct in respect to slavery. The old standards defined in the queries had required Friends to have nothing to do with the slave trade and to treat slaves in a Christian manner. Even these rules were ignored, as the replies to queries revealed. After much pondering, the yearly meeting in 1769 decided that the old rules had been self-contradictory because a Christian should not own a slave. The yearly meeting's committee insisted that all Quakers must free their slaves. If a Quaker failed to do so, he or she would be disowned by the monthly meetings. This moral reform led indirectly to the separation of Quakers from public office. Several men in high places were expelled from their meetings; other Friends could no longer serve in places where they would administer the law of slavery.[16]

The campaign to insist on conformity to Quaker standards led to new clarification of the rules of membership in the church and expulsion of many persons who did not meet the test. The reformers accepted a loose definition of who was a Quaker and tried to make it logical. People considered themselves Friends because their parents had been or because they had married under the supervision of a monthly meeting. Probably some who began to attend meetings had been casually assimilated as members. The yearly meeting committee prevailed upon monthly meetings to cull out reputed or self-styled Quakers who failed to live by Quaker standards and to accord formal membership to those who qualified for it but lacked any outward sign of obtaining it. For the first time, monthly meetings drew up lists of members, expelled incorrigible sinners or people who had drifted away, and sifted the rest. The Aquidneck Friends reluctantly agreed to follow these procedures only in 1771.[17]

Then the yearly meeting could proceed to codify regulations on the subject of membership. Birthright membership, long a matter of common expectation, was extended only to children born of two Quaker parents in good standing who had married in meeting. Any others could become members only by formal admission. They had to be examined by a committee of a monthly meeting and be found to know and endorse Quaker teachings, live by them, attend meetings for worship, and accept the church discipline for themselves and their families. Furthermore, in the future, no couples might marry in meeting unless they both were members in good standing and approved for marriage by the men's and women's meetings.[18]

Parallel to the tightening of discipline among the membership at large, the meetings of ministers and elders, or select meetings, improved their organization beginning in 1755. The yearly meeting in that pyramid required written replies to a slate of queries from all subordinate meetings and insisted that all meetings have elders. Wherever they were missing, select meetings were created to complete a parallel to the meetings for discipline at all four levels. Though the select meetings remained somewhat inchoate until 1770, they soon accepted responsibility to preserve orthodoxy within the fold and ceased to have duties to present Quakerism to outsiders. Proselytizing was an odd victim of reformist rigor. But Quakers decisively turned against any blurred edges around their church. Members had to be in conformity with sectarian rules or be expelled. No laxity could be tolerated. Purity must come before numbers.[19]

Urban Churches, Property, and Incorporation

While the spiritual ferments of the late colonial period led the affected churches to rule-mindedness, as well as some institutional modifications and denominational consciousness, older tendencies led to more significant results. Respect for traditional Christianity advanced along with the search for ways to give churches a place in a legal system where religious liberty prevailed. The search culminated in new institutional devices, especially the incorporation of a church or something close to it. Seven urban churches won incorporation in three distinct varieties, and the Newport Friends contrived a similar means to manage their property. The three varieties highlight both the differing purposes of the churches concerned and also the religious conundrum that resulted from seeking a secular declaration of the rules for conducting a spiritual association.[20]

The Anglican churches of Newport and Providence presented the simplest cases. They found their circumstances less than satisfactory in both theory and practice. The Church of England in the parent country enjoyed the benefits of taxation and endowments, ascribed (or common law) corporate standing that facilitated management of property, and a partnership with government that gave the church coercive and judicial powers and a near monopoly of royal favor. None of these privileges except a trifling endowment existed in Rhode Island, but the Anglicans yearned for them. Without involuntary support they had to depend on pew taxes, subscriptions to annual contributions, weekly collections, and donations from the Society for the Propagation of the Gospel in Foreign Parts (S.P.G.).

Trinity Church in Newport found these sources inadequate, and in 1767 it sought a charter of incorporation. The congregation voted for a special pew tax to pay part of the price for repairing the steeple and then obtained permission to raise twice as much more by a lottery. Next, the vestry found it hard to collect the tax to pay the minister and had to sue for overdue rent on some of the church's property and borrow more. Conditions grew worse the next year, when the lottery was a disappointment and the carpenters had to be paid with more borrowed money.[21] At that point, the vestry petitioned for a charter, primarily to strengthen the pew tax.

There could have been little doubt that the Assembly could gratify this wish. It had chartered secular corporations already, and colonial governors had chartered Anglican parishes in other colonies. At most, somebody in England might object to the terms or the lack of cooperation with the episcopal hierarchy. Massachusetts, however, in 1755 had authorized a coercive pew tax for Anglican churches without making them comparable to English parishes.[22]

The church's petition came close to complaining of the religious liberty in Rhode Island. The Newport Anglicans traced their woes to "their not being able by any Laws of this Colony to carry into Execution any Laws or Rules that may be agreed to by the Majority of the Congregation." They wanted a power to coerce negligent members and so asked that the minister, wardens, vestry, and congregation be made a body corporate and politic, empowered to make bylaws by majority vote. The charter would do no more; it would have no effect on the organization of the church or on outsiders. The petition included a promise, backed by the signatures of the wardens and seventy others, that granting it would not contravene colonial policy.[23]

The Assembly complied, allowing the church to make bylaws by majority vote, provided "[t]hat such Laws, Rules and Ordinances be not repugnant to any Laws of this Colony."[24] It is hard to see how the proviso could be met while Trinity Church used corporate powers to enforce a pew tax.

Regardless of how the act might be construed, it did in fact achieve its purpose. The congregation chose a committee, including a lawyer, to prepare a slate of bylaws. The church revised the tax and within a year directed the wardens to sue delinquent pewholders, a step that was repeated before long.[25] The Anglicans of King's Church in Providence followed nearly the same path as those of Trinity. Disappointed in their efforts to raise money by lotteries, they obtained a charter in 1772 almost identical to that for the Newport church.[26]

The near silence of the acts of incorporation on the internal polity of the corporation deserves comment. The Assembly, surely acting at the churches' request, accepted the existing form of ecclesiastical government. The main elements of the Trinity bylaws clearly came from Anglican tradition as adapted to Rhode Island. The inclusion of the congregation expressed a religiously straightforward, if practically vague, concept of who formed the church. (It also differed from Massachusetts law, which had incorporated the church wardens alone.)[27] Membership was not clearly defined. Regardless of this foggy point, incorporation was intended to create a legal obligation to promises by members, and therefore the entire congregation had to be made members of the corporation.

A second sort of incorporation appeared in two cases during the colonial period, one connected with the older Congregational church in Providence and the other with the Baptist church there.[28] These organizations sought incorporation for a money-raising society distinct from the church or congregation or even the traditional society. The religious fellowship as such formed no overt connection to secular authority and thus preserved the tradition of religious liberty better than the other two kinds of incorporation did. All the same, various clauses, including ones on disposition of the assets of the corporation in the event of its demise, sketched the institutional forms and basic beliefs of the related churches.

Providence's first Congregational organization had the usual elements of church, congregation, society, and executive committee. However, it was almost dying of apathy and poverty. It struggled along with aid from a Boston committee, a feeble pew tax, subscriptions, and gifts, until in 1762 it finally secured the services of a reasonably effective pastor, David Sherman Rowland. But then the Bostonians cut off subsidies, and Rowland's salary went unpaid. In hope of curing these woes, Jonathan Badger, a wealthy member, proposed the creation of a distinct institution to raise money, the Benevolent Congregational Society. It formed in 1770 and soon obtained a charter of incorporation. Badger and the Congregational clergymen of nearby churches thought along thoroughly traditional lines about the function of a corporate charter. They expected this official sanction to encourage contributions, partly by prestige and partly by assuring the donors that their gifts would go to the end they intended. Badger and his friends also thought the scheme would overcome the difficulties imposed by Rhode Island's law on religious liberty.[29]

The new society had the usual corporate attributes: power to act by majority vote, have a corporate name, hold and improve property of all kinds, act as a party in litigation, use a seal, make bylaws, and so forth. The charter specified the basic routines of internal operation, such as the time of the annual meeting and essential officers.[30]

The corporation quickly began to deviate from the founders' vision. The turn in a new direction was almost implicit in the charter's clauses on the capital fund. The society was to raise money with dues and donations, first to accumulate a stock that would be invested to provide income to pay the minister's salary and beyond that for other pious purposes. The assets of the corporation, if it dwindled below the charter quorum of seven members, would devolve upon the Congregational society—that is, the male members of church and congregation. A slate of bylaws and early decisions by the corporation elaborated the charter provisions.[31] The society in truth was little more than a fund-raising club.

Badger's device proved its worth to the Baptist flock in Providence. Upon the choice of James Manning as pastor, this church changed abruptly from its old rural ways to a radically different tone, marked by a paid ministry, a costly meetinghouse (with steeple!), and important ancillary property. The institutional expression of the metamorphosis was not only a more precise definition of the elements within the ecclesiastical complex than had been useful before but also the incorporated Charitable Baptist Society, technically outside it. The sudden shift in Providence had an obvious occasion, the location of the college in town. Leading members of the flock wanted President Manning to have a salary as well as a pulpit in a meetinghouse where commencements might be held.

Even the process of erecting the new meetinghouse required institutional innovation. The organization of the ecclesiastical complex had to be clarified, primarily to give the society scope for action. The Baptists needed the Assembly's permission to seal the site of the old meetinghouse, contrary to the stipulations of the donors, and buy a lot for the new one.[32] The society used an old-fashioned subscription to raise part of the fund and expected to raise more by sale of the previous site and of pews in the new edifice, but it still had to close a gap and provide for Manning's salary. To get the money, the Baptists obtained permission for a lottery, which was successful, and petitioned for a charter for a society like the Benevolent Congregational Society, this one to be the Charitable Baptist Society.[33]

The charter for the new corporation was in most respects like the older one, but it specified more about the internal organization and less about the associated ecclesiastical institution. The corporation was to accumulate a fund, invested as it saw fit, for religious uses as the Providence Baptist Church. The first £100 in annual income would support the pastor or pastors. Other clauses allowed the society to respect the wishes of donors, thus letting it hold property for a variety of purposes.[34]

At once, the society began to do more than accumulate a ministerial endowment. It charged its members dues and fines for absences from meetings. It circulated a subscription paper and took the occasion to renounce any intention of invoking the authority of the courts. It opposed both compulsion by the state and "the majority of a particular Society disfranchising any member or members who refuse to pay any Tax or proportion." Both methods were called "antichristian and intolerant."[35] The corporation obviously conceived of itself simply as a property-managing affiliate of the church. Thus, its intention was roughly the opposite of the Anglicans who had procured charters. The corporation for the benefit of a church could be reconciled with religious liberty. In this case, too, the corporation was a great success.

While the Providence flock departed from the ways of other Baptists, the Newport churches and even some rural Six Principle congregations headed in the same direction. After the Revolution, financial hardship and growing reliance on adherents outside the church proper led several Six Principle churches to seek incorporation, but most predestinarian Baptists looked on this expedient, as they had long looked on lotteries, as an improper allocation of power to the unregenerate, if not subordination to secular authority.[36]

The third kind of ecclesiastical corporation grew out of the interactions (1) between some members of the second Congregational flock in Newport and its pastor, Ezra Stiles, and (2) between their proposal and the General Assembly's objections to it. The result was a charter that neither gave teeth to a pew tax in the Anglican fashion nor incorporated a society distinct from the spiritual association as in Providence. Rather, the document served mainly to give a legal description to the ecclesiastical complex of church, congregation, and society. This plan was imitated during the colonial period by the other Congregational flock in Newport and the new one in East Greenwich.

The occasions and the results were different in the two places and so cast doubts on the practical value of this form of incorporation. The people in East Greenwich wanted a charter to stimulate formation of a church and accumulation of property for it, but little came of these hopes for many years. Certainly, the charter was no magic wand.[37] On the contrary, neither Newport congregation faced a financial crisis or any other special need to solidify the basic organization. The impulses, as known in Stiles's flock, were to preserve property more effectively than before and to guard against deviation from existing religious principles, but no threat loomed to either, so the effectiveness of the charter remains problematical.

Action began in Stiles's flock in 1770, when the society set out to tidy up its arrangements to control property. Some members suggested adopting Badger's plan for Providence, by incorporating either a new society or the existing one, composed of the men in the church and congregation. Stiles objected to both ideas, insisting that the church proper must be recognized and assured of its rights. Indeed, he thought incorporation was unnecessary and might inadvertently make mischief for the future even if it could be done in accord with Christian principles. Nevertheless, he agreed to draft a document to submit to the General Assembly. After prayerful cogitation, he decided that governmental endorsement could be harmless. In contrast to some, he favored letting the congregation join with the church in the choice of a minister, for the pastor should be *"totally dependent on his Flock . . . at all Times,"* even if he might suffer at their hand undeservedly. Advocates of incorporation yielded to Stiles on making the church a vital element in the plan.[38]

In turn, Stiles yielded to them, accepting a clause to authorize a pew tax to finance repairs of the meetinghouse and manse, though he thought a compulsory tax would be useless. It would drive away opponents when it was needed and would be unnecessary when everyone paid voluntarily. Besides, it would antagonize the General Assembly, to which "every Thing that had the Appearance of a Taxation for Religion, enforceable at Law, was obnoxious." In the end the Assembly gave the corporation no more than a power to make regulations on a pew tax.[39]

Early in the deliberations, Stiles wrestled with other desires of the laymen. Some of them wanted to protect the doctrinal tenets of the church by putting them into the charter. At first Stiles worried that such stipulations might be tailored to the General Assembly's views. But he decided that "we did not consider the Gener[eral] Assem[bly] as having power to constitute us as a Church of Christ, or of their own Authority to define the Ministry therein: but we had a right to declare ourselves and to define the Ministry, to whose use we requested a legal (as well as spiritual) Corporation." As he pondered the history of New England Congregationalism, he produced formulations that would accommodate all the varieties within it that he thought were legitimate and yet would rule out what he thought were the lurking dangers, such as Baptist or Catholic principles.[40] Eventually, the congregation agreed to ask for a charter "to secure the Perpetuity of the Grant."[41]

When the church and society approved the draft, a committee put it before the Assembly. Stiles feared that all other denominations would oppose it, especially Baptists and Quakers, who militantly opposed any whiff of establishment. He interpreted the debate and vote in the House of Deputies with these thoughts in mind, but his report revealed a more complex response. The opposition appeared, and much of it indeed came from Baptists and Quakers, but it also clearly emanated from the Hopkins party in the northern towns. Both Hopkins himself and his ally, Moses Brown, opposed the charter. However, the Newport delegation, composed of men of both parties, favored it, which Stiles explained by saying that although most of them were Anglicans they feared losing the votes of his parishioners. When Moses Brown proposed to substitute a parallel to the incorporation of Trinity Church, Stiles's chief representative, Henry Marchant, replied that to squeeze Congregationalists into the Anglican mold would violate religious liberty. Finally, the deputies gave the charter a majority of three votes. Governor Wanton, a Newport Anglican and nominal chief of the Hopkins party, steered it easily through the upper house.[42]

The resulting charter covered the main structural features of the ecclesiastical complex and brushed aside old difficulties in defining the congregation. The document made the "Church and Congregation," not just the church and society, "a Body Corporate and Politick, with perpetual Succession," under the name of "the *Second Congregational Church in Newport Rhode Island*." The corporation might own and improve all sorts of property and use it for the support of pastors, relief of the poor, and other religious uses. The charter gave a special standing to an institutional arm that had grown without much definition, the "Committee of said Body Corporate and politic" or their successors in office. In their names, the congregation might be a party in any kind of litigation.

The charter defined the congregation as those who at any time "usually assemble together for public Worship in the *Meetinghouse in Clark Street* in Newport . . . belonging to the second Congregational Church," and included no formal requirements for admission. Anyone departing from belief in presbyterian ordination or the prevailing mode of worship of the church, however, would cease to be a member. The document included no rules on voting, but it endorsed the existing practice of calling or dismissing pastors by concurrent majority votes of church and congregation (the charter meant the men) and prescribed a procedure for summoning meetings for this purpose. The church proper might own property separate from the congregation. Additional provisions dealt with regular officers. Though not explicitly, the charter made the society the chief governing institution. Nothing in the charter made ordinary congregational decisions binding on the minority, but the binding nature could have been argued from the wording all the same.[43]

This tactful document adjusted the Congregational polity as it had developed in Massachusetts to circumstances in Rhode Island. Strong theological underpinnings had always sustained the church proper, but the rest of the system had grown awkwardly out of the assumption that a church was in a territorial parish where it held a religious monopoly. The Massachusetts practice, whereby voters in the parish had levied ecclesiastical taxes and gained a voice in management of temporalities and hiring a minister, had accommodated realities when the church came to comprise a small portion of the resident adults. Nothing but the denominational custom of exclusive communion had extended this system to Rhode Island. The charter bridged the gap. It gave a legal rather than theological or traditional territorial foundation for the congregation or society while preserving a distinct existence for the church composed of those admitted to communion.

When the other Congregational flock in Newport in 1773 asked for a charter, it asked for one "incorporating this first congregational Society into a Body Politic similar to that granted to Dr. Stiles Society." The result was nearly a duplicate, but a few changes of wording improved the text.[44] The Revolution disrupted the church before implementation of these rules had more than begun. Nevertheless, they revealed a more extensive value for incorporation than had appeared in Stiles's flock.

The Quaker Variant

In view of the flexibility of the corporate device, the question arises of why Quakers did not make use of it during the colonial period. They had been the canniest denomination in Rhode Island in management of temporalities. They had an ingrained opposition to seeking governmental recognition, but they surely availed themselves of the courts and the law. More likely, they found it possible to achieve as much as they reasonably could expect by developing means already familiar to them. In doing that, the Newport Friends came remarkably close to creating a counterpart of a society in either the usual or the Providence version.

Reliance on trustees to hold church property served most meetings well enough but produced something like a society in the Congregational fashion in connection with the endowment lands at Easton's Point in Newport. The story resembled that of the Grand Committee. For years, the property was a cornucopia of benefits for the Rhode Island Monthly Meeting. No difficulties arose from the easygoing system by which the meeting set policy when it wished and chose an advisory committee and a collector for the trustees (rather like the Keeper of the Grand Committee's office). The meeting even strengthened the trustees' hands by disowning members who refused to pay back rents. Midcentury wars slowed collection; peace only seemed to improve things.[45]

Trouble began with the deterioration of the old-tenor pound and was aggravated by practices of at least one collector (reminiscent of Jahleel Brenton). The trustees began to set rents in silver on lands they sold after 1752, but that was too late to prevent the declining value of rents in currency. When the colony began the switch to Lawful Money, it provided the trustees with legally enforceable rates of conversion of old-tenor obligations to the new standard, with the cooperation of the monthly meeting. The Friends began a campaign of persuasion and litigation to halt the erosion of their assets.[46] Evidently, they had no difficulty in bringing actions without benefit of corporate standing.

The efforts to overhaul the system led to an inspection of the accounts of the collector, Samuel Easton, and his dismissal. After resisting for a while, he finally transferred his papers and duties to Edward Thurston, who had been the trustees' attorney.[47]

The meeting reorganized the system in 1773. It installed new trustees and a new advisory committee; the two panels together were called the proprietors, and they took a more active role than their predecessors had done and may have contributed generously on assuming office.[48] They conducted business with their own committees and kept close watch over the collector's books. For all their energies, however, the Revolution reduced their affairs to a shambles. They never fully recovered. Nevertheless, the reorganization of 1773 created an unincorporated counterpart of the Charitable Baptist Society—or more loosely, the societies of the various Congregational churches. The proprietors had trouble in suits to adjust the rents, but not for lack of a charter. They could act in a collective capacity quite safely. The reorganization and the processes leading up to it also resembled the Assembly's treatment of the Grand Committee. The meeting's committee had a part like the Assembly's audit committees; the collector, like the Keeper's. The Quakers, however, had the superior reform.

Conclusion

The religious institutions in Rhode Island during the late colonial period illustrated the variety or even Babel lurking in religious liberty, yet the record reveals more. The effects of the Awakening in this colony were less disruptive, whether to churches or the social fabric or political ties, than in many others because liberty left no solid walls to be knocked down. There was no establishment to attack or take over. The spiritual tone of most revivalist Baptists harmonized with local tradition. Controversy merely encouraged formalization in the conduct of churches, whether they were for or against the Awakening.

The theme of rambling diversity might be extended in several directions, such as the continuing tendency to stratify religion in social levels or in the distinctions between urban and rural. Clearly, the religions and churches reflected secular society more than they shaped it. Still, the stratification had not yet reached extremes. If the wealthy, powerful, ambitious, and British-oriented gravitated to the Church of England in disproportionate numbers, they joined a mixed assortment. People of prominence, like others, embraced all persuasions or none.

Freedom and the possibilities opened by the social order created in the early eighteenth century accounted for much of the institutional development. Congregationalists (or most of them) and Anglicans continued to want a framework of law and denominational rules. So they kept ties to Boston and London, respectively. They learned to use Rhode Island law to serve their own purposes, however, and the urban flocks found a substitute for establishment in incorporation. Baptists followed them only in Providence, nearly adopting Congregational ways, and then eschewing compulsion under any guise. Especially in the incorporated society theoretically outside the ecclesiastical complex, a few Rhode Island churches found a model for inserting a church into the legal system for practical matters and controlling mundane affairs, a model that they adapted to religious organizations throughout the United States. Even charters designed to give force to a church's internal government kept a clear barrier between the fellowship and the secular state. The legislature would approve the ecclesiastical polity, sometimes over the objections of those who saw a charter as a violation of the policy of soul liberty, and let the courts enforce the organization's rules in limited ways.

All the same, Rhode Island's practice gave reasonable safety to a variety of churches without charters and without impairing liberty. The casual methods of the early Baptists still served many flocks. The Quaker methods of trustee-ship, adapted by some Congregationalists and Baptists, successfully used land law and a sympathetic judiciary.[49] Churches could use as much formality as they liked and form associations with each other according to their lights. The whole spectacle illustrated the possibilities for freedom of action within a centrally managed legal system.

Retrospect

In Rhode Island, the last decades of the colonial period brought to flower many of the possibilities opened in the early eighteenth century and made places for a few new forms of organization. A growing population with ambitions to enrich its life or bring predictability to a turbulent time produced methods of collective action suited to a great variety of ends. The basic decision to make government the one institution capable of imposing a collective decision on an individual, already implemented in most respects, required some elaboration of the governmental organs to accomplish an increasing number of tasks. An elastic fabric of colonial law kept town government within the system without destroying localism. The General Assembly, furthermore, began to use governmental authority to support nongovernmental collectivities in two ways: deliberately by authorizing lotteries and chartering corporations and indirectly by sanctioning judicial enforcement of private agreements. Social policy loosely guided how these aids should be applied, but acceptance of the main traits of English law made private action in several respects seemingly independent of the Assembly's wishes.

The final pattern of institutions exhibited a blend of central control and looseness, a pattern quite different from the one outlined in the colonial charter. That document, read literally, prescribed a central government of wide powers, mentioned towns briefly, and limited legislative discretion by stipulations such as those requiring religious liberty and approximate concord with English law. As usual in the seventeenth century, the charter gave the Governor and Council predominance that they could not in fact exercise. Rather, the representative link to the towns gained significance; but even so, the colonial government could act only in limited spheres—and not very effectively in them. Towns, frail as they were, remained the arenas for more public action. The eighteenth-century reforms subordinated towns and built up the importance of the deputies in the General Assembly and, by the 1740s, elaborated the central government in so many ways as to create specialized organs under control of the Assembly as a whole.

All the same, towns remained vital in the system. If the special qualities implanted by their founders had faded away, the towns cultivated new distinctive traits even though colonial law made their governments formally alike. Commercial Newport and agricultural Middletown, for instance, for all their interlinked interests, could not remain united. Beyond the basic plan of organization, general law, even when it had a peremptory tone, often did no more than enable towns to act if they saw fit. The price of successful central government in the eighteenth century was accommodation to localism, which contributed to restraints on public authority in many ways.

And if the diversity of town government was palpable, the diversity of nongovernmental action was wider by far. Only a few towns could put their poor in workhouses; only Newport could support institutions like the Redwood Library and the Fellowship Club. Urban and rural churches took strikingly different courses, nowhere more obvious than among the predestinarian Baptists. In Providence they had a paid and learned clergy, civil incorporation, and a lottery; their rural brethren avoided all these reforms.

Apart from a few features dictated in Whitehall, Rhode Island's institutions throughout the colonial period acted with the consent of the active participants, rather than by such determinants as status or hereditary right. The consent was to the terms of association. This qualification was important. The concept of consent had settled into a broad meaning that it has kept ever since. Status implied a set of duties and prerogatives according to place in a hierarchy. High status or hereditary authority produced an undifferentiated power to command those below and generally required personal loyalty from them. But consent on set limits to rights and obligations required loyalty to correct procedures.

By the eighteenth century, consent covered a broad spectrum. It might be to a marriage, where the vows resulted in an association largely governed by custom, but in Rhode Island the Assembly and the courts treated the agreement between spouses as a contract rather than an objectification of divine or natural law. Entering the contract required observance of forms prescribed by law, and release from it required a judicial ruling that the contract had been broken by failure of one party to meet the terms. Consent also might be to articles of agreement that created a mercantile firm or some other kind of partnership. Or it might be to join a church fellowship, which rested on shared principles, often formulated in a covenant or other formal declaration of adherence to the ecclesiastical rules.[1] The new nongovernmental corporations were grounded on consent blessed by a delegation of authority from the colonial government. The terms of association had to be accepted by the participants and changed only by methods to which they agreed. The consequences of breaking the agreements in secular organizations that controlled property often were decided in court, but religious fellowships could do no more than expel the wayward.

Government alone was monopolistic and exerted power over persons who did not participate in it. For the voters, subjection to its powers might be involuntary in the sense that it came with residence or ownership of land within the jurisdiction, but residence and ownership were formally voluntary. To be sure, a majority of the population fell outside the category of active participants in government. In addition to children, all women, slaves, Indians, free non-Whites, poor Protestant White men, and all Catholics and Jews, no matter how prosperous, were excluded from the suffrage. The laws applied to them all the same. The only known objections to these exclusions came from a few Jews. Yet the body politic proper comprised a large portion of the adult male population by eighteenth-century standards, and it had an extraordinary control over its affairs, whether in town meetings or in the election of officials. Thus, it approximated government by consent.

The forms of private organizations suited their purposes but usually had a variant of one basic pattern. Most often the members, as equals, chose a few officers and perhaps an executive committee and adopted some basic bylaws; yet they often continued to make day-to-day decisions. This simple plan served such diverse institutions as the parents' associations to operate schools, Anglican parishes, the Fellowship Club, and the Redwood Library after its building was completed. Even organizations that could apportion voting rights to shares often did not. Baptist and Congregationalist churches, however, produced more elaborate structures when they accepted the consequences of an exclusive membership in the spiritual body by making places in the governance for the male members of the church proper and the congregation, as well as part of a society.

The pyramids of Quaker meetings, as always, remained a special case. Their basic design was a product of a different place and time, when Friends had sought to achieve an effective ecclesiastical discipline without giving up a spiritist religion as a defense against hostility from the surrounding population. Rhode Island Quakers had no need to defend themselves, but the structure worked well there nevertheless and could be revised to suit changing aspirations in the fellowship. Alone in the colony, Quakers had a hierarchical arrangement and specialized organs comparable to the government's.

In nearly all institutions except the family, explicit rules came to govern association and so to limit collective power. The more rules, bylaws, articles of agreement, or contracts an institution observed, the less it could expand and change shape freely, the less it could be an all-embracing social entity.

The Quakers afforded a good example. In the early days, they had used only rudimentary written regulations. Epistles by leading Friends, formally no more than advisory, often were more explicit than minutes agreed to by the meetings. The meetings provided close to a comprehensive social setting for the members. With the elaboration of rules came limitation as well as precision in the church's demands on the members.

Changes in the forms of institutions, like the tendency to base them on individual consent, took place in the presence of a social configuration that distorted the meaning of equality of voices. Laws were written to serve the wishes of the rich. Political apathy kept many ordinary inhabitants away from elections and town meetings. In Newport, often only a tiny portion of the freemen attended. Prominent men in the cities and the Narragansett towns had a disproportionate influence on public business. The corresponding concentration of power, however, never got a legal underpinning in Rhode Island and so remained unsolid. The colony lacked a legally privileged class, an established church, a substantial tenantry. Even servitude for Whites was limited to a term of years. Among Protestant White men, only a property qualification separated the freemen from the rest, and this was a barrier that could be crossed. No Old World class structure distributed power. Rather, a color and a gender line—and in the case of Catholics (if there were any) and Jews, a religious line—marked off the minorities ineligible for the franchise.

Similarly, government smiled on more than a ruling class. Except when they included all people in a congregation as members, corporate charters during the colonial period went no further down the social scale than sea captains and up-and-coming commercial people of the middle ranks, but others probably had no ability to take advantage of such benefits. When the Assembly faced pleas from towns for subsidies for roads, from operators of mills for rights to use rivers, or from the many petitioners (including bankrupts and impecunious Baptist churches) who wanted to raise money by lotteries, it distributed the favors freely.

Institutional forms, of course, revealed less than the whole truth. Participation in most nongovernmental associations had some potential for creating or strengthening social bonds. Marriage did so on a broad scale, of course. But so did collective action for ostensibly narrow purposes, such as forming a true church of Christ or making money. Neighbors in one church ran a water system. Business partnerships, begun in friendship or a tutelary relation, led to tight personal bonds or family alliances through marriage. Churches recognized only vague boundaries to their operations and often accepted traditional duties, such as educating children, without demanding tight logic to connect them to their primary spiritual functions. They accepted a broad social role while justifying it on religious grounds. The ties formed in these associations might extend across the generations. Reliance on consent and contract certainly did not atomize society, but neither did it create rigid stratification.

* * *

When taking a retrospective look at Rhode Island, it should be possible to form some estimates of how closely the pattern of institutional changes there resembled other mainland colonies.

The developments around Narragansett Bay during the colonial period could not wholly replace the original ways of life. Organizational practices had moved at a fitful pace away from the world that had fostered the first settlements and that had once seemed possible, even inevitable for the colonists to imitate. Granted that there was great variety among English villages and towns, yet they had a consistency of style. The Rhode Island founders imagined that they could adopt some traits of Old World communities for their own purposes. They could abandon many common elements they had known at home, such as a monopolistic church, the remains of the manorial system, and the hierarchy of justice and administration under royal authority. Thus, they could design still further variations on familiar patterns, even in the distinctly utopianized manner of Providence.

They could adopt many practices that had been common in the parent country, such as the arrangement of houses and fields or the rudiments of self-government. They could allocate land to create any pattern of social ranks they favored. They could award monopoly privileges to men who would promise to use them to supply what their neighbors wanted, such as a gristmill or tavern, at prices set by the community. But they could not offer the settlers the essence of traditional sanctions. Old World villages rested on the subconscious belief that they were real entities and that what was done in the past was right because it had been done time out of mind and therefore should be continued. The Rhode Island founders, on the other hand, had to seek quite different justifications for what they did, and they thought about them hard and deeply.

At first they invoked the universal and timeless, whether in abstract ideas, the will of God, or the common practices of mankind. The practical attributes of village life, no matter how traditional they appeared, could not be stabilized on these foundations. The settlers resisted equality or inequality of land allocations as well as the methods of self-government. They disputed the justifications they themselves had created. Nor could the founders achieve much by a coalition of towns to create a theoretically higher source of authority than the village. They had to appeal to something with a traditional validity, the English monarchy, but unfortunately they did so at the very time when the monarchy was being defeated in a revolution. Only fears of hostility by their neighbors—more the English colonials than the Indians—held the young towns together.

On the mundane level, these fears that focused on the issue of internal quarrels over rights and external threats from claims by adjoining colonies could be countered by redefining political or communal association based on a shared control of land. What had been at the outset the product of group decision became its foundation. This redefinition took place just before a genuine attachment to the monarchy became possible.

On the religious level, the founders feared forcible interference with their forms of leading a godly life. They rejected most of what other English people held to be sanctioned by the past or by divine revelation; they made no avowed selection among Old World practices but instead appealed to their own understandings of the history and inner meaning of Christianity. Precedent sanctioned by God's will might fit an abstract formula of tradition, but it was only a dead theory, because in practice it called for radical novelties. Detested by practically everyone else and usually fighting among themselves, the Rhode Island dissidents, to live with each other, had to reject the tradition of unity in religion and affirm soul liberty.

Distinctive though the record of early Rhode Island was, it shared important features with other English colonies. Notoriously, no two of these jurisdictions ever were quite alike, so similarities must be sought at ascending levels of abstraction. The four towns that later formed New Hampshire afford the closest parallel. They, like the four Rhode Island towns, were founded as independent communities characterized by discordant religions. Their settlers quarreled over land and self-government. They too acted together somewhat ineffectually, as a result of fears of outside interference. They too sought a connection with an external source of authority—in their case, a merger with Massachusetts and, in their case, because of fears of Indians rather than English neighbors.[2]

Yet virtually all New England towns formed in the first half century or more devised their own social and governmental arrangements and came to shift their senses of themselves from shared pursuit of a good community to shared control of land. In many places, proprietary rights became distinct from residency; limits had to be set on the use of commons. The specifics differed, but the phenomena were pervasive. For all, colonial governments had limited functions distinct from local, with town government operating in its own ways in its own ample sphere. Even the seemingly homogeneous congregations of Connecticut and Massachusetts were in fact characterized by considerable variety.[3] Throughout the region, people were making selective use of the Old World past and the precedents of Christian history to create social arrangements that bore a visible likeness to English ways while at the same time serving to make what the organizers believed would be improvements on or purifications of what they had known before emigration. Quite consistently, the settlers rejected all the trappings of manorialism and reduced the variety of authority-wielding institutions found in England to a simple hierarchy.[4]

Nor were the New England settlers unique in their use of the familiar. The record of early Virginia displays a different kind of confidence that solid truths of English life could be transported across the Atlantic even while the corporate sponsors dictated a set of relations among people quite out of the ordinary for England. That is, the Virginia Company expected rank in the Old World to inhere in its employees or servants, though that rank might be suspended for the purpose of putting these men into a table of organization. Later, the company assumed that the European family was a fact of natural law that would automatically cross the ocean and remain intact. The company later assumed that it could use any traditional social relations that served its purposes while creating innovations when they were desirable.[5] Later still, the planters, rather in the New England fashion, adopted an assortment of English practices to use in the counties and parishes.

This widespread confidence that Old World ways could be imported in any combination was wishful thinking of a sort that was nearly unavoidable. The strength of tradition lay in the subconscious; so in consciousness, the traditional seemed to inhere in visible behavior or innate rank, which could be transferred anywhere. The result was the beginning of a process of change. This process was not one determined in the initial moment, as theologians have said the fall of man was put into action with the creation of Adam and the Garden of Eden, though it had its dialectical features. Too many influences came from external events to allow depiction of the process as one following entirely from an internal dynamic.

In Rhode Island, the resort to seeing social groupings as undergirded by land had a deceptively traditional quality. Land rights, indeed, corresponded with most social attributes in England, so it was easy to think that a social order, complete with institutions, could be designed—or redesigned—by an artful distribution of land. The settlers, at first pitching their ambitions no higher than ample shares in villages of the usual several square miles' extent or an estate worked by a flock of servants, then discovered that they might have potential duchies by manipulating governments well within their reach and by getting rid of Indians. Englishmen obtained royal grants or dusted off dormant claims to land and tried to use their government against the colonials. The burst of land lust—and the consequent breakdown of the self-restraints necessary to create a harmonious society—occurred everywhere.[6] To the dismay of many people, mere ownership of land guaranteed nothing without the ability to use it in a way that would guarantee a steady income.

Less uniform than the rush for land was the response to the restoration of the English monarchy in 1660 and the beginnings of imperial control that followed. Even in New England, variation ran rampant. But no colony seriously modified its internal order to obey the king. Even the Rhode Island charter was framed in terms that represented the wishes of those who sought it.

South of New England, the record was similar in important respects. Royal authority ostensibly, if not vigorously, backed central colonial governments. The superficial stability of William Berkeley's administration in Virginia masked an ambiguous reality. The king and Parliament embarked on policies inimical to Virginian interests, policies that Berkeley opposed with mixed success. Royal tolerance, however, let the Virginia Assembly regularize the system of local government that had come into being despite English wishes. Eventually, the appearance of steadiness went up in smoke in Bacon's Rebellion. The king's officials responded with their own blend of repression, paternalism, and indifference. The institutional pattern of the colony, though shaken, survived. And the county and parish, in the usual seventeenth-century fashion, operated almost on their own and in spheres distinct from the central government. The king's support for proprietary colonies, of course, left the proprietors great latitude. The resulting semblance of endemic anarchy may indeed have been deceptive. Undue interest in central colonial governments may distract attention from the less volatile routine of county or neighborhood as it had settled down in the Chesapeake region but properly brings to view the tensions between the settlers and the Carolina proprietors.[7]

The similarity of Rhode Island to other colonies becomes harder to appraise after the late seventeenth century, partly because scholarship has not yet provided enough useful material. Comparison, however, is well grounded on one point: the growing value of ecclesiastical organization whenever the social fabric was loose. Quaker meetings and a few other places regulated life in Pennsylvania and west New Jersey much as they did in Rhode Island around the turn of the century.[8] Later, churches more often provided social solidarity and discipline in conjunction with—indeed, to preserve—ethnic loyalties outside Rhode Island than they ever did inside. From Dutch Reformed congregations in New Netherland maintaining an ethnic identity against the effects of English conquest to Huguenot and Jewish settlements to the many German faiths and Scotch-Irish groups of the eighteenth century, religious belief seemed inseparable from the culture that had shaped it. So a church became the institution to preserve both. In Pennsylvania or North Carolina, by around 1750, the population could be analyzed almost as a mosaic of ethnic-religious blocks.

Rhode Island's experience with the Dominion of New England and the confusion verging on anarchy thereafter, resembled what happened in the other affected jurisdictions and most of those farther south. The turbulence in the English monarchy was thrust into the American scene, where the pre-existing institutions lacked the inertia of those in the parent country and therefore fell the more easily into disarray. Rhode Island probably suffered at least as much as anywhere else. Unfortunately, historians have left largely unexamined the extent to which the local governments and parishes managed to continue in a normal fashion.[9] Maryland constitutes an exception: the modest disruptions of 1688–1690 have been evaluated with care.[10] Probably many of the basic institutions throughout rural New England suffered seriously, especially if they depended on tax money and confidence in titles to land, if not so much as in Rhode Island. The Delaware River colonies and Carolina were too young and disorderly to allow comparison.

The heavy assertions of imperial control, of which the Dominion was the heaviest and clumsiest, continued after 1689 and eventually brought vital changes in colonial institutions. This subject has been investigated extensively, so it is possible to see the elaboration of a system based in London, with agencies in America that assumed some functions previously performed by colonial authorities or not performed at all. Customshouses proliferated to undertake new duties and crowd colonial naval officers out of some of theirs. Vice-admiralty courts were commissioned to take over from colonial courts or augment them. And the number of royally appointed offices multiplied to expand government or to reduce choice by proprietors or local election. Rhode Island and Connecticut experienced less of this than most other places did, if only because they managed to keep their charters and were not important enough to warrant a large corps of customs and vice-admiralty court officers. Still, subjection to imperial authority brought Rhode Island into a new arena of politics. As in the other colonies, attention to the imperial capital became routine, with the Americans relying on a new official, an agent residing in London and always ready to speak for his employers.[11]

Rhode Island, like Connecticut and Maryland, remained exempt from a royal disallowance of its legislation but had to accept some infringements on its legislative autonomy from royal orders or acts of Parliament. Like all other colonies, it had to allow judicial appeals to the monarchy's privy council.

More important, however, was the internal reorganization of the colony that was only partly a response to an assertive imperial government. Probably nowhere else was there a comparable metamorphosis, and probably this was true because nowhere else did a previously insignificant jurisdiction manage to keep its separate existence and also build up a major port. The obvious comparison is with Plymouth Colony, which was submerged in Massachusetts after 1691; it was rather poor and never developed a city in the colonial period. As argued above, Rhode Island revamped its institutional arrangements beginning in the 1690s to keep as much of its autonomy as it could and to make the whole territory serve Newport.

Elements in the process were duplicated elsewhere, however. In New York, for instance, an even more sudden adoption of the technicalities of English law took place.[12] In all but a few colonies technical law and lawyers entered the scene in this period. Appeals to the privy council and expanding commerce made something close to an imperial standard necessary.

Likewise widespread were several changes in the operations of colonial government. Legislatures adopted the procedures and privileges of the British Parliament as much as they could. And, as we have been told well past the point of tedium, lower houses gained power by a variety of maneuvers. Both of these phenomena took place in Rhode Island, though it did not experience the common conversion of the governor into an agent of an external authority. Whereas royal and proprietary governors received their appointments and therefore their political responsibilities from outsiders, Rhode Island elected all its high officials. Only Connecticut did likewise. So these central colonial governments served their constituents with no more than a wary eye on the officialdom in Great Britain. Political aspirations consequently produced an internal dynamic in Rhode Island early in the eighteenth century, resulting in the proto-parties that lasted until the Revolution.[13] By contrast, the appointive nature of many high offices in other jurisdictions made politics swirl around use of their powers and drove colonials to gain influence in Whitehall to guide appointments and tune policy, thus producing an intense imperial politics far beyond any counterpart in Rhode Island.

The change in the relation of central to town government was crucial to eighteenth-century Rhode Island. Local autonomy remained in many respects, especially to promote local economic ambitions, but colonial law ironed out differences in procedure, added duties, imposed restraints, harnessed town to central governmental objectives, and began to act directly on the inhabitants much oftener than it had before. And the towns obeyed colonial law and judicial rulings far oftener than before. Similar if less profound or abrupt changes took place elsewhere. In Virginia, for example, roughly the same alterations took place in the operations of counties. There, the distinctive novelty in local government was the tobacco warehouse, which served both to further overseas trade and exert local control over it. The story was almost the same in Maryland but less dramatically told in New Jersey.[14] But in Pennsylvania and South Carolina, there was only a transition from the confusion of the early years to a fairly durable pattern in the eighteenth century.

Nevertheless, Rhode Island most resembled its neighbors in New England. On the occasion of its new charter in 1692, Massachusetts began to legislate extensively for the towns and the proprietors of common lands. Connecticut took a more gradual pace in the same direction. Both of these jurisdictions developed the county unit before Rhode Island did, though in different forms. They had far less to accomplish, however, to put local government in a clear hierarchy under the provincial government and to subject it to uniform laws.[15]

The similarity among the New England colonies grew in most respects after the fall of the Dominion, more so than can be explained merely by response to imperial assertiveness. Rhode Island diminished its exceptional traits. It no longer feared crusades against religious liberty, and although its controversies over boundaries continued, it began to follow the lead of Massachusetts in a surprising number of ways. Massachusetts set the pace on topics as diverse as paper money and proprietary organizations. The full scope of this leader-follower relation needs to be explored. Connecticut and New Hampshire were followers, too. Presumably, the smaller jurisdictions fell into line because of the advantages of regional consistency (the uniform standard and resulting intercolonial circulation of paper currency was an obvious example), because Massachusetts had led the way due to its earlier complexity and involvement in large-scale commerce, and because the much greater size and concentration of its trade gave the colony the initiative.

Rhode Island deviated significantly from the rest of New England in the relations between towns and proprietors of undivided land. To be sure, it followed roughly the same chronological pattern in the original towns—separation of proprietary business from town business between the late seventeenth and early eighteenth centuries, with a definition of proprietary organization by colonial statute at some point along the way. But after the early fracas in Portsmouth, there was no campaign by the excluded townsfolk to gain shares, unlike many other places in the region.[16] The main conflicts in Rhode Island were those between proprietors, or in Westerly against Connecticut grants as much as proprietary control of undivided territory.

Rhode Island also deviated in ecclesiastical organization. By embracing religious freedom, it rejected the traditional sharing of authority between church and secular government and so avoided the complexities and the frequent antagonisms spawned by the arrangements in colonies that created some form of establishment. Around Narragansett Bay, churches organized as they saw fit, and dissidents had no recourse to governmental power to dispute levies, alleged errors in doctrine, methods of calling pastors, location of meetinghouses, or definitions of parish bounds. Nothing restrained the introduction of new faiths. Still, Baptists assimilated some of the structure of Massachusetts Standing Order churches, notably the restricted communion and consequent design of church, congregation, and society. Congregationalists did so even more, to the extent of treating the Cambridge Platform as their constitutional law.

More difficult to assess is the representative quality of the large outline of eighteenth-century developments in Rhode Island. The colony reduced authority-wielding institutions to secular government, roughly integrated governmental organs into a hierarchy under centrally written law, and then created a profusion of agencies that were intermediary between the government and the individual or the family. They had voluntary membership yet were protected and defined in crucial ways by public authority. Often having the air of an improvisatory response to advancing social complexity, this exploration of new forms of association had a fairly consistent quality that marked a change from the assumptions of the founders in the seventeenth century. The result was a system to protect individual rights, facilitate nongovernmental associations, limit government, and give the residents a loud voice in public affairs if they wished to use it. Old ideas about authority gave way to tacit or explicit reliance on consent. Public power reinforced such voluntary associations on their own terms.

Rhode Island may have been an extreme case. On the whole, however, this record probably was similar at best, in its broad outlines, to those in other colonies. As local government fell under legal regulation, increasing definition emphasized procedures and limits, much as in Rhode Island. Probably most colonies developed a more elaborate governmental system, notably by adding the complex officialdom burgeoning around fiscal policies and imperial wars, more or less in the fashion of Rhode Island.

The reduction of the scope of public authority and its growing reliance on general laws rather than specific rulings was common in the mainland jurisdictions. Salient examples in several colonies showed the failures of governmental action in the comprehensive fashion taken for granted in the founding years. For instance, the Free Society of Traders, chartered by William Penn to be a vital agency in Pennsylvania's economy, failed quickly. It could not achieve the intended dominance in commerce or exploitation of land and never reaped the benefits of Penn's plan to award it three seats in the provincial council or the appointment of its leaders to other positions. Instead, the economy prospered as the result of individual action. Even prominent members of the company went on their own.[17] Wherever they were tried, schemes to regulate trade with Indians by award of privileges or licenses proved ineffectual.[18] With the division of commons and separation of town government from control over undivided land, New England communities lost the capacity to give comprehensive direction to their economies or to award privileges through collective decisions. By their own voluntary decisions, ethnic settlements in the eighteenth century could design communal life in ways reminiscent of New England towns a century earlier, though the special grants with restrictive privileges and obligations for the Palatine Germans in New York and North Carolina in the early years of the century were fiascos.[19]

In most colonies, however, government was not completely stripped down to a purely secular agency operating through general laws. Most supported a church, though religious toleration reduced, inch by inch, the practical significance of establishment. Still, Anglican parishes in Virginia and elsewhere were responsible for the poor.[20]

Rhode Island's record in creating a new approach to nongovernmental institutions in the colonial period is especially hard to assess. The usual shortcomings of institutional history, the confinement of attention to one institution or type of institution, and the emphasis on function to the neglect of form make generalization risky.

On the whole, the more visible intermediary institutions that appeared in the eighteenth century were urban. So Rhode Island's large proportion of urban dwellers—roughly a quarter of the total in 1776 as compared to a tenth or much less in all other colonies—meant a corresponding prominence for noncommercial corporations, schoolhouse proprietors, and even gentlemen's clubs. (Lotteries, of course, had their appeal to people of all kinds.) So the catalogs of fire companies, distilleries, workhouses, and the like in modern urban histories fail to put into context the significance of such forms of collective action.[21] Yet passing remarks on rules and formalities suggest the prevalence of habits such as those observed in Rhode Island. At least, the evidence points to a pervasive increase of interest in rules and procedural correctness on the part of churches.[22]

Although Rhode Island authorized lotteries and granted corporate charters in uncommon profusion, it usually did so for purposes similar to those elsewhere. The Penns' awards of charters to a school, college, hospital, library, and several churches afford a good example.

The procession of college foundations probably dramatized the record fairly well, however, and revealed the uncertainties of the process. In the seventeenth century Massachusetts made Harvard College an emanation of the colonial government. The legislature or General Court chose the president and board of overseers, chose public officials to the governing body, appropriated money, heard charges against the first president and fired him, and kept changing the organization and powers of the governing boards as though they were executive offices of the colony. The colonial government granted a succession of charters without explaining in all cases whether the later ones were to supersede or augment the earlier ones. In the 1680s, colonial government stopped this free-wheeling supervision of the college, significantly due to London's disapproval. The colony tried and failed to obtain royal approval of a new charter on terms that would be acceptable to Congregationalists, and then in 1707 it reaffirmed an early version when Whitehall's vigor diminished.[23] So Harvard drifted into the gray area between public and private control.

The later colleges roughly followed the tide in institutional matters. William and Mary, founded during the upsurge of imperial initiative, enjoyed a royal charter, a seat in the House of Burgesses, and a firm alliance with the established church. Thereafter, though new colleges usually had denominational connections, they were meant to be less attached to government. The College of Rhode Island probably typified the degree of autonomy in its cumbersome assignment of seats on the governing boards to men of prescribed persuasions and the appointment of governmental dignitaries to the board of trustees. Colleges were regarded as public institutions to some extent throughout the colonial period and never could attain the autonomy of some other corporations.

Rhode Island had its quirks, as everybody knows, but its institutional development shared many traits with those of the other mainland colonies. To say that it reached a configuration of a kind that would prove adaptable to a great range of purposes today would both exaggerate the case and reduce it to banality. Neither Rhode Island nor any other colony, for example, had a discernible vision of a general incorporation statute or a modern governmental regulatory agency. The use of colonial paper currency, so important in the eighteenth century, turned out not to be the pioneer of any later institution or practice. So the eighteenth century was not the pattern for the twentieth in public administration, though it nearly set the plan for the relation of churches to secular government.

And if we look at the last part of the colonial period, we find that Rhode Island once again went off on its own. The founders of the original towns tried to find basic principles to justify creating societies with a coercive government and kept shifting to different ones when they could not agree on the first principles. Most other settlers were spared such hard thinking because they came to their colonies with charters or something similar. But at the end of the colonial period, Americans throughout the British colonies explored basic principles and kept expanding their ideas until they abandoned English legal doctrines for pure philosophical concepts and then plunged into a twelve-year period of creativity to set new governments on new foundations.

Ironically, Rhode Island took little part in this intellectual excitement. Early in the prerevolutionary era, Governor Stephen Hopkins and a few others debated the constitutional and economic structure of the British Empire without arriving at any new conclusions. Then debate on these subjects dwindled to sloganeering and was overshadowed by political action.[24]

Nor did independence reawaken the old concern for hard thinking. The Declaration of Independence, approved by the General Assembly on July 18, 1776,[25] telescoped ideas in a way that never would have escaped the critical eye of many seventeenth-century founders. It proclaimed that all men have "certain unalienable rights" and that "to secure these rights, governments are instituted among men, deriving their just powers from the consent of the governed." If rights were strictly individual and unalienable, consent to government had to be voluntary—and could be withdrawn. So government at all times had to act by unanimous consent. The Declaration leaped over the step in between, the step clear to some social contract theorists of the seventeenth century, that produced an agreement to form a society. Only a society based on unanimous consent could create a government with the power to rule by majority vote or some other mechanism. That middle step had been the difficult one for the founders of Providence, Portsmouth, and Newport and had been dodged in Warwick. The middle step had seemed easy to some thinkers, from Aristotle to Puritan divines: for them, society was natural. But to their sorrow, the pioneers around Narragansett Bay had learned better. Their descendants conveniently forgot the lesson. In 1776, society had come to seem natural, as the result of a long, turbulent colonial history.

Moreover, Rhode Island silently had got what it first lacked, its own tradition. At the outset, drawing on the support of tradition had seemed to mean no more than adopting specific English practices. That had been a delusion. By 1776, however, after a series of experiments, the colony had created its own methods to create institutions that worked. What once had been its most radical and socially disruptive choice, religious freedom with the diversity it allowed, had become the local tradition. At the outset, government by consent, whether obtained by signatures on a compact or over approval of somebody's understanding of the will of God or the law of nations, had been a necessity. Yet it failed, for all the intensity of thought lavished on it. By 1776, the practice of creating and operating institutions by individual choice had become routine. As earlier, people thought the forms mattered much more than the underlying beliefs, making it easy to disregard theoretical rigor. The efficacy of consent came from the source it originally had lacked; it had become tradition.

Rhode Island, accordingly, saw no need to construct a new state government. The revered old charter seemed adequate, though it lacked the new-fashioned separation of powers, checks and balances, and bill of rights. All the same, it satisfied several requirements that the revolutionaries advocated and could be twisted to satisfy others. By the eighteenth century, it had been interpreted as a constitution, as Americans came to use the term—that is, as a description of the organs of government and a prescription of their powers and certain immovable principles for the protection of individual citizens. It had become a bulwark against domineering government. And it had operated by a system of direct or indirect election of its officials. So it could be seen as embodying the principles of limited government, enumerated powers, and action by the citizens' consent. Moreover, it could be redefined to embody a somewhat archaic approximation of the principle of popular sovereignty. When the General Assembly decided to sever its ties to the British Empire on May 4, 1776, it rewrote the formulas for official action to stop invoking royal sovereignty. Instead, the government would act by the "authority of the Governor and Company . . . of the English Colony of Rhode Island and Providence Plantations."[26] In other words, by authority of the citizens, but in the old mode—not as so many independent persons but as a collectivity. That was enough.

Thus, in the end, Rhode Island produced a last outburst of its maverick ways. In doing so, it tacitly expressed a belief that the institutional development of the colonial period had been a success. The Revolution was to guard, not reshape it.[27]

Notes

Abbreviations

Ct.	Court
ER	Early Records
Gen. Ct. Tr.	General Court of Trials
Inf. Ct.	Inferior Court
JCB	John Carter Brown Library, Brown University, Providence, R.I.
LE	Land evidence volumes (i.e., manuscript records of deeds, mortgages, etc.); see town entries for comments on specific ones.
NHS	Newport Historical Society, Newport, R.I.
PGA	Proceedings of the General Assembly
RI	Rhode Island
RICR	*Records of the Colony of Rhode Island*
Sup. Ct.	Superior Court
TC	Manuscript town council records; see town entries for comments on specific ones.
TM	Manuscript town meeting records; see town entries for comments on specific ones.

See also "Key to Short Citations," page 313.

1. Customary Ways and Radical Ideas in the Original Town (pp. 14–37)

1. Theodore Dwight Bozeman, "Religious Liberty and the Problem of Order in Early Rhode Island," *New England Quarterly* 45 (1972): 44–64; Dennis Allen O'Toole, "Exiles, Refugees, and Rogues: The Quest for Civil Order in the Towns of Providence Plantations, 1636–1654" (Ph.D. diss., Brown University, 1973); and Bruce C. Daniels, *Dissent and Conformity on Narragansett Bay: The Colonial Rhode Island Town* (Middletown, Conn., 1983), 3–9, 16–22; all treat the difficulties that early Rhode Island people encountered in trying to achieve order. These authors, however, considered order mainly in its modern sense, a prevalence of law-abiding behavior, and overlooked some of the older dimensions of the subject that emphasized hierarchy and interdependence as keys to faithful fulfillment of individual duties to a social compound. For a broader view, see Robert deV. Brunkow, "Love and Order in Roger Williams' Writings," *Rhode Island History* 35 (1976):115–25. Timothy H. Breen, "Persistent Localism: English Social Change and the Shaping of New

England Institutions," in *Puritans and Adventurers: Change and Persistence in Early America* (New York, 1980), 4–8, 16–18, makes the valuable observation that the specific English backgrounds of the first settlers of Massachusetts influenced their conceptions of how to organize a village. The most prominent founders of Rhode Island towns, curiously, all came from cities, so their understanding of rural villages presumably came from observation rather than experience. The early townsfolk came from a variety of places and were drawn together by religious beliefs rather than acquaintance in the parent country. Breen's suggestion in "Moving to the New World: The Character of Early Massachusetts Immmigration," in *Puritans and Adventurers*, 67, that "early New Englanders may have adopted an unusual system of land division, in part because many of them were amateurs at agriculture," is also valuable. Detailed investigation of the backgrounds of the first settlers in Providence, for instance, might reveal a tension between the experienced and inexperienced—or between those experienced in different kinds of agricultural methods—lying behind the quarrels over spatial arrangement of allocations.

2. Testimony of Roger Williams, 13 Dec. 1661, in John Russell Bartlett, ed., "The Letters of Roger Williams," *The Complete Writings of Roger Williams*, ed. Reuben A. Guild et al. (New York, 1963 [vols. 1–6 orig. publ. Providence, 1866–1874]), 6, 316–17.

3. Brunkow, "Love and Order," 116–18, explains this point well.

4. Roger Williams to John Winthrop, c. Sept. 1636 or a few months later, in John Winthrop et al., *Winthrop Papers* (Boston, 1929–1947), 3:296; Roger Williams, *The Bloudy Tenet of Persecution, for cause of Conscience . . .* , 2nd ed. rev. (London, 1644), 132; Providence Early Records (hereafter Providence ER), 1:2–4; 2:1–2; Roger Williams to town of Providence, c. Aug. 1654, Providence Town Papers (hereafter PTP), 2nd ser., 5:01310. Williams's concept of natural law, of course, was not in opposition to divine law. Rather, it was the law implicit in God's creation. Though Williams's ideas on the relation of the commonwealth to the constituent families were commonplace in his day, his corrollary on the natural authority of the assembled (equal) patriarchs was not. See Gordon T. Schochet, *Patriarchalism in Political Thought: The Authoritarian Family and Political Speculation and Attitudes Especially in Seventeenth-Century England* (New York, 1975), 37–84.

5. Roger Williams to John Whipple Jr., 24 Aug. 1669, RIHS (Rhode Island Historical Society) Manuscripts, 5:921. See also Brunkow, "Love and Order," 117, 121–24.

6. Roger Williams to John Winthrop, c. Sept. 1636 or a few months later, *Winthrop Papers*, 3:296–97; Providence ER, 1:1; Howard M. Chapin, *Documentary History of Rhode Island* (Providence, 1916, 1919), 1:96–97.

7. John Russell Bartlett, ed., *Records of the Colony of Rhode Island and Providence Plantations* (1856–1862; reprint, New York, 1968), 1:18–21 (hereafter *RICR*); Providence ER, 1:3; 2:53; 3:90–91, 110–11; Roger Williams to Thomas Hinckley, 18 June 1678, MS, JCB.

8. Providence ER, 2:29.

9. Providence ER, 15:2–5.

10. Petition of John Field to inhabitants of Providence, n.d. (c. 1641 or 1642), PTP, 2nd ser., 5:01253; Edw.[ard] Winslow, *Hypocrisie Unmasked: By A true Relation of the Proceedings of the Governor and Company of the Massachusets against Samuel Gorton . . .* (London, 1646), 56–58.

11. Roger Williams to John Winthrop, c. Sept. 1636 or a few months later, *Winthrop Papers*, 3:296–97; Williams to Winthrop, c. 1638, *Winthrop Papers*, 4:2; John Winthrop, *The History of New England from 1630 to 1649*, ed. James Savage, 2nd ed.

rev. (Boston, 1853), 2:71, 102; Nathaniel B. Shurtleff, ed., *Records of the Governor and Company of the Massachusetts Bay in New England* (Boston, 1853–1854), 2:26, 27; Chapin, *Documentary History*, 2:144–47; Providence ER, 4:160–62; Roger Williams to John Mason, 22 June 1670, in Williams, *Complete Writings*, 6:340; Samuel H. Brockunier, *The Irrepressible Democrat: Roger Williams* (New York, 1940), 135. Williams probably sought the patent under parliamentary rather than royal authority for three reasons: the English civil war made a choice necessary, his sympathies were with the Puritan opponents of Charles I, and he could obtain a favorable hearing from Parliament's commission.

12. Providence ER, 1:114; 2:45–46, 59–60, 67, 85–89, 91–92, 151–57; 15:19–20, 27–30, 32; Writ of Execution signed by Robert Williams and Thomas Harris, 4 Feb. 1649/50, PTP, 39:16611; copy of Robert Williams and Thomas Harris to William Arnold, 16 July 1649, PTP, 39:16614; Declaration of Richard Harcut, plaintiff, against William Arnold, n.d. (probably 1650), PTP, 2nd ser., 5:01105; Robert Williams, "Quaeries, presented unto the serious Consideration of this Towne, [of Providence] in points of Law," n.d. (c. 1649 or 1650), PTP, 2nd ser., 5:01138. Actually, the town founded its court shortly before the colonial government granted the charter.

13. Providence ER, 2:112.

14. Roger Williams to John Winthrop, c. Sept. 1636 or a few months later, *Winthrop Papers*, 3:297; Providence ER, 1:2, 3; 2:40, 47, 50, 55, 65, 76–77, 81, 84;15:4, 9; Report of Chad Browne et al., 14 Apr. 1641, PTP, 39(C), 17708; Colony Records, 1 (pt. 2):213; *RICR*, 1:154.

15. Providence ER, 2:94, 95, 98, 105, 106, 108, 109, 111–12.

16. On conditions attached to ownership: e.g., Providence ER, 1:3; 2:1–3. On taxes and roads: Providence ER, 2:40, 44. On grants to sponsor tanning and mills: Providence ER, 2:41, 42, 61, 66, 83; 3:239–40; Draft of Articles of Agreement between Alice Smith and John Smith, on one side, and town of Providence on the other, 1649, PTP, 39:16616; Petition of Anna Smith to Town of Providence, n.d. (probably before 1649), PTP, 2nd ser., 5:01123. On damage by livestock: Providence ER, 2:98, 111–12.

17. Some famous passages are in Williams, *Bloudy Tenet*, 25, 80, 105, 121, 203, 210–11.

18. Edmund S. Morgan, *Visible Saints: The History of a Puritan Idea* (New York, 1963), 20–60, 102–4; Edmund S. Morgan, *Roger Williams: The Church and the State* (New York, 1967), 21, 52.

19. Stephen Hopkins, "The Planting and Growth of Providence," in Rhode Island Historical Society, *Collections* (Providence, 1885), 7:56–58; John Winthrop, *The History of New England from 1630–1649*, ed. James Savage, 2d ed. rev. (Boston, 1853), 1:352–53; Matt. 3:13–16.

20. Chapin, *Documentary History*, 1:96; Morgan, *Roger Williams*, 44–56; Roger Williams to John Winthrop Jr., 9 Dec. 1649, *Winthrop Papers*, 5:376–77; Crawford Leonard Allen, "'The Restauration of Zion': Roger Williams and the Quest for the Primitive Church" (Ph.D. diss., University of Iowa, 1984), 96–103 and passim; W. Clark Gilpin, *The Millenarian Piety of Roger Williams* (Chicago, 1979), 138, 148.

21. Roger Williams to John Winthrop Jr., 24 Feb. 1649/50, in Williams, *Complete Writings*, 6:192.

22. Ibid., Historical Records Survey, Division of Community Services Projects, Work Projects Administration, *Inventory of the Church Archives of Rhode Island Baptist* (Providence, 1941), 183.

23. Untitled Records of the Island of Rhode Island, 1638–1644, called the "Clasp Book," MS, State Archives, Providence (hereafter cited as Island Records), 1. The

texts cited in the covenant were Exod. 24:3, 4; 2 Chron. 11:3; and 2 Kings 11:17. Surely 2 Chron. 11:3 was a mistake for 1 Chron. 11:2, 3.

24. Island Records, 2.

25. O'Toole, "Exiles," 140–53; *RICR,* 1:55–56, 59, 61.

26. Island Records, 7.

27. Ibid., 8.

28. Samuel Gorton, *An incorruptible Key Composed of the CX: Psalme . . .* (London, 1647; because the book has a series of five page sequences unrelated to the printers' signatures, they will be designated by letters A through E), D80, D87, E78–E83; Portsmouth ER, 1–8; O'Toole, "Exiles," 199–200.

29. Portsmouth ER, 7–9; Island Records, 15–16.

30. Island Records 1:34, 36; Portsmouth ER, 41.

31. Island Records, 4, 5, 7–8; *RICR,* 1:61, 64; Portsmouth ER, 3, 4, 6, 41, 43–44, 45. No record of the town's choice of officers for several years survives.

32. Portsmouth ER, 41–44, 62, 75.

33. Ibid., 34, 42, 70, 322–24.

34. Ibid., 4, 6, 12–14, 19–24, 47, 57–58.

35. Island Records, 1:3; Portsmouth ER, 4.

36. Island Records, 4, 6, 36; Portsmouth ER, 14, 17–18, 35–36, 48–50; Portsmouth LE, 1:10.

37. Portsmouth ER, 10, 24–25, 34.

38. John Callender, *An Historical Discourse on the Civil and Religious Affairs of the Colony of Rhode-Island and Providence Plantations in New-England in America: From the first Settlement 1638, to the End of first Century* (Boston, 1739), 62; Island Records, 3.

39. Winthrop, *History of New England,* 1:338. Winthrop got his information secondhand. What he wrote should be subjected to critical evaluation.

40. Callender, *Historical Discourse,* 62; Portsmouth ER, 27. For examples of the radical style in religious fellowship, see Philip F. Gura, "Samuel Gorton and Religious Radicalism in England, 1644–1648," *William and Mary Quarterly* 3rd ser., 40 (1983):121–23.

41. Island Records, 11.

42. Ibid., 12–13, 15, 16, and later.

43. Ibid., 13, 15–16.

44. Ibid., 34.

45. Ibid., 34, 36.

46. The basic concept of democracy stemmed from ancient Greek political thought, probably by way of Renaissance interpreters. Aristotle left the best-known commentary on Greek democracy. See his discussion of the best type in *Politics,* book 4, chap. 4, and book 6, chaps. 4 and 5, rather than his analysis in book 2, chaps. 6 and 7. On publicizing the laws and obligations of men on Aquidneck: Island Records, 28–29, 36, 63. On extension of freeman's rights: Chapin, *Documentary History,* 2:117–20; William Coddington to John Winthrop, 11 Nov. 1646, *Winthrop Papers,* 5:118.

47. Island Records, 28, 30; O'Toole, "Exiles," 213–17.

48. Island Records, 27, 34, 37, 38, 58, 63, 64.

49. Ibid., 28–29, 32, 36–37, 39, 57–58. On the Massachusetts plan: Timothy H. Breen, "The Covenanted Militia of Massachusetts Bay: English Background and New World Development," in *Puritans and Adventurers,* 33–36. When the General Court allowed the towns to buy military supplies with money from the colonial treasury, the gesture was less than it seemed. The treasury had little money, and the General Court had already decided that each town might use half. Island Records, 30, 39.

50. O'Toole, "Exiles," 231, 235–53; Thomas Lechford, "Plain Dealing: or, Newes from New-England" (1642), in Massachusetts Historical Society, *Collections*, ser. 3 (Cambridge, Mass., 1833), 3:96–97; Winslow, *Hypocrisie Unmasked*, 54–55.

51. Chapin, *Documentary History*, 1:164–65; Island Records, 68; Portsmouth ER, 31–32.

52. Island Records, 15–16, 18, 34.

53. Middletown Proprietors, 1, 7–9; Attested Copy of Decision (on p. 29 of now missing first book of Newport proprietors' transactions) of proprietors, 25 Jan. 1659/60, in papers of *Job Carr v. Samuel Carr et al.*, Gen. Ct. Tr. papers, box 1719. Formal records of the proprietors before 1701 (two volumes) have disappeared. Without either those records or the contemporaneous town records, the operations of the proprietors and their trustees can be known only in fragments.

54. Philip F. Gura, *A Glimpse of Sion's Glory: Puritan Radicalism in New England, 1620–1660* (Middletown, Conn., 1984), 64, 66; Colony Records, 1 (pt. 1):45.

55. William Coddington to John Winthrop, 9 Dec. 1639, *Winthrop Papers*, 4:161; Callender, *Historical Discourse*, 62; Thomas Lechford, "Plain Dealing," 3:96; Winthrop, *History of New England*, 2:48–49, *RICR*, 1:119.

56. John Clark[e], "Ill Newes from New-England: or, A Narrative of New-Englands Persecution. Wherin is Declared That while old England is becoming new, New-England is become Old" (1652), in Massachusetts Historical Society, *Collections*, ser. 4, 2 (Boston, 1854), 19–20, 25–26; John Comer, "The best, Most Correct, and Exact account of the first Settlement of the Baptist Churches in Newport in Rhode Island, together with their Progress Down to the Year 1730," Backus Papers, RIHS; historical note by John Comer, in "The Book of Records belonging to the Church of Christ in New-port under the Pastoral Cear of mr. William Peckam and mr. John Comer," MS, NHS (hereafter cited as Newport First Baptist Records), 129.

57. Callender, *Historical Discourse*, 64; Comer, "The best, Most Correct, and Exact account"; Samuel Hubbard, "Samuel Hubbard's Journal, *Circa* 1633–1686: Manuscripts relating to Samuel Hubbard of Newport Rhode Island," transcribed by the Rhode Island Historical Records Survey Project, Division of Professional and Service Projects, Work Projects Administration (Providence, 1940), 9.

58. Historical note by John Comer, Newport First Baptist Records, 131; Comer, "The best, Most Correct, and Exact account." It is tempting to interpret the controversy over laying on of hands as either a cause or manifestation of internal discord in town and colony, but there is no evidence to substantiate a connection. There was, however, a strong association between the laying on of hands for all believers, antipredestinarian views, and confidence in a ministry by inspiration of the Holy Spirit. Together, these departures from mainstream Puritanism undermined its emphasis on fixed categories in society and moved people toward hope in a more direct relation with God than ordinary Puritans dared to believe in.

59. [Samuel Gorton], *Simplicities Defence against Seven-Headed Policy. . . .* (London, 1646), 4–10, 14, 26, 28n, 34–35, 55; *RICR*, 1:130–31.

60. [Gorton], *Simplicities Defence*, 25, 34, 36; Winslow, *Hypocrisie Unmasked*, 44–46; Gorton, *An incorruptible Key*, E45–E50.

61. [Samuel Gorton], *An Antidote Against the Common Plague Of the World. Or, An Answer to a small Treatise, . . .* (London, 1657), 6, 17, 124–27, 132–33, 286; Samuel Gorton, *Saltmarsh Returned from the Dead, In Amico Philalethe. . .* (London, 1655), 149–50.

62. [Gorton], *Simplicities Defence*, 74, 76.

63. Warwick ER, 35–36.

64. Ibid., 34–35.

65. The surviving record, as published and read literally, says that the inhabitants would admit no more. This is out of keeping with the usual conduct of affairs in Warwick. The text probably is defective and should read: "no p[ar]t of this Common shalbe aproproated to anny [but] by the major p[ar]t of all the Inhabitants." See Warwick ER, 34.

66. When the territory west of the Four Mile Common became accessible to White occupation after King Philip's War, it fell into private ownership in a haphazard pattern. Some got large blocks; others, smaller tracts, whether because of subdivision of share rights among heirs or sales. Besides, the connection between patterns of ownership and the society of the town had changed.

67. Warwick ER, 89, 91, 100–101, 103–4, 107, 111–12; Warwick LE, 2:13.

68. Warwick ER, 32, 36–37, 40, 43–45, 47–48, 100, 252–54.

69. Ibid., 3, 34–35, 37–38, 41–43, 46, 49–51, 56, 60.

70. Ibid., 3, 46, 50, 58, 67, 96, 129.

71. Ibid., 2–3, 36, 38, 44–46, 50, 57, 58, 72, 89, 97, 101–2, 107, 112, 124, 127, 128, 130, 132.

72. Samuel Gorton, untitled (and incomplete) exposition on the Lord's Prayer, MS, RIHS, 8, 90, 123; Gorton, *Saltmarsh Returned*, 141–42.

73. Gorton, *An incorruptible Key*, A3–A4, D15–D16, E19–E20; Gorton, *Saltmarsh Returned*, 73, 79; [Gorton], *Simplicities Defence*, 68–71; [Gorton], *Antidote*, [xxvi–xxvii]; Gorton, exposition on Lord's Prayer, 31–33.

74. Gorton, *Incorruptible Key*, E112; Gorton, exposition on Lord's Prayer, 1, 28–29, 56–57, 85; [Gorton], *Antidote*, 27.

75. Gorton, exposition on Lord's Prayer, 19.

76. Warwick ER, 79–82; Providence ER, 15:50–61; *RICR,*, 1:250–55; Samuel Gorton et al. to town of Providence (?), 22 Mar. 1652/53, RIHS Manuscripts, 10:134; O'Toole, "Exiles," 510–14; Copy of Deed, Taccomanan to Randall Holden et al., 13 July 1654, Warner Papers, RIHS, no. 6; Copy of Deed, Wompattucke and Waysook to Randall Holden et al., 9 Aug. 1654, Warner Papers, RIHS, no. 7.

2. The Colonial Governments in the Seventeenth Century (pp. 41–63)

1. Timothy H. Breen, "Persistent Localism: English Social Change and the Shaping of New England Institutions," in *Puritans and Adventurers: Change and Persistence in Early America* (New York, 1980), 3–24, argues that Massachusetts localism was strengthened by a reaction against centralizing policies in England under Charles I and that some tensions in that colony came from widespread resistance to central authority exerted by those men who had in England taken part in the institutions of county or higher levels. Rhode Island had no settlers from as high as the gentry level and very few with any experience with English county or central institutions. So the settlers may have created a colonial government to do very little and then lacked skills to make it do even that much very well.

2. Howard M. Chapin, *Documentary History of Rhode Island* (Providence, 1916, 1919), 1:214–17.

3. Ibid., 1:217.

4. Ibid., 1:216.

5. Edw.[ard] Winslow, *Hypocrisie Unmasked. . .* (London, 1646), 83; Chapin, *Documentary History*, 1:227–30; 2:152–60; Roger Williams to Major John Mason, 22 June 1670, in John Russell Bartlett, ed., "The Letters of Roger Williams," *The*

Complete Writings of Roger Williams, ed. Reuben A. Guild, et al. (New York, 1963 [vols. 1–6 orig. publ. Providence, 1866–1874]), 6:341; Samuel Gorton, *An incorruptible Key Composed of the CX: Psalme*. . . (London, 1647; because the book has a series of five page sequences unrelated to the printer's signatures, they will be designated by lettter A through E), title page.

6. Winslow, *Hypocrisie Unmasked*, 82–85; Winthrop, *History of New England* 2:270, 308–9; Dennis Allen O'Toole, "Exiles, Refugees, and Rogues: The Quest for Civil Order in the Towns and Colony of Providence Plantations, 1636–1654" (Ph.D. diss., Brown University, 1973), 366–67, 375–78; William Bradford et al. to John Winthrop, 6 June 1646, MS, JCB; Providence ER, 15:10; William Coddington to John Winthrop, 5 Aug. 1644, *Winthrop Papers* (Boston, 1929–1947), 4:490; Coddington to Winthrop, 11 Nov. 1646, *Winthrop Papers*, 5:118.

7. Chapin, *Documentary History*, 1:223; *RICR*, 1:147–48.

8. Colony Records, 1 (pt. 2):215.

9. Ibid., 211–12; Providence ER, 15:22.

10. Colony Records, 1 (pt. 2):211–12, 243.

11. Ibid., 1 (pt. 2):232–39, 244.

12. Providence ER, 15:10 (missing letters supplied in brackets).

13. Colony Records, 1 (pt. 2):212–13, 226, 229–30, 240; Portsmouth ER, 35, 37.

14. Colony Records, 1 (pt. 2):214; Providence ER, 15:16; Portsmouth ER, 45, 59, 64, 70, 74.

15. Colony Records, 1 (pt. 2):216.

16. Ibid., 213.

17. Ibid., 215–39; Gerald B. Warden, "The Rhode Island Civil Code of 1647," in *Saints and Revolutionaries in Early American History*, ed. David D. Hall, et al. (New York, 1984), 138–51; John T. Farrell, "The Early History of Rhode Island's Court System," *Rhode Island History* 9 (1950):107–8. Warden and Farrell differ on the origins of the texts used in the code. On the whole, Farrell is the more persuasive. Warden asserts (p. 149) that the order of the categories of crimes corresponded to the "Second Table"—i.e., the fifth through tenth of the Ten Commandments (Exod. 20:12–17). That was not entirely true. In the code, sexual offenses came after instead of before stealing, and other Mosaic categories were used loosely, if at all.

18. The most interesting statement of theory came from Robert Williams, Roger's brother, and Thomas Harris. As judges of the Providence town court, they justified obstructing jurisdiction of the colony's Court of Trials by saying that they were obliged to uphold the laws of town and colony—and so, the town's liberties—while the colonial officers must be confined within the letter of the colony's law, "ffor the Generall [colonial government] having life in perticulars, holds forth the peoples ffreedome" only so long as the officials abide by laws either passed as statutes or assimilated from English rules for "the Common pleas." They saw the colony as based on a compact between the towns rather than as the product of the freemen as individuals or as a function of the English state. See copy of prohibition by Robert Williams and Thomas Harris, 25 Feb. 1649/50, PTP, 39:16615; copy (?) of petition of Robert Williams to town of Providence, c. 1649 or 1650, PTP, 2nd ser., 5:01150; Robert Williams to town of Providence, c. 1650, PTP, 2nd Ser., 5:01274.

19. The complexities of this interlude, which never have been detailed fully in historical literature, need not be unraveled here. The curious may consult, inter alia, Warwick ER, 73–74; Providence ER, 2:70–71; 15:34, 50–61; *RICR*, 1:250–55, 261, 268–72, 274; Portsmouth ER, 59; Newport TM (A), preceding p. 1; draft of towns of Providence and Warwick to Roger Williams, c. Feb. 1652/53, PTP, 2nd ser., 5:02184; "A Briefe Remonstrance of the two Towns of Providence and Warwicke beinge at

present the Colony of Providence Plantations; . . . ," MS, John Hay Library, Brown University, A53999; photostat of commission to William Dyre and John Underhill, authorizing military action against the Dutch, given in Newport, 24 May 1653 (original in Towns and Lands, 1, no. 76, Connecticut State Archives), RIHS Manuscripts, 1:160; Declaration of Fidelity to Commonwealth of England by Twelve Providence men, 7 Mar. 1652/53, Peck Collection, RIHS, Box 2:5; William Baulston et al. to town of Providence, 2 Mar. 1652/53, Moses Brown Papers, RIHS, Miscellaneous, box 4:108; town of Warwick to deputies of Providence, 22 Mar. 1652/53, Moses Brown Papers, RIHS, Miscellaneous, box 4:109. The closest thing to a full use of the surviving evidence, which surely reveals less than the whole story, is in O'Toole, "Exiles," chap. viii.

20. On Warwick: Samuel Gorton et al. to unknown, 22 Mar. 1652/53, RIHS Manuscripts, 10:134; Providence ER, 15:65; Warwick ER, 79–81; Nicholas Easton and Randall Holden to head warden of Portsmouth, 9 Aug. 1653, Moses Brown Papers, RIHS, Miscellaneous, box 4:112. On Providence: Providence ER, 15:66–67. On the island government's efforts: Colony Records, 1 (pt. 1):48.

21. Roger Williams to town of Providence, c. 1654, PTP, 2nd ser., 5:[01310]; *RICR*, 1:276–77, 279, 283, 351–52, 402; copy of decision by Portsmouth and Newport, 21 Aug. 1654, to send commissioners to a General Court at Warwick, RIHS Manuscripts, 1:8; Portsmouth ER, 64; Colony Records, 1 (pt. 1):55, 58, 61–65, 112, 115, 123, 126, 143; Roger Williams, et al., summons to Court of Commissioners, 2 Nov. 1654, Moses Brown Papers, RIHS, Miscellaneous, box 4:113; Providence ER, 2:84.

22. Colony Records, 1 (pt. 1):55; Providence ER, 15:34; *RICR*, 1:299–302, 401–2, 429.

23. Isaac Backus, *A History of New-England, With particular Reference to the Denomination of Christians Called Baptists* . . . (Boston, 1777; the two subsequent parts of this work appeared under somewhat different titles), 1:302; Providence ER, 15:122; *RICR*, 1:364, 365; Copy of Warrant to arrest William Harris, signed by Roger Williams, 12 Mar. 1656/57, Moses Brown Papers, RIHS, Miscellaneous, box 4:224; Colony Records, 1 (pt. 1):115–16. Harris's paper has vanished. The hostile characterization of it by Roger Williams, if accurate, suggests that Harris out-Gortoned Gorton.

24. *RICR*, 1:307, 314, 316–17. 321. 327–33, 346–47, 349, 356–57, 387–90, 403, 425; Backus, *History of New England*, 1:303–4; Portsmouth ER, 67, 78, 81–82, 84, 87.

25. Roger Williams to Gov. John Endicott, 27 Sept. 1656, MS, Peck Collection, RIHS, box 2:2; Williams to Endicott, 1 Dec. 1656, MS, JCB; Roger Williams to Arthur Fenner, 24 Feb. 1656/57, MS, JCB; Roger Williams to General Court of Massachusetts, 12 May 1656, *Complete Writings*, 6:301–2; Providence ER, 15:72; unknown writer to town of Providence, c. Feb. or Mar. 1652/53, PTP, 2nd ser., 5:01302; Bradford F. Swan, *Gregory Dexter of London and New England, 1610–1700* (Rochester, N.Y., 1949), 81; Bradford F. Swan, *The Case of Richard Chasmore, alias Long Dick* (Providence, 1944); *RICR*, 1:367–69, 369n-373n, 405–6.

26. *RICR*, 1:280; O'Toole, "Exiles," 537–38.

27. For an analysis of part of the phenomenon, see Robert deV. Brunkow, "Officeholding in Providence, Rhode Island, 1646 to 1686: A Quantitative Analysis," *William and Mary Quarterly*, 3rd ser., 37 (1980):242–60. Apart from some errors in fact and uncertainty in analysis, this is a valuable study and not confined to the dates in the title. Brunkow seems inclined to regard as undemocratic the concentration of "major offices" in the hands of the older and wealthier (generally the same) freemen but concludes that this concentration came from a desire by the voters for experienced and proven leadership, rather than a preference for oligarchy, especially as some men were elected frequently but not in unbroken sequences of terms. In view of the absence

from high office of about 40 percent of the wealthiest men, it might be advantageous to add a self-selection factor. That is, almost half of the most eligible probably avoided public office, some others sought it, and still others felt a duty to serve from time to time.

Unless we set up an Aristotelian standard of extreme democracy, in which all citizens are equally likely to be chosen to all offices, ideally by lot, the pattern that Brunkow found in Providence should scarcely be taken either as proving or disproving democratic qualities. Reputed democracies of recent times hardly can match the record of early Providence—or indeed, almost any early New England town—in distributing public responsibilities among the citizens. The standard must be refined. Besides, classifying some men as among the wealthiest suggests a greater spread of wealth than was there. Surely, it was narrower than in Newport or even Portsmouth. Granted, in virtually any community, some had more possessions than others, but the absolute difference, as well as the relative, must be taken into account.

28. *RICR*, 2:18–20. The best analyses in print are mostly the same, both being by Richard S. Dunn: "John Winthrop, Jr., and the Narragansett Country," *William and Mary Quarterly*, 3rd ser., 13 (1956):68–86; and *Puritans and Yankees: The Winthrop Dynasty of New England, 1630–1717* (Princeton, N.J., 1962), 117–42.

29. *RICR*, 2:3, 6.

30. Ibid., 2:3–21.

31. Ibid., 4–6. The echo of the Declaration of Breda was pointed out by Thomas W. Bicknell, *Story of Dr. John Clarke, the Founder of the First Free Commonwealth of the World on the Basis of "Full Liberty in Religious Concernments"* (Providence, 1915), 182–83, 193. Of course, the king had quite different aims from those of the Rhode Island colonists.

32. *RICR*, 2:9, 11, 472–73; (draft of?) petition of Warwick to General Assembly, 26 Oct. 1664, RIHS Manuscripts, 10:140; Warwick ER, 145–46; Portsmouth ER, 127; Colony Records, 1 (pt. 1):191. The petition of Warwick was especially interesting. The town advocated a bicameral form because it was "the comendable forme used in our Native Countrey as well as in the collinies about us" and because "the trueth of our Patent houldes it forth because the Governor Deputy Governor and Assistants are not elected by the people as their representatives but are Instituted by his Majesties speciall order in our Patent which doth the more lively sett forth that most renowned way of our Native countrey to bee atended unto."

33. *RICR*, 2:26, 30–32, 171; Colony Records, 1 (pt. 1):180.

34. *RICR*, 2:27, 32.

35. Colony Records, 1 (pt. 2):203, 333; Providence ER, 15:112; *RICR*, 2:113.

36. *RICR*, 2:14.

37. Ibid., 2:171–72, 189–90, 213–15, 217–19, 221, 489–99; Governor and Council, 1:34; Edmund Calverly to council of war in town of Warwick, 12 Apr. 1670, RIHS Manuscripts, 10:146; draft of order by Warwick town council of war, 4 Sept. 1671, RIHS Manuscripts, 10:149.

38. *RICR*, 2:10, 57–58.

39. Warwick A2, 19; petition of town of Warwick to General Assembly, 7 May 1673, RIHS Manuscripts, 10:148 or 149; Providence ER, 8:46–47; *RICR*, 2:103.

40. *RICR*, 2:13–14, 27, 64, 184.

41. Ibid., 1:518; 2:65–70. From this time on, the term Narragansett country generally meant the land south of the Shawomet purchase, though this meaning was without a sufficient grounding in historical fact to be precise or invariable. Originally, the term had meant the territory inhabited by Narragansett Indians, probably in turn derived pragmatically from a high estimate by English colonials of which villages

acknowledged the superiority of the chief sachems, Canonicus and Miantonomi. Thus considered, the Narragansett country plainly included most of Warwick and Providence and probably a little of southern Massachusetts but not the southwestern part of Rhode Island, where Niantics and Pequots were distinct peoples. The distinctness of the Pequots became fixed in English minds quite early, but the Niantics often were grouped casually with the Narragansetts before the distinction actually vanished around the end of the seventeenth century. The Indians themselves usually regarded land as connected to villages but gave honor to certain august lineages. The intertwined genealogies of the royal families of Narragansetts, Pequots, and Niantics can be traced in some detail.

The basis for using the term Narragansett country to mean the mainland south of Warwick came from the dispute between Connecticut and Rhode Island. Connecticut at times used sweeping terms to insist on the full literal force of the boundary clauses in its charter but in practical ways wrote off claims to Providence and Warwick, which were nests of heretics who would have been hard to assimilate into Connecticut. Besides, after the deaths of Canonicus and Miantonomi, the disintegration of their web of allegiance actually reduced the territorial extent, particularly on the north. Various villages became autonomous, whatever the later principal sachems liked to think. While the northern expanse of the Narragansett country thus ceased to figure in the dispute, the Niantic and Pequot lands along Block Island Sound were casually lumped with the proper Narragansett country.

42. *RICR*, 2:59–60, 93–95; 3:128–32, 135–37, 140–49; J. W. Fortescue, ed., *Calendar of State Papers, Colonial Series, America and West Indies, 1681–1685* (London, 1898), nos. 1941 and 2017.

43. *RICR*, 2:63–64, 78n-80n; Warwick ER, 146.

44. Copy of Roger Williams to people of Rhode Island, 1 Jan. 1665/66, RIHS Manuscripts, 10:25; General Assembly to freemen of Warwick, 27 Mar. 1666, RIHS Manuscripts, 10:141.

45. Colony Records, 1 (pt. 2):313–15; Warwick A2, 31–33, 35, 36, 43–44, 50–51, 66–67, 72, 79; town of Warwick to Governor William Brenton, 1 June 1668, RIHS Manuscripts, 10:138; copy of town of Warwick to Governor Benedict Arnold, 20 Nov. 1671, RIHS Manuscripts, 10:143; Providence ER, 3:149–51; *RICR*, 2:337–38, 358–60, 438; Irving B. Richman, ed.,"Harris Papers," RIHS, *Collections* (Providence, 1902), 10:104–18, 118n-119n.

46. The two advocates of concessions to Connecticut were Richard Smith and Francis Brinley, who shared in the land claims that Connecticut backed. The opinions of other magistrates and many deputies are hard to pin down. See *RICR*, 2:449–52, for the roster of officials, and pp. 417 and 434 for other pertinent details. For efforts at interpretation, see Clarence Saunders Brigham, untitled general history, in Edward Field, ed., *State of Rhode Island and Providence Plantations at the End of the Century; A History* (Boston, 1902), 1:121, 121n-122n; Richman, ed., "Harris Papers," 10:118n; J. William Frost, "Quaker versus Baptist: A Religious and Political Squabble in Rhode Island Three Hundred Years Ago," *Quaker History* 63 (1974):39–52; and Arthur J. Worrall, "Persecution, Politics, and War: Roger Williams, Quakers, and King Philip's War," *Quaker History* 66 (1977):74–77.

47. *RICR*, 2:531–32, 535–40, 543–48, 550–51; copy of town of Warwick to Governor William Coddington, 1676, RIHS Manuscripts, 10:152. An adequate narrative of the war, if not one sufficiently sensitive to the positions of White and Indian Rhode Islanders, may be found in Douglas Edward, Leach, *Flintlock and Tomahawk: New England in King Philip's War* (New York, 1958), esp. 16–26, 41, 57–63, 112–47, 167–72, 210–12.

48. Colony Records, 2:63, 73.

49. Providence ER, 8:102, 104–7, 113, 124, 126, 127; Colony Records, 2:100; copy of writ issued by John Sanford (General Recorder) to Edmund Calverly (General Sergeant) to seize property of town of Providence, 29 Sept. 1682, PTP, 1:20.

50. *RICR*, 3:76n–77n; Colony Records, 2:66–67, 97, 110.

51. Ibid., 3:153–55, 191–92.

52. David S. Lovejoy, *The Glorious Revolution in America* (New York, 1972), 200; *RICR*, 3:193–98; copy of address of Thomas Field et al. to king, 11 Oct. 1686, in transcripts of documents in the British Public Records Office made for John Carter Brown, JCB, 2, no. 217.

53. Lovejoy, *Glorious Revolution in America*, chaps. 9–11.

54. General Court of Trials, 1:81–83, 86, 88, 91–92, 95, 100–102, 106, 197. On appointment of local officers: General Court of Trials, 1:81–83, 100–101.

55. Providence ER, 8:175–76. For examples of the actions of the county court: General Court of Trials, 1:90, 91. On actions concerning land by the governor and council: "Land Warrants under Andros," Colonial Society of Massachusetts, *Publications* (Boston, 1920), 21:294–96, 299–300, 358; attested copy of patent in king's name issued by Dominion of New England for land conveyed to Richard Wharton on quit rent tenure, 29 June 1687, RIHS Manuscripts, 10:86.

56. E.g., Providence ER, 8:172, 174–75; Portsmouth ER, 235–39.

57. General Court of Trials, 1:101–2, 107–9.

58. *RICR*, 3:257n, 259; W C [Walter Clarke] and J C [John Coggeshall] to freemen at large, 23 Apr. 1689, RIHS Manuscripts, 5:29.

59. PGA, 5:2. The text of the king's order to Sir Edmund Andros is in Providence ER, 17:72. The date given there, 11 March 1684/5, must be too old by two years. Of course, the royal advocacy of religious toleration in the colonies applied to all of them. See, e.g., *RICR*, 3:199.

60. PGA, 5:3. *RICR*, 3:267–68, presents the decision on resuming government as made in 1690. Cf., *RICR*, 3:258, 266.

61. PGA, 5:5, 7, 8; petition of Rose Wickes to Warwick town council, 4 June 1689, RIHS Manuscripts, 10:64; Portsmouth LE, 1:282, 296.

62. Richard Smith and John Fones to Arthur Fenner and Thomas Olney, 1 Apr. 1690, RIHS Manuscripts, 5:944; John Greene to freemen of Providence, 15 Apr. 1690, RIHS Manuscripts, 5:945.

63. New Shoreham TB, 121–22; Thomas Brinley to Francis Brinley, 24 May 1690, RIHS Miscellaneous Manuscripts, B-722; Brinley to William Blathwayt, 29 Dec., Blathwayt Papers, Colonial Williamsburg, 11; Sir William Phips to William Blathwayt, 20 Feb. 1692/93, Blathwayt Papers, 5.

64. *RICR*, 3:275–77, 279–80.

65. *RICR*, 3:265–66, 575–76.

66. Copy or draft of affidavit, unsigned, by Warwick men, rreporting events of 30 May 1692, Warner Papers, RIHS, 118; *RICR*, 3:285–88.

67. *RICR*, 3:288–90. The land claims certainly figured in the opposition to the revived charter, but it is hard to determine how extensive their effects were. The claimants opposed by Rhode Island took themselves very seriously and were at this time appealing to imperial authority to get their way. See Francis Brinley to Capt. Samuel Gorton, 21 Nov. 1693, RIHS Manuscripts, 10:147; Samuel Greene Arnold, *History of the State of Rhode Island and Providence Plantations* (1859–1860; reprint, Spartanburg, S.C., 1970), 1:525.

68. Francis Brinley to Capt. Samuel Gorton, 21 Nov. 1693, RIHS Manuscripts, 10:147; *RICR*, 3:340, 387.

69. *RICR*, 2:33; Colony Records 1 (pt. 1):184, 191.
70. *RICR*, 3:288–90.

3. Disintegration of the Communal Ideal in the Original Towns (pp. 66–79)

1. Warwick ER, 109 and passim; Warwick A2, passim.
2. E.g., Portsmouth ER, 85, 218–19; Newport TM, 1:1, 6; 2:10; Newport TM (A), 1.
3. Warwick ER, 134, 138–39; Warwick A2, 42; Portsmouth ER, 153, 169–70; Newport TM, 2:6. On care of the needy: Warwick A2, 49–50; Providence ER, 2:140–41; 3:32; 8:66, 88–90, 95–96; Portsmouth ER, 153.
4. Portsmouth ER, 172–74, 207, 209, 221; Providence ER, 3:42–44; 8:42–44, 51–53, 55–56, 61–64, 145–46; Warwick ER, 134–35. 138–40, 180–81; Warwick A2, 178–79; Newport TM, 2:5, 10.
5. Providence ER, 3:161–65, 224–25; 4:70; 8:66–67, 78; 15:81; Warwick A2, 5; Warwick Town Papers, City Hall, Warwick, R.I.; Newport TM, 2:10; PTP, passim. Items formerly in the Providence town papers are in the RIHS Manuscripts; the Moses Brown Papers, RIHS; the collections of the John Hay Library at Brown University; and maybe elsewhere.
6. Providence ER, 6:110–11; Warwick ER, 133.
7. Portsmouth ER, 93; Providence ER, 3:18, 84; 14:68.
8. Newport TM (A), 5; Providence ER, 3:55, 62–63, 83; Warwick ER, 135–36, 146; Warwick A2, 176; Warwick GR, 2.
9. Portsmouth ER, 116, 119–21, 130, 142–43, 153–54, 160–64, 167, 181, 210, 222–23; Providence ER, 3:51–52, 57–58, 60, 71, 92, 125; 8:25–26, 28–29, 80–81, 118–19; 15:140, 169; 17:8, 9; Warwick ER, 166–67; Warwick GR, 27; Newport TM (A), 11–12; Newport TM, 1:7.
10. Colony Records, 1 (pt. 2):305; 2:74; PGA, 4:426–27; Portsmouth ER, 84, 168; Warwick ER, 155; Providence ER, 6:28–30; New Shoreham TB, 43, 217.
11. Warwick A2, 154; Samuel Stafford to town of Warwick, 9 Dec. 1690, RIHS Manuscripts, 18:51; Warwick LE, 1:122, 138, 139; 2:108–9; 3:7a; Frank Greene Bates and Charles M. Perry, "The Shawomet Purchase in the Colony of Rhode Island and Providence Plantations in New England," n.d., MS, RIHS, 119n.
12. For an example of a mill site being converted to simple private property: Portsmouth ER, 186. For examples of control of mills by agreements among partners embedded in deeds and wills: Warwick GR, 43a-44a; Warwick LE, 1:116, 179, 186.
13. Portsmouth ER, 170–72.
14. These allocations, of course, were made by the Gortonian settlers and expressed their long-range intentions. The planners knew perfectly well that an Indian village occupied part of the land.
15. On restrictions on livestock that might be turned out on the commons, e.g., Newport TM, 1:33, 37; Portsmouth ER, 189. On contradictory votes on commons: e.g., Providence ER, 3:17, 21–22; Portsmouth ER, 77–81.
16. For fairly traditional town grants, e.g., Warwick A2, 138, 184. On Newport's projects: Newport TM (A), 25, 63–64; Newport TM, 1:14, 25, 33, 34, 37, 51–52; Middletown Proprietors, 13; papers of Smith v. Smith et al., Gen. Ct. Tr. papers, Box 1716 and 1717. On Portsmouth's: Portsmouth TC, 5:1–3; Portsmouth LE, 1:332–33; Portsmouth TM, 1:9, 17–19. On Providence's: Providence ER, 8:62, 79, 83–84, 94, 95, 100, 105, 107, 109, 111, 117, 119, 121, 125, 128; 15:203, 204, 226, 227, 229, 239.

17. Newport TM, 1:54; Newport TM (A), 89; Middletown Proprietors, 9; Portsmouth ER, 97–101, 134, 242–43; Portsmouth TM, 1:3, 6, 8, 10–12, 45, 46, 48–49, 51.

18. Newport TM (A), 25; Newport TM, 1:33, 34, 37, 51–52; Middletown Proprietors, 13; copy of deed from freemen of Newport to Bartholomew Martin, 10 Oct. 1695, in papers of Smith v. Smith et al., Gen. Ct. Tr. papers, boxes 1716 and 1717.

19. Newport TM, 1:33, 37, 54; Newport TM (A), 89; Middletown Proprietors, 9.

20. Middletown Proprietors, 11–13, 43.

21. Portsmouth ER, 77–81, 189.

22. *RICR*, 3:153–54.

23. Portsmouth ER, 231–32; draft of patent to Thomas Wilson, authorized by Sir Edmund Andros, 24 Oct. 1687, Henry W. Greene Papers, RIHS, 52.

24. Portsmouth ER, 252–54; Portsmouth TC, 5:1–3; Portsmouth LE, 1:332–33.

25. The best versions are those in Samuel H. Brockunier, *The Irrepressible Democrat: Roger Williams* (New York, 1940), 225–63, 277–78; Irving B. Richman, "The Land Controversies of William Harris," in "Harris Papers," RIHS, *Collections* (Providence, 1902), 10:11–12, and notations to documents; Irving B. Richman, *Rhode Island: Its Making and Meaning* (New York, 1902), chap. 14; and Bates and Perry, "Shawomet Purchase," 54–70. Among the earlier versions, the most interesting is Henry C. Dorr, "The Proprietors of Providence, and their Controversies with the Freeholders," RIHS, *Collections* (Providence, 1897), vol. 9, which twisted the story into a fable to defend Thomas Wilson Dorr.

26. Colony Records, 1 (pt. 1):141; Richman, ed., "Harris Papers," 48–49; Providence ER, 2:126–28; 3:2–3, 8; 5:283–86, 297–306.

27. John R. Bartlett, ed., "The Letters of Roger Williams," in Reuben A. Guild, et al., eds., *The Complete Writings of Roger Williams* (1866–1874; reprint, New York, 1963), 6:318; Providence ER, 2:134–35; 3:19, 22, 46, 47; Joshua Winsor to town of Providence, 20 Sept. 1662, Loutitt photostats, RIHS, 460; Roger Williams to John Whipple, Jr., 24 Aug. 1669, RIHS Manuscripts, 5:921–23; James N. Arnold, ed., *The Records of the Proprietors of the Narragansetts, Otherwise Called the Fones Record*, vol. 1 of *Rhode Island Colonial Gleanings* (Providence, 1894), 1–16.

28. For lists of law books that Harris owned at the time of his death: Providence ER, 6:82–84, 89; receipt signed by Susan Harris and Howlong Harris, 2 June 1682, RIHS Manuscripts, 1:57; note by John Whipple Jr., n.d., RIHS Manuscripts, 10:136; Colony Records, 1 (pt. 2):292–93; Thomas Olney, Sr., to town of Providence, 15 Feb. 1668/69, Loutitt photostats, RIHS, 464a.

29. On the compromises: Providence ER, 3:60–62; 15:105; copy of minutes of Providence town meeting, 31 Mar. 1665, PTP, 39(A), 16630. On town meetings: copy of Arthur Fenner et al., "The ffirebrand discovered," 10 June 1667, RIHS Manuscripts, 10:136; Providence ER, 3:102–6, 147–48; 15:117–18, 149; Thomas Olney, Sr., to town of Providence, 15 Feb. 1668/69, Loutitt photostats, RIHS, 464a. On appeals to the General Assembly: Colony Records, 1 (pt. 2):292–93, 313–15.

30. Providence ER, 2:72–75; 3:11–12, 17, 18, 20–22, 31, 37–38, 48–49, 53–56, 66–74, 84, 93, 94, 105, 156, 180–85; 8:28, 115–16; 15:130–32, 169, 233, 238; Cyrus Walker, "The History of Scituate, R.I., from the Acquisition of the Territory in 1659, to the Close of the Nineteenth Century," microfilm at RIHS of MS reportedly at Town Hall, Scituate, R.I., 1:1; surveyor's return on land in Providence, 18 Dec. 1684, RIHS Manuscripts, 1:74. In 1668 the Williams side offered to compromise with the Harris side on a rule requiring the presence of at least twenty-one men with purchase rights to qualify as a session of the town meeting to dispose of land and approve transfers of ownership. See Bradford F. Swan, *Gregory Dexter of London and New En-*

gland, 1610–1700 (Rochester, N.Y., 1949), 89–90; Richman, ed., "Harris Papers," 91; Providence ER, 3:118.

31. Richman, ed., "Harris Papers," 38–39, 198–245, 261–65, 278–99, 317–18; Providence ER, 8:21, 60–61; 15:170, 174–75; copy of John Whipple, Sr., et al. to town of Providence, 27 Apr. 1678, Loutitt photostats, RIHS, 470q.

32. Richman, ed., "Harris Papers," 40, 321–23, 326, 337–41, 350–51; Providence ER, 15:214–15; Francis Brinley to Arthur Fenner, 12 Aug. 1686, PTP, 39(A), 16650; Francis Brinley to Richard Smith, n.d. (c. Oct. 1680), RIHS Manuscripts, 5:935.

33. Providence ER, 8:120, 130–31, 160–61; 15:236–38; memorandum (by Arthur Fenner?) on lands in Providence, 1 Jan. 1703/04, PTP, 39(A), 16675. On separation of town government from land allocation: Providence ER, 8:177–78; 11:6, 7, 19, 36, 39, 79–80, 83–85, 93–95; 14:54–55.

34. Most of the relevant sources are in Richman, ed., "Harris Papers"; Warwick ER; *Records of the Court of Trials of Providence Plantations*, 2 (Providence, 1922); Providence ER; RIHS Manuscripts; and *RICR*, 1–3. In addition, a few important documents are in PTP, especially vol. 39(A); the unpublished Harris Papers, RIHS; Warner Papers, RIHS; and other collections at RIHS. Bates and Perry, "Shawomet Purchase," provides a careful analysis of these matters.

35. Copy of deed from Wompattucke and Waysoote to Randall Holden et al., 9 Aug. 1654, Warner Papers, RIHS, 7; Warwick ER, 158; Warwick A2 LE, 152.

36. Warwick A2, 161–62, 165, 167; Warwick GR, 3–5, 9–11, 15–17. For examples of partnerships: Warwick GR, 28a–33a, 46a–49a; articles of agreement among Nausauket proprietors, 27 Jan. 1681/82, Henry W. Greene Papers, RIHS, 30; Eliza Collins et al. to town of Warwick, 15 Feb. 1682/83, RIHS Manuscripts, 10:134; John Gorton to town of Warwick, 18 Mar. 1681/82, RIHS Manuscripts, 18:48; agreement of John Greene, Sr., et al., 18 Apr. 1682, Shepley Papers, RIHS, 4:147; copy of Benjamin Gorton to town of Warwick, 19 Apr. 1682, Warwick Town Papers, City Hall; Stephen Arnold to town of Warwick, 19 Apr. 1682, Warwick Town Papers, City Hall; copy of decision by Warwick town meeting, 30 Jan. 1682/83, Warwick Town Papers, City Hall; agreement between Thomas Greene, Benjamin Gorton, and John Warner, 12 Apr. 1682, RIHS Manuscripts, 10:196. On revision of the terms of holding land and voting rights in the Four Mile Common: Warwick A2, 161 (second time the number was used), 200ff. For example of Four Mile Commons proprietors' meeting as a distinct body: copy of decision by proprietors of Four Mile Common, 19 Mar. 1706/07, Warner Papers, RIHS, 186. On separation of Potowomut into a distinct proprietary system: Warwick A2, 156–57, 189, 201–4; accounts of money from townsmen in Warwick to defend Potowomut, 1677, Warner Papers, RIHS, 57. On further difficulties in securing Potowomut: Warwick A2, 161–62 (second time these numbers were used), 164–65; Harrison S. Taft, unfinished and untitled studies of Warwick, R.I., MS, RIHS, 1:40, 41; Warwick GR, 6–8, 13–14, 17–21, 26, 64a–65a; report of Benjamin Barton et al. to town of Warwick, 23 Feb. 1681/82, RIHS Manuscripts, 10:51; *RICR*, 3:109–10; Warwick LE, 1:59–60, 65–66, 79, 85; Rouse Helm to town of Warwick, 19 Apr. 1682, and decision by Warwick town meeting, 11 Mar. 1684/85, Warwick Town Papers, City Hall.

37. Warwick A2, 100, 210.

38. Copy of Shawomet purchasers' decision on Cowesett, 27 Nov. 1672, and draft of agreement, 23 Oct. 1706, Warwick Manuscripts, RIHS, 12:1; Warwick A2 LE, 103, 104.

39. Copies(?) of decisions by Shawomet purchasers, 15 Mar. 1689/90 and 29 Mar. 1690, Shepley Papers, RIHS, 4:139; copy of decision by Shawomet purchasers, 16 Jan. 1688/89, Warner Papers, RIHS, 103; copy of decision by Shawomet purchasers, 10 Feb. 1690/91, Warner Papers, 110.

40. Providence ER, 8:160–61; 11:164; 21:10–11. For an example of a summons for a meeting: Providence ER, 17:234.

41. Providence ER, 8:120, 130–31; 14:145–47; 15:236–38; 17:183; agreement of Pawtuxet proprietors, 27 Nov. 1682, PTP, 1:22; memorandum (by Arthur Fenner?) on running Seven Mile Line, 1 Jan. 1703/04, PTP, 39(A), 16675; copy of confirmation of division of Pawtuxet east of Pocasset River, 4 May 1689, Harris Papers, RIHS, 78; copy of records of Pawtuxet proprietors east of Pocasset River, 15 Dec. 1718, 4 Mar. 1718/19, 17 Mar. 1718/19, Harris Papers, RIHS, 326; papers in *Rex v. Samuel Byles*, Prov. Ct. of Gen. Sessions, June 1749; copy of Rocky Island Proprietors' records, MS, John Hay Library, Brown University, 2–21.

42. Warwick GR, 19, 52a-54a; copy of Shawomet purchasers' agreement on Cowesett, 25 Feb. 1674/75, Warner Papers, RIHS, 56; copy of surveyor's report on Cowesett lots, 8 Mar. 1678/79, Warner Papers, 59; copy of decision by Shawomet purchasers, 8 Mar. 1678/79, Warner Papers, 61; copy of decision by Shawomet purchasers, 26 Mar. 1680, Warner Papers, 62; Bates and Perry, "Shawomet Purchase," 94; Warwick A2 LE, 157–58, 200–205; Warwick LE, 1:129; 5:253–57.

4. Land Promotions and New Towns (pp. 84–98)

1. Recent work by historians and ethnohistorians has explored much of this record. See Neal Salisbury, *Manitou and Providence: Indians, Europeans, and the Making of New England, 1500–1643* (New York, 1982); Alden T. Vaughan, *New England Frontier: Puritans and Indians, 1620–1675*, rev. ed. (New York, 1979); William Cronon, *Changes in the Land: Indians, Colonists, and the Ecology of New England* (New York, 1983); Francis Jennings, *The Invasion of America: Indians, Colonialism, and the Cant of Conquest* (Chapel Hill, N.C., 1975); Douglas Edward Leach, *Flintlock and Tomahawk: New England in King Philip's War* (New York, 1958); and for a further guide, Neal Salisbury, *The Indians of New England: A Critical Bibliography* (Bloomington, Ind., 1982). An even more detailed analysis of the Narragansetts, as well as as review of secondary writings, will appear in the annotations by Roger Williams, *The Corrrespondence of Roger Williams*, ed. Glenn W. LaFantasie (Hanover, 1988). Ethnohistorians have done much to illuminate the disintegration of Narragansett solidarity but have shed no light on why the Narragansetts acquiesced to the arrogation by the United Colonies of a supreme judicial power over them or how White people understood what was happening among them.

2. Portsmouth ER, 66; Roger Williams, *An Answer to a Scandalous Paper . . . dated 25 August 1658*, ed. Bradford F. Swan (Providence, 1945). Williams wrote his letter in response to a somewhat obscure political controversy over the shift from working for the towns to working strictly for the shareholders. John Easton, Rhode Island's attorney general, accused Coddington and Arnold of perfidy, but he presented his accusations to the governor of Massachusetts, who passed them along to Williams.

3. Articles of Agreement and early proceedings of the Conanicut company, Potter Papers, RIHS, 4–10.

4. Articles of Agreement of the Conanicut company, Potter Papers, RIHS, 11–19, 13–14.

5. Walter L. Watson, "A Short History of Jamestown, on the Island of Conanicut, Rhode Island," RIHS *Collections* (1933), 26:48–49; Jamestown Proprietors, 3–7, 10, 11, 13, 21, 27, 35, 36, 42–43; Colony Records, 2:69; untitled accounts of treasurer of

Rhode Island, 1 (1672–1711), MS, State Archives, Providence, 52; Jamestown LE, 1:1–40.

6. New Shoreham TB, 57, 96–97.

7. Ibid., 58–60.

8. *RICR*, 2:32; Colony Records, 1 (pt. 1):187–89, 207; RI LE, 1:7.

9. RI LE, 1:7, 25, 26, 172–73, 427.

10. Colony Records, 2:22–24; New Shoreham TB, 24, 72–74, 205, 396, 399, 580.

11. New Shoreham TB, 15, 16, 32–33, 49, 173, 174, 217, 394, 423, 511–17.

12. Ibid., 15, 40, 163–64, 236, 256, 279, 579, 580. On leased ministerial land: New Shoreham TB, 201–2, 337–42, 518–20; Samuel T. Livermore, *History of Block Island* (Hartford, Conn., 1877), 241, 312, 314–15.

13. New Shoreham TB, 221–23, 231–32, 399, 423, 427, 456, 569, 572–75.

14. James N. Arnold, ed., *The Records of the Proprietors of the Narragansett, Otherwise Called the Fones Record* (Providence, 1894), 1–9, 15–16.

15. Arnold, ed., *Fones Record*, 10–15, 20, 23; Francis Brinley, "A Briefe Narrative of that Part of New England called the Nanhiganset Countrey," RIHS *Publications* 8 (1900–1901): 76; Elisha R. Potter Jr., *The Early History of Narragansett; with an Appendix of Original Documents, Many of Which are Now for the First Time Published* (publication data on this title are misleading: the title page identifies the book as published in Providence, 1835; it also has been considered as RIHS *Collections*, 3 [Providence, 1835], but pp. 314–423 contain material added to the original version by William H. Potter, and the preface is dated 1 May 1886), 61, 62; King Charles II to the New England Colonies, 21 June 1663, "Trumbull Papers," Massachusetts Historical Society *Collections*, 5th ser. (Boston, 1885), 9:54–55.

16. *RICR*, 1:518; 2:93–94, 127; Samuel Greene Arnold, *History of the State of Rhode Island and Providence Plantations* (1859–1860; reprint, Spartanburg, S.C., 1970), 1:282–83, 379, 381; Arnold, ed., *Fones Record*, 24–25; Potter, *Early History of Narragansett*, 62; J. Hammond Trumbull, ed., *The Public Records of the Colony of Connecticut, . . .* (Hartford, 1850), 1:407. Rhode Island continually maintained that the commissioners had nulllified the claims based on the mortgage to the United Colonies, but the commissioners only allowed the Narragansetts to redeem the mortgage at any time, which they failed to do. Robert C. Black III, *The Younger John Winthrop* (New York, 1966), 287.

17. Arnold, ed., *Fones Record*, 5, 17, 18, 21, 25–29; copy of agreement to divide and promote settlement on land north of Richard Smith's trading post, 15 June 1660, Warner Papers, RIHS, 13; *RICR*, 2:478.

18. Rhode Island, too, wanted to change the decision in order to get direct and unquestioned jurisdiction over the Narragansett country. "The Clarendon Papers," *Collections of the New-York Historical Society for the Year 1869* (New York, 1870), 2:139–49, 153–56.

19. Arnold, ed., *Fones Record*, 29–30, 32–37, 59–75, 77–83, 104–5, 110–11; *RICR*, 2:567, 579, 593–98; 3:127–34, 139–49; J. Hammond Trumbull, ed., *The Public Records of the Colony of Connecticut, . . .* (Hartford, 1852), 2:315–16; Brinley, "Briefe Narrative," 89; copy of proclamation, Boston, 22 Mar. 1685/86, Warner Papers, RIHS, 86. See also Bernard Bailyn, *The New England Merchants in the Seventeenth Century* (Cambridge, Mass., 1955), 172; Colony Records, 2:106. The royal commission of 1683 decided that Connecticut had jurisdiction in the Narragansett country.

20. Arnold, ed., *Fones Record*, 35; Elisha R. Potter, *Memoir Concerning the French Settlements and French Settlers in the Colony of Rhode Island* (Providence, 1879), 23–24, 29; *RICR*, 3:184–85, 228; Theodore B. Lewis, "Land Speculation and

the Dudley Council of 1686," *William and Mary Quarterly*, 3rd ser., 31 (1974): 267; Richard S. Dunn, *Puritans and Yankees: The Winthrop Dynasty of New England, 1630–1717* (Princeton, N.J., 1962), 245.

21. On the woes of the French: Potter, *French Settlements*, 14–17. Examples of maneuvers between the two opponents: *RICR*, 2:356; Brinley, "Briefe Narrative," 93–94; warrant signed by John Greene for asrrest of Gideon Crawford, 17 Mar. 1695/96, Warner Papers, RIHS, 131; John Greene, Jr., to Capt. (Nathaniel?) Coddington, 5 July 1697, Henry W. Greene Papers, RIHS, 54. The dispute had the added complilcation of the claims from a third side, the heir of the Marquis of Hamilton, who had received the territory in a grant from the Council for New England in 1635. The claim had been raised sporadically without consequences before the royal commission of 1683 took it seriously or pretended to. *RICR*, 3:145. After various maneuvers, Rhode Island and Connecticut collaborated to oppose this claim and won a ruling against it by the Board of Trade. See J. W. Fortescue, ed., *Calendar of State Papers, Colonial Series, America and West Indies, 1696–1697* (London, 1904), nos. 962–64, 985, 992, 1151, 1234; "Trumbull Papers," Massachusetts Historical Society *Collections*, 5th ser. (Boston, 1885), 9:180–85. On the maneuvers between Rhode Island and the Narragansett Proprietors in the early eighteenth century: copy of proclamation by John Saffin et al., 14 May 1701, Warner Papers, RIHS, 161; *RICR*, 3:474, 518; Gen. Ct. Tr., 1:147, 149, 155; RI LE, 2:190–95, 204–5; Nathaniel(?) Coddington to Gideon Crawford, 15 July 1707, PTP, 39(A), 16757; PGA, 7:210–11, 256–57.

22. Potter, *Early History of Narragansett*, 275–76; *RICR*, 1:403–4. The Court of Commissioners of the mainland towns had enacted a similar law in 1651, but despite the ambiguous terms of the reunion in 1654, it lapsed into oblivion, as did the law against slavery. *RICR*, 1:236, 243, 276–77.

23. Potter, *Early History of Narragansett*, 275–77; RI LE, 3:254.

24. Potter, *Early History of Narragansett*, 279–81, 291–92, 394; copies of grants by Pettaquamscut purchasers to William Haviland (1 May 1663), William Bundy (1 May 1663), and Jireh Bull (25 July 1667), Potter Papers, *RIHS*, folder on Pettaquamscut purchasers; copy of minutes of Pettaquamscut purchasers, 4 June 1668, Shepley Papers, RIHS, 4:35; copy of deed from Pettaquamscut purchasers to Jahleel Brenton, 7 Sept. 1693, Shepley Papers, RIHS, 4:39; South Kingstown LE, 6:43–45.

25. Colony Records, 2:43.

26. Potter, *Early History of Narragansett*, 53; Westerly LE, 1:48; Colony Records, 1 (pt. 1):141; untitled records of Misquamicut purchasers, Westerly Public Library, Westerly, R.I. (hereafter cited as Misquamicut), 1:1.

27. Misquamicut, 1:7.

28. Copy of Articles of Agreement of Misquamicut purchasers, 22 Mar. 1660/61, Shepley Papers, RIHS, 4:31; Misquamicut, 1:8, 13, 15, 17, and passim. See also the list of shares, transcribed from Westerly records, in file of papers of *Daniel Stanton v. William Champlin et al.*, April 1749 term of King's Inf. Ct.

29. Copy of Articles of Agreement of Misquamicut purchasers, 22 Mar. 1660/61, Shepley Papers, RIHS, 4:31; Misquamicut, 1:6, 14, and passim.

30. Misquamicut, 1:4, 13–15.

31. Potter, *Early History of Narragansett*, 62, 63, 67–68; *RICR*, 1:455–57, 472; Misquamicut, 1:16, 17, 21–23; Colony Records, 1 (pt. 1):157; (pt. 2):305.

32. Westerly LE, 1:5, 6, 7, 9, 10; 9:283. On conflicting jurisdictions: Samuel Hubbard, "Samuel Hubbard's Journal Circa 1633–1686: Manuscripts Relating to Samuel Hubbard of Newport Rhode Island," transcribed by the Rhode Island Historical Records Survey Project, Division of Professional and Service Projects, Work Projects Administration (Providence, 1940), 69; *RICR*, 2:225–34, 299–300.

33. Westerly LE, 1:6–8, 10–12, 14; Arnold, ed., *Fones Record,* 73; Colony Records, 2:117; "Land Warrants under Andros, 1687–1688," Colonial Society of Massachusetts, *Publications* (Boston, 1920), 21:294–96; *RICR,* 3:172, 260, 270. Later, it was said that the extension of the town's jurisdiction was authorized as a stratagem in the contest with Connecticut. See Nathaniel(?) Coddington to Gideon(?) Crawford, 15 July 1707, PTP, 39(A), 16757.

34. Nathaniel(?) Coddington to Gideon(?) Crawford, 15 July 1707, PTP, 39(A), 16757; Westerly LE, 1:16–17; Potter, *Early History of Narragansett,* 70; copy of deed of Cochainaquant (Cojanoquant) to Richard Knight and Henry Hall, 19 Jan. 1664/65, Warner Papers, RIHS, 35; deposition of Joseph Dauel, 31 July 1711, Shepley Papers, RIHS, 4:28.

35. Westerly LE, 1:15–18, 38, 75, 77–79, 81–82, 84–85; deposition by Joseph Dauel, 31 July 1711, Shepley Papers, RIHS, 4:28.

36. Circular letter from William Field et al. (Court of Commissioners' committee to acquire land) to towns, 26 May 1660, Loutitt photostats, RIHS, 457; *RICR,* 1:418, 424.

37. *RICR,* 1:424; Providence ER, 2:132, 138–39; 15:78; list of men, mostly of Warwick, willing to buy shares of land at Aquidnesset or Potowomut, n.d., RIHS Manuscripts, 10:18; Warwick ER, 120, 124; William Field et al. to towns, 26 May 1660, Loutitt photostats, RIHS, 457.

38. Copy of deed from Awashouse to William Vaughan et al., 8 May 1662, PTP, 39(A), 16628; Warwick LE, 1:205; deposition of Nicholas Utter, 18 June 1678, in papers of *Jeremiah Spink and Thomas Hopkins v. Nathaniel French,* Providence Inf. Ct., December 1730 term; Deposition of Jeremiah Clarke, 26 March 1723, and copy of articles of agreement, in papers of *Job Lawton v. Joseph Knight,* September 1723 term, Gen. Ct. Tr. papers; "The Minutes of the Westconnaug Purchase," transcribed by Theodore G. Foster, RIHS *Collections* (Providence, 1932), 25:121–22; *RICR,* 3:446.

39. Colony Records, 2:57–58. On efforts to take advantage of the offer: Daniel H. Greene, *History of the Town of East Greenwich, from 1677 to 1877* (Providence, 1877), 29–30.

40. Colony Records, 2:61–62; East Greenwich TC, 1:5.

41. William Davis Miller, *Notes and Queries Concerning the Early Bounds and Divisions of the Township of East Greenwich As Set Forth in William Hall's Plat, 1716* (Providence, 1937?), 11; Harrison S. Taft, unfinished and untitled studies of Warwick, R.I., MS, RIHS, 1:50; *RICR,* 3:8–9, 11–121, 55–56; East Greenwich TC, 1:10; papers of *John Rice v. John Peirce and Thomas Peirce,* September 1750 term, Providence Sup. Ct.; Potter, *Early History of Narragansett,* 76; Warwick GR, 91a. The colony interfered again in 1685, requiring the town to take in three more men. See petition of Samuel Bennet et al. in MS schedule of General Assembly actions, 21 Oct. 1685, Warner Papers, RIHS, 91; *RICR,* 3:179.

42. East Greenwich TC, 1:4, 7, 8, 15, 23, 38, 45, 73,103.

5. *Religious Association Replacing Secular (pp. 102–110)*

1. Edwin Barrows, "Historical Sketch of the First Baptist Church, in Newport," in *Minutes of the First Rhode Island Baptist Anniversaries, 1877* (Providence, 1877), 20; Portsmouth ER, 113; John Richardson, *An Account of the Life of that Ancient Servant of Jesus Christ, John Richardson, . . .* (London, 1757), 97; Samuel Hubbard,

"Samuel Hubbard's Journal, *Circa* 1633–1686: Manuscripts relating to Samuel Hubbard of Newport Rhode Island," transcribed by the Rhode Island Historical Records Survey Project, Division of Professional and Service Projects, Work Projects Administration (Providence, 1940), 119.

2. John Comer, "The best, Most Correct, and Exact account of the first Settlement of the Baptist Churches in Newport on Rhode Island, together with their Progress Down to the Year 1730 . . . ," Backus Papers, RIHS, no. 21; Hubbard, "Journal," 9–10, 22, 52–55, 60–62; untitled narrative of schism of Seventh Day Baptists, in hand of John Comer, "The Book of Records belonging to the Church of Christ in New-port on Rhode-Island under the Pastoral Cear of mr. William Peckam and mr. John Comer," NHS (hereafter cited as Newport First Baptist Records), 137. In view of the Seventh Day Baptists' later correspondence with Edward Stennet, a minister of that persuasion in London, Mumford may have had some association with Fifth Monarchists. Stennet had been in that loosely definable category. See Bernard S. Capp, *The Fifth Monarchy Men: A Study in Seventeenth-Century English Millenarianism* (London, 1972), 173.

3. On Hubbard's and Hiscox's view of the Ten Commandments: Hubbard, "Journal," 52–55. On preaching against the seventh day observance: Newport First Baptist Records, 139, 141; Hubbard, "Journal," 64–65; Comer, "The best, Most Correct, and Exact account," Backus Papers, RIHS. On arguments on the Commandments and God's covenant: Newport First Baptist Records, 143, 145, 147, 149, 151, 153; Hubbard, "Journal," 65–66, 113.

4. Newport First Baptist Records, 153; Comer, "The best, Most Correct, and Exact account," Backus Papers, RIHS; Hubbard, "Journal," 10, 68, 97–101, 113. In broad terms, the religious practices (speaking in tongues, etc.) were consistent with Stennet's background. See Capp, *Fifth Monarchy Men*, 173. On the sense of affinity with other Baptists: e.g., Hubbard, "Journal," 104. The recognition of the Baptist category appeared in correspondence and various other ways. Nor was it one-sided. When the Dominion of New England loomed, the Swansey, Massachusetts, Baptists—no Sabbatarians—urged the Seventh Day flock to join in a meeting of all New England Baptist churches to consider what to do "in this day of distress and trouble." Hubbard, "Journal," 138.

5. Copy of "Records of the First Seventh Day church of Hopkinton, R.I.," RIHS, 2, 7, 18, 20, 23, 55–56, 61, 62; Historical Records Survey, Work Projects Administration, *Inventory of the Church Archives of Rhode Island; Baptist* (Providence, 1941), 147–48.

6. Hubbard, "Journal," 121, 131.

7. Thomas Olney Jr., "Ambition Anatomized . . . ," ed. J. William Frost, *Quaker History,* 68 (1974): 48– 49.

8. By that time, there was a "monthly mans meetinge" embracing Quaker men on Aquidneck and perhaps on the mainland to the east as well. Portsmouth LE, 1:116. There was no women's meeting. A few years later, women surely met with the men; later still, the women met separately. See Arthur J. Worrall, *Quakers in the Colonial Northeast* (Hanover, N.H., 1980), 63–64.

9. Records of Rhode Island Monthly Meeting of Friends (mostly men), MS, NHS (hereafter cited as RI MM, with reference to specific session by date, given as day and year separated by month in Roman numerals), 1:12/X/1676/77, 6/XII/1676/77; Worral, *Quakers in the Colonial Northeast,* 70.

10. RI MM, 1:30/II/1677, 29/III/1677.

11. Ibid., 1:24/II/1681.

12. Ibid., 1:12/X/1676, 6/XII/1676/77, 6/I/1676/77; Worrall, *Quakers in the Colonial Northeast,* 64–65.

13. RI MM, 1:19/VI/1679. The focus here is on the institutional manifestations of the disagreement. As the dissidents' statements implied, profound religious principles lay behind the schism. Readers familiar with early Quakerism will recognize in the disagreements at Newport the New England echoes of the Wilkinson-Story separation in England.

14. RI MM, 1:21/IV/1681, 31/XI/1681/82, 25/II/1682, 27/XII/1682/83, 27/I/1683, 14/VI/1683, 11/VII/1683, 9/VIII/1683, 5/X/1683, 13/VI/1684, 9/VIII/1684, 1/IX/1684, 11/VI/1685, 2/IX/1686, 1/X/1686, 25/XI/1686/87, 22/XII/1686/897, 9/II/1687, 17/III/1787. Hodgson also faced discipline for his part in a controversy over keeping a hat on in meeting when another person was at prayer. See Worrall, *Quakers in the Colonial Northeast*, 65.

15. RI MM, 1:23/III/1682, 11/IV/1682. A separate book of minutes for the Yearly Meeting was opened the following year.

16. For examples of meetings where discussion of Aquidneck business predominated: RI MM, 1:13/V/1686, 29/VII/1691, 4/II/1699, 2/III/1699. On "Reeding of friends Epistles: " RI MM, 1:14/XII/1692/93, 4/V/1693.

17. Ibid., 1:14/XII/1692/93. Mary Maples Dunn, "Saints and Sisters: Congregational and Quaker Women in the Early Colonial Period," in Janet W. James, ed., *Women in American Religion* (Philadelphia, 1980), 45.

18. RI MM, 1:24/XII/1684/85.

19. Portsmouth LE, 1:116, 317; RI MM, 1:6/VII/1687, 5/V/1692, 30/VI/1692, 22/IX/1692, 30/V/1695, 2/III/1699.

20. RI MM, 1:30/V/1695, 5/I/1696, 2/IV/1696, and 1697–1703, passim; RI LE, 2:104.

21. RI MM, 1:1700–1707, passim; 2:1710–1711, passim; "A Book of Records Belonging to the Proprietors of Eastons Point Newport," MS, NHS, 3, 5–8; RI LE, 2:269–71.

22. Arnold Lloyd, *Quaker Social History, 1669–1738* (London, 1950); Sydney V. James, *A People among Peoples: Quaker Benevolence in Eighteenth-Century America* (Cambridge, Mass., 1963), esp. chap. 1. For an example of declarations and precepts on conduct: Minutes of New England Yearly Meeting of Men Friends, MS, Archives of New England Yearly Meeting, RIHS, 1:1708.

23. Reference to Jews living in the colony: Untitled Accounts of Treasurer of Rhode Island (1672–1711), MS, State Archives, Providence, 1:32. Quotation at Colony Records, 2:111.

24. L. Effingham de Forest, trans. and ed., "Records of the French Church at Narragansett, 1686–1691," *The New York Genealogical and Biographical Record*, 70 (1939):236–41, 359–65; 71 (1940):51–61.

25. Ibid., 70:237, 240–41; 71:51–54.

26. Ibid., 70:239–41; 71:52.

27. Ibid., 71:56–60.

6. The Rise of the Colonial Government and a New Direction for Institutional Development (pp. 114–134)

1. The record is not entirely clear. Carl Bridenbaugh, *Fat Mutton and Liberty of Conscience; Society in Rhode Island, 1636–1690* (Providence, 1974), esp. 93–130, paints an overly rosy picture, as the quantities in the lists he gives (pp. 121–122) demonstrate. The contrasting picture in Gov. Samuel Cranston's reports to the Board

of Trade in 1708 (*RICR*, 4:53–60) possibly understates the extent of Newport trade, either from ignorance or from ignorance plus a desire to generate the impression that his colony could not have been guilty of much of anything contrary to British interests. Though of oblique relevance, the data in Bernard Bailyn and Lotte Bailyn, *Massachusetts Shipping, 1697–1714* (Cambridge, Mass., 1959) harmonize with Cranston's reports. In any case, Newport served a small population, even after the decline of early trading ventures based in Providence and Warwick and the growth of White settlement in the late seventeenth century. The volume of imports to supply a White population of under 6,000 and the nearby Indians must have been small, as was that of their exports. In most respects, Newport was a satellite of Boston. Lynne Withey, *Urban Growth in Colonial Rhode Island: Newport and Providence in the Eighteenth Century* (Albany, N.Y., 1984), 17–29, offers a judicious interpretation of the surviving information. Her comment that "sometime between 1715 and 1740, . . . Newport reached . . . [the] level of size and importance" to engage in trade directly with England is particularly telling.

It is intriguing, but in the end futile, to pursue Timothy Breen's suggestion in "Persistent Localism: English Social Change and the Shaping of New England Institutions," *Puritans and Adventurers: Change and Persistence in Early America* (New York, 1980), 21, that most early New England settlers, by virtue of their experiences in England, were oriented to local concerns and only a few toward county or national ones. Possibly, nobody in the early communities in Rhode Island had direct experience with the more inclusive levels, except Roger Williams. In Providence, nevertheless, he could be as village-minded as anybody. It follows that the great changes of the early eighteenth century should have been a product of the arrival on the scene of men who thought in wider contexts. Evidence can show conflicts between persistent localism and the assertions of colonial government. So little is known, however, about most of the new colonial political figures that no base exists for understanding how they thought other than the record of official actions. Therefore, the record to be explained must be used as the evidence for the mentality to explain it. The circle cannot be broken by speculating that commerce broadened consciousness. No one can say that it did so any more than emigration had done for the founders—indeed, no one can determine precisely what effect it did have.

Nor does it help to examine those who are easiest to see. A few individuals attract attention. Francis Brinley, like his brother-in-law, William Coddington, probably had some association with the higher levels of English society or at least developed pretensions. Coddington's sons may have imagined themselves a local gentry. When they and Brinley cooperated with the Winthrops, the pretensions may have seemed justified. The Sanfords genuinely were part of a family network that included prominent Bostonians and even the venerated John Cotton. Jahleel Brenton attained the highest position in the imperial customs service in New England. All these people had intercolonial and transatlantic connections. So one can posit a ruling class outlook, derived from experience or ambition, in such persons. But they were either leading opponents of the men who accomplished the great changes in Rhode Island or stood on the sidelines.

2. Richard R. Johnson, *Adjustment to Empire; The New England Colonies, 1675–1715* (New Brunswick, N.J., 1981), 183–21, covers the New England scene very well.

3. *RICR*, 3:310–11, 313.

4. Ibid., 3:313.

5. On speaker and clerk: *RICR*, 3:313, 326, 342. On the rules of the House of Deputies: Journal of the House of Deputies (hereafter, Journal H of D), 16 and 18 June 1729.

6. *RICR*, 3:288–89, 297, 298.

7. *RICR*, 3:450, 506–7, 517–19, 524–26, 566, 557–58, 565, 590; 4:5–6, 43, 52, 59, 70, 71, 74, 75, 81–83, 93–95, 98–101, 103, 107, 116–17, 175, 197, 249, 297, 344, 491, 506. Along the way, the Assembly also wrangled over town watches and councils of war. The issue with regard to watches and similar measures for local defense lay in Cranston's desire to assert central authority against the towns. By laws of 1700 and 1701, the Assembly empowered colonial officials to direct a town to set a watch, but a few years later it gave towns power to create their own garrisons and later still let town councils post peacetime watches and join the militia officers in posting wartime ones. The importance of these measures is problematical. See *RICR*, 3:424–25, 431–32, 506–7; Colony Records, 4:215–16, 423–24.

8. Colony Records, 4:185.

9. *RICR*, 3:432–33; 4:179; Colony Records, 4:179, 184; 5:45; PGA, 8:213.

10. *RICR*, 4:173, 211, 377–79, 496; PGA, 6:439; 7:42; 8:125–28, 213–14; Colony Records, 4:179, 494; 5:14, 19–20, 279, 293, 334–35, 422–23; Journal H of D, 22 June 1728, 1 Nov. 1728, 27 Feb. 1728/29, 20 June 1729, 21 June 1734, 17 June 1736, 6 May 1737, 21 June 1737, 23 Nov. 1737, 28 Feb. 1739/40, 8 May 1741; Rhode Island Quarterly Meeting of [Men] Friends to General Assembly, 25 Mar. 1729, RI Petitions, 1:53; same to same, 10 Oct. 1729, RI Petitions, 1:62; Warwick men to General Assembly, Feb. 1734/35, RI Petitions, 3:37; Newport men to General Assembly, 1 Oct. 1735, RI Petitions, 3:43; Samuel Gardner et al. to General Assembly, Oct. 1735, RI Petitions, 3:76; eighty-six men to General Assembly, May 1737, RI Petitions, 3:120.

11. Journal H of D, 7 May 1730, 6 May 1731; Colony Records, 5:45, 94; Providence ER, 6:47, 118–19; New Shoreham TB, 286; Westerly TM, 1:16, 22; Westerly TC, 1:48; 2:162; North Kingstown Probate, 5:95.

12. Journal H of D, 23 Feb. 1736/37. On pacifists: Newport men to General Assembly, Oct. 1735, RI Petitions, 3:43.

13. *RICR*, 3:321–22, 326–27, 330, 337, 339–42, 346, 351–53, 363–67, 373–74, 376–78, 382–83, 385–99, 493, 507, 534–35, 558, 546–49; 4:12–16, 92.

14. Ibid., 3:330, 346, 350–51, 376, 378, 382–83, 396–97, 425. As altered in the compilation of 1719, this act was made even vaguer, although the mysteries of custom and the like were omitted. RI *Laws* 1719, 45.

15. *RICR*, 4:194–95.

16. Ibid., 4:209, 225–26, 234.

17. As in the draft of 1706, the laws had been revised by the Assembly's committee, so the text is often a false guide to legislative history. Indeed, the committee probably inserted new measures under old dates.

18. E.g., North Kingstown Probate, 5:91, 96–97.

19. They were the Governor, Deputy Governor, ten assistants, wardens in Jamestown and New Shoreham, and the conservators of the peace chosen by the Assembly for the Narragansett towns. About this time, the Assembly began to add justices of the peace for Newport and other towns.

20. Samuel Greene Arnold, *History of the State of Rhode Island and Providence Plantations* (1859–1860; reprint, Spartanburg, S.C., 1970), 2:49. On the General Assembly's functions, see Dorothy S. Towle, ed., *Records of the Vice-Admiralty Court of Rhode Island, 1716–1752*, American Legal Records (1936; reprint, Millwood, N.Y., 1975), 105.

21. Colony Records, 5:13, 38.

22. RI *Laws* 1730, 113; RI *Laws* 1706 (?), 70–72; *RICR*, 3:435.

23. RI *Laws* 1730, 13, 164. For a time the appeal on liquor licenses was to the Court of Trials. RI *Laws* 1730, 179–80.

24. Appeals from the councils' decisions in emergencies, such as epidemics, also lay to the Governor and Council. On the exclusion of justices and others from ex officio memberships in councils: Journal H of D, 6 Dec. 1733.

25. *RICR*, 2:477–79; Colony Records, 4:617–22; 5:6a, 7.

26. On selection of judges: *RICR*, 4:484; RI *Laws* 1745, 210. On appeals: RI *Laws* 1730, 247–48. On justice of the peace duties: RI *Laws* 1730, 262–63.

27. On events before 1705: *RICR*, 3:508–9, 536–39; Arnold, *History of Rhode Island*, 2:49; jotting by Samuel Cranston (?) on swearing in of William Atwood as vice-admiralty judge, 23 Oct. 1701, in almanac for 1670, Cranston Papers, RIHS.

28. *RICR*, 3:481–82, 550–51; 4:26, 29–30, 39–40, 48–49, 80–81, 90, 115–16, 136–37, 157, 199, 262, 268–69, 289, 294, 312–13, 320; Edward Stinnes, "The Struggle for Judicial Supremacy," in Edward Field, ed., *State of Rhode Island and Providence Plantations at the End of the Century; A History* (Boston, 1902), 3:120.

29. RI *Laws* 1730, 106; Colony Records, 6:28; RI *Laws* 1752, 30.

30. On authorization of new rates and procedures for collection: *RICR*, 3:300–303, 308–9, 318–19, 324, 343–45, 347–49, 368–69, 378, 401, 417–18, 436–37. 441–42, 448, 450–51, 456–57, 466–68, 484–87, 489–91, 500–503, 520, 532–34, 541–42, 557–59, 562, 564–65; 4:24–25, 33–34, 46, 65, 70, 75, 84–85, 100–101, 106, 164–66, 170; PGA, 5:171–72; Providence ER, 17:180–81, 186–87; RI *Laws* 1706 (?), 101–4. On town actions (or heel-dragging): Newport TM, 1:38, 75, 86, 91, 101, 113; Portsmouth TM, 1:4, 5, 21, 23, 26, 28, 32; Providence ER, 11:86, 99, 109, 117, 132, 147–48, 156, 163, 167, 174; Westerly LE, 1:38, 39, 40; Westerly TM, 1:4, 8, 11, 13, etc.; East Greenwich TC, 1:54; North Kingston TC, 1:7, 11; New Shoreham TB, 425, 448, 455. On disputes over town boundaries: *RICR*, 3:307, 314–15. On the limited success of collection: Providence ER, 17:161–62; RI Treasurer's Accounts, 1:87–88; *RICR*, 3:323–24, 532–33; 4:84–85, 165.

31. *RICR*, 4:100–101; RI *Laws* 1730, 59–64; John Blanchard MacInnes, "Rhode Island Bills of Public Credit, 1710–1755" (Ph.D. diss., Brown University, 1952), 103. On shortfalls of receipts: *RICR*, 4:164–65; summary at end of Oct. 1734 session, Journal H of D.

32. RI *Laws* 1719, 75–79. The fees were modest, potentially a total of £133 6s 8d for the Trustees in that capacity, £66 13s 4d for the town committees, including the Trustees acting as the committee for Newport.

33. Colony Records, 4:451. On extension of loans to ten years: Colony Records, 4:250–51, 451. The uncommonly slipshod drafting of the law allowed a reading to give the town committees still wider discretion, but probably it was not exploited. On trustees' practices: file papers of *John Wanton v. Benjamin Ellery*, in Gen. Ct. Tr. papers, box 1721.

34. Colony Records, 4:136, 261; MacInnes, "Rhode Island Bills," 138, 176. Journal H of D, 4 May 1728.

35. Colony Records, 4:450–52.

36. Suits began in the 1730s on a small scale. At once, the Assembly decided that the colony should claim no interest on overdue interest. See Journal H of D, 4 Nov. 1736; RI *Laws* 1730, 281. On the prevailing interest in retirement of wartime bills of credit: accounts at end of Oct. 1734 session, Journal H of D; MacInnes, "Rhode Island Bills," 228–30, 604.

37. Accounts at end of Oct. 1734 session, Journal H of D; MacInnes, "Rhode Island Bills," 221–25, 228–30, 604.

38. As power ordinarily has among its first objects building monuments to itself, so Rhode Island used its paper money to strengthen the fortifications on Goat Island and erect the handsome Colony House at Newport. See *RICR*, 4:487, 551, 559.

39. MacInnes, "Rhode Island Bills," 142.

40. Ibid., 124, 132–35, 151–54, 169–71, 215–19, 237–71; Colony Records, 4:258–59, 264, 296, 400, 437, 531–32, 556; 5:71, 132, 134, 322. Because the bills never would circulate readily outside New England, they did little good when Newport trade reached to farther ports, especially across the Atlantic. Hence, as Newport merchants tried to build on their successes by developing exchanges on an ever-widening scale, they first lost enthusiasm for the paper pounds and then sometimes opposed them. These converts to hard money feared losses, such as erosion of capital, by the paper pound's decline in value.

41. *RICR*, 3:334–35, 349–50; PGA, 4:597–98; 6:420–21; 7:140–42, 143, 282; 8:39; Colony Records, 4:136; 5:60–61, 65–66, 70–71; various merchants of Newport to General Assembly, June 1730, RI Petitions, 2:24; RI *Laws* 1706 (?), 82–83; RI *Laws* 1730, 141–42; Newport TM, 1:61, 91, 109, 141, 151, 181, 249, 254; Newport TM (A), 95; Portsmouth TM, 1:23, 28, 144; Providence ER, 11:49; 13:37, 66; Warwick TM, 2:4, 14; Westerly LE, 1:22, 39; North Kingston TC, 15, 144; Jamestown Proprietors, 36. Laws requiring all towns to elect vendue masters or let them do so if they saw fit, like a law authorizing regulated fairs (probably of interest only to commercially ambitious Providence and Portsmouth), had little or no effect. See Colony Records, 4:222–23; PGA, 7:90; Providence ER, 11:26–27, 35, 40; 13:65; Portsmouth TM, 1:27, 144.

42. On tax on itinerant traders: *RICR*, 3:357–58, 421–23, 438; 4:162–63; Providence ER, 17:177; Colony Records, 4:558–59. On regulations concerning fees and use of the port: *RICR*, 3:437–39, 487–89, 504–5; 4:101, 104–5, 111, 236–37; Colony Records, 5:15–16; Newport TC, 6:144; town council of Newport to General Assembly, Feb. 1729, RI Petitions, 2: A; Journal H of D, 7 May 1730.

43. The General Recorder's series of books, opened to record land evidences, began, in vol. 2, to include maritime papers, which supplanted the deeds entirely in the eighteenth century, a rather accurate reflection of the shift in preoccupations in the populace.

44. *RICR*, 3:373, 405–6, 415–16, 449–50, 454, 471; 4:76, 152; PGA, 5:210, 294–95; Portsmouth TM, 1:106–8; Colony Records, 4:514.

45. Portsmouth TM, 1:5, 20; *RICR*, 3:384–85, 493–94, 505–6, 529–30, 568–69; 4:83, 85, 142–43, 150, 151; Colony Records, 4:129–30; Francis Brinley, "A Briefe Account of Mister Samuell Cranstons proceedings to gaine Bridget Sanfords Land, that was Originally laid out by John Greene as per the draught may be seene," MS, NHS, box 117, folder 1; Jamestown Proprietors, 65; Gen. Ct. Tr., 1:142; papers of *Oliver Arnold v. Thomas Northrop*, replaced as defendant by his landlord, Josiah Arnold, document 14, Gen. Ct. Tr. papers, box 1713–1715; Jamestown proprietors to General Assembly, c. 1731, RI Petitions, 1:38. Portsmouth had begun to impanel juries to lay out roads before authorized to do so by colonial law. See Portsmouth TM, 1:3, 6. Examples of special variations: Portsmouth TM, 1:46–47, 65–67; Colony Records, 4:167, 207, 289, 496–95a [*sic*]; Journal H of D, 6 Dec. 1733. Examples of appeals: Colony Records, 4:161–62; Journal H of D, 19 Feb. 1728/29, 18 June 1736; Job Tripp et al. to General Assembly, c. 10 Oct. 1727, RI Petitions, 1:69; men in North Kingstown to General Assembly, c. 1731, RI Petitions, 2: B. On subsidies: PGA, 7:449–50; 8:20, 301–2; Colony Records, 4:170, 195, 251–252, 412, 420, 444, 447, 469, 570–71; town of Westerly to General Assembly, Feb. 1730, RI Petitions, 2:32.

46. John Whipple, Jr., to town of Providence, n.d. (probably c. 1700), PTP, 2nd ser. 5:01070. See also Portsmouth TM, 1:132; Middletown Proprietors, 96; Jamestown Proprietors, 194, 197, 209.

47. PGA, 7:193; *RICR*, 4:24; Providence ER, 11:54, 102–3; Westerly LE, 3:106; Westerly TM, 1:8; East Greenwich TC, 1:105.

48. Papers of *Stephen Northrop v. Thomas Mumford*, Gen. Ct. Tr. papers, box 1722M, 1723S; South Kingstown TM, 1:11; *RICR*, 4:382–83; North Kingstown Probate 6:209.

49. RI *Laws* 1730, 264–66; William Randall et al. to General Assembly, Oct. 1737, RI Petitions, 3:109; Thomas Harris et al. to General Assembly, 21 Nov. 1737, RI Petitions, 3:122.

50. On fishing privileges: North Kingstown Probate, 6:3, 92; South Kingstown TC, 2:42–43, 64, 75, 96, 105, 130; 3:22, 37; Westerly LE, 1:39. On regulating weirs: *RICR*, 4:263; RI *Laws* 1719, 110; Journal H of D, 4 May 1734. On complaints and subsequent action: *RICR*, 4:511; RI *Laws* 1744 or 1745, 185; Samuel Barton and Samuel Bennet to General Assembly, Feb. 1739/40, RI Petitions, 4:3; Henry Gardner et al. to General Assembly, Jan. 1739/40, RI Petitions, 4:13; Thomas Northup et al. to General Assembly, Oct. 1739, RI Petitions, 4:35; Colony Records, 5:249, 283, 602.

51. Record of Justices' Court at Providence, 20 May 1729, RIHS Manuscripts, 1:16; Warwick Wills, 1:56–57.

52. Colonial rules for town government: *RICR*, 3:306; 4:195–96, 207–8. On plans to synchronize election meetings: Journal H of D, 6 Nov. 1734, 22 Feb. 1734/35, 3 Nov. 1736; Colony Records, 5:525. On the franchise: RI *Laws* 1730, 131; Journal H of D, 28 Feb. 1729/30; Colony Records, 5:9. The law of 1723/24 was a substitute for one that remained on the books for only three months, restricting the vote for colonial officials to men who had been given freemen's rights by the Assembly. See Colony Records, 4:423, 428.

53. Colony Records, 4:176.

54. Ibid., 4:616. For an example of seven freemen calling for a vote: Portsmouth TM, 1:139.

55. On the councils' responsibilities: *RICR*, 3:350; 4:64–65, 250, 452–53; Colony Records, 4:170, 221; Journal H of D, 25 June 1729, 19 Feb. 1734/35, 21 Feb. 1734/35. On composition of the councils and town responses to colonial laws on this subject: RI *Laws* 1719 22; *RICR*, 4:497; Westerly TM, 1:28; East Greenwich TC, 1:112; Samuel Carr et al. to General Assembly, 3 July 1733, RI Petitions, 2:116; fifteen men to General Assembly, Dec. 1733, RI Petitions, 2:119; Journal H of D, 6 Dec. 1733; Colony Records, 5:149; Portsmouth TC, 3:41; Newport TM, 1:267. In New Shoreham and Jamestown, the wardens were to continue to be considered among the basic six.

56. E.g., *RICR*, 3:446–47.

57. *RICR*, 3:525–26; Newport TM, 1:83.

58. PGA, 7:146, 180; Portsmouth LE, 1:5.

59. Johnson, *Adjustment to Empire*, chaps. 3–7.

60. *RICR*, 3:288–300.

61. On Governor Clarke's position: *RICR*, 3:315, 321–26, 329–31; Arnold, *History of the State of Rhode Island*, 1:539–40. On Cranston's policies: *RICR*, 3:333–37, 346, 373–77, 397–99, 416, 419–20, 460, 462, 509; 4:53–60; Towle, *Records of the Vice-Admiralty Court*, 14n, 83–84.

62. In the seventeenth century, the colony sometimes sent men to represent it for quite specific purposes. Towns and private interests did likewise. There are a few hints of the colony's employment of a resident English agent, a mysterious Nathaniel Colson or Colston. See Gov. John Cranston to Sir Robert Southwell, 1 Aug. 1679, Blathwayt Papers, Colonial Williamsburg, 11; John Greene, Sr., to William Blathwayt, 18 Dec. 1680, Blathwayt Papers, 11. A cryptic reference to Colson is in *RICR*, 3:19. For Wharton's career: "The Winthrop Papers," Massachusetts Historical Society, *Collections*, 6th ser. (Boston, 1889), 3:254, 286, 288–89, 377–80, 467n; (Boston, 1892), 5:218.

63. *RICR*, 2:10; 3:386, 543.
64. Massachusetts Historical Society, *Collections*, 6th ser., 3:286.
65. Ian K. Steele, *Politics of Colonial Policy; The Board of Trade in Colonial Administration, 1696–1720* (Oxford, 1968), 109–11.
66. *RICR*, 4:458–61. Jenckes's theory was an interesting one, a grotesque echo of the notion that a colony was parallel to an English municipality. He thought that the prevalence of a veto power in the hands of colonial governors elsewhere implied that it was in his power regardless of the charter.

7. Subduing the Conflicts over Land (pp. 139–150)

1. RI *Laws* 1719, 36. The Rhode Island law was probably inspired by Massachusetts laws of 1692 and 1713 giving corporative status to proprietors of undivided lands and similar groups, though Rhode Island took an oddly surreptitious approach to the subject. Oscar Handlin and Mary Flug Handlin, *Commonwealth, a Study of the Role of Government in the American Economy: Massachusetts, 1774–1861* (New York, 1947), 96.
2. Many of Newdigate's points came from "Shepard's Abridgment." See Newdigate Manuscripts (a ledger containing miscellany), RIHS, 2k.
3. *RICR*, 3:289; Nathaniel (?) Coddington to Gideon (?) Crawford, 15 July 1707, PTP, 39(A), 16757; facsimile of plat of Stanton's and Gardner's Purchase in Susan Stanton Brayton, "The Stanton Purchase," Rhode Island Historical Society, *Collections* 28 (1935): 80–81, 101–4; Westerly LE, 2:69, 182, 225, 246–47; 4:72–73; 5:162–63; agreement between Henry Hall and others, 12 Aug. 1701, Warner Papers, RIHS, 163. The contemporary description in Sarah Kemble Knight, *The Journal of Madam Knight*, ed. George P. Winship (1920; reprint, New York, 1935), 13–25, offers no commentary on habitation except to point out the rarity of accomodations for travelers along the new Post Road. She seldom commented on the extent of settlement along her journey from Boston to New York and back, from which it is plausible to conclude that she saw nothing out of the ordinary in the Narragansett country, apart from the crude manners at an inn and the primitive dwelling next to the Pawcatuck at Westerly, as compared with other parts of New England.
4. Proclamation, 14 May 1701, Warner Papers, RIHS, 161.
5. On the colonial government's willingness to compromise: RI Laws 1706 (?), 76–77; Nathaniel (?) Coddington to Gideon (?) Crawford, 15 July 1707, PTP, 39(A), 16757; James Greene, Jr., to Capt. Nathaniel (?) Coddington, 5 July 1697, H. W. Greene Papers, RIHS, 54. The citation of laws here is to a resolution of uncertain date but probably refers to May 1696, because the rest of the item into which it was placed by the compilers came from Feburary 1698/99, while the date given to the whole was May 1696. It promised fair adjudication of all land claims. On the agreement with Connecticut: *RICR*, 3:474. On litigation: Gen. Ct. Tr., 1:147, 149, 155. Unfortunately, the court documents on the case have disappeared, so it is impossible to determine the basis of the opposing claims. If the Narragansett Proprietors were suing for part of the Quidnesset purchase, which Rhode Island had sanctioned in 1672, and the opposing claim rested on the Fones Purchase, sanctioned by the colony in 1677, the judgment had a narrow implication. If, however, the Narragansett Proprietors sued on the basis of the foreclosed mortgage, the incident had a quite different meaning.
6. The gambit with Ninigret had an immediate precedent in Connecticut. See

Richard L. Bushman, *From Puritan to Yankee; Character and the Social Order in Connecticut, 1690–1765* (Cambridge, Mass., 1967), 84–99; Nathaniel (?) Coddington to Gideon (?) Crawford, 15 July 1707, PTP, 39(A), 16757. On the Assembly's actions and the deed: *RICR*, 4:31–32, 35–36, 50–52, 229–33; Report of committee on vacant lands, 27 Oct. 1708, "Rhode Island Reports" (committee reports to General Assembly), MS, State Archives, Providence, 1: A; RI LE, 3:273–76.

7. *RICR*, 4:61–63; RI LE, 3:39–41, 231; Westerly LE, 2:35, 36, 41, 47–49, 114, 147, 156; Potter Papers, RIHS. Cf. figures for Andover, Massachusetts, where prices of "wilderness land and unbroken land" usually ran from 10 to 20 shillings per acre between 1660 and 1710, while other land (except meadow) never went over £3 per acre. Philip J. Greven Jr., *Four Generations; Population, Land, and Family in Colonial Andover, Massachusetts* (Ithaca, N.Y., 1970), 128–29.

8. *RICR*, 4:75, 161–62, 175, 344, 364, 380–81, 426.

9. Elisha R. Potter Jr., *The Early History of Narragansett; with an Appendix of Original Documents, Many of which are Now for the First Time Published* (publication data on this title are misleading: the title page identifies the book as published in Providence, 1835; it has also been regarded as Rhode Island Historical Society, *Collections*, vol. 3 [Providence, 1835], but pp. 314–423 contain material added to the original version by William H. Potter, and the preface is dated 1 May 1886), 214–19, gives a list of the sales that is nearly complete. On the sawmill: Westerly LE, 2:48, 106–10. On Mumford: RI LE, 3:40–43, 46, 321. It is all but inconceivable that Mumford paid cash in full for the land.

10. Westerly LE, 2:37, 47, 58–65, 71, 84, 89, 104, 113–15, 117. On the more complex dealings: Westerly LE, 2:193–95, 198, 239; 4:94, 258; 5:72; 6:179; surveyor's plat of Bly's Purchase, 7 Mar. 1725/26, Potter Papers, RIHS; Pierce Records, RIHS, 1:103, 116, 120. The practical results of many of these purchases cannot be reconstructed because of the inadequacy of land records, notably the destruction of those in North Kingstown.

11. Copies of East Greenwich Proprietors Papers, MS, Town Hall, East Greenwich, R.I. (the material includes three bundles, with page sequences differentiated by a, b, and c), 1a.

12. Warwick LE, 2:46. By 1713, shares were freely alienable (e.g., East Greenwich LE, 2:145–46). On voting for those holding more than one share: Warwick LE, 2:46–47. On the functions of a general meeting: East Greenwich Proprietors Papers, 2a–3a, 7a–8a, 11a–14a, 20a–21a.

13. East Greenwich Proprietors Papers, 17a, 21a, 26a, 28a, 30a–32a, 35a–36a, 38a–39a, 42a, 44a–45a, 47a; *RICR*, 4:439, 441; Journal H of D, 18 June 1730.

14. Westerly LE, 2:69, 182; 4:36–39, 42–43, 80–81; *RICR*, 4:151–52, 211, 220–21, 229–34, 236, 396, 450–51, 550, 562; lease from William Wanton et al., to Samuel Clarke and Edward Larkin, 4 Feb. 1717/18, RIHS Miscellaneous Manuscripts, C-55.

15. "Letter-Book of Samuel Sewall," Massachusetts Historical Society, *Collections*, ser. 6 (Boston, 1888), 1:25, 40, 105–6, 108, 135; South Kingstown LE, 6:43–45; Agreement of Pettaquamscut Purchasers, 8 Nov. 1704, Shepley Papers, RIHS, 4:29; Agreement of Pettaquamscut Purchasers, 2 Dec. 1704 , Shepley Papers, 4:30; Copy of decisions of Pettaquamscut Purchasers, 8 Apr. 1692, Shepley Papers, 4:38; Deed from other Pettaquamscut Purchasers to Jahleel Brenton, 7 Sept. 1693, Shepley Papers, 4:39; RI LE, 2:8–21, 102, 106, 107, 147–57; Potter, *Early History of Narragansett*, 290; Papers of *Sion Arnold et al. v. Thomas Potter et al.* (or Potter v. Arnold in the second hearing), Gen. Ct. Tr. papers, box 1720; Gen. Ct. Tr., 1:292.

16. East Greenwich TC, 1:106; East Greenwich LE, 2:277–78; East Greenwich TC, 2:27 Aug. 1793, 1 Jan. 1794.

17. Middletown Proprietors, 11–13, 17, 18, 21–23, 29, 40–42, 44, 54–63, 71.

18. On Goat Island: RI LE, 1:110; Middletown Proprietors, 72–79, 85; Newport TM, 1:165, 193, 266; Newport TM (A), 151, 214, 392, 661; Newport TC, 3:141; 5:13. On Sachuest Point beach: Newport TM, 1:118, 167–70, 172, 191–92, 211, 215, 255, 261, 264, 270–73, 282; Newport TM (A), 188–89, 209–10, 228–29, 263k, 266; Middletown Proprietors, 88–90, 94–102; Middletown TM, 1:15–16, 18–20, 23, 76–77, 78–79, 98, 99, 103; Middletown TC, 1:37, 230–31 (first so numbered), 234, 236, 243; 2:48, 50; *RICR*, 5:275–76.

19. *RICR*, 3:493–94; papers of *Oliver Arnold v. Thomas Northrop* (replaced by landlord, Josiah Arnold), nos. 15, 18, and 26, in Gen. Ct. Tr. papers, box 1713–1715. See also Francis Brinley, "A Briefe Account of Mr. Samuell Cranstons proceedings to gaine Bridget Sanfords Land, that was Originally laid out by John Greene as per the draught may be seene," MS, NHS, box 117, folder 1.

20. Jamestown Proprietors, 65. The roads at issue included the one connecting the ferries to Newport and Kingstown. These were vital to town and colony alike so may have occasioned some of the vigor in governmental action on them.

21. Papers of *Oliver Arnold v. Thomas Northrop*, Gen. Ct. Tr. papers, box 1713–1715; copy (?) of Samuel Cranston to committee of Conanicut proprietors, 12 Apr. 1710, Henry W. Greene Papers, RIHS, 51; Gen. Ct. Tr., 1:228; Brinley, "A Briefe Account"; copy of declaration and complaint of Thomas Carr (by Nathaniel Newdigate, attorney) to General Court of Trials, Sept. 1725, Shepley Papers, RIHS, 15:15; Francis Brinley to General Assembly, May 1728, RI Petitions, 1:57; copy of the case of *David Greene et al. v. Clarke Rodman et al.* (Newport Inferior Court of Common Pleas, Nov. 1740), NHS, box 117, folder 1.

22. Brinley, "A Briefe Account." Unfortunately, no information survives on the voting system of the original Conanicut proprietors.

23. Westerly TC, 1:37.

24. "The Purchasers book of the Purchasers Mettings," MS, Westerly Public Library, Westerly, R.I. (hereafter cited as Misquamicut, 2); Westerly LE, 2:38, 122, 137, 142, 147, 149, 153, 163, 178–79, 212, 214, 235, 242, 244.

25. Misquamicut, 2:4, 6–7.

26. *RICR*, 3:446.

27. One assistant, Randall Holden, was a secret partner and was rewarded for his help later. Decisions of the committee of the Westconnaug proprietors, 7 Feb. 1721/22, Warwick Manuscripts, RIHS, 1:12.

28. Providence ER,17:227–28, 230–33, 235–36; *RICR*,4:18, 41–42; Memorandum on plea against Westconnaug proprietors, n.d., PTP, 39(A), 16627; Copy of deed from Newcom and Awashouse to William Vaughan et al., PTP, 39(A), 16628; Two memoranda probably by Arthur Fenner, 1 Jan. 1703/04, PTP, 39(A), 16675; draft (?) of plea and complaint of justices of the peace in Providence to town or to General Court of Trials, n.d. (after 1 May 1707), PTP, 39(A), 16749; Notes of expenses of Providence proprietors in contest with Westconnaaug, PTP, 39(A), 16750, Nathaniel (?) Coddington to Gideon (?) Crawford, 15 July 1707, PTP, 39(A), 16757; Deposition by Nathaniel Cahoone, 11 Mar. 1707/08, PTP, 39(A), 16775 (verso); Nathaniel Coddington to Gideon Crawford, 16 July 1707, PTP, 39(D), 18049; Samuel Greene Arnold, *History of the State of Rhode Island and Providence Plantations* (1859–1860; reprint, Spartanburg, S.C., 1970), 2:29–30.

29. Providence ER,17:239–40; "The Minutes of the Westconnaug Purchase," transcribed by Theodore G. Foster, Rhode Island Historical Society, *Collections* (Providence, 1933), 26:29–31, 33n, 34–36, 95; Attested copy of the case of *Job Randall v. Richard Steere*, Prov. Sup. Ct. papers for 1763, pp. 39–42; Photostat of petition, 11

October 1711, in RIHS, from Connecticut Archives, Colonial Boundaries, 1662–1827, 1: Document 200, pp. ab. The published minutes of the Westconnaug proprietors, unfortunately, are not derived immediately from originals. No originals have come to light in recent times. The publication is of a copy made by Theodore Foster, probably around 1800. A few entries in the copy, however, agree with better-authenticated documents on incidents in the early eighteenth century.

30. "The Minutes of the Westconnaug Purchase," Rhode Island Historical Society, *Collections*, 26:30, 34, 35, 94, 97n–98n; RI LE, 3:223–25, 308–9.

31. Compare papers of *Andrew Harris v. William Randall*, Gen. Ct. Tr. papers, box September 1722, with papers of *Toleration Harris v. John Randall*, Gen. Ct. Tr. papers, box 1732.

32. Providence ER, 11:28–31, 36, 39, 79–80, 83, 93–95, 141, 146; Walker, "History of Scituate," Appendix, 43–44. Possibly, the town's actions on wharf lots were thought to be justified by their allocation of rights on fill extended from the original shoreline pursuant to authorization to the town by the colonial government. The proprietors got an exclusive right to grant warehouse lots.

33. Providence ER, 11:88–90; 17:192–93, 197, 239, 250. Actually, some of the beds remained undivided by their owners for many years.

34. Providence ER, 2:117; 3:21–22, 66, 68; 7:157–59; 11:56–57; report of committee to town of Providence, 4 June 1764, PTP, 158:A36; "An account of the Divisions of the Lands in Providence: on the East side of the seven Mile line . . . ," in hand of Richard Browne, RIHS Miscellaneous Manuscripts, Se-82; list of divisions of Providence east of the Seven Mile Line to 1751, RIHS Manuscripts, 10:58; papers of *John Smith v. Robert Williams*, Providence Inf. Ct., June 1744 (box 3). The division of the stated common was often omitted from later lists of the proprietors' divisions.

35. Walker, "History of Scituate," 3:15–16; receipt by Thomas Harris, 25 Nov. 1717, PTP, 34:14640; William R. Staples, *Annals of the Town of Providence, from its First Settlement, to the Organization of the City Government, in June 1832* (Providence, 1832), 592; RIHS, M-Pl, A.

36. For examples of lawsuits: Gen. Ct. Tr., 1:265, 268, 277, 305. On adjusting disputes: Gen. Ct. Tr., 1:306, 317, 327, 336; Sup. Ct., 1:663; Papers of *Thomas King and Agnes King v. Joseph Whipple*, Gen. Ct. Tr. papers, box 1721; Papers of *Henry Harris v. Silas Williams and Elizabeth Sheldon*, Providence Inf. Ct., June 1739. On the town's backing of a claimant: Providence Proprietors' plats, RIHS, M-Pl, P; Providence Inf. Ct., 2:476.

37. Warwick LE, 2:16; copy of decisions by proprietors of Four Mile Common, 19 Mar. 1706/07 and 15 Apr. 1707, Warner Papers, RIHS, 186; copy of deliberations of proprietors of Four Mile Common, 9 Jan. 1710/11, Warner Papers, 204; list of shares in the Horse Neck land, 19 Feb. 1716/17, Warner Papers, 246; copy of decision by proprietors of Four Mile Common to divide Horse Neck land, 20 Feb. 1716/17, Warner Papers, 247; Harrison S. Taft, untitled set of nine notebooks (some of which have their own titles) on land divisions in Warwick, MS, RIHS, 1:63.

38. Warwick LE, 3:5a, 6a; Warwick GR, 90a; Copy of decision by proprietors of Four Mile Common, 29 Apr. 1710, Warner Papers, RIHS, 201; copy of decision by proprietors of Four Mile Common, 11 May 1710, Warner Papers, 202; copy of deliberations of proprietors of Four Mile Common, 24 Jan. 1712/13, Warner Papers, 228; copy of decision by proprietors of Four Mile Common, Warner Papers, 308; decision of proprietors of Four Mile Common, 1 July 1714, Shepley Papers, RIHS, 6:113.

39. Warwick LE, 3:6a, 7a; copy of decisions by proprietors of Four Mile Common, 20 Feb. 1716/17, Warner Papers, RIHS, 247; report of committee to proprietors of Four Mile Common, 8 Apr. 1717, Warner Papers, 248; working paper of clerk

of proprietors of Four Mile Common, 11 Feb. 1717/18, Warner Papers, 258; copy of decisions by proprietors of Four Mile Common, 22 Jan. 1722/23, Warner Papers, 380; rough minutes of proprietors of Four Mile Common, 10 Jan. 1725/26, Warner Papers, 409; copy of list of lots drawn in Four Mile Common, 30 Jan. 1726/27, Warner Papers, 424; copy of decisions by proprietors of Four Mile Common, 30 Jan. 1726/27, Warner Papers, 437; copy of minutes of proprietors of Four Mile Common, for various dates, 7 Jan. 1735 to 11 Nov. 1751, Warner Papers, 666; Taft, Warwick notebooks, 1:63, 66, 68.

40. Lawyer's argument for John Warner, n.d. (after 1697), Warner Papers, RIHS, 140; lawyer's notes on case for John Warner, n.d. (after Apr. 1717), Warner Papers, 249; lawyer's notes on evidence, n.d. (1718 or later), Warner Papers, 274; John Warner to General Assembly, 29 Oct. 1718, Warner Papers, 289; lawyer's notes, n.d. (probably Sept. 1722), Warner Papers, 307; copy of "Plea and Answer of John Gereardy" by Daniel Updike, attorney, Gen. Ct. Tr., Mar. 1727, and notes by Nathaniel Newdigate for rebuttal for plaintiff, John Warner, Warner Papers, 433; note of judgment for defendant in *John Warner v. John Gereardy*, Gen. Ct. Tr., Sept. 1727, Warner Papers, 438; Papers of *John Warner v. Mary Smith*, Gen. Ct. Tr. papers, box September 1722; Gen. Ct. Tr., 1:378; 2:55, 58, 80, 132, 150.

8. Town Ambitions and Town Government (pp. 154–168)

1. Newport LE, 10:135–36 (new series; rerecord made in 1807); Newport TM, 1:112.

2. Newport TM, 1:34, 37, 38, 42, 57, 60, 73, 77, 90, 92–94, 100, 128, 160, 220, 224; Newport TM (A), 91, 93, 108, 122, 124, 151–52, 181.

3. On the town's desire for water frontage lots: Newport TM, 1:89, 90; Newport TM (A), 124; PGA, 7:193. On the new special committee: Newport TM, 1:123–25; Newport TM (A), 149–51.

4. Newport TM, 1:260, 307; Newport TM (A), 209, 261.

5. Newport TM, 1:14, 64; Newport TM (A), 97. Cf. Newport TM, 3:364.

6. Newport TM, 1:66–67; Newport TM (A), 98–100, 101.

7. Newport TM, 1:59, 60; Newport TM (A), 90–93.

8. Newport TM, 1:133, 134, 159, 206, 217–18, 226, 232, 235–36, 244, 288; Newport TM (A), 239, 244, 246, 251–51a, 287; Colony Records, 4:136.

9. RI *Laws* 1706 (?), 81–82; Newport TM, 1:45, 60, 221, 277, 288, 289; Newport TM (A), 235–36, 249, 287; *RICR*, 4:538.

10. On night watch and other features of town government: Newport TM, 1:74; Newport TM (A), 105, 263; Newport TC, 2:31, 133, 209; 3:240; 4:6, 37; Newport town meeting to General Assembly, 3 Dec. 1733, RI Petitions, 2:118; Newport men to General Assembly, Dec. 1735, RI Petitions, 3:44; Colony Records, 5:149–50, 288; Journal H of D, 21 Aug. 1735, 22 Feb. 1736/37, 17 June 1737. On restraint of outsiders in local commerce: Newport TM, 1:114, 141–42, 243, 273, 281, 284, 308; Newport TM (A), 142–43, 229, 251; RI *Laws* 1706 (?), 82–83; Newport TC, 7:91.

11. Newport TM, 130, 161, 202, 209, 210; Newport TM (A), 155, 225.

12. Newport TC, 6:144; town council of Newport to General Assembly, Feb. 1729, RI Petitions, 2: A; Journal H of D, 7 May 1730; Colony Records, 5:15–16. Like the law on waterfront improvements, this one extended the same benefits to all towns, but it was sought by and chiefly useful to Newport.

13. Portsmouth TC, 5:1.

14. Portsmouth TC, 5:2–3, 17–22; Portsmouth LE, 1:414; 2:1–15; Gen. Ct. Tr., 1:403; papers of *William Hall et al. v. William Earle*, Gen. Ct. Tr. papers, box 1722M.

East Greenwich succeeded in creating a port village by methods similar to Portsmouth's but left management mainly to the proprietors. They reserved the site at the northeast corner of their territory until 1711 and then appointed a committee to subdivide it. They took half of the two hundred lots and let the committee grant the others for a small fee under confining terms. After several years, the committee began to review compliance with the terms and gave title to those who had met them. Copies of East Greenwich Proprietors Papers, MS, Town Hall, East Greenwich, R.I. (the material includes three bundles, with page sequences differentiated by a, b, and c), 1b–4b; East Greenwich TC, 1:146, 173; 2:12 Oct. 1711, 6 Nov. 1725, 5 April 1726, 11 March 1726/27, 2 Sept. 1727, 27 May 1729, 27 May 1730, 25 March 1734.

15. East Greenwich TC, 1:135, 139, 156, 255–57; 2:13 April 1754; East Greenwich TM, 26 May 1752; East Greenwich Proprietors Papers, 50b.

16. Providence ER, 11:22, 26–27, 42, 53, 56–57, 79–80, 83, 88–90, 158–59; 8:177; 17:198–99, 241–42.

17. Providence ER, 13:37–38; 17:239, 250; Providence Proprietors Documents, RIHS, M-Pr; committee reports on streets to town council of Providence, Feb. 1737/38 ff., PTP, 158:A9–A29; plan of house lots laid out in 1717, PTP, 154:B3; list of divisions of Providence east of Seven Mile Line to 1751, RIHS Manuscripts, 10:58.

18. Portsmouth TM, 1:38–39.

19. The councils were quite different from boards of selectmen. Their capacity as probate courts, together with town supervision of such things as land records, made local units carry more of the burdens of government in Rhode Island than in a place like Massachusetts. For a different view of the shift of power, see Edward M. Cook Jr., *The Fathers of the Towns; Leadership and Community Structure in Eighteenth-Century New England* (Baltimore, 1976), 8. Cook also sees the growing devotion to formality in town business. His data on length of service in councils and boards of selectmen (pp. 56–59) show councilmen serving longer—and sometimes being older—than selectmen. These data suggest the greater weight of the councils.

20. Providence ER, 15:152–55; John A. Sainsbury, "Indian Labor in Early Rhode Island," *New England Quarterly* 48 (1975):378–88.

21. On seventeenth-century laws against slavery: *RICR*, 1:243; 2:535. On the growth of the Rhode Island slave trade: Jay Coughtry, *The Notorious Triangle; Rhode Island and the African Slave Trade, 1700–1807* (Philadelphia, 1981), 25–27, 241–43, and passim.

22. Jamestown Proprietors, 97; Warwick TM, 2:2; Newport TM, 1:219, 287, 289; Newport TM (A), 288; South Kingstown TM, 1:10, 13, 80–81; South Kingstown TC, 2:140.

23. E.g., Newport TM, 1:60; Westerly TM, 1:26, 71.

24. On screening potential inhabitants: North Kingstown Probate, 5:11; 6:122; South Kingstown TC, 3:80–81; Portsmouth TC, 2:13; Newport TC, 1:15. On posting bonds: *RICR*, 3:117; Portsmouth TC, 2:50. On colonial laws regulating admissions: Portsmouth TC, 2:59; North Kingstown Probate, 7:282; Colony Records, 4:176.

25. On the right of settlement: Colony Records, 6:118–19. Portsmouth requested clarification of the foggy statute in 1740. See Portsmouth town council to General Assembly, Feb. 1739/40, RI Petitions, 4:11. See also Lynne Withey, *Urban Growth in Colonial Rhode Island; Newport and Providence in the Eighteenth Century* (Albany, N.Y., 1984), 57. On town use of the concept of right of settlement: e.g., Portsmouth TC, 2:1, 15, 27, 50; Warwick Wills, 1:15; North Kingstown Probate, 5:11; 6:92; East

Greenwich TC, 4:25 August 1733; Jamestown Proprietors, 256; South Kingstown TC, 2:137–38, 140, 144.

26. E.g., East Greenwich TC, 1:197.

27. East Greenwich TC, 1:64, 197. On other towns: New Shoreham TB, 24, 580; Jamestown Proprietors, 7; North Kingstown TC, 15, 25, 32, 35, 50–51, 93, 116; South Kingstown TM, 1:2; Westerly LE, 1:36, 40; Westerly TM, 1:52; Portsmouth ER, 255–56; Portsmouth TM, 1:28, 31; Warwick TM, 2:1, 10, 13, 14, 20, 45, 46, 81; RIHS Manuscripts, 2:40.

28. PGA, 5:176; Colony Records, 4:616.

29. South Kingstown TM, 1:43.

30. Providence ER, 11:152–54, 166–67; East Greenwich TC, 1:194.

31. Examples of fence requirements: Portsmouth TM, 1:6, 45. Examples of other measures to restrain livestock: Westerly LE, 1:15; Westerly TM, 1:28; North Kingstown TC, 25, 29; Newport TM, 1:74, 84, 134, 141; Providence ER, 11:14–15, 146, 154; 13:3; Richard Knight et al. to town of Providence, 27 Apr. 1734, PTP, 2nd ser., 3:0742; Portsmouth TM, 1:62; Jamestown Proprietors, 117, 118, 267, 305; East Greenwich TC, 1:122, 156, 183. 196, 207; South Kingstown TM, 1:3. On pounds and poundkeepers: Portsmouth TM, 1:1, 11–12, 22; Jamestown Proprietors, 35, 117; East Greenwich TC, 1:70, 122; Westerly LE, 1:21–22, 25; Westerly TM, 1:28; North Kingstown TC, 49; South Kingstown TC, 1:2; Warwick TM, 2:13–14, 116–17. On field drivers: Portsmouth TM, 1:45, 49, 52, 54, 63; Jamestown Proprietors, 127, 169, 207; South Kingstown TM, 1:2, 13, 20, 21–24, 32, 38–40; North Kingstown TC, 116–18; East Greenwich TC, 1:208–10, 214, 215, 223. On earmarks: Newport TM, 1:107–8, 155–57, 287; Newport TM (A), 174, 177–78, 288; South Kingstown TM, 1:10. On control of pests and predators: Portsmouth ER, 309–10; Portsmouth TM, 1:27; North Kingstown TC, 43, 93, 94, 127, 174, 169; Westerly TM, 1:9; Westerly LE, 1:24; Jamestown Proprietors, 7, 169; East Greenwich TC, 1:91; Providence ER, 13:2, 19–20, 29, 42–43, 64; Warwick TM, 2:3, 9; South Kingstown TM, 1:2, 6, 27, 96–97; Newport TM, 1:115, 149.

32. E.g., Providence ER, 11:64–65, 140–41, 165; East Greenwich TC, 1:176–77, 195.

33. Roads of the older sort remaianed, but they no longer were roads. In Rhode Island parlance, they became driftways.

34. Portsmouth TM, 1:51; South Kingstown TM, 1:25–29, 33–34, 65–67, 77, 83, 88, 90, 320, 246; South Kingstown LE, 4:141–43.

35. East Greenwich TC, 1:61, 75, 82, 85, 99, 152; Westerly TM, 1:24, 43, 51; Portsmouth TM, 1:51, 110–11; Newport TM, 1:51–52, 119, 186; Newport TM (A), 152–53; Warwick TM, 2:7, 8, 45–47; South Kingstown TM, 1:51–52; Jamestown Proprietors, 97.

36. E.g., Newport TM, 1:119; Newport TM (A), 152–53; East Greenwich TC, 1:99, 181; Westerly TM, 1:37–38, 43; Warwick TM, 2:9; Jamestown Proprietors, 27, 145, 173, 229, South Kingstown TM, 1:1, 28; Portsmouth TM, 1:54, 127; North Kingstown TC, 87–88.

37. Westerly LE, 1:39; Westerly TM, 1:16, 17, 24; RI *Laws* 1719, 23; Newport TM, 1:133–34, 148, 226, 235–36, 268, 274; Newport TM (A), 239, 244, 246; East Greenwich TC, 1:171; Jamestown Proprietors, 145, 149, 152, 153, 157, 173, 197; South Kingstown TM, 1:20, 77; Providence ER, 9:24; 13:10; North Kingstown TC, 50–51.

38. RI *Laws* 1706(?), 81–82; Newport TM, 1:45, 60, 221; Newport TM (A), 235–36, 277, 279, 288–89; *RICR*, 4:538.

39. Newport TM, 1:74, 114, 243, 262; Newport TM (A), 105, 142–43, 251, 263; Newport TC, 2:31, 133, 209; 3:240; 4:6, 37; Samuel Carr et al. to General Assembly, 3

July 1733, RI Petitions, 2:116; Newport town meeting to General Assembly, 3 Dec. 1733, RI Petitions, 2:118; petitions to General Assembly, Dec. 1735 and 22 Feb. 1735/36, RI Petitions, 3:44; sixty-four Newport men to General Assembly, June 1742, RI Petitions, 4:119; petition from men in "woods part" of Newport to General Assembly, June 1743, RI Petitions, 5:11; Colony Records, 5:149–50, 288.

40. Warwick TM, 2:13–14; Westerly TM, 1:71; Portsmouth TM, 1:154–55; Newport TM, 1:291–92; RI *Laws* 1719, 23. Cook, *Fathers of the Towns*, describes a norm of five to fifteen "minor offices," i.e., other than moderator, selectman, clerk, treasurer, and constable. His count may have omitted officers chosen only when need arose, rather than annually. Sometimes, Rhode Island towns, instead of electing a full list of sealers, packers, cullers, etc., chose at the annual election only to make necessary replacements.

41. Providence ER, 11:58–59.

42. North Kingstown Probate, 5:9; Portsmouth TC, 2:11; Jamestown Proprietors, 65, 95, 306; East Greenwich TC, 1:59; Westerly LE, 1:18, 21; Westerly TC, 1:14–16, 19, 24, 31, 36, 37, 72–73; 2:278–81, 306.

43. On monthly meetings: e.g., Portsmouth TC, 2:1; Westerly TC, 1:1; Providence ER, 10:42. On council seals: Portsmouth TC, 2:35; East Greenwich TC, 3:15; Jamestown Proprietors, 116. On benefits for service: Westerly LE, 1:37; Westerly TM, 1:30; East Greenwich TC, 1:140, 156, 207; 2:77–78; South Kingstown TC, 2:123; Jamestown Proprietors, 289, 326. On selection of a president: South Kingstown TC, 3:79, 153.

44. On councils suing on executors' bonds: e.g., Jamestown Proprietors, 76, 91, 110; Portsmouth TC, 2:24–25. On the old flexibility: Providence ER, 10:76–81; Westerly TC, 2:199; East Greenwich TC, 4:23 Feb. 1739/40, 29 March 1740; North Kingstown Probate, 5:91, 96–97. On changing statutes and their results: e.g., Providence ER, 12:76; RI *Laws* 1719, 13–15, 95–98; RI *Laws* 1730, 162.

45. On paternalistic flexibility: e.g., Warwick Wills, 1:19, 33–34. Examples of requesting authority to sell real estate: *RICR*, 3:440–41; Journal H of D, 19 Feb. 1728/29; Peter Davis to General Assembly, Feb. 1729, RI Petitions, 2:18. In an interesting example, the Providence council planned use of the land of John Paine, who died intestate, to let his widow raise the minor children. His older children then asked for equal division of the lands outside Providence, which the council agreed to. Providence ER, 12:6, 11;16:88–92. This kink in the law was partly ironed out in 1745. After then, creditors could sue heirs at law or devisees (not the estate) and, if successful, get paid by the sheriff, who could choose and sell land to raise the amount. Executors still had to go through the routine of the petition. See *PS* 1768, 71–72.

46. Examples of wards choosing their own guardians: Portsmouth TC, 2:1; Warwick Wills, 1:5. On binding out fatherless children: e.g., Providence ER, 10:31–35.

47. Example of a town meeting's action: Providence ER, 11:3, 7–8. Examples of usual practice of councils' authorizing expenditures: Portsmouth TC, 2:3, 7, 10–11, 17; South Kingstown TC, 2:127; North Kingstown Probate, 5:12. On councils taking assets of the poor and compelling them to bind out children: Providence ER, 21:48–49; Warwick Willls, 1:7, 12, 46; Portsmouth TC, 2:1, 38, 39, 41; North Kingstown Probate, 7:358. On the colonial law: Colony Records, 5:433.

48. On Newport's pioneering: Newport TM, 1:31, 86, 132, 237; Newport TM (A), 67–68, 85–86. On the colonial law: RI *Laws* 1719, 10. On overseers elsewhere: e.g., Jamestown Proprietors, 141; East Greenwich TC, 3:22–23; Warwick Wills, 1:55. Several towns elected the same set of men to the council and the panel of overseers.

49. South Kingstown TC, 2:13; Jamestown Proprietors, 31, 59, 88. On councils' powers over Indians elsewhere: Westerly TC, 2:216; Portsmouth TC, 3:20, 54, 263.

50. On unwed mothers: e.g., North Kingstown Probate, 5:104. On the councils' regulation of apprenticeship: e.g., Newport TC, 2:36; 4:134; Portsmouth TC, 2:70, 72; East Greenwich TC, 4:31 Jan. 1735/36. On children being compelled to support their parents: South Kingstown TC, 2:2, 107–8, 127, 132, 136; 3:7, 9, 15, 25, 35, 39.

51. On the ordinary practice: e.g., Newport TC, 5:15. On special laws for Providence and its divisions: RI *Laws* 1730, 136; Journal H of D, 24 June 1731; Colony Records, 5:69. On the use of these laws: e.g., Providence ER, 9:49–63; committee reports on streets to town council of Providence, 1737/38 and 1738, PTP, 158:A7, A8, A9; committee report on laying out highway to town council of Providence, 1733, PTP, 164:B5.

52. E.g., Newport TC, 2:31, 209; 3:41, 102, 240; 7:91; Westerly TC, 2:78; South Kingstown TC, 2:36; East Greenwich TC, 4:26 May 1733; Providence ER, 12:89; Colony Records, 5:195. Pursuant to colonial statutes, some councils passed ordinances restricting the citizens' freedom to own dogs.

53. On quarantine responsibilities for magistrates: PGA, 8:29–33; Colony Records, 4:268–70, 274–75; 5:10, 24–26, 32; Newport TC, 3:141; 5:13. On the legislation of 1738 and shortly thereafter: Colony Records, 5:321, 328, 355–66. Examples of town councils' actions after these laws: South Kingstown TC, 3:69; Jamestown Proprietors, 289–95.

9. *Sacred Fellowship in Relation to Time and Space (pp. 171–184)*

1. Document on the early history of Newport First Congregational church in the handwriting of Thomas Browne, NHS, box 4, folder 6; Copy of Nathaniel Clap, Newport 9 May 1739, to Henry Flynt, NHS, box 40, folder 70.

2. Document on the early history of Newport First Congregational church, NHS, box 4, folder 6; Clifford K. Shipton, "Nathaniel Clap," *Sibley's Harvard Graduates; Biographical Sketches of Those Who Attended Harvard College* (Cambridge, Mass., 1933), 4:36.

3. Document on the early history of Newport First Congregational Church, NHS, box 4, folder 6; copy of Nathaniel Clap, Newport, 9 May 1739, to Henry Flynt, NHS, box 40, folder 70.

4. Confession of faith and covenant, both in NHS, box 40, folder 6.

5. Document on the early history of Newport First Congregational Church, NHS, box 4, folder 6; Shipton, "Nathaniel Clap," 4:37; Shipton, "Benjamin Bass," *Sibley's Harvard Graduates* (Boston, 1942), 6:73; copy of Clap to Flynt, 9 May 1739, NHS, box 40, folder 70; copy (by Ezra Stiles) of Boston ministers to Benjamin Ellery and Samuel Vernon, 12 Jan. 1726/27, in "A Book Containing The Affairs and Proceedings of the second Congregational Church in Newport . . . ," MS, NHS (hereafter cited as Newport Second Congregational Record), 79.

6. Draft of result of council, 3 April 1728, RIHS Miscellaneous Manuscripts, SE-24; copy of result of the council, Newport Second Congregational Record, 3–6.

7. On church decisions: Newport Second Congregational Record, 7–11, 16. On Adams's troubles: copy of John Coddington, 28 Apr. 1729, to Thomas Foxcroft, RIHS Miscellaneous Manuscripts, SE-24; Ezra Stiles's narrative and copy of John Adams, 25 Feb. 1729/30, to church and congregation, in Newport Second Congregational Record, 81–83; Shipton, "John Adams," *Sibley's Harvard Graduates*, 6:425–26. On further confining bylaws: Newport Second Congregational Record, 19–20, 83. On the resolution of differences between the churches: Proceedings of church meetings,

14 Apr. 1728 and 9 July 1730, Newport Second Congregational Record, 10, 81, 84; John Adams, 10 May 1728, to Thomas Foxcroft, RIHS Miscellaneous Manuscripts, SE-24; John Coddington, 23 July 1728, 23 December 1728, and 28 April 1729, to Thomas Foxcroft, RIHS Miscellaneous Manuscripts, SE-24; Subscription paper, Jan. 1728/29, RIHS Miscellaneous Manuscripts, SE-24.

8. The background of this system need not be rehearsed here *in extenso*. Briefly, it was a method to reconcile the conflicting interests in a "converted membership" and a territorial parish, and it was legitimized by a theological distinction between "saving faith" in the church members and "historical faith" or merely intellectual assent by members of the congregation. Further difficulties lay in defining what the two elements were to gain from religious fellowship. The church was to be the object of preaching and pastoral care in general, as well as church discipline, and the congregation presumably was to have its historical faith nurtured and expanded, while the children of both groups might receive some advantages in being brought into historical faith. By the time this system was introduced into Rhode Island, it had no bearing on old problems of the parish in Massachusetts and had become embedded in New England folkways.

9. Proceedings of the society, 18 Dec. 1733, Newport Second Congregational Record, 177; copy of indenture deed 11 March 1733/34, in Newport Second Congregational Record, 139–41.

10. On Block Island: New Shoreham TB, 337–42, 518–20; Shipton, "Samuel Niles," *Sibley's Harvard Graduates*, 4:485–86. On Providence: copy of Nathaniel Clap, 9 May 1739, to Henry Flynt, NHS, box 40, folder 70; Shipton, "Samuel Moody," *Sibley's Harvard Graduates*, 4:362; Shipton, "Josiah Cotton," *Sibley's Harvard Graduates* (Boston, 1945), 7:50–51; William R. Staples, *Annals of the Town of Providence, from its First Settlement, to the Organization of the City Government, in June, 1832* (Providence, 1843), 432–38, 440; Arthur E. Wilson, *Weybosset Bridge in Providence Plantations, 1700–1790* (Boston, 1947), 32–33, 47–48, 50–56, 73; Copy of deed, 2 July 1722, and other papers, Providence First Congregational Society Papers, RIHS, box 1. On the Kingstowns: South Kingstown LE, 2:153–55; or North Kingstown LE, 1:135–36, for surviving portion of slightly variant text; Jahleel Brenton, 9 Aug. 1711, to Samuel Sewall, Shepley Papers, RIHS, 4:35; Documents in "Torrey v. Gardner" papers, Prince Library, Boston Public Library, 1:13, 45, 59, 93, 99–101; 2:12, 14–19, 28, 29, 55–59; James Honyman, 27 April 1716, to Samuel Sewall, Shepley Papers, RIHS, 4:34; Shipton, "Joseph Torrey," *Sibley's Harvard Graduates* (Boston, 1951), 8:498–507. On Westerly: Westerly LE, 7:228, Shipton, "Joseph Park," *Sibley's Harvard Graduates*, 7:416.

11. *RICR*, 4:490.

12. George Champlin Mason, ed., *Annals of Trinity Church, Newport, Rhode Island. 1698–1821* (Newport, R.I., 1890), 10–13, 18.

13. Ibid., 11, 13–16, 76, 79.

14. Ibid., 18, 19, 54, 57, 59.

15. "The Register Book Belonging to the Church of St Pauls in Naragansett," MS, St. Paul's Parish House, Wickford, R.I., 1–2, 5, 9, 12, 21, 25, 29–30.

16. Mason, ed., *Trinity Church*, 30–34; "Register Book . . . of St Pauls," 27, 28–29, 36, 48, 132.

17. Mason, ed., *Trinity Church*, 37, and passim; "Register Book . . . of St Pauls," 23, 26–27.

18. Arthur L. Cross, *The Anglican Episcopate in the American Colonies* (New York, 1902), 100–101; Mason, ed., *Trinity Church*, 26. The reasoning and even the phrasing may have been drawn from a letter written by a Pennsylvania clergyman, Evan Evans, in 1707; see Cross, *Anglican Episcopate*, 95–97.

19. Mason, ed., *Trinity Church*, 27.

20. *RICR*, 4:205–6.

21. Copy of Francis Nicholson, 23 Dec. 1714, to James Honyman, MS, JCB; "Register Book . . . St Pauls," 7, 26–27; Wilkins Updike, *A History of the Episcopal Church in Narragansett Rhode Island Including a History of Other Episcopal Churches in the State With a Transcript of the Narragansett Parish Register, from 1718 to 1774; . . .*, 2nd ed., enlarged by Daniel Goodwin (Boston, 1907), 1:374, n. 104; "Torrey v. Gardner" papers, Prince Library, Boston Public Library, 1:55. On the parish's decision to go to court: "Register Book . . . of St Pauls," 7.

22. Declaration and complaint by Henry Bull, attorney; Testimony of Henry Gardner, 21 March 1722/23; Deposition of George Gardner, 13 March 1722/23; Deposition of Philip Briggs, 8 March 1722/23; all in copy of the case of James MacSparran v.George Mumford, Gen. Ct. Tr. papers, box March 1724; copy of minutes of Pettaquamscut purchasers, 4 June 1668, Shepley Papers, RIHS, 4:35.

23. Plea and answer by Nathaniel Newdigate, attorney, at General Court of Trials, September 1723, in copy of the case of *James MacSparran v. George Mumford*, Gen. Ct. Tr. papers, box March 1724.

24. Gen. Ct. Tr., 1:409, 421; Shipton, "Joseph Torrey," *Sibley's Harvard Graduates*, 8:500; Sup. Ct. 1:443; decision of privy council, 16 July 1734, entered in South Kingstown LE, 3A, 674–77.

25. Sup. Ct., 1:499, 511, 527, 652; "Register Book . . . of St Pauls," 38–39.

26. Shipton, "Joseph Torrey," 8:506; "Register Book . . . of St Pauls," 59; South Kingstown TM, 1:233.

27. Providence ER, 11:55; John Comer's report on acquisition of land and erection of meetinghouse, in "The Church Records: 1729 Containing the [illegible] of the Church [illegible] by the Rev. John Comer," MS, NHS (hereafter cited as Newport Six Principle Records, 1); cf. Newport LE, 24:480–81; Photostat of deed of land for meetinghouse, North Kingstown, 1703, in possession of Mrs. Edwin H. Huling of that town; Historical Records Survey, Division of Community Service Projects, Work Projects Administration, *Inventory of the Church Archives of Rhode Island: Baptist* (Providence, 1941), 30–31; South Kingstown LE, 3A, 47–49; Cyrus Walker, "The History of Scituate, R.I., from the Acquisition of the Territory in 1659, to the Close of the Nineteenth Century," MS, said to be in Scituate Town Hall but consulted on microfilm at RIHS, 8:23–24.

28. The South Kingstown deed was an exception in resorting to a trusteeship arrangement such as Quakers used. South Kingstown LE, 3A, 47–49.

29. Copy (by John Comer) of "The form of the Agreement of the Church In Building a Meeting House," 23 Jan. 1706/07, Newport Six Principle Records, 1; Newport LE, 24:480–83.

30. "The Church Records of the sevent[h] day sabbath keepers on Rhod Island," MS, NHS (hereafter cited as Newport SDB), 22, 24, 76; Deed from Hezekiah Carpenter et al. to William Packcom et al., 6 Sept. 1737, NHS, box 103, folder 3; Rerecorded in Newport LE, 10:19–21; Proceedings of meeting of the society, 12 May 1737, "The Book of Records belonging to the Church of Christ in New-port on Rhod-Island under the Pastoral Cear of mr. William Peckam and mr. John Comer," MS, NHS (hereafter cited as Newport First Baptist Records), 39–40.

31. Church meeting, 15 Nov. 1725, and note on ordination of John Comer, 19 May 1726, including his declaration of faith, Newport First Baptist Records, 7, 9; Isaac Backus, *A History of New England. With Particular Reference to the Denomination of Christians Called Baptists*, 2nd ed. (Newton, Mass., 1871), 2:16–17, 17n–18n.

32. Church meeting, 8 Jan. 1728/29, Newport First Baptist Records, 33; Shipton, "John Callender," *Sibley's Harvard Graduates*, 7:150–51; Joseph Jenckes, 19 March 1729/30, to James Brown, Backus Papers, RIHS; John Walton, 17 June 1731, to church council, Backus Papers, RIHS; copy of James Brown, "A Memarandum of a separation in the bapt[ist] congregation in Prouidenc made chifly by Elder Place deacon Winsor and Timothy Sheldon . . ." in 1731, Backus Papers, RIHS; Newport SDB, 20.

33. Note on ordination of deacons, 20 Oct. 1724, Newport First Baptist Records, 13; Copy of treatise by John Clarke "Containing his Judgment and the Judgment of the Church respecting that Soul Supporting Doctrine of Personal Election . . . ," Newport First Baptist Records, 173, 175; Backus, *History of New England*, 2:19n, 23; John Comer's copy of Reuben Packcom, "Seven queries propounded to the Church . . . 5 June 1731"; Joseph Jenckes, 19 March 1729/30, to James Brown; John Walton, 17 June 1731, to a church council; copy of James Brown, "A Memarandum of a seperation . . ."; all in Backus Papers, RIHS; Backus, *History of New England*, 2:23; Sydney V. James, "Ecclesiastical Authority in the Land of Roger Williams," *New England Quarterly* 57 (1984):341–43.

34. The petition in 1733 asking for a statute to let Baptist and "Presbyterian" (i.e., Congregationalist) ministers perform marriage ceremonies asserted blandly that marriage should be religiously performed; it went on to make the proposal a matter of giving equal treatment to denominations in the jurisdiction, then presented an argument for the General Assembly's power to gratify the petitioners. The Assembly granted the petition. Petition of Baptists and "Presbyterians" to General Assembly, Oct. 1733, RI Petitions, 2:131. See also *RICR*, 4:490.

35. John Comer's entry of "A Coppie of what was Drawn up by mr. Daniel Wightman Pastor and presented to the Church at the time when a Record of Affairs relating to the Church was first Set up. December the 31. 1726," Newport Six Principle Records, 1; Church meeting, 24 Dec. 1724, Newport First Baptist Records, 23; Disciplinary cases, 1726–1728, Newport First Baptist Records, 23–29; Church meetings, 21 Apr. 1726 and 22 May 1726, Newport First Baptist Records, 43; Church decisions on "Days of Fasting and Thanksgiving . . . ," Newport First Baptist Records, 87; Notes on gifts to church, Newport First Baptist Records, 179.

36. Copy of "Records of the First Seventh Day church of Hopkinton, R.I.," MS, RIHS, 2, 18, 20, 23–24, 45, 55–56; Newport SDB, 4–5, 6, 22, 24, 29–32, 39–40, 42, 82–84, 97; copy made in late nineteenth century of records of Newport Seventh Day Baptist Church, 1708–1736 and 1770–1771, MS, NHS, 5, 7–11, 18, 48; copy made in 1898 of "Records of the Seventh-day Baptist Church of Newport, R.I. from 1692 to 1836, comprising three Volumes," MS, Westerly Public Library, Westerly, R.I., 199–200.

37. Newport SDB, 10, 12, 72, 85.

38. Backus, *History of New England*, 2:27; church meeting, 24 Jan. 1733/34, Newport First Baptist Records, 38. For examples of church councils called on vexing issues: Copy (by John Comer) of Daniel Everitt, 31 Dec. 1729, to Daniel Wightman; copy (by John Comer) of Joseph Jenckes, 3 Feb. 1729/30, to Daniel Everitt; Questions from John Tefft and others, 26 Aug. 1731, to James Brown and messenger of Baptist church at Providence; all in Backus Papers, RIHS.

39. Little need be said on the methods for controlling land. After the introduction of the trusteeship, it only had to be perfected. In 1708 a traveling Friend from England, Thomas Story, introduced the device of adding to a conveyance a document in which the trustees signed a promise to each other (on behalf of themselves, their heirs, and assigns) not to divide the property and not to sue on a writ of partition.

Moreover, the conveyance went to them as joint tenants with right of survivorship and not as tenants in common. With variations, this scheme was used for many years. See records of Rhode Island Monthly Meeting of Friends (men), MS, NHS (hereafter cited as RI MM with volume number plus date of session given as number of day and year separated by month in Roman numerals), 2:18/III/1708, 25/XI/1709/09, 14/VII/1728, 29/XI/1733/34, 28/VII/1736; Portsmouth LE, 2:16–17, 623–24; 4:83–84; Jamestown LE, 1:139–40; 2:271–75; 3:296–300; Indenture deed, 28 December 1736, for Tiverton meetinghouse site, papers of Rhode Island Monthly Meeting of Friends, MS, RIHS; East Greenwich LE, 2:92–93; South Kingstown LE, 2:165–67; Providence ER, 20:284–87; Warwick LE, 2:303–4; Indenture, 17 December 1719, in box "Deeds, Burying Grounds," papers of New England Yearly Meeting of Friends, MS, Yearly Meeting Archives, RIHS; Indenture, 31 January 1726/27, New England Yearly Meeting papers, RIHS.

40. RI MM, 2:28/VII/1714, 26/VIII/1714, 25/XI/1714/15, 26/II/1715, 28/IX/1715, 28/XI/1717/18, 27/VI/1723, 31/I/1724, 25/III/1725, 25/IV/1728, and later entries; "A Book of Records Belonging to the Proprietors of Eastons Point Newport," MS, NHS, 11–13.

41. Greenwich Monthly Meeting, established in 1699, at first embraced all the mainland but later was subdivided to set off South Kingstown and, later still, Smithfield. Minutes of the Monthly Greenwich Meeting of Friends (men), MS, New England Yearly Meeting Archives, RIHS (hereafter cited as Greenwich MM, with volume number followed by date of session given in numbers for day and year separated by month in Roman numerals), 1:?/V/1699; 1:7/II/1705, 2/IV/1718.

42. Greenwich MM, 1:22/VIII/1705, 19/IX/1705, 16/V/1705; 2:4/XI/1719/20, 2/XI/1727/28, 6/I/1727/28; RI MM, 1:26/I/1706; 2:7/VII/1708, 5/VIII/1708; 2:25/X/1739, 25/I/1740.

43. Greenwich MM, 1:20/VIII/1701.

44. RI MM, 1:1/II/1701, 22/V/1701, 27/II/1703, 13/V/1708, 10/VI/1708; Minutes of New England Yearly Meeting of Friends (men), New England Yearly Meeting Archives, RIHS (hereafter cited as NE YM, with date of session given in number of year), 1701, 1708, 1709, 1720; Greenwich MM, 1:17/I/1706/07, 16/XII/1717/18; quarterly meeting epistle to monthly meetings, 7/VIII/1736, in box "Smithfield Monthly: Epistles to: 1716–1860," in New England Yearly Meeting Papers, New England Yearly Meeting Archives, RIHS; Rhode Island Monthly Meeting, "Testimonials of denial and Condemnation by Individuals," New England Yearly Meeting Archives, RIHS.

45. Although previous minute books sometimes had designated sessions as men's meetings, in fact the sexes met together for many years and did so on occasion as late as 1709 in Rhode Island Monthly Meeting to deliberate on a couple's fitness for marriage. See, e.g., RI MM, 2:4/VIII/1709. The same practice was used in Greenwich Monthly Meeting. On the work of the women's meetings: NE YM, 1706, 1708, 1709; RI MM, 1:25/I/1707, 22/II/1707; 2:31/XI/1715/16.

46. Arthur R. Worrall, *Quakers in the Colonial Northeast* (Hanover, N.H., 1980), 76–77.

47. On methods of managing ecclesiastical business: NE YM, 1692, 1699. From time to time, various comments in minutes mentioned categories of members not to be encouraged to attend, such as those who "slight and unnder value the service of the visiters." RI MM, I2:31/XI/1715/16. See also RI MM, 1:25/I/1707, 22/II/1707; Epistle of William Edmundson in NE YM, 1711. For an example of constituent meetings: Greenwich MM, 1:5/III/1701.

48. The Yearly Meeting was not the only institutional voice for speaking to secu-

lar authority. In the first half of the eighteenth century, no regular practice existed. Rhode Island Monthly Meeting (men's) sent delegates to the General Assembly with petitions in support of pacifist principles, both as a plea "that friends may have their former Liberty to watch without arms" in 1706 and as a protest against the colony's participation in Queen Anne's War in 1709. RI MM, 1:21/III/1706; 2:17/III/1709. Later, Rhode Island Quarterly Meeting (men's) sent a petition for relief from penalties for Friends refusing to train with militia companies. Rhode Island Quarterly Meeting of Friends (men) to General Assembly, Oct. 1729, RI Petitions, 1:62.

49. On control over publication: NE YM, 1699, 1703, 1708, 1720. On rulings by the yearly meetings: NE YM, suitable years; Greenwich MM, 2:15/IX/1716, 3/X/1716, 7/XI/1716/17; RI MM, 1:15/VI/1704, 21/III/1706; 2:28/V/1713, 27/X/1715, 28/IV/1720; Minutes of Smithfield Monthly Meeting of Friends (men), MS, New England Yearly Meeting Archives, RIHS, 1:4/VIII/1721, 9/VII/1730.

50. Minutes of Rhode Island Quarterly Meeting of Ministers and Elders, MS, New England Yearly Meeting Archives, RIHS, 1:11/IV/1708, 3/VII/1730; Greenwich MM, 1:21/I/1702, 21/II/1707.

51. Greenwich MM, 1:19/VI/1706; 2:6/VI/1716, 4/VII/1721, 6/IX/1721; RI MM 2:29/XII/1710/11, 29/III/1711; NE YM, 1716.

52. On raising the young: RI MM, 2:31/XI/1715/16. On the importance of marriage within the fold: NE YM, 1707; RI MM, 2:31/XI/1715/16, 27/X/1737. On status of children: NE YM, 1707. On responsibility of parents: RI MM, 2:31/XI/1715/16.

53. Fifth query in 1701 version, as transcribed at back of Greenwich MM, 1.

54. Testimony against superfluity: NE YM, 1708, as revised in NE YM, 1709.

55. Greenwich MM, II, 19/I/1710/11; RI MM, I, 27/II/1703, 25/III/1703, 22/IV/1703; II, 30/III/1710, 21/VIII/1710, 25/X/1711, 26/XII/1711/12, 29/V/1718, 26/VI/1718, 28/II/1719, 25/II/1727, 25/V/1727, 26/I/1734, 24/XII/1735/36, 29/IV/1736, 2/VI/1736, 28/I/1738, 25/II/1738, 26/VII/1738; III, 29/VI/1749; Minutes of Rhode Island Monthly Meeting of Friends (women), MS, New England Yearly Meeting Archives, RIHS, 25/V/1727.

56. RI MM, II, 25/V/1727, 26/I/1728; NE YM, 1728.

57. On slavery: e.g., Greenwich MM, 7/XI/1716; RI MM, II, 27/IX/1716; NE YM, 1717, 1718; Minutes of New England Yearly Meeting of Ministers and Elders, New England Yearly Meeting Archives, MS, RIHS, 15/IV/1717, 17/IV/1717. On universal salvation: RI MM, III, 27/IX/1739, 24/IV/1740.

10. The Framework of Government after 1738 (pp. 187–204)

1. On property qualifications for voting: RI *Laws* 1730, 131; Journal H of D, 28 Feb. 1729/30; Colony Records, 5:9; 6:32–33; *PS* 1760, 36. On propounding a man to the town meeting: Journal H of D, 28 Feb. 1729/30; Colony Records, 6:32–34; RI *Laws* 1752, 24; *PS* 1761, 193–194. On challenging a man's right to vote: Colony Records, 5:522–23; Sup. Ct., 2:215, 228–29. Measures against corruption: Journal of House of Magistrates (hereafter Journal H of M), 21 Dec. 1738; RI *Laws* 1730, 209, 280; RI *Laws* 1745, 217–18, 252–253; RI *Laws* 1752, 12–16; Colony Records, 5:535; 6:32–33, 40; Journal H of D, 22 Aug. 1746, 30 Oct. 1746, 30 Jan. 1746/47; *PS* 1761, [192]-194, *PS* 1770, 28. On coordination of colonial elections in the towns: Journal H of D, 6 Nov. 1734, 19 Feb. 1734/35, 22 Feb. 1734/35, 17 June 1736, 3 Nov. 1736, 21 June 1737, 23 Aug. 1738, 25 Aug. 1738, 26 Nov. 1742; Journal H of M, 23 June 1738, ? Nov. 1742; Colony Records, 5:525; RI *Laws* 1745, 255. Laws on procedures for

voting: RI *Laws* 1719, 1–2; RI *Laws* 1745, 287; RI *Laws* 1752, 15–16; *PS* 1760, 36; *RICR*, 4:207–8. Debate over method of voting: Journal H of D, 6 Nov. 1734, 4 May 1737, 21 June 1737, 29 Nov. 1737, 30 Nov. 1737, 6 Feb. 1737/38, 16 Feb. 1737/38, 17 Feb. 1743/44; Journal H of M, 30 Nov. 1737, 1 Dec. 1737, 14 Feb. 1737/38. On further political wrangling: Journal H of M, 12 May 1761, 13 May 1761, 4 May 1762; Journal H of D, 9 May 1761, 11 May 1761, 12 May 1761, 14 May 1761, 15 May 1761, 16 May 1761, 5 May 1762; *PS* 1761, 196.

2. In 1738 the colony had thirteen towns and a total population of c. 22,000. In 1770 it had twenty-nine towns and nearly 60,000 people. The number of deputies climbed from thirty-six to sixty-eight. While the ratio of towns to people and people to deputies at the two times were not exactly equal, they were in the same range. Much greater discrepancies existed between the ratios of people to deputies within the various towns at any given time, and these inequalities increased between 1738 and 1770. See David S. Lovejoy, *Rhode Island Politics and the American Revolution, 1760–1776* (Providence, 1958), 15–18.

3. *PS* 1748, 30, 34, 41–42; Journal H of D, 24 Aug. 1749, 13 June 1750, 25 Aug. 1750, 1 Nov. 1750, 2 Nov. 1750; Colony Records, 6:208; *PS* 1750, 63; deposition of Rouse Helme, 14 June 1753, RIHS Manuscripts, 12:5; *RICR*, 7:227–28.

4. The upper house successfully objected to the deputies' having their own committee for other purposes, too, and sometimes initiated the business of setting up a committee. E.g., Journal H of D, 1 Nov. 1729, 25 Feb. 1729/30, 27 Feb. 1729/30, 12 June 1771, 20 Aug. 1771, 30 Oct. 1771, 7 May 1773; Journal H of M, 30 Oct. 1747, 31 Oct. 1747.

5. Most of the record is explained in John Blanchard MacInnes, "Rhode Island Bills of Public Credit, 1710–1755" (Ph.D. diss., Brown University, 1952); the whole record is summarized in Sydney V. James, *Colonial Rhode Island: A History* (New York, 1975), 168–73, 275–83, 303–8.

6. Journal H of D, 18 Feb. 1743/44, 14 Feb. 1744/45; Colony Records, 5:586, 589–94, 604, 621, 627; RI *Laws* 1752, 8–10.

7. Journal H of M, 13 May 1746; *PS* 1750, 95; *PS* 1772, 5. After 1751, the town committees were not abolished but generally were not replaced when vacancies occurred. *PS* 1750, 95; *PS* 1753, 13

8. Colony Records, 5:418, 556, 644.

9. Colony Records, 5:486, 493, 541; MacInnes, "Rhode Island Bills," 307–9; Journal H of D, 18 Sept. 1742, 11 Nov. 1742, 30 Sept. 1743, 28 Oct. 1743; *PS* 1759, [78]–[80].

10. Journal H of D, 3 (?) May 1770; *PS* 1770, 41, 75–76.

11. Journal H of M, 9 May 1772; *PS* 1772, 69–70; *PS* 1773, 62, 66; *PS* 1774, 19; Journal H of D, 6 May 1774, 25 Aug. 1774, 8 Dec. 1774.

12. E.g., *PS* 1758, 14–16, 27–29, 48, 53; Journal H of D, last page of volume for May 1758 to March 1759 (report dated 6 May 1758), 25 Aug. 1758, 26 Aug. 1758; Journal H of M, 25 Aug. 1758, 26 Aug. 1758.

13. On Cranston's powers: *RICR*, 4:70, 78, 94, 122. On the Commisssary-General: *RICR*, 4:71, 82–83, 100, 121, 145. On appointment of officers: *RICR*, 4:94, 122.

14. Colony Records, 5:359, 369, 373, 380–81, 391, 391, 394, 444, 632–35, 686, 719; 6:15, 19, 30; *RICR*, 4:94, 122. Presumably, one reason for departure from the example of Governor Cranston's role in Queen Anne's War was the fact that the Governor at the outbreak of the War of Jenkins' Ear was a Quaker.

15. Colony Records, 6:15, 30, 35, 42, 49, 75; *PS* 1747/48, 10–11; Journal H of M, 1 Nov. 1748, 11 June 1755.

16. *PS* 1754, 78–79, 81.

17. *PS* 1754, 77, 85; *PS* 1755, 16–18, 30, 39–40, 44, 48, 49, 57; *PS* 1756, 16, 18, 36, 41, 42, 67, 71–77, 112, 139, 149–51; *PS* 1757, 17–18, 106.

18. On the draft of troops, etc.: *PS* 1756, 73–74, 149–51; *PS* 1757, 17–18, 42–43, 45, 46. Examples of curtailing the committee's powers: *PS* 1757, 106–8; *PS* 1758, 78; *PS* 1759, 12, 25–26, [85], and August session, n.p.; *PS* 1760, session of March 1761. n.p.; *PS* 1761, 93; Journal H of M, 1 Apr. 1761.

19. On the committee's composition: *PS* 1755, 62–64; *PS* 1756, 93–94; *PS* 1757, 24–25; *PS* 1758, 12, 64, etc. On the abolition of the Commissary: *PS* 1755, 17; *PS* 1758, 11, 14, 104, 106; *PS* 1760, March session 1761, n.p.; *PS* 1761, 75.

20. Certainly when the Assembly chose to decentralize administration, it brought on the profiteering that came to light. Not only did Colonel Henry Babcock, who got the old Commissary's duties, come under accusations but also two members of the Committee of War. These men (from Providence and Warwick) could not settle their accounts to the colony's satisfaction. Their obvious trouble was losing when they expected to gain by use of office, but below that lay the precariousness of men of political connections and insufficient capital trying to fill the function previously filled by leading Newport merchants. See *PS* 1758, 74–77, 86–101; *PS* 1760, 22–24, Feb. session 1761, n.p.; *PS* 1761, 26–27, 41–42, 44–45, 80–81, 86–87, 169–76, 196–98, 212–16, 219–20; *PS* 1763, 12–26, 33–35, 37–41, 64, 74–80, 85–88, 105; *PS* 1764, 87–88; Journal H of D, 30 Oct. 1762, 4 March 1763, 5 March 1763.

21. RI *Laws* 1730, 14; Journal H of M, 18 June 1748; Colony Records, 6:126; Mary Patterson Clarke, *Parliamentary Privilege in the American Colonies* (New Haven, Conn., 1943), 29. Briefly, the Assembly showed a desire to divest itself of appellate functions on personal actions. In 1741 it authorized what it called a Court of Equity, with a bench of five judges to sit twice annually to hear appeals from the Superior Court and give "judgment and determination" "agreeably to law and equity," subject to appeals to the privy council. The tribunal duly heard the appeals within its purview and dispensed what the justices regarded as substantive justice. They bent the strict implications of law, as equity indeed does, but made no effort to observe the procedures of the Court of Chancery in England or prescribe its remedies. The Court of Equity fell qickly upon attack by a disgruntled loser in litigation before it, a man who had many friends. See Journal H of D, 22 Aug. 1735, 18 Feb. 1735/36, 16 June 1736, 17 September 1740, 18 Feb. 1743/44; *RICR*, 5:23; Zechariah Chafee Jr., "Records of the Rhode Island Court of Equity, 1741–1743," Colonial Society of Massachusetts, *Publications* (Boston, 1951), 35:95–97, 117–18; Simon Ray et al. to General Assembly, 14 Feb. 1743/44, RI Petitions, 5:45; Simon Ray to General Assembly, Oct. 1743, RI Petitions, 5:52; Colony Records, 5:611, 623; RI *Laws* 1745, 282–84.

22. On proposals concerning the Superior Court: Journal H of D, 8 Feb. 1733/34, 5 Nov. 1734, 22 June 1737, 24 Nov. 1737, 30 Nov. 1737, 22 Aug. 1738; RI Petitions, 3:A. On the intransigence of the upper house and final acquiescence: Journal H of D, 9 July 1746, 20 Aug. 1746, 20 Feb. 1746/47. Measures defining the new Superior Court's powers and operations: RI *Laws* 1752, 27–29; Colony Records, 6:97, 174; *PS* October 1747, 2; *PS* 1754, 23. Grounds for dissolution of marriage included desertion for seven years or other "breach of the Marriage Covenant," which included adultery.

23. *RICR*, 2:26–27; RI *Laws* 1730, 111–12, 168; RI *Laws* 1745, 253–54, 284–85; RI *Laws* 1752, 6; Colony Records, 5:732; 8:35–36; *PS* 1752, 30; *PS* 1755, 71; *PS* 1756, 40; *PS* 1757, 59, 100; *PS* 1760, 25, [49]; Journal H of D, 24 Aug. 1762, 25 Aug. 1762.

24. Colony Records, 6:28, 59–60; *PS* 1750, 56, 65–66; *PS* 1763, 123–24; *PS* 1769, 42; *PS* 1771, 36.

25. *PS* 1749, 18–24; *PS* 1757, 73, 80–81; Journal H of D, 1 Nov. 1728, 22 Aug. 1735; Journal H of M, 29 Oct. 1757, 22 Dec. 1758, 23 Dec. 1758; Dorothy S. Towle, "The Rhode Island Vice-Admiralty Court," in *Records of the Vice-Admiralty Court of Rhode Island, 1716–1752,* American Legal Records, vol. 3 (1936; reprint, Millwood, N.Y., 1975) 89, 90; Gertrude S. Kimball, ed., *The Correspondence of the Colonial Governors of Rhode Island, 1723–1775* (1902–1903; reprint, Freeport, N.Y., 1969), 2:273–76, 291–93, 304, 306; RI *Laws* 1745, 188, 268–70. The contrast between the situation before and after 1735 merits notice. After that date, prohibitions were the function of the Superior Court, which of course became separate in staffing from the Governor and Council a few years later. Before 1735 the Governor and Council as such issued temporary prohibitions pending action by the General Assembly. Curiously, the route of appeals from the vice-admiralty court changed in an opposite way, at least as regarded prizes. Instead of going to the High Court of Admiralty in England, by 1740 appeals went to the Board of Trade, presumably for a binding judgment by the privy council at the board's recommendation. Charles M. Andrews, "Vice-Admiralty Courts in the Colonies," in Towle, ed., *Records of the Vice-Admiralty Court of Rhode Island,* 20–22; [Towle], "Records of the Vice-Admiralty Court of Rhode Island," in Towle, ed., *Records of the Vice-Admiralty Court of Rhode Island,* 154, 198, 480.

26. E.g., Edward Clinton Stiness, "The Struggle for Judicial Supremacy," in Edward Field et al., *State of Rhode Island and Providence Plantations at the End of the Century; A History* (Boston, 1902), 3:98–104, 139–40, 161–62.

27. Middletown TM, 1:1.

28. Colony Records, 6:103; Middletown TM, 1:3–9, 22, 24, 27, 43–45, 48; Middletown TC, 1:48–49, 88.

29. On general laws: Colony Records, 5:431–32; *PS* 1754, 77–78. On examples of decisions by towns: East Greenwich TM, 16 Apr. 1760; Westerly TC, 4:55; Portsmouth TC, 10:40; Portsmouth LE, 5:326–30; South Kingstown TM, 1:66, 77, 83, 90, 230, 246; South Kingstown LE, 4:131–43.

30. On general law: Colony Records, 5:594–95; 6:278–79. Town actions: e.g., East Greenwich TC, 2 Jan. 1753, 8 Jan. 1753, 17 March 1770; Westerly TC, 4:131; Middletown TC, 2:56; Newport TM (A), 542; South Kingstown TC, 5:27–28, 31–36.

31. Copy of the case of *Daniel Stanton v. William Champlin, Oliver Babcock, and Elias Thompson,* papers of Kings Inf. Ct., April 1749 term; Westerly TM, 1:172; 2:25, 28; Westerly TC, 4:56, 124, 159, 173, 185, 196, 202, 274, 400, 472–73, 484, 488, 502, 1°, and passim; Elias Thompson to General Assembly, June 1757, RI Petitions, 9 (pt. 1):185; Journal H of D, 12 June 1757; Journal H of M, 16 June 1757; Colony Records, 6:554–55.

32. Westerly TM, 2:66; copies of Westerly town records pertaining to Cedar Swamp, copies of documents on litigation, and petition from "a Number of Freemen and part of the Inhabitants of the town of Westerly" to General Assembly, 27 Feb. 1764, RI Petitions, 11 (pt. 2):77.

33. Newport TM (A), 364, 366, 370, 372–76.

34. Newport TM (A), 502, 556, 558, 732, 752, 754, 798.

35. Order from multitown committee to build almshouse and workhouse to ratemakers of Providence, 29 June 1753, Shepley Papers, RIHS, 6:94; William R. Staples, *Annals of the Town of Providence from its First Settlement to the Organization of the City Government, in June, 1832* (Providence, 1843), 194–95; East Greenwich TM, 21 Apr. 1773; Warwick TC, RIHS, 1:84–87.

36. Middletown TM, 1:29, 30, 33, 35, 37, 41, 43, 46; East Greenwich TC, 1:208, 222, 238, 250, 256; East Greenwich TM, 29 May 1753, 15 April 1761, 31 May 1763,

29 May 1770; Newport TC, 10:149, 208; Newport Sup. Ct., 1:171–72; Newport TM, 2:50, 56, 64; Newport TM (A), 433–34, 546, 742, 744, 746, 748, 848, 862; *Newport Mercury*, 6 Oct. 1763; 9 July 1764; 29 Apr. 1765; 31 March, 1768.

37. Daniel Abbot et al. to Providence town meeting, 5 June 1758, PTP, 2nd ser., 3:0874; Daniel Abbot et al. to Providence town meeting, 7 June 1742, PTP, 2nd ser., 3:0945; Staples, *Annals*, 200–202; Newport TM (A), 482, 502, 566, 786, 1054. Newport in 1732 took over a faltering private project. The town meeting chose a committee to finish construction of a market house with funds from the treasury. Newport TM, 1:253.

38. Carl Bridenbaugh, *Cities in the Wilderness: The First Century of Urban Life in America, 1625–1742*, 3d ed. (London, 1971), 370; Newport TM, 1:275, 289; Bridenbaugh, *Cities in Revolt: Urban Life in America, 1743–1776*, 2d ed. (London, 1971), 104–5; Staples, *Annals*, 199–200.

39. Cf., Gen. 3:13.

40. PS 1748, 30, 34, 41–42; Journal H of D, 24 Aug. 1749, 13 June 1750, 25 Aug. 1750, 1 Nov. 1750, 2 Nov. 1750; Colony Records, 6:208; PS 1750, 63; deed from Daniel Coggeshall et al. (committe of General Assembly) to Stephen Wilcox, 25 Oct. 1750, RIHS Manuscripts, 12:5.

41. The money was collected by the naval officer, who was the most blatantly political appointee in the jurisdiction, the only one chosen by the Governor alone. Anything he touched was inspected for corruption by opposing politicos. Besides, the operator of the lighthouse was usually suspected of padding his accounts. PS 1753, 30–31; PS 1754, 41–42; PS 1758, 39 (second page with that number), 44–45; Journal H of D, 26 Feb. 1760, etc. On the financial arrangements, see especially: Journal H of M, 4 Dec. 1766; PS 1767, 44–45, 56; Lovejoy, *Rhode Island Politics and the American Revolution*, 63–64.

42. E.g., William Robinson and Robert Hassard, Jr., to General Assembly, 18 Feb. 1736/37, RI Petitions, 3:96; four Warwick men to General Assembly, 5 Sept. 1740 RI Petitions, 4:66; Samauel Perry and Christopher Champlin to General Assembly, June 1741, RI Petitions, 4:144; William Robinson and Jonathan Haszard to General Assembly, c. June 1742, RI Petitions, 4:144; PS 1748, 56; PS 1750, 92, 93; Journal H of M, 20 March 1750/51; Journal H of D, 12 June 1771, 20 Aug. 1771, 31 Oct. 1771.

43. On the statute of 1745: Colony Records, 5:729. On its flaws and modifications: Colony Records, 6:97; PS 1771, 76–77; PS 1772, 91; PS 1773, 32.

44. E.g., Colony Records, 5:43, 218, 433–34, 453, 524; 6:138–39, 143–44, 253, 261–62; 7:19–20; PS 1755, 76; PS 1764, 74; PS 1768, 20; PS 1769, 86–87; PS 1773, 22–25, 35–36, 39; PS 1774, 42; Journal H of D, 4 May 1734, 21 Feb. 1734/35, 20 Aug. 1735, 2 Nov. 1736, 23 Feb. 1736/37, 18 June, 1737, 25 Aug. 1738, 2 Nov. 1754, 5 March 1763, 30 Nov. 1764, 11 Sept. 1765, 13 Sept. 1765, 27 Feb. 1767; Journal H of M, 13 Sept. 1765, 14 Sept. 1765, 3 July 1767, 4 Sept. 1767; men of South Kingstown to General Assembly, 8 June 1736, RI Petitions, 3:93; Joseph Edmunds to General Assembly, 22 Feb. 1738, RI Petitions, 3:135; men of North Kingstown to General Assembly, Oct. 1739, RI Petitions, 4:35; James Greene et al. to General Assembly, Jan. 1740/41, RI Petitions, 4:70; twenty Warwick men to General Assembly, Apr. 1741, RI Petitions, 4:105; Block Island men to General Assembly, May 1743, RI Petitions, 5:22; two petitions from men of North Kingstown to General Assembly, Oct. 1743, RI Petitions, 5:43; subscription by men in Providence toward price of fire engine, 21 Sept. 1754, RI Petitions, 8:196; Benjamin Arnold et al. to General Assembly, Feb. 1755, RI Petitions, 9 (pt. 1):16; Stephen Hopkins et al. to General Assembly, Feb. 1769, RI Petitions, 13 (pt. 1):77; John Littlefield and John Sands to General

Assembly, RI Petitions, 15:31; list of subscribers "for Opening the Breach," n.d., Ward Manuscripts, RIHS, 1:15; RI *Laws* 1730, 264–66; RI *Laws* 1772, 13–14.

45. *PS* 1768, 71–72.

46. *PS* 1769, 90–94. The new law on intestacy was elaborate far beyond its forerunners. It acknowledged that some social conditions (unspecified) might justify deviation from equal division but claimed that Rhode Island had no such conditions and could not get them "for a long time."

47. Daniel Updike et al. to General Assembly, RI Petitions, 2:108; Journal H of D, 8 Dec. 1733, 14 June 1754, 15 June 1754, 23 Aug. 1754; Journal H of M, 14 June 1754, 23 Aug. 1754; *PS* 1771, 50–59; *PS* 1772, 16; Peter J. Coleman, "The Insolvent Debtor in Rhode Island, 1745–1828," *William and Mary Quarterly*, 3d ser., 22 (1965):413–16.

48. Journal H of D, 22 June 1728, 17 June 1732, 25 Feb. 1767, 1 July 1767; *PS* 1767, 132–33.

49. Newport TM (A), 649, 654, 702, 704, 776, 998, 1000.

50. The discussion of parties in this and ensuing paragraphs is a commentary on the description given in Lovejoy, *Rhode Island Politics and the American Revolution*, esp. chaps. 1, 3, 5, and 7; and Mack E. Thompson, "The Ward-Hopkins Controversy and the American Revolution in Rhode Island," *William and Mary Quarterly*, 3d ser., 16 (1959):363–75. The categories of analysis, however, have been drawn more from William Nisbet Chambers, *Political Parties in a New Nation; The American Experience, 1776–1809* (New York, 1963), chap. 2. See also James, *Colonial Rhode Island*, chap. 12; Robert J. Dinkin, *Voting in Provincial America; A Study of Elections in the Thirteen Colonies, 1689–1776* (Westport, Conn., 1977), esp. pp. 83–86, 161–72, 192–99, 205–6.

51. Lovejoy, *Rhode Island Politics*, 28.

52. A somewhat more extended discussion of the controversy over fiscal policy is in James, *Colonial Rhode Island*, 303–8.

53. Providence *Gazette*, 6 Nov. 1762, 20 Nov. 1762, 5 Feb. 1763, 26 Feb. 1763, 2 Apr. 1763, 9 Apr. 1763; Newport *Mercury*, 10 Jan. 1763, 21 Feb. 1763, 28 Feb. 1763; *PS* 1761, 227; *PS* 1763, 28–32, 122–23; *PS* 1766, 40, 56–58; *PS* 1770, 50–51; Joseph G. Wanton, *Observations and Reflections on the Present State of the Colony of Rhode Island, In which the Cooper's Letter is Particularly Taken Notice of—Addressed to the Freemen of the Said Colony* (Newport, R.I., 1763), 3.

54. *PS* 1765, 82–83; *PS* 1766, 20, 76–77; *PS* 1767, 11–12, 67; *PS* 1768, 42, 60; *PS* 1769, 13; *PS* 1771, 37; *PS* 1773, 12; Journal H of M, 11 Sept. 1766, 31 Oct. 1766, 3 Dec. 1766, 4 Dec. 1766, 5 Dec. 1766; Journal H of D, 12 Sept. 1766, 30 Oct. 1766, 1 Nov. 1766, 5 Dec. 1766, 25 Feb. 1767, 27 Feb. 1767.

11. Steps toward the Private Corporation (pp. 207–223)

1. It is possible to find precedents for many of these new entities in other colonies and to conclude rashly that there is no need to explain their appearance in Rhode Island. If they were not wholly novelties, then perhaps the idea of creating them was in the air and the legal rationale for them already established. On the contrary, what was in the air needs more explanation than does an oddity.

2. In the sense of limitation on competition, the system of licensing ferries continued the old ways; the licenses tended to be regarded as privileges that could not be revoked without proof of wrongdoing on the part of the licensee.

3. Something close to this view of the corporation had been expressed by Roger Williams in 1670: "patents, grants and charters, and such like royal favors, are not laws of England, and acts of Parliament, not matters of propriety and *meum* and *tuum* between the King and his subjects, which, as the times have been, have been sometimes triable in inferior Courts; but such kind of grants have been like high offices in England, of high honor, . . . yet revocable or curtable upon pleasure, according to the King's better information." Roger Williams to John Mason, 22 June 1670, John Russell Bartlet, ed., "The Letters of Roger Williams," in Reuben A. Guild et al., eds., *The Complete Writings of Roger Williams* (New York, 1963 [vols. 1–6 originally published 1866–1874]), 6:348–49.

4. L'Estrange Ewen, *Lotteries and Sweepstakes* (London, 1932), 68. Cf. John S. Ezell, *Fortune's Merry Wheel: The Lottery in America* (Cambridge, Mass., 1960).

5. In the colony, the absolute ban extended only from January 1733 to 1744. Ewen, *Lotteries and Sweepstakes*, 32; Colony Records, 5:108. If people in Rhode Island organized lotteries before 1733, no record survives of them.

6. Daniel Jenckes et al. to General Assembly, Oct. 1744, RI Petitions, 6:3; Colony Records, 5:648–49.

7. Colony Records, 654–55, 735; 6:11, 185.

8. Friends of Joseph Fox to General Assembly, Oct. 1748, RI Petitions, 7:33; Joseph Pendleton to General Assembly, Feb. 1749/50, RI Petitions, 7:99; *PS* 1759, 16–18, 29–30, [77].

9. *PS* 1761, 52, 224; Cranston Baptists to General Assembly, Oct. 1770, RI Petitions, 14:41; John Smith and John Innes Clarke (wardens of St. John's Church, Providence) to General Assembly, Oct. 1771, RI Petitions, 14:99.

10. See notation by the clerk of one of the houses of the Assembly on a petition for a lottery, saying it was granted "under the Usual Restrictions of giving Bond etc." Note on petition of North Providence men to General Assembly (asking permission to raise money for road), Oct. 1771, RI Petitions, 14:101.

11. *PS* 1761, 106–7; *PS* 1763, 70–71; committee of first Congregational society in Providence to General Assembly, Oct. 1771, RI Petitions, 14:100; Augustus Johnston et al. to General Assembly, Dec. 1772, RI Petitions, 15:17; Reserved Peirce et al. to General Assembly, May 1774, RI Petitions, 15:100. A few lotteries differed from the basic pattern in instructive ways, showing how responsibility for these schemes could be intertwined with institutions other than the colonial government. Arrangements could be quite flexible when a recognized collectivity wanted a lottery. One to pave streets in Newport put the money for the project in the hands of the town, to be expended on order of any three of the directors. A lottery to repair and extend Long Wharf in Newport made the directors synonymous with the proprietors, who included at least one woman, and allowed them to decide by majority vote on the method of administration. They chose to let volunteers from their own ranks serve as directors under bond to the General Treasurer. Newport TM (A), 502; *PS* 1768, 85–86; untitled records of the Proprietors of Long Wharf, 1739–1801 (with gaps), MS, NHS, 138.

12. On secular examples: *PS* 1759, 16–18, [77]; *PS* 1760, 13–14. When gratifying churches, the Assembly was especially easygoing in prescribing accountability. It stipulated only a financial plan to the Johnston Baptists in 1761 and implied that the beneficiary would be the Six Principle society of that town. *PS* 1761, 52–53. In fact, the Assembly let religious organizations, regardless of how misty their legal standing might be, raise money to spend on acquiring or improving real estate. This practice stood in such contrast to the cases of the Masons and the Providence library as to suggest that these latter two organizations used the lottery to acquire legal recognition of

power to hold property, whereas the churches or religious societies were content with arrangements that already existed. Some religious organizations did in fact get incorporation about the same time, but only the Providence Congregationalists did so before seeking permission for a lottery.

13. In strict formal respects, none of these actions had qualified as incorporation. The town charters of 1649 lacked several elements; those of later years were brief statutes, sometimes extremely simple. The statute allowing corporative traits to proprietary syndicates neither defined a full slate of attributes of a corporation nor resulted in the issuance of any charters. Formal respects, however, were not all that mattered.

14. The statutes of Massachusetts probably inspired Rhode Island. Roy H. Akagi, *The Town Proprietors of the New England Colonies: A Study of Their Development, Organization, Activities and Controversies, 1620–1770* (Philadelphia, 1924), 55–60. Akagi was misled by Henry C. Dorr, who failed to find out that the date (1682) on the colonial laws concerning proprietors, as published in 1719, referred only to the oldest sections. See also Oscar Handlin and Mary Flug Handlin, *Commonwealth, a Study of the Role of Government in the American Economy: Massachusetts, 1774–1861* (New York, 1947), 96.

15. Newport TM, 1:13, 153.

16. Newport TM, 1:64, 66–67; Newport TM (A), 97–100.

17. See fragments of petition from the new organization to the town, c. 3 Oct. 1739, in Newport TC, 18:45–46.

18. On the record of the proprietors in general: Newport TM, 1:305; Newport TM (A), 312–15, 325, 327; Untitled records of the Proprietors of Long Wharf, 1739–1801 (with gaps), MS, NHS, esp. 27–66; Untitled account book of Proprietors of Long Wharf, 1750–1801 (with gaps), MS, NHS, 1, 10, 14, 22, and passim; Newport Sup. Ct., 2:204.

19. On divisions: Records of the Proprietors of Long Wharf, 33, 57, 59, 60, 62, 65–66, 72, 74, 78, 79, 83, 84. On management of the remainder: e.g., records of the Proprietors of Long Wharf, 31, 35, 38; Newport *Mercury*, 17 March 1764, 24 March 1766.

20. Samuel Wickham and Fones Nichols for proprietors of Long Wharf to General Assembly, Feb. 1745/46, RI Petitions, 6:94; Journal H of D, 13 Feb. 1745/46; Colony Records, 5:738–39; records of the Proprietors of Long Wharf, 60–61.

21. Records of the Proprietors of Long Wharf, 53–54, 79–83; PS 1759, 81–82; Carl Bridenbaugh, *Peter Harrison, First American Architect* (Chapel Hill, N.C., 1949), 111.

22. Joesph Stancliffe Davis, "Corporations in the American Colonies," in *Essays in the Earlier History of American Corporations* (1917; reprint, New York), 1:25–26; Armand B. DuBois, *The English Business Company after the Bubble Act, 1720–1800* (New York, 1938), 2, 25–32, 87, 138.

23. Davis, "Corporations in the American Colonies," 1:20–25. The doubts at the time of the founding of the Redwood Library are implicit in the basic documents, including the deed to the site.

24. Massachusetts had created the Ancient and Honorable Artillery Company in 1637. Rhode Island had authorized a few other special units in the eighteenth century, notably the Providence Country Troop of Horse in 1711, which may have had some tangible existence though in 1729 it had been inactive "of Late for wont of Reselute men" as officers. *RICR*, 4:119; Joseph Brown et al. to General Assembly, May 1729, RI Petitions, 1:68. In 1756 some Providence men proposed to found a new one because the old one was inactive. It had not mustered for several years and served only to exempt its members from service in the regular town companies. Colony

Records, 6:466, 468. In 1718 the Assembly decided to authorize a second troop of horse on the mainland. See documents on dispute over alleged malfeasance by the captain of second troop of horse on mainland, authorized 7 May 1718, RI Petitions, 2:85. It and others probably never organized. *RICR*, 4:178–79.

25. Colony Records, 5:468, 476–77. Davis, "Corprations in the American Colonies," 1:103, is unduly rigid in rejecting incorporation of elite military units as true corporations.

26. Colony Records, 5:476–77; Transcript of charter in untitled Newport Artillery Company records, 1741–1794, MS, NHS, n.p.

27. Newport Artillery Company Records.

28. Twenty-eight Providence men to General Assembly, May 1744, RI Petitions, 6:46; Twenty-five Westerly men to General Assembly, 8 Oct. 1754, RI Petitions, 8:198; Benjamin Sherburne et al. to General Assembly, Feb. 1755, RI Petitions, 9 (pt. 1):12; John Rogers et al. to General Assembly, May 1755, RI Petitions, 9 (pt. 1):83; Colony Records, 5:628; 6:402–3, 407–8, 466.

29. George Champlin Mason, ed., *Annals of the Redwood Library and Athenaeum, Newport, R.I.* (Newport, R.I., 1891), [9], 12–18.

30. Abraham Redwood et al. to General Assembly, Aug. 1747, RI Petitions, 6:144.

31. Colony Records, 6:79.

32. Mason, ed., *Annals of the Redwood Library*, 34–35.

33. Newport LE, 34:524–27; or Mason, ed., *Annals of the Redwood Library*, 485–87.

34. Mason, ed., *Annals of the Redwood Library*, 38–71.

35. Ephraim Bowen et al. to General Assembly, Feb. 1754, RI Petitions, 8:157; Colony Records, 6:352.

36. *PS* 1759, 29–30, [77]; *PS* 1760, 13–14; Gertrude S. Kimball, *Providence in Colonial Times* (Boston, 1912), 211–12.

37. Benjamin Wickham et al. to General Assembly, June 1754, RI Petitions, 8:175; Colony Records, 6:381; Rough minutes of the Fellowship Club or Marine Society, 1752–1824, loose sheets and unbound books, MS, NHS, meetings from Dec. 1752 to June 1754.

38. Colony Records, 6:381; *Charter of the Fellowship Club, Instituted at Newport (R.I.) Dec. 5th, A.D. 1752, And Incorporated by the Name of the Marine Society* (Newport, R.I., 1819), 4–7; *Laws of the Marine Society: Instituted at Newport, Dec. 5, 1752, under the Title of Fellowship Club, Anno 1754 under said Title, and a new Charter granted, Anno 1785, altering said Title, and entitling them the Marine Society* (Newport, R.I., 1785), 2–6.

39. *PS* 1759, 16–18.

40. The story has been told adequately in the narratives and documents in Reuben A. Guild, *Early History of Brown University, Including the Life, Times, and Correspondence of President Manning* (Providence, 1897); and in Walter C. Bronson, *The History of Brown University, 1764–1914* (Providence, 1914). See also Edmund S. Morgan, *The Gentle Puritan: A Life of Ezra Stiles, 1727–1795* (Chapel Hill, N.C., 1962), 204–6.

41. Richard Hofstadter, *Academic Freedom in the Age of the College* (New York, 1961), 114–51; Peter Dobkin Hall, *The Organization of American Culture, 1700–1900: Private Institutions, Elites, and the Origins of American Nationality* (New York, 1982), 102–6.

42. *RICR*, 6:387–90. Some members of each governing board were from outside Rhode Island.

43. *RICR*, 6:387; Minutes of meetings of the Brown University corporation,

1764–1810, MS, Archives, Brown University, 1–13, 15–19, 31; "Miscellaneous Papers Concerning Rhode Island College, 1763–1804," MS, Archives, Brown University, 1:21, 23.

44. Minutes of Brown University corporation, 19, 23, 28, 30.

45. Copy of narrative by M. B. [Moses Brown], in "Miscellaneous Papers Concerning Rhode Island College," 1:55; Minutes of Brown University corporation, 40–45; James B. Hedges, *The Browns of Providence Plantations; Colonial Years* (Cambridge, Mass., 1952), 197; Richard Luftglass, ed., "Nicholas Brown to Isaac Backus: On Bringing Rhode Island College to Providence," *Rhode Island History* 44 (1985):121–25. Defeat of the Ward party and Newport's ambitions stimulated the plan for a second college to be located in the capital, but not even all of Ward's backers would support it. David S. Lovejoy, *Rhode Island Politics and the American Revolution, 1760–1776* (Providence, 1958), 149–50, 152.

46. On commencement: Arthur E. Wilson, *Weybosset Bridge in Providence Plantations, 1700–1790* (Boston, 1947), 191–92. On connection with the colonial treasury: Attested copy of the decision by the General Assembly, Sept. 1768, in "Miscellaneous Papers Concerning Rhode Island College," 1:39. Example of a corporate suit to recover a legacy: Prov. Sup. Ct., 2:182–83, 420–22.

47. Charles Keen et al. to General Assembly, Oct. 1768, RI Petitions, 13 (pt. 1):46; John Jenckes et al. to General Assembly, Feb. 1770, RI Petitions, 13 (pt. 1):129.

48. Davis, "Corporations in the American Colonies," 1:94, by a combination of credulity and error credited Rhode Island with creating corporations to operate saw and flour mills. The colony did nothing of the sort. Persons operating installations of such a kind sometimes did refer to themselves as a company, but the term did not imply legal corporation necessarily.

49. Wilson, *Weybosset Bridge*, 182–83; Samuel Wiley et al. to General Assembly, Oct. 1772, RI Petitions, 14:134; Draft of "An Act incorporating Cooke's fountain Society," RI Petitions, 15:107; *PS* 1772, 8–11, 55–57; *PS* 1773, 76–78.

50. Untitled records of Rawson's Fountain Society, 1772–1843, MS, RIHS, 2.

51. Ibid., 2–3.

52. Ibid., 3.

53. Ibid., 6–7.

54. Samuel Wiley et al. to General Assembly, Oct. 1772, RI Petitions, 14:134; Records of Rawson's Fountain Society, 7–10.

55. Records of Rawson's Fountain Society, 23. Cf. pp. 10–17 for style used before incorporation.

56. Ibid., 20–22.

57. Ibid., 31–32, 34, 38, 39, 41, 43, 44, 46, 47, 50, 51.

58. Ibid., 39–41, 44, 48, 53, 54; Sale of share by Thomas Jones as treasurer, 16 Sept. 1793, Shepley Papers, RIHS, 4:42; Bill of sale of share from John Clifford et al. to Samuel Butler, Jr., 3 Nov. 1795, Shepley Papers, 5:68. The priority of Rawson's Fountain Society as a public utility may be open to question. Davis, "Corporations in the American Colonies," 1:89, mentions a similar water company authorized in Boston in 1652 but says, "It never accomplished the objects intended."

12. Ecclesiastical Organization and Civil Incorporation (pp. 226–240)

1. Sydney V. James, "Religion and the Amarican Revolution: The Development of the Federal Style in the Relations between Religion and Civil Authority," in Jaroslaw

Pelenski, ed., *The American and European Revolutions, 1776–1848: Sociopolitical and Ideological Aspects* (Iowa City, Iowa, 1980), 9–12, 19–24.

2. It is beside the point here to deliberate on the main spiritual effects of the Great Awakening. Plainly, Rhode Island Baptists and Congregationalists were stirred by the revival and often took sides for or against it. Some, however, could respond to it almost casually. The few schisms that resulted were much like earlier ones. Neither did the organization of new churches differ greatly from what had been done before. So the institutional consequences of the Awakening lacked the novelty or drama chronicled elsewhere. The reason was the absence of either of two conditions that caused shocking turbulence in other colonies. First, Rhode Island lacked the establishment found in adjoining New England jurisdictions and Virginia, which created an institutional framework to be captured or flouted or overthrown. Religious liberty allowed no barriers to institutional revision. Second, Rhode Island lacked the ethnic cleavages of the Middle Atlantic colonies, which in various ways added fuel to the animosities aroused by the revival. Neither differing spiritual traditions (e.g., New England v. Scotch-Irish) nor devotion to a non-British language and culture (e.g., among Dutch Reformed and assorted German faiths) could intensify the polarization occasioned by the revival in Rhode Island. All in all, the record in that colony casts doubt on recent interpretations of the Awakening that present it as crucial to the onset of the Revolution and an essential event in fashioning a national mentality for the United States.

3. Arthur E. Wilson, *Weybosset Bridge in Providence Plantations, 1700–1790* (Boston, 1947), 99–100, 110–15, 124–26, 128, 137–44, 149–51, 153; assorted documents in First Congregational Society [of Providence] Manuscripts, RIHS, box 1, esp. Joseph Snow, Jr., and Joseph Snow to Josiah Cotton, 29 Sept. 1743, and Church Meeting Records (item 20) of 17 July 1741, 17 Sept. 1741, 21 Nov. 1742, 14 Jan. 1742/43, 29 June 1743, 9 Sept. 1743, and 14 Nov. 1746; Decisions by Second Congregational society, 9 Mar. 1743/44, collection of documents on churches, RIHS, C.

4. Decision of prospective members, June 1743, untitled Church Record of the Six Principle Baptist Church in East Greenwich, R.I., 1743–1937, RIHS. Cf. the copy of declaration of the North Kingstown church, 2 June 1740, Potter Papers, RIHS, Pettaquamscut Purchase folder.

5. Cheesebrough, "Historical Sketch of the Second Baptists Church, Richmond," *Minutes of the Rhode Island Baptists Anniversaries, 1884* (Providence, 1884), 22–24.

6. This statement is a vague summary. Ordination ceremonies solemnized the relation of pastor to flock and increasingly eroded congregational autonomy by relying on the consent of nearby pastors to perform the ritual. Baptists, once they chose their candidate, preferred to have an elder elevated by imposition of hands by a few other elders, a crucial point surrounded by sermons, prayers, and several other events, such as an elder giving the charge and the right hand of fellowship. At such occasions, the visiting elders in some cases participated as individuals, in others as representatives of churches in the Congregationalist or Presbyterian fashion. The standing of an elder had a certain ambiguity. As the Richmond example illustrates, he might administer the sacraments outside his own church and so might be considered to have a spiritual rank independent of his relation to his flock. Yet Baptists churches often broke up when they ceased to have an elder, and elders who left for some reason were ordained again if they found a new flock.

The tendency to think of a church as existing only when it had an elder affected even the Newport Sabbatarians, some of whom thought their church had been disembodied in 1783 when Elder Maxson died. The majority assured the brethren in

Westerly and Hopkinton, however, that "we never thot the elder of a church was the same head of it but that Jesus Christ was the only head of the church and the Elder if he knows his place is the servant of the church, and that when an Elder dies or leaves a society that the members of the church that are destitute have power to elect another in his place." Copy made in 1898 of "Records of the Seventh-day Baptist Church of Newport, R.I. from 1692 to 1836, comprising Three Volumes," MS, Westerly Public Library, Westerly, R.I., 189–90.

Ezra Stiles, a Congregationalist (or self-styled Presbyterian) minister, claimed that Baptist elders normally participated in ordinations as individuals ordained by the poor of Christ to a spiritual office or rank of unlimited geographical jurisdiction, which he said was the basis for their administering the sacraments outside their own churches, but that revivalist Baptists gravitated to the Congregationalist or Presbyterian view of a minister's participating in an ordination as a representative of a church. Evidently, Stiles forgot about the administration of baptism in the predecessor to his own church, the flock under Clap, by outsiders from Massachusetts when Clap refused. Ezra Stiles, *The Literary Diary of Ezra Stiles, D.D., L.L.D.*, ed. Franklin Bowditch Dexter (New York, 1901), 1:29, 40, 40n-41n, 43, 81, 213, 225, 326, 334, 504. Some of the Baptists ways are illustrated by the Old Baptist Church in Warwick. Historical Records Survey, Division of Community Service Projects, Work Projects Administration, *Inventory of the Church Archives of Rhode Island; Baptist* (Providence, 1941), 35.

A few eccentric ordinations occurred. When Henry Dawson formed a church in Newport, the only elder who would assist him was a man of obscure credentials, said to have had strictly lay ordination himself. Dawson had to give the first hymn and offer the prayer. Nobody gave him the charge or imposition of hands, but the visitor did extend the right hand of fellowship. This was a reversion to the seventeenth century. Stiles, *Literary Diary*, 1:18, 19, 101–2.

7. Church meeting, 29 Apr. 1742, untitled records of Newport Six Principle Baptist Church, MS, NHS (hereafter cited as Newport's Six Principle Records, 2), 2:33; church meeting of 3 March 1747/48, "The Church Records: 1729 Containing the [illegible] of the Church [illegible] by the Rev. John Comer," MS, NHS (hereafter cited as Newport Six Principle Records, 1).

8. E.g., "Records of the First Baptist Church, of South Kingstown. R.I. From 1781 to 1839," transcribed by Julia Stedman in 1877–1879, MS, Town Clerk's Office, Wakefield, R.I., 30–31; copy of Daniel Everitt on behalf of Baptist church in South Kingstown to Robert Willcox, 30 Sept. 1742, Shepley Papers, RIHS, 9:104.

9. E.g., Thomas Burlinggame, Jr., et al. to John Gorton, 9 May 1756 (certificate of transfer of John Treadwell from Cranston Baptist Church), John Gorton Manuscripts, RIHS, 123; Samuel Winsor on behalf of Glocester Baptist Church to John Gorton, May 1766 (note on transfer of William Wood), John Gorton Manuscripts, 160. The General Assembly of this denomination in 1762 endorsed written certificates or letters of commendation signed by several men in the church from which someone moved. Copy of decision of assembly of Baptist elders and messengers, 25 June 1762, John Gorton Manuscripts, RIHS, 139.

10. Meeting of 6 May 1759, Newport Six Principle Records, 1; List of members and minutes of church meetings of 4 Feb. 1768, 2 Jan. 1772, and 3 Sept. 1772, Newport Six Principle Baptist Records, 2:11–16, 29, 31; Church meeting, 6 Jan. 1786, and note on dismission, 15 Sept. 1788, "The Book of Records belonging to the Church of Christ in New-port on Rhod-Island under the Pastoral Cear of mr. William Peckam and mr. John Comer" (First Baptist Church), 62, 64.

11. William G. McLoughlin, *New England Dissent, 1630–1833: The Baptists and*

the Separation of Church and State (Cambridge, Mass., 1971), 1:281; Historical Records Survey, *Inventory of the Church Archives of Rhode Island: Baptist*, 26.

12. McLoughlin, *New England Dissent*, 1:322, 428–30, 433–35, 502–8, 510–11; 2:705; copy of decisions by "General meeting at Providence," 24 June 1764, John Gorton Manuscripts, RIHS, 148; variant of the same, Newport Six Principle Records, 2:276.

13. Minutes of New England Yearly Meeting of Friends (men), MS, New England Yearly Meeting Archives, RIHS (hereafter cited as NE YM, with date of session given in number of year), 1755, 1762, 1769, 1775, 1776, 1782; Epistles of (men's) Rhode Island Quarterly Meeting to monthly meetings, 8/VII/1756, 12/VII/1759, box: Smithfield Monthly: Epistles to: 1716–1860, in NE YM Papers, RIHS; Minutes of Smithfield Monthly Meeting of Friends (men), MS, NE YM, RIHS (hereafter cited as Smithfield MM, with date of session given in numbers of days and years separated by month in Roman numerals), 30/III/1758; minutes of Rhode Island Monthly Meeting of Friends (men), MS, NHS (hereafter cited as RI MM, 3, with volume number plus date of session given in numbers of day and year separated by month in Roman numerals), 25/XII/1759; minutes of Greenwich Monthly Meeting of Friends (men), MS, NE YM, RIHS (hereafter cited as Greenwich MM, with volume number plus date of sessions given in numbers for day and year separated by month in Roman numerals), 3:8/IX/1760 and later; "Records of the Meeting for Sufferings from 1775 to 1793 10th Month Inclusive," MS, NE YM, RIHS, 14/VIII/1775, 15/VIII/1775, 13/VIII/1776.

14. NE YM, 1763, 1765. The Quaker schooling even in Newport was intermittent. After departure of the regular schoolmaster in 1749, the meeting's records reveal only two subsequent uses of the meetinghouse for schooling, both of unknown duration. RI MM, 3:29/VI/1749, 31/I/1764, 25/VI/1771, 27/VIII/1771.

15. RI MM, 3:24/II/1750; Greenwich MM, 2:8/II/1751; NE YM, 1774, 1775. For examples of distributing books and keeping a monthly meeting library: Greenwich MM, 3:3/IV/1769, 6/VIII/1772.

16. NE YM, 1744, 1753, 1769. On the expulsion of some prominent men, see, e.g., RI MM, 4:28/II/1775, 27/VI/1775, 26/IX/1775, 28/XI/1775; Smithfield MM, 25/III/1773.

17. Smithfield MM, 31/XII/1761, 25/II/1762, 28/X/1762; Greenwich MM, 3:8/X/1764, 3/XII/1769; minutes of South Kingstown Monthly Meeting of Friends (men), MS, NE YM, RIHS (date of session given in numbers for day and year separated by month in Roman numerals), 28/XII/1761, 31/V/1763; RI MM, 3:25/XII/1769, 29/I/1771, 25/V/1773.

18. NE YM, 1772, 1774.

19. Minutes of the Yearly Meeting for Ministers and Elders, MS, NE YM, RIHS (date of session given in numbers for day and year separated by month in Roman numerals), 8/VI/1770, 11/VI/1770; Additional report of New England Yearly Meeting for discipline, Epistle to quarterly and monthly meetings, 1770, in box: Smithfield Monthly: Epistles to: 1712–1860, NE YM papers, RIHS; South Kingstown MM, 1/XI/1762; NE YM, 1773, 1774, 1775, 1777, 1783.

20. Churches with a thoroughgoing objection to mixing earth and heaven have been uneasy over or flatly opposed to any relation to the state, no matter how convenient for the church.

21. George Champlin Mason, ed., *Annals of Trinity Church, Newport, Rhode Island. 1698– 1821* (Newport, R.I., 1890), 134–37; Simon Pease and Francis Brinley on behalf of "The Minister, Church Wardens, Vestry and Congregation of Trinity Church in Newport" to General Assembly, June 1767, RI Petitions, 12:75; PS 1767, 19–20.

22. Kirk G. Alliman, "The Incorporation of Massachusetts Congregational Churches, 1692–1833: The Preservation of Religious Autonomy" (Ph.D. diss., University of Iowa, 1970), 121–22.

23. Andrew Hunter, et al., on behalf of Newport Anglicans to General Assembly, Feb. 1769, RI Petitions, 13:74.

24. *PS* 1768, 75, 77 (there was no p. 76). The entry both in the manuscript and printed records of the session may have omitted the full text of the intended charter. It appears to allude to an act that is not there. The text as given was defective compared with some other charters; it contained almost nothing of the traditional verbiage on power to use a seal, sue and be sued, and so forth.

25. Mason, ed., *Annals of Trinity Church*, 138, 140, 141, 149, 153.

26. *PS* 1761, 91; *PS* 1772, 62–63, 71–73; John Smith and John Innes Clarke (wardens of King's Church, Providence) to General Assembly, Oct. 1771, RI Petitions, 14:99; "Ministers, Church-Warden, Vestry, and a Number of the Congregation of King's Church, in Providence, in Behalf of said Church" to General Assembly, 28 Oct. 1772, RI Petitions, 15:3; Charter to King's Church in Providence, 1772, RI Petitions, 15:12. Strange to say, Governor Wanton, himself an Anglican, never issued the charter. By 1790, "some doubt . . . [had] arisen whether . . . [the previous act of the Assembly] is not thereby vacated." So doubt arose also concerning the validity of actions by the minister, wardens, vestry, and congregation "under Authority" of the act. The Assembly then declared that the conduct of business by the church and its officers had been as valid as though the intended charter had been issued, and it authorized Governor Arthur Fenner to issue the document. See the original in the possession of St. John's Church, Providence, a copy of which has been provided by courtesy of the archivist and William G. McLoughlin.

27. Alliman, "Incorporation of Massachusetts Congregational Churches," 121–22.

28. Just after the Revolution, the Congregational church in Bristol and the second Congregational church in Providence followed this pattern.

29. William Dexter, et al., to General Assembly, RI Petitions 14:37; Wilson, *Weybosset Bridge*, 132–33; Copy of minutes of Rhode Island Association of Congregational ministers, 21 May 1771, RIHS Manuscripts 16:93; *The Act of Incorporation of the Benevolent Congregational Society, In the Town of Providence, in the Colony of Rhode-Island, etc. Together with Rules of said Society. To which is prefixed, A short Account of the Congregational Society in said Town, under the Pastoral Care of the Rev. Mr. Rowland* (Providence, 1771), ii–vi.

30. *Act of Incorporation of the Benevolent Congregational Society*, 1–5.

31. Ibid., 4–7; Rules and Orders adopted 25 Dec. 1770; Minutes of the Benevolent Congregational Society, 1:8 Jan. 1771, 5 Feb. 1771, 1, 19 Feb. 1771, 19 Mar. 1771, and 16 Apr. 1771; in First Congregational Society Manuscripts, RIHS, Box 1.

32. Gertrude S. Kimball, *Providence in Colonial Times* (Boston, 1912), 360–61; Copy of petition to General Assembly, Aug. 1773, by members of the church and society in Providence, RIHS Manuscripts, 16:58, 59; Attested copy of act of General Assembly authorizing sale of old meetinghouse site, Aug. 1773, RIHS Manuscripts, 16:60; Deed from Ephraim Wheaton to Nicholas Brown, et al., 14 Sept. 1784, RIHS Deed Book, 2:89.

33. List of subscribers, various dates from 13 Feb. 1774 on; Summary of accounts of building the Meetinghouse, Aug. 1774, in Papers of the Charitable Baptist Society, MS, JCB; Providence Baptists to General Assembly, May 1774, RI Petitions, 15:90; *PS* 1774, 66; Kimball, *Providence in Colonial Times*, 361.

34. Charter of the Charitable Baptist Society, Papers of the Charitable Baptist Society, JCB.

35. Transactions of 28 July 1774, and copies of first subscription paper, 13 June 1774, Papers of the Charitable Baptist Society, JCB.

36. McLoughlin, *New England Dissent*, 1:646–48, explains this point of view chiefly on the basis of evidence from Massachusetts. In Rhode Island, the record of nonresort to lotteries by predestinarian Baptist churches was almost perfect. Providence was the obvious exception, and it was a special case.

37. *PS* 1774, 73–75; East Greenwich LE, 9:290–91.

38. Ezra Stiles, "Memoir of Transactions in procuring the Charter from the General Assembly 1771," 16 Aug. 1771, in "Moses Pitmans Book 1740" (miscellaneous records of second Congregational Church in Newport, 1741 to 1771 or later), MS, NHS, 45–48.

39. Ibid., 50–51, 62–63.

40. Ibid., 50–57.

41. Ibid., 59.

42. Ibid., 63–67.

43. Church meeting, 10 June 1771, and text of charter, "A Book Containing The Affairs and Proceedings of the second Congregational Church in Newport . . . ," MS, NHS, 148–49.

44. Meetinghouse Booke of the Reverend Mr. Clap Commencing September 5, 1743," or First Congregational Church, Records, 1743–1831, MS, NHS, meeting of 25 Oct. 1773; copy of the charter of the first Congregational Church in Newport, NHS, box 40, folder 13.

45. RI MM, 3:25/I/1746, 31/I/1747, 29?/I/1748, 28/I/1749, 31/III/1761, 28/V/1765.

46. A Book of Records Belonging to the Proprietors of Eastons Point Newport," MS, NHS (hereafter cited as Newport Quaker Proprietors Records), 16 and passim; RI MM, 3:29/IX/1767.

47. RI MM, 3:28/IV/1767, 26/V/1767, 24/XI/1767, 26/I/1768, 26/IV/1768, 31/V/1768.

48. Newport Quaker Proprietors Records, 13, 17–20; RI MM, 4:31/VIII/1773; Deed of Peter Barker, et al., to Thomas Gould, Jr., et al., 13/III/1773, RI MM Papers, RIHS; Newport LE, 3:278–85.

49. Trusteeships in Rhode Island differed radically in form from contemporaneous arrangements in Britain. Moreover, in the colony, churches encountered neither hostility of Anglicans and the courts nor grasping behavior of trustees, both of which bedeviled use of trusteeships in England. Still, England Dissenters—except Quakers, of course—met and had to cope with the growing importance of the society in the ecclesiastical complex, just as Rhode Island Congregationalists and Baptists did. See Edwin Welch, "Nonconformist Trust Deeds," *Journal of the Society of Archivists* 3:(1968):397–403.

Retrospect (pp. 242–255)

1. In theology, of course, the authority of any Christian church or minister was derived from the kingship of Christ, and ordination of a clergyman commonly was done by other clergymen. Yet in a practical sense, the minister's authority came from his selection by the flock, and a church's power over its members came from their willingness to be under its discipline. In this respect, the churches paralleled the colonial government, which in theory derived its powers from the monarch of England but elevated its officers by election and enjoyed its effectiveness by a prevalent (if often passive) consent to its procedural correctness.

2. David E. Van Deventer, *The Emergence of Provincial New Hampshire, 1623–1741* (Baltimore, 1976), 5–30. Cf. Jere R. Daniell, *Colonial New Hampshire: A History* (Millwood, N.Y., 1981), 17–51, which presents a happier view and describes the effects of merger with Massachusetts as producing a working hierarchy of governmental agencies far more successfully than did the combination of the Rhode Island towns into one colony.

3. Timothy Breen, "Persistent Localism: English Social Change and the Shaping of New England Institutions," in *Puritans and Adventurers: Change and Persistence in Early America* (New York, 1980), 16–24. Many items in the great array of articles and monographs on early New England might be cited to support or elaborate on Breen's comments.

4. Bruce C. Daniels, *The Connecticut Town: Growth and Development, 1635–1790* (Middletown, Conn., 1979), 45–88, argues that Connecticut towns were more alike than Massachusetts towns because Connecticut towns (in spite of appearances) were created by the colonial government rather than the other way around. He shows, however, a range of variation, occasions when towns chose their own methods of self-government and then got the sanction of colonial law and the prevalence of the distinction that Breen, "Persistent Localism," points out between the functions of town and colony.

5. Sigmund Diamond, "From Organization to Society: Virginia in the Seventeenth Century," *American Journal of Sociology* 68 (1957–58):457–75, makes this point brilliantly if perhaps too schematically.

6. E.g., Van Deventer, *Emergence of Provincial New Hampshire*, 40–82; Bernard Bailyn, *The New England Merchants in the Seventeenth Century* (Cambridge, Mass., 1955), 102–3, 117; Edmund S. Morgan, *American Slavery, American Freedom* (New York, 1975), 218–20.

7. Darrett B. Rutman and Anita H. Rutman, in *A Place in Time: Middlesex County, Virginia, 1650–1750* (New York, 1984), present a fairly unchaotic process of a stratified society settling down and suggest that the spectacle of disorder given by Morgan, for instance, in *American Slavery, American Freedom*, is misleading. In a different way, Jon Kukla, "Order and Chaos in Early America: Political and Social Stability in Pre-Restoration Virginia," *American Historical Review* 90 (1985):275–97, has a cognate argument. Lois Green Carr and David William Jordan, *Maryland's Revolution in Government, 1689–1692* (Ithaca, N.Y., 1974), esp. 1–45, 180–231, argues both an impressive continuity in institutional practices and also a cluster of well-focused controversies over them. It would be hard to make such an argument for the Penn territories or Carolina.

Curiously, the Rutmans and Kukla believe in the dominance of a self-assured nascent gentry that is reminiscent of what was taking hold in the Aquidneck towns and part of the Narragansett country at the same time.

8. Edwin B. Bronner, *William Penn's "Holy Experiment": The Founding of Pennsylvania, 1681–1701* (New York, 1962), 50–56; Sydney V. James, *A People among Peoples: Quaker Benevolence in Eighteenth-Century America* (Cambridge, Mass., 1963), 1–70, 144–55; Arthur J. Worrall, *Quakers in the Colonial Northeast* (Hanover, N.H., 1980), 107–10 and passim.

9. Even Richard M. Johnson, *Adjustment to Empire: The New England Colonies, 1675– 1715* (New Brunswick, N.J., 1981), has little to offer on the local scene. Michael Kammen, *Colonial New York: A History* (New York, 1975), 117–27, considers only high politics. Van Devanter, *Emergence of Provincial New Hampshire*, barely touches the subject.

10. Carr and Jordan, *Maryland's Revolution in Government*, 86–93, 103–9,

138–39, 228–230, analyze the scene in detail and conclude that continuity and stability should be emphasized.

11. Michael G. Kammen, *A Rope of Sand: The Colonial Agents, British Politics, and the American Revolution* (Ithaca, N.Y., 1968), 7–11; Johnson, *Adjustment to Empire*, 306–63.

12. Kammen, *Colonial New York*, 128–31.

13. In Rhode Island, political controversy polarized sides over the land banks as early as 1714. The two sides persisted until the Revolution. The contests always were over secular matters, whether legislation or patronage. The extent of party-like organization before the 1750s remains obscure. In Connecticut, with a similar governmental system, party-like polarization and associated organizations began only after 1740—and then over religious disagreements, though secular affairs became involved, too. Richard L. Bushmam, *From Puritan to Yankee: Character and the Social Order in Connecticut, 1690–1765* (Cambridge, Mass., 1967), 235–66.

14. Robert Wheeler, "The County Court in Colonial Virginia," in Bruce C. Daniels, ed., *Town and County: Essays in the Structure of Local Government in the American Colonies* (Middletown, Conn., 1978), 125–28. Cf. Lois Green Carr, "The Foundations of Social Order: Local Government in Colonial Maryland," in *Town and County*, 91–92; Carr and Jordan, *Maryland's Revolution in Government*, 228–30; John E. Pomfret, *Colonial New Jersey: A History* (New York, 1973), 131, 292–93.

15. Benjamin W. Labaree, *Colonial Massachusetts: A History* (Millwood, N.Y., 1979), 126–29; Robert J. Taylor, *Colonial Connecticut: A History* (Millwood, N.Y., 1979), 44–46.

16. Roy H. Akagi, *The Town Proprietors of the New England Colonies: A Study in Their Development, Organization, Activities, and Controversies, 1620–1770* (Philadelphia, 1924), 44–165, remains the standard treatment. It is flawed.

17. Gary B. Nash, *Quakers and Politics: Pennsylvania, 1681–1726* (Princeton, N.J., 1968), 19–28, 56–67.

18. E.g., M. Eugene Sirmans, *Colonial South Carolina: A Political History, 1663–1763* (Chapel Hill, N.C., 1966), 82–83, 90, 92–94, 124, 136–37.

19. E.g., Kammen, *Colonial New York*, 177–78; Hugh T. Lefler and William S. Powell, *Colonial North Carolina: A History* (New York, 1973), 59–65, 106.

20. E.g., Rhys Isaac, *The Transformation of Virginia, 1740–1790* (Chapel Hill, N.C., 1982); William G. McLoughlin, *New England Dissent, 1630–1830: The Baptists and the Separation of Church and State* (Cambridge, Mass., 1971).

21. E.g., Carl Bridenbaugh, *Cities in the Wilderness: The First Century of Urban Life in America, 1625–1742*, 3rd ed. (London, 1970); Carl Bridenbaugh, *Cities in Revolt: Urban Life in America, 1743–1776*, 2nd ed. (London, 1970).

22. E.g., Dietmar Rothermund, *The Layman's Progress: Religious and Political Experience in Colonial Pennsylvania, 1740–1783* (Philadelphia, 1961), esp. 16–56; Jack D. Marietta, *The Reformation of American Quakerism, 1748–1783* (Philadelphia, 1984), 3–72, 150–86.

23. Samuel Eliot Morison, *The Founding of Harvard College* (Cambridge, Mass., 1935), 168, 193–94, 232–35, 325–27; Samuel Eliot Morison, *Harvard College in the Seventeenth Century* (Cambridge, Mass., 1936), 3–15, 292–302, 314–19, 398–99, 474, 484, 487–93, 509–30, 549, 555–56, 654–61.

24. *RICR*, 5:393–94; Bernard Bailyn, ed., *Pamphlets of the American Revolution, 1750–1776* (Cambridge, Mass., 1965), 1:500–544.

25. *RICR*, 7:581.

26. Ibid., 7:522–26.

27. This is not to deny the intermittent objections to the basic institutional arrangements voiced by men throughout the colonial period, including those who advocated royal government and acquiescence to the Stamp Act in 1765 and the many Loyalists in 1776. Nor is it to deny the vigor of debate over the Constitution. For the sake of simplicity, however, the preponderant voice is taken for the whole.

Bibliographical Notes and
Key to Short Citations

So far, no better bibliographical guide has been published for materials on colonial Rhode Island than my bibliographical essay in *Colonial Rhode Island: A History* (New York, 1975), 385–411. Roger Parks, ed., *Rhode Island: A Bibliography of Its History*, vol. 5 of *Bibliographies of New England History*, ed. T. D. Seymour Bassett and John Borden Armstrong (Hanover, N.H., 1983), has some value, but it contains no guide to archives, excludes much of the best material on one policy or another, includes a vast number of marginal publications, and offers very little help in distinguishing them from the most useful ones. Clarence S. Brigham, "Report on the Archives of Rhode Island," in American Historical Association, *Annual Report*, 1 (1903):543–655, remains quite useful. Some items mentioned by Brigham no longer can be found—I looked in vain for some of them at Warwick and Coventry, for instance. Some town records have been relocated. I saw the early West Greenwich ones, for example, in the State Archives in Providence. The State Archives themselves have been moved and improved under the fine direction of Phyllis Silva. The court records have undergone a variety of relocations and disruptions.

At present, the court records are still undergoing change. The most important repository is the library at Providence College, Providence, R.I., where the materials are being put back in proper order. That repository is now the first place to go when hunting for court records. Some remain in the Providence County Court House, however, and others can no longer be located. So I have mentioned locations and guides to arrangement as I found them at various times, hoping that this information may provide additional clues for efforts to track them down. The court records, including the records proper in ledgers, the daybooks, dockets, and file papers, are an immensely rich collection of sources of great potential value. The file papers contain a profusion of information otherwise unavailable. Use of these materials has been inhibited not only by their inaccessibility and forbidding quantity but also by the frustration they promise to anyone with a fairly specific quest. Every such search is like one for a duplicate snowflake. The affidavits, depositions, and sworn interrogations, to mention one category of unexploited treasure, contain fascinating insights into ordinary life, even sexual mores. Yet there is no means of finding items pertaining to a particular subject.

For other purposes, the papers baffle research because they include almost no reports of viva voce testimony in court. At times, it is even impossible to figure out which party produced certain evidence. Rarely did the judges write down any reasoning for their judgments. So research in basic legal history will remain extremely difficult. So far, some efforts at quantification of kinds of actions or parties have yielded necessarily limited results.

Town records fall into six categories: land evidence, town council proceedings, town meeting proceedings, vital records, file papers, and others. Most, but not all, of these are in ledgers and entered by hand. By the middle of the eighteenth century, some town clerks began using printed blank deeds for the land evidence records, completing them by hand and binding the sheets into volumes.

Land evidence records mainly consist of records of deeds but also contain documents on divisions by proprietors, special agreements (e.g., on operating a mill) among partners when land rights were concerned, mortgages, and the like. In a few cases, clerks opened special books for purposes such as recording mortgages to the colony.

Town council records consist of records of transactions and basic documents in probate proceedings—wills, inventories, letters and bonds of administration, and so forth—but almost never acquittances. Because of the distinct character and documentary paraphernalia of probate jurisdiction, town clerks often segregated it from the other transactions. The most common result was to begin entries in a ledger from opposite ends, which creates a complication for citation. Occasionally, the clerks kept separate series of ledgers. Historians often have assumed that probate proceedings resulted in distribution of an estate exactly in accord with the will. Surely that happened often, but the rarity of acquittances or documentary evidence of transmissions of land, together with the usual absence of any list of real properties of the estate and the rarity of documents on the satisfaction of debts of the estate, ordinarily leave the outcome uncertain.

Town meeting records were recorded minutes of decisions by town meetings, occasionally with miscellaneous supplementary information.

Vital records were those of births, deaths, and marriages. They were kept with growing care throughout the colonial period. At the start, they were neglected, and even when a separate series of ledgers became common, some clerks continued to jot down vital records here and there in older volumes of town meeting or town council deliberations.

File papers, as illustrated by those in Providence (see PTP and other items at RIHS, as commented on in the list of short citations below) contain a great variety of materials. Such things as "bills" by the freemen (i.e., proposals to the town meeting), protests or messages from other towns, or tax lists can be very useful. In general, the file papers not only contain information on what the townsmen voted down but also reveal much more than the formal minutes do about who wanted what. The Providence town papers are enriched by the accumulation of private papers, the largest single bundle being a donation from the Fenner family (vols. 39(A)–39(D)). As illustrated in Portsmouth and Warwick, clerks kept files of probate documents, where acquittances are most likely to turn up, as are discharges of bonds from executors and administrators. Unfortunately, over the years many file papers have drifted away from clerks' custody, so even when they survive elsewhere, their function in town business can be hard to ascertain.

In the miscellaneous category fall such things as records of earmarks or streets.

The materials in the State Archives in Providence, so far as they have been cited in the notes, have been described below in the "Key to Short Citations." Other documents of great importance are to be found there also, such as the records of the Grand Committee.

Documents in the collections of the Rhode Island Historical Society in Providence (RIHS) and the Newport Historical Society in Newport (NHS) are in various states of arrangement or presentation. I have not listed all the specific collections I examined. Two series need comment and are explained in the "Key to Short Citations" below: RIHS Manuscripts and Miscellaneous Manuscripts, RIHS. I have tried to achieve accuracy in describing documents, as to both technical terms and location. Nevertheless, I surely have made mistakes. For one thing, my knowledge of technical terms and my ability to distinguish holograph from copy increased as the work progressed. For another, librarians have relocated documents in ways that change the most useful specification of location. At RIHS, relocations have been made with proper records of what was done, so outmoded specifications can be interpreted. Odd notations on page numbers of manuscript sources (e.g., 139A), unless otherwise explained in the "Key to Short Citations" or the notes, indicate pages numbered out of strict sequence or a second sequence in one volume—for example, probate records as distinct from other town council business. Anyone consulting the original will find the anomaly without difficulty.

Dates used in the notes are in Old Style before September 1752 and in New Style thereafter. I have supplied double dating for dates from January 1 to March 24, regardless of the form in the original. I have used a special form for minutes of Quaker meetings: except for New England Yearly Meeting (sessions identified by year only), citations are to date of session given in number of day and year in the usual numerals, separated by number of month in Roman numerals (e.g., 13/III/1731). This form, which has been used commonly when citing these materials, serves well because it supplies information and because Quakers used numbers instead of names for months and days of the week. So no mental translation is needed to go from note to original. Page and volume numbers also have uses—minutes for one session required more than one page oftener than less—yet introduce confusion when two sets of page numbers exist, as they do in some volumes.

Key to Short Citations

(N.B. Titles of published items or abbreviations of them are italicized to distinguish them from manuscripts.)

Colony Records Manuscript records of the transactions of the Court of Commissioners (under its various names) of the government under the Providence Plantations patent of 1644 and of the General Assembly under the charter of 1663. The first volume has two parts. Other volumes continue the series (with a break from 1685 to 1715) until the Revolution. State Archives, Providence, R.I.

East Greenwich LE, TC, TM LE: land evidence records (and miscellany). MS, town clerk's office, East Greenwich, R.I. Vol. 1 is paged from front and back, designated in notes by A for front and B for back (e.g., 54B).
TC: a series of volumes under misleading title for the first two. MS, same location. Vol. 1 is mainly town meeting records (and miscellany); vol. 2 is mainly records of the committee on small lots; vol. 3 and thereafter properly contain town council records. Vols. 4 and 5 have no page numbers, so citations are to date of session. TM: town meeting records, 1752–1793. MS, same location. Citations are to date of session.

Gen. Ct. Tr. Records (i.e., ledgers containing judgments, orders, etc., in chronological order) of the General Court of Trials, 1671–March 1741, 2 vols. MS, formerly at office of the clerk of the Superior Court, Newport. Beginning with the September 1730 term, the tribunal gloried in the name of Superior Court of Judicature, Court of Assize and General Goal Delivery.

Gen. Ct. Tr. papers File papers accumulated in the hands of the clerk of the Court of Trials. When consulted, these were in the office of the clerk of the Superior Court in Newport and arranged in boxes bearing year numbers, some divided into separate boxes for the sessions in a given year. Citation, therefore, is to the label on the box. Subsequent removal of these materials from Newport may have resulted in disruption of the system formerly observed.

Governor and Council Transactions of the Governor and Council of Rhode Island. MS, State Archives, Providence. The first volume began in 1667. Entries included military and emergency business and, by the middle of the eighteenth century, appeals from rulings on probate or tavern license rulings by town councils.

Island Records Records of the Island of Rhode Island, 1638–1644, called "Clasp Book." MS, State Archives, Providence. Most of this volume is fairly well transcribed in RICR, vol. 1.

Jamestown LE, Proprietors, TC, TR LE: land evidence volumes. MS, town clerk's office, Jamestown, R.I. The numbering of volumes can be misleading. Vol. 3 contains some records of the proprietors of Dutch Island.
Proprietors: This is the first book of town records. In one page sequence (the one cited), it contained records of proprietors' meetings, town meetings, and town council meetings, with chronology often disregarded; the other pagination contained vital records. MS, same location.
TC: town council proceedings. MS, same location. Vols. 1 and 3 (bound together) included general business; vol. 2 contained probate proceedings.
TR: a medley of town meeting and town council records beginning in 1744. MS, same location. This volume follows Jamestown Proprietors.

JCB John Carter Brown Library, Brown University, Providence, R.I. Included in the collection are manuscript copies of documents in the Public Record Office of Great Britain pertaining to Rhode Island (designated JCB Transcripts in notes). Most of them were published in RICR or partly published in Calendar of State Papers, Colonial Series, America and West Indies.

Journal H of D Journals of the House of Deputies, or lower house, in the General Assembly of Rhode Island, 1728ff. MS, State Archives, Providence. Usually unpaginated, these volumes are cited by date of session. These documents seldom revealed much about deliberation.

Journal H of M Journals of the House of Magistrates, or upper house: Governor and Deputy Governor and assistants when acting as part of the General Assembly of Rhode Island, 1733ff. MS, State Archives, Providence. After the judicial reorganization in 1747, the name House of Magistrates fell out of use. These documents are remarkably skeletal. Citations are to date of session.

King's Inf. Ct. or King's Sup. Ct. Records, dockets, daybooks, and file papers of King's County (now Washington County) courts. MS, consulted in fourth-floor vault, Providence County Courthouse, but since removed. The formal record ledgers are designated by a Roman numeral (e.g., King's Inf. Ct., I).

Middletown LE, Proprietors, TC, TM LE: land evidence records of town of Middletown, 1743ff. MS, town clerk's office, Middletown, R.I.
Proprietors: Proprietors: proprietors' records. MS, same location. Virtually all of the volume pertains to transactions before Middletown was set off from Newport in 1743. The earliest entries concern the division begun in 1701/02. Miscellaneous evidence shows that this was the third book of Newport proprietors' records.
TC: town council records of Middletown. MS, same location. Vol. 1 has pagination errors; vols. 2 and 3 segregate probate from other transactions, beginning at opposite ends of the book. The pages in the probate series are designated A (e.g., 82A).
TM: town meeting records of Middletown. MS, same location.

New Shoreham TB New Shoreham Town Book No. 1. Presumably, the original is in town clerk's office, New Shoreham (Block Island), R.I. The version consulted was a typescript by George R. Burgess at RIHS. All sorts of town records.

Newport LE, TC, TM, TM (A) LE: land evidence volumes, new series. MS and modified MS, City Hall, Newport, R.I. The remains of the colonial series are at NHS; they have not been cited.

TC: original town council records. MS, NHS. They were reassembled badly after the damage done to them when all the colonial town records went overboard in Hellgate during the Revolution. Though given volume and page numbers, the pages often are not in any plausible sequence, let alone the original.

TM: original town meeting records. MS, NHS. They were reassembled in nearly the original order. The first volume contains fragments from 1679 and entries almost continuously from 1682 to 1739.

TM (A): transcript made from the original colonial town meeting records. MS, NHS. Probably made by Benjamin F. Howland. When he made the transcript, more could be read in the originals than can be now, though he made out less than can be now in some passages.

Newport Sup. Ct. Records of the Superior Court of Judicature Court of Assize and General Goal Delivery . . . within and for the County of Newport. MS, consulted at office of clerk of the Superior Court, Newport, R.I.

North Kingstown Probate, TC Probate: town council transactions, beginning with the predecessor town of Kingstown and continuing with North Kingstown. MS, town clerk's office, Wickford, R.I. These records were damaged by fire in the nineteenth century. They are not entirely confined to probate transactions. The first volume (1698ff.) is designated vol. 5. The original pagination no longer corresponds to the index, indicating some lack of success in efforts at restoration.

TC: mostly town meeting records, 1699ff. MS, same location. These volumes also contain some town council transactions and miscellany.

PGA Proceedings of the General Assembly of Rhode Island. MS, State Archives, Providence. Nineteenth-century copies of older documents, mostly Colony Records, but for 1686 to 1715, copies of the "schedules" or reports of actions by the Assembly sent to clerks of the towns. Presumably regular records either were not kept in that interval or, much more likely, were lost. In the order of authority, PGA stands below Colony Records and PS, except for the years 1686–1715, for which interval it is the most authoritative.

Portsmouth ER Clarence Saunders Brigham, ed., The Early Records of the Town of Portsmouth (Providence, 1901). A very scrupulous transcription.

Portsmouth LE, TC, TM LE: land evidence volumes. MS, town clerk's office, Portsmouth, R.I. Variant titles or none. Some oddities in pagination. The first volume, indexed as the first, bears the title, "Land Evidence 2nd Book No. 1." Citations include a volume and page number.

TC: town council proceedings. MS, same location. Vol. 1 is an eighteenth-century copy. By vol. 6 (1763–1781), the clerk began segregating probate from other proceedings in a separate pagination, which is cited as Portsmouth TC Probate.

TM: own meeting proceedings. MS, same location. Vol. 1 (1697–1786) began where Portsmouth ER ended.

Providence Ct. of Gen. Sessions Formal records, dockets, daybooks, and file papers of Providence County Court of General Sessions. MS, consulted in office of clerk of Providence Superior Court, fifth floor, Providence County Courthouse. Since removed.

Providence Inf. Ct. or Sup. Ct. Records, dockets, daybooks, and file papers of the Providence County courts with jurisdiction over civil actions. MS, consulted in office of clerk of Providence County Superior Court, fifth floor, Providence County Courthouse. Since removed. Formal records are designated by Roman numerals (e.g., Prov. Sup. Ct., 2).

Providence ER Horatio Rogers et al., eds., The Early Records of the Town of Providence, 21 vols. (Providence, 1892–1915). A comprehensive index has been published.

PS Untitled printed "schedules" or sessional reports of the General Assembly of Rhode Island, October 1747ff. These publications contained most of what was in the Colony Records. Copies were sent to each town clerk and a list of other officers after each session. Beginning in May 1748, the page numbers were in sequence for a whole year, beginning with the May sessions (apart from some errors, minor variations, and a two-year sequence beginning in May 1761) and continuing until the Revolution. Citations are to sequence designated by year number (e.g., PS 1758 means the sequence started in May 1758) except where variant identification is necessary.

PTP Providence Town Papers, c. 169 vols. MS, RIHS. Thousands of items mounted in large ledgers. In two series. Citations are to first series, unless otherwise indicated, and include a volume number and an item number. Some of the papers have been published in Providence *ER*, 15 and 17.

RI Laws 1706? "Laws and Acts made From the [first Setling?] of His Majestyes Colony of Rhode Island and Providence Plantations by the General Assembly of said Colony and Confirmed [by] authority thereof according to his Majestyes Gracious [charter] granted to said Colony in the fifteenth year of his Reign anno [Domine] 1663." N.d., but probably 1706 or 1707. MS, State Archives, Providence.

RI *Laws* 1719, 1730, etc. Acts and Laws of his Majesties Colony of Rhode-Island, and Providence-Plantations in America. Variant titles after first four words. Boston, 1719; Newport, 1730 (and continuation in 1736), 1745, 1752, 1767, 1772. In most of these publications, the charter came first, with its separate page sequence and title page.

RI LE "Rhode Island Land Records." MS, State Archives, Providence. Vols. 1–3 (designated somewhat loosely as comprising 1648–1721) were in fact almost entirely public recording of documents pertaining to land. Beginning with vol. 4, other kinds of documents came to predominate, and the series is called "Rhode Island Public Notary Records" from then on.

RI Petitions Volumes containing mounted petitions to the General Assembly and a few supplementary documents. MS, State Archives, Providence. According to the late archivist, Mary Quinn, one of her predecessors discarded all the petitions that were denied but missed a few. Also, petitioners could retrieve their petitions, so the series is far from complete. Citations are to the description of the document, volume (sometimes volume and part), and page.

RI Treasurer's Accounts Colonial treasurer's accounts. MS, State Archives, Providence. The ledgers called vols. 1 and 2 (1672–1711 and 1711–1812) surely are incomplete. Vol. 2 contains allusions to another book.

RICR John Russell Bartlett, ed., Records of the Colony of Rhode Island and Providence Plantations (1856–1862; reprint, New York, 1968). These volumes are primarily the records of the General Assembly of the colony but contain both more and less than the manuscript originals. See also Colony Records, Island Records, PGA, PS, and JCB Transcripts.

RIHS Manuscripts RIHS Manuscripts is the name of a series of documents, for many years mounted in scrapbooks, where they were identified by page or item number. Some or all have been dismounted and placed in boxes, but the old identifications by volume and page number have been preserved.

RIHS Miscellaneous Manuscripts RIHS Miscellaneous Manuscripts is the name of a huge series of documents with short code descriptions of place in series. Many parts of the series go under names of their own (e.g., Harris Papers) and are identified that way in the notes. Others, however, are isolated items or in small clumps under the code labels. Ordinarily, these items are in boxes.

South Kingstown LE, TC, TC Probate, TM LE: land evidence records. MS, town clerk's office, Wakefield, R.I. The volumes containing the oldest entries are copies from the records of the antecedent town of Kingstown, for some reason called vols. 2 and 3. The third in the series, here designated 3A, begins in 1723. TC, TC Probate: town council records. MS, same location. The first volume contains copies from Kingstown records—probate documents, lists of freemen, earmarks, births, and marriages. Subsequent volumes contain town council proceedings of a general nature from one end and probate (here designated South Kingstown TC Probate) from the other.
TM: town meeting proceedings, 1723ff. MS, same location.

Sup. Ct.: Records of "Superior Court of Judicature, Court of Assize and General Goal Delivery . . . for . . . Rhode Island and Providence plantations . . ." MS, consulted at the office of the clerk of the Superior Court, Newport. Since removed. This court was the former General Court of Trials, renamed when the county courts were instituted. The records, in fact, began in vol. 2 of the ledger begun by the predecessor. This part of the volume is designated Sup. Ct., 1. The next volume is entirely for the Superior Court, but the third volume, after 39 pages, becomes the record of the Superior Court for Newport county (Newport Sup. Ct.).

Warwick A2, A2 LE Untitled town records of Warwick, R.I. MS, designated A2 at one time. The original, presumably once at City Hall, Apponaug, R.I., has not been seen for some time. Microfilm at RIHS. Warwick A2 designates the pagination, beginning at one end of the volume with an entry for the town meeting of 18 Apr. 1668; Warwick A2 LE designates the pagination, beginning at the other end, containing land evidence entries.

Warwick ER Howard M. Chapin, ed., The Early Records of the Town of Warwick (Providence, 1926).

Warwick GR Warwick records of miscellaneous kinds. MS, City Hall, Apponaug, R.I. Mainly late seventeenth century. At one time designated A1. The pagination from one end (town orders, proceedings of town meetings and town council, and miscellany) is designated by a plain number. The pagination from the other end (deeds, indentures, and miscellany) is designated by a number plus a (e.g., 3a, 10).

Warwick LE, TC, TM, Wills LE: land evidence volumes. MS, City Hall, Apponaug, R.I. The series begins with vol. 2 (see microfilm, RIHS), an earlier book of town records (probably Warwick A2 LE) being considered vol. 1 Vol. 2 starts with a deed dated in 1682 but contains older items, plus some pertaining to Portsmouth land. Vol. 3, in addition to documents on land titles, contains some records of the town meeting, mainly 1689–1709/10. Thereafter, the series is straightforward.
TC: town council proceedings. MS, same location, except for what probably were two books of clerk's rough minutes, now at RIHS.
TM: town meeting minutes. MS, same location.
Wills: probate documents. MS, same location. The town meeting decided on a separate set of records for probate documents in February 1708/09 (see Warwick LE, 3, 2), but Wills, 1, begins with entries dating from 1703, probably entered after the town meeting's decision.

Westerly LE, TC, TM LE: land evidence records. MS, town hall, Westerly, R.I. The first three volumes are numbered by folio rather than page. Vol. 1 contains some town meeting and town council records.
TC: town council records, 1699ff. MS, same location. Vol. 1 contains some deeds; vol. 4 contains miscellaneous documents interleaved, indicated in notes by asterisk on number of preceding page.
TM: town meeting records, 1707ff. MS, same location.

Index

Absentee ownership, 144, 145, 149
Adams, John, 172
Admiralty court, 121–22
Advowson, 174, 175
Akagi, Roy H., 302n.14
Alcock, John, 86
Alimony, 193
Allocation of land. See Land distribution
Almshouses, 198
Ancient and Honorable Artillery Company (Massachusetts), 302n.24
Andover (Massachusetts), 283n.7
Andros, Sir Edmund, 57, 58, 61, 71, 92, 96
Anglicans. See Church of England
Animals, domestic. See Livestock
Antinomianism, 33
Apathy, political, 244
Apology for the True Christian Divinity, An (Barclay), 184
Appeals (judicial), 121, 193, 297n.21
Apportionment, 123
Apprenticeship, 69, 167, 205
Aquidneck commonwealth, 29–31; Coddington on allying with Massachusetts, 31, 42–43; Coddington patent as governor, 41, 45, 46; General Court, 30, 31, 260n.49; as pattern for colonial government, 41; Portsmouth in, 25
Aquidneck Island: commons and proprietors on, 70–72; growing prosperity of, 114; Middletown, 144, 163, 195–96, 198, 242; new town promoters from, 82; Quakers on, 105, 108; vestigial commons on, 144. See also Aquidneck commonwealth; Newport; Portsmouth
Aquidnesset (Quidnesset), 88, 89, 93, 141
Arnold, Benedict, 84, 271n.2
Assembly, General. See General Assembly

Atherton, Humphrey, 88
Atherton syndicate. See Narragansett Proprietors
Attorney General, 188, 190, 191, 205

Babcock, Henry, 297n.20
Bacon's Rebellion, 248
Badger, Jonathan, 233
Balston, William, 27
Bankruptcy, 202
Baptism, 22, 32, 106, 171, 179, 228
Baptists: Charitable Baptist Society, 234; church records kept by, 179–80; clergy, 179; and College of Rhode Island, 218; compulsion eschewed by, 239; denominationalism in, 227–29; in early eighteenth century, 178–80; elaborate structures created by, 243; the Great Awakening dividing, 226, 239, 305n.2; and incorporation, 11, 226, 234–35; land ownership by, 178; lotteries run by, 210, 301n.12; on marriage, 179, 293n.34; and Massachusetts Standing Order churches, 251; meetinghouses built by, 178; in Newport, 28, 32, 178–79, 180, 228, 235; old and new, 102–4; ordination in, 228, 305n.6; in Providence, 22, 178, 179, 234–35, 242; religious fellowship among, 180; and traditional Christianity, 9; trusteeships used by, 240; urban versus rural, 178, 184, 228, 242; in Westerly, 180. See also Seventh Day Baptists; Six Principle Baptists
Barclay, Robert, 184, 230
Bellomont, Richard Coote, earl of, 133
Benevolent Congregational Society, 233–34
Berkeley, George, 216
Berkeley, William, 247–48
Bicameralism, 51, 117

Binding out children, 167
Birth records, 67, 105, 113
Blacks, 159
Blathwayt, William, 133
Block Island: Congregationalists on, 173; considering other allegiance, 60; garrison sent to, 118; Indians on, 83; proprietary syndicate on, 83; self-contained quality of, 88. *See also* New Shoreham
Board of Trade, 119, 133, 134, 298n.25
Boards of selectmen, 158, 287n.19
Boston Neck, 88, 89, 93, 141
Boundaries, town, 131
Bound servitude, 69, 159, 244
Bowen, Ephraim, 217
Breen, Timothy H., 257n.1, 262n.1, 277n.1, 310n.3
Brenton, Jahleel, 124, 189, 238, 277n.1
Brenton, William, 54
Bridenbaugh, Carl, 276n.1
Bridges: General Assembly subsidizing, 127, 195, 201; lottery for financing, 209–10; towns in building and maintaining, 67, 161, 163
Brinley, Francis, 57, 60, 62–63, 145, 266n.46, 277n.1
Bristol, 10
Brown, Moses, 236
Brown University (College of Rhode Island), 218–20, 234, 253, 304n.45
Brunkow, Robert deV., 264n.27
Bubble Act of 1720, 213–14
Bull, Henry, 107

Callender, John, 179
Cambridge Platform (Congregationalism), 227, 251
Canonicus, 84, 141, 266n.41
Carolina, 248, 249
Carré, Ezekiel, 110
Catholics, 243, 244
Charitable Baptist Society, 234
Charles II, 48, 50
Charter of 1644. *See* Parliamentary charter of 1644
Charter of 1663. *See* Royal charter of 1663
Charters, corporate. *See* Corporate charters
Chasmore, Richard, 47

Children: binding out of, 167; birth records, 67, 105, 113; churches rearing their children in the faith, 170, 184; orphans, 166. *See also* Schools
Christianity: baptism, 22, 32, 106, 171, 179, 228; Catholics, 243, 244; confirmation, 106, 174; direct inspiration, 102, 104; French Protestants, 92, 98, 101–2, 109, 110–11, 248; laying on of hands, 22, 32, 102, 103, 178, 261n.58; Puritans, 13, 21, 22, 89, 254; sacraments, 38, 171; traditional, 9, 111, 184, 231. *See also* Baptists; Church of England; Congregationalists; Gortonians; Predestination; Quakers; Religious institutions
Church and state: Congregationalists and Anglicans wanting legal backing, 171, 185; separation of, 6, 7, 27, 251
Churches. *See* Religious institutions
Church of England (Anglicans): adapting rules to their own circumstances, 113; in charter of 1663, 50; clergy, 174; corporate charters sought by, 11, 226, 231–33; in early eighteenth century, 173–78; imperial loyalty represented by, 174; introduced into Rhode Island, 9, 173; King's Church in Providence, 232, 308n.26; in Kingstown, 174; lotteries run by, 210; in Newport, 173, 174, 175–76; official standing wanted by, 171, 185, 239; parishes in, 174, 175, 226, 227, 242, 252; permanence of, 184; the powerful gravitating toward, 238; in Providence, 174; St. Paul's Church in Narragansett, 175, 176, 177; schools, 176; Trinity Church in Newport, 173, 175–76, 231–33
Church property, 170, 238
Church records, 179–80, 181, 227
Civil code of 1647, 45
Clap, Nathaniel, 171–72
Clarke, John: agreement with Winthrop, 53, 89; in London to procure royal charter, 49, 54; Newport Baptists suing over estate of, 179; in the Newport church, 32; on total immersion, 22
Clarke, Walter, 58–59, 133
Class, 158, 244

Clergy (ministry): advowson, 174, 175; Baptist, 179; charismatic, 38; in the Church of England, 174; Congregationalist, 173; Gorton on, 36; ordination, 228, 305n.6, 309n.1; Quaker, 106, 181, 183, 184; university-trained, 21; in Providence, 22

Coasters Harbor Island, 144, 167–68

Coddington, William: coup against in Portsmouth, 25; in Jamestown's founding, 84, 271n.2; on merging Aquidneck commonwealth with Massachusetts, 31, 42–43; in Newport, 29; patent making him governor of Aquidneck, 41, 45, 46; as Pocasset Judge, 24; and reunion of 1654, 47; in town church of Newport, 31–32

Coggeshall, John, 58–59

Coggeshall, Joshua, 106

College of Rhode Island (Brown University), 218–20, 234, 253, 304n.45

College of William and Mary, 253

Colleges: College of Rhode Island, 218–20, 234, 253, 304n.45; Harvard College, 171, 173, 179, 253; legislative creation of, 218; as public institutions, 253; William and Mary, 253; Yale College, 179, 214

Collins, Henry, 217

Colonial government: administrative arms of, 188–93; Attorney General, 188, 190, 191, 205; centralization of, 8–9, 131, 135; charter of 1644 authorizing, 20, 41–45; coercion exercised by, 113–14; collective action regulated by, 224; Colony House in Newport, 171, 279n.38; confusion from 1690 to 1694, 58–61; as a corporation, 214; as creation of the original towns, 15, 40; division and reunion from 1648 to 1654, 45–48; in the early eighteenth century, 112–36; economic development policy, 125–29; feeble government from 1654 to 1686, 53–56; finance of, 122–25; formal changes in, 117–22; General Treasurer, 124, 188, 190–91, 211; Governor and Council, 121, 191, 193, 202, 241, 298n.25; imperial pressure on, 116, 117, 132–34; and land acquisition, 83; land conflicts subdued by,

137–52; as limited government, 208; Newport as capital of, 53; oaths of office, 52; political parties, 11, 202–4, 250, 311n.13; under the royal charter of 1663, 48–53; in the seventeenth century, 40–63; after 1738, 186–206; specialized organs created, 10; town government regulated by, 129–31; and the "vacant lands," 140–43; as weak, 41, 64, 99. *See also* General Assembly; Judiciary

Colony House (Newport), 171, 279n.38

Color line, 158–59, 244

Colson (Colston), Nathaniel, 281n.62

Combination (1638), 17

Comer, John, 32, 179, 293n.35

Commerce. *See* Trade

Commercial centers, development of, 10, 154–58, 200

Commissary-General, 191

Committee of War, 188, 191–93, 297n.20

Commons: in the communal ideal, 14; decline of, 69, 168, 207, 252; in new towns, 83; proprietary syndicates managing, 70; and proprietors on Aquidneck Island, 70–72; Providence dismantling, 149; recording divisions of, 67; selling of, 144, 145; Stanton suit in Westerly, 197; Warwick restricting use of, 35. *See also* Four Mile Common

Communal ideal: disintegration of, 64–81; in establishment of Rhode Island settlements, 13–15

Conanicut Island: Indians on, 83; as pasture for Newport and Portsmouth, 88; proprietary syndicates dividing, 138, 144, 145. *See also* Jamestown

Confirmation, 106, 174

Congregationalists: adapting rules to their own circumstances, 113; Benevolent Congregational Society, 233–34; on Block Island, 173; Cambridge Platform, 227, 251; clergy, 173; corporate charter sought by, 11, 226, 233–34, 235–37; denominationalism in, 227; in early eighteenth century, 170–73; in East Greenwich, 235; elaborate structures created by, 243; the Great Awakening dividing, 226,

Congregationalists (*continued*)
305n.2; introduced into Rhode Island, 9, 171; in Kingstown, 173, 177, 185; lotteries run by, 210, 302n.12; in Newport, 171–73, 235–37; official standing wanted by, 171, 185, 239; permanence of, 184; in Providence, 173, 227, 233–34; schism in Newport, 171–72; schools, 172; the society, 172, 291n.8; trusteeships used by, 240; in Westerly, 173
Connecticut: attempting to extend its borders to Narragansett Bay, 39, 49, 53, 54–55, 59, 62, 74, 266nn. 41, 46; as charter colony, 214; colonial government and imperial policy in, 40; common land allocated to individuals in, 71; electing all its high officials, 250; institutional variety in, 246, 310n.4; legislating for towns and proprietors of common lands, 250; Massachusetts followed by, 251; Misquamicut claims of, 95–96; and Narragansett Proprietors, 88, 89, 92, 93, 140, 141; political parties in, 311n.13; in regional monetary system, 125; royally appointed officers in, 249; Yale College, 179, 214
Consent: becoming a tradition, 255; colonial government dependent on, 41, 113; in the Declaration of Independence, 254; in nongovernmental institutions, 242–43; old ideas about authority giving way to, 252; in Providence Plantations, 43; in religious institutions, 309n.1; Rhode Island founders appealing to, 5; and social stratification, 244; town government and, 38
Constables, 164
Constitutionalism, 113
Cook, Edward M., 287n.19, 289n.40
Cooke's Fountain Society, 221
Corporate charters: allowed for public purposes, 209; for churches, 226, 231–37; and class, 244; enduring bodies created by, 224–25; functions of, 11, 224; General Assembly granting, 214–23, 241; in other colonies, 253. *See also* Corporations; Town charters

Corporations, 207–25; colonial government as, 214; general statute of incorporation lacking, 254; as legal persons, 209; nongovernmental, 211–23; public versus private, 213; as subsidiaries of towns, 186, 197; two types of, 139; Williams on, 301n.3. *See also* Corporate charters
Corruption, 161
Cotton, John, 27
Cotton, Josiah, 173
Counties: creation of, 121; Massachusetts and Connecticut developing, 250
Court of Elections. *See* General Assembly
Court of Equity, 193, 297n.21
Courts. *See* Judiciary
Cowesett, 77, 79
Cranston, 210
Cranston, Samuel: accommodation with London, 133; in admiralty court dispute, 122; in development of colonial government, 115; in Jamestown commons' division, 145–46; on military organization, 119; and Misquamicut land division, 146; in Newport commons' division, 144; opposition to, 116; in Queen Anne's War, 191; report on Newport trade, 276n.1; and the "vacant lands" dispute, 140, 142; in Westconnaug land division, 146–47
Criminal code of 1647, 45, 263n.17
Cromwell, Oliver, 47
Customshouses, 249

Dams, 129
Danforth, John, 171
Daniell, Jere R., 310n.2
Daniels, Bruce C., 310n.4
Dawson, Henry, 306n.6
Death penalty, 133
Death records, 105, 113
Declaration of Breda, 50
Declaration of Independence, 254
Democracy: Aquidneck commonwealth as, 25, 29–30, 260n.46; and the charter of 1663, 62; direct versus representative, 41–42, 49; General Court of Election of 1647 on, 43; in Providence, 264n.27

Denominationalism, 227–31
Direct inspiration, 102, 104
Distribution of land. *See* Land distribution
Divorce, 193
Domestic animals. *See* Livestock
Dominion of New England, 56–58; colonial government replaced under, 7, 40; as exhibiting evils to be avoided, 114; imperial control asserted in, 249; Narragansett Proprietors in, 92; noncompliance with, 62, 63
Dorr, Henry C., 302n.14
Driftways, 288n.33
Dudley, Joseph, 56–57, 133
Dutch Reformed congregations, 248
Dyer, William, 46

East Greenwich: colonial government in establishment of, 62, 83; commercial center development in, 154, 157–58, 287n.14; Congregationalists in, 235; Cooke's Fountain Society, 221; economic ambitions of, 10; establishment of, 55, 62, 83, 97–98; gaining territory, 100; mad dogs destroyed in, 196; map of, 90–91; and Narragansett Proprietors, 92; road controversy in, 196; school management in, 198; Six Principle Baptists in, 227; undivided lands in, 143–44; workhouse in, 198
Easton, John, 140, 271n.2
Easton, Samuel, 238
Easton's Beach, 144
Easton's Point (Newport), 108, 181, 238
Economic development policy, 125–29; commercial center development, 10, 154–58, 200; Newport affected by success of, 200
Economic enterprises: British practices adopted by, 9; partnerships, 242, 244; taverns, 14, 27, 41, 68, 165, 207. *See also* Mills; Trade
Education. *See* Colleges; Schools
Elite military companies, 214–16
English law: abandonment of, 254; charter of 1663 giving the colony a place in, 50; codes of 1647 derived from, 45; colonial courts implementing, 224; colonial courts made compatible

with, 9, 133, 168; equity, 122; local usage developing along with, 119; main traits accepted in Rhode Island, 241; Newdigate turning to, 139; in New York, 249; Portsmouth resorting to, 23; and proprietary syndicates, 152; religious institutions placing themselves within, 170
Equality: of freemen, 48; Gorton on, 34; in Providence, 16, 17, 23; in Warwick, 34. *See also* Inequality
Equity, 122
Ethnicity, 248, 252
Evans, Evan, 291n.18
Excise on wine and liquor, 54
Eyres, Nicholas, 179

Family, the: in the communal ideal, 13, 37; Gortonians on, 33; law as embracing, 38, 113; as private arrangement, 205; public dimension of, 224; Williams on, 16. *See also* Marriage
Farrell, John T., 263n.17
Federalism, 45
Fenner, Arthur, 308n.26
Fenner, Thomas, 147
Ferries: General Assembly regulating, 127; to Jamestown, 188, 201, 213; licensing of, 300n.2; at Portsmouth, 27; roads to, 284n.20
Field, John, 221
Field's Fountain Society, 221
Fifth Monarchists, 275n.2
Fire fighting, 156, 163, 199, 253
Fish, Daniel, 227
Fishing, 128
Fones, John, 59
Founders of Rhode Island. *See* Rhode Island founders
Four Mile Common (Warwick), 34; reserved for collective use, 69, 262n.65; town versus proprietary management of, 75, 76, 77, 150
Fox, George, 105, 107, 183
Franchise: broadening of, 48; colonial regulation of, 129; General Assembly as unable to control, 52; majority of the population excluded from, 243, 244. *See also* Voting
Freedom of conscience, 6, 7
Freedom of religion. *See* Religious liberty

Freemanship: under charter of 1663, 52; equality of freemen, 48; establishment in Providence, 17, 20; free inhabitants compared with, 158; property qualification for, 129, 159

Free Society of Traders, 252

French and Indian War, 190–92, 215

French Protestants (Huguenots), 92, 98, 101–2, 109, 110–11, 248

Friends. *See* Quakers

Friendship Club (Newport), 217–18, 242, 243

Gazette (newspaper), 203

General Assembly: ad hoc committees of, 117–18, 187–88; bicameral form adopted by, 117–18; colonial government reestablished in August 1654, 46; Committee of War, 188, 191–93, 297n.20; corporate charters granted by, 214–23, 241; Declaration of Independence approved by, 254; after Dominion of New England, 59–61; elections to, 129; as feeble between 1654 and 1686, 54; Grand Committee, 123–24, 187–90, 205; and Harris land claim, 74; House of Deputies, 117, 188; House of Magistrates, 118, 188; itinerancy of, 53; and the Jews, 109; and the judiciary, 193–94; as keeping a hand in all branches of government, 205; in King Philip's War, 55; in Newport, 31; of Providence Plantations, 43; under royal charter of 1663, 49–50, 51; after 1738, 186, 187–88; severing its ties to British Empire, 255; specialized organs created in eighteenth century, 10; working majorities in, 206

General Court (Aquidneck commonwealth), 30, 31, 260n.49

General Court (Providence Plantations), 43

General Court of Election (1647), 43

General Court of Trials, 44, 51, 53, 121, 139, 193

General redemption, 102

General Sessions of the Peace, 121

General Treasurer, 124, 188, 190–91, 211

Goat Island, 70, 144, 279n.38

Gorton, Benjamin, 60

Gorton, Samuel: captured by Massachusetts, 31; in Portsmouth judiciary defied by, 26, 28; Providence Combination defied by, 17; religious views of, 36–37; secular conception of government of, 24–25; in Warwick, 33–34, 37–38

Gorton, Thomas, 27

Gortonians: as Antinomian, 33; Newport alarmed over, 31; in Portsmouth, 26; and Quakers, 105; religious beliefs of, 36–37, 54; in Warwick, 33–34, 75–76, 268n.14

Gospel order, 103

Governmental institutions. *See* Colonial government; Town government

Government finance, 122–25

Governor and Company of the English Collonies of Rhode-Island and Providence Plantations, in New England, in America, 49, 62

Governor and Council, 121, 191, 193, 202, 241, 298n.25

Grand Committee, 123–24, 187–90, 205

Great Awakening, 187, 226, 227–28, 239, 305n.2

Greenwich Monthly Meeting (Quakers), 182, 183, 294n.41

Hamilton, Marquis of, 273n.21

Harris, Thomas, 263n.18

Harris, William: essay to the Court of Election of 1655, 47; land claim of, 55, 72–74, 75, 76, 79, 138, 269n.30

Harvard College, 171, 173, 179, 253

Hierarchy, social, 13, 14, 38, 247

High justice, 133

Highways. *See* Roads

Hiscox, William, 103

Hodgson, Robert, 107, 276n.14

Holden, Randall, 284n.27

Holliman, Ezekiel, 22

Honyman, James, 175

Hopkins, Stephen: British institutions debated by, 254; as College of Rhode Island chancellor, 220; political rivalry with Ward, 202, 203, 204; Providence *Gazette* launched by, 203; and Providence library, 217; Stiles opposed by, 236

House of Deputies, 117, 188
House of Magistrates, 118, 188
Hubbard, Samuel, 103, 104
Huguenots (French Protestants), 92, 98, 101–2, 109, 110–11, 248
Hull, John, 93
Hutchinson, Anne, 23, 25, 27, 28, 31, 32

Incorporation. *See* Corporate charters
Indians: in bound servitude, 69, 159; commandeering labor of, 167; the franchise denied to, 243; Niantics, 141, 266n.41; Pequots, 94, 266n.41; Warwick compensating for damages from livestock, 36. *See also* Narragansett Indians
Individual rights: becoming clearer in eighteenth century, 10; and collective action, 224; colonial government sustaining, 137; in colonial regulation of town government, 129; in the Declaration of Independence, 254; Rhode Island creating a system for protecting, 251; traditional intermediary institutions limiting, 207
Inequality: in new towns, 82; in Portsmouth, 24, 25; in proprietary syndicates, 99
Inferior Court of Common Pleas, 121
Inhabitant labor, 35
Initiative and referendum, 43, 45, 53
Inns (taverns), 14, 27, 41, 68, 165, 207
Inoculation against smallpox, 202
Institutions: definition of, 2; in English colonies in America, 1–2; five traits of, 2; parts influencing and limiting each other, 1. *See also* Colonial government; Economic enterprises; Nongovernmental organizations; Religious institutions; Town government
Interest income, 122, 124, 126
Intestacy, 201, 300n.46

James II, 59, 62
Jamestown: commons divided in, 144, 145–46; deputies sent to General Assembly, 55; after Dominion of New England, 59, 60; establishment of, 84–85; ferries to, 188, 201, 213; lighthouse at, 201; non-Whites in, 159; Perpetual Council, 85; taking control

of its own affairs, 100; town council functions in, 167; wardens as justices of the peace in, 278n.19
Jenckes, Joseph, 134, 282n.66
Jews, 101–2, 109, 243, 244, 248
Johnston, 210, 301n.12
Judiciary: admiralty court, 121–22; appeals, 121, 193, 297n.21; corporations supported by, 208; Court of Equity, 193, 297n.21; General Court of Trials, 44, 51, 53, 121, 139, 193; General Sessions of the Peace, 121; high justice, 133; Inferior Court of Common Pleas, 121; justices' courts, 121; justices of the peace, 44, 120, 165, 193, 203; as more elaborate than necessary in 1650s, 48; particular courts, 30; probate, 67, 121, 165, 166, 193, 289n.45; reform of, 119–22; after 1738, 193–94; Superior Court, 121, 193–94, 298n.25; town councils' judicial role, 165; vice-admiralty courts, 194, 249, 298n.25. *See also* Town courts
Justices' courts, 121
Justices of the peace, 44, 120, 165, 193, 203

Keeper of the Grand Committee's Office, 189–90
King George's War, 215
King Philip's War, 6–7, 55, 69, 76, 80, 84, 92
King's Church (Providence), 232, 308n.26
King's Province, 53, 57, 272n.18
Kingstown: Church of England in, 174; Congregationalists in, 173, 177, 185; control lacking in, 100; after Dominion of New England, 59, 60; establishment of, 93–94; General Assembly selling vacant lands in, 142; North Kingstown, 162, 177; on road development, 127. *See also* South Kingstown
Knight, Sarah Kemble, 282n.3
Kukla, John, 310n.7

Land: Newport conflicts over, 65; Portsmouth conflicts over, 65; in probate, 166; Providence conflicts over,

Land *(continued)*
65, 72–75, 148–50, 269n.30; subduing conflicts over, 137–52; Warwick conflicts over, 65, 75–77, 150. *See also* Commons; Land distribution; Land rights; Proprietary syndicates
Land banks, 123–24, 188, 189, 311n.13
Land distribution: challenges to, 38; first settlers' backgrounds affecting, 258n.1; Harris land claim in Providence, 72–75; in Newport, 29, 31; in Portsmouth, 24, 26–27; in Providence, 16, 20, 21; social consequences of, 14, 247; in Warwick, 34
Land rights: and charter of 1663, 8; under Dominion of New England, 57; and freeman status, 20; Harris land claim in Providence, 72–75; proprietary rights becoming, 151; proprietary syndicates, 77–80; recording of, 67; Rhode Island founders on, 15; social distinctions as based on, 14, 48, 247; town government separated from, 65; towns as based on, 6; in Warwick, 75–77; Williams setting new foundation for, 17
Law: civil and criminal codes of 1647, 45; compilation of, 9, 120, 278n.17; liability, 68; maritime law, 44; mercantile law, 44–45; natural law, 16, 258n.4. *See also* English law; Judiciary
Lawful Money of New England, 189, 190, 204
Laying on of hands, 22, 32, 102, 103, 178, 261n.58
Lenthall, Robert, 32
Liability, 68
Liberty, religious. *See* Religious liberty
Lighthouses, 201
Livestock: colonial government in regulation of, 195; General Court in regulation of, 44; Newport laying down rules on, 31; New Shoreham regulating, 87; pasturing on commons, 70; Portsmouth raising for export, 29; swine, 21, 162; town government regulating, 67–68; Warwick's measures on damage caused by, 36
Local government. *See* Town government

Localism: Breen on, 277n.1; colonial government's accommodation with, 241, 242; freemen as sensitive to, 44; and judicial reforms of 1647, 119; on the mainland, 114; and the militia, 118
Lockyer, John, 173
Long Wharf (Newport), 155, 169, 208, 212–13, 224, 301n.11
Lotteries, 209–11; Baptists using, 234, 309n.36; colonial government authorizing, 11, 223, 241, 253; flexibility in arrangements for, 301n.11; for Masons, 211, 218, 301n.12; for the Providence library, 211, 217, 301n.12; temporary collectivities created by, 224
Lucar, Mark, 22

MacSparran, James, 175, 177
Majority rule, 254, 301n.11
Manning, James, 218, 219, 234
Marchant, Henry, 236
Maritime law, 44
Markets, supervision of, 155, 199
Marriage: for Baptists, 179, 293n.34; as a contract, 205, 224, 242; divorce, 193; a public dimension given to, 224, 242; Quaker requirements for, 230–31; records of, 67, 105, 113; social bonds strengthened by, 244
Mary, Queen, 7, 60, 132
Maryland, 248, 249, 250
Masons, 210, 211, 218, 301n.12
Massachusetts: Ancient and Honorable Artillery Company, 302n.24; Anglican pew tax authorized in, 232, 233; attempting to extend its borders to Narragansett Bay, 39, 73; Cambridge Platform, 227, 251; central authority resisted in, 262n.1; charter of 1692, 250; in charter of 1644, 42, 43; common land allocated to individuals, 71; and Congregationalists in Rhode Island, 170, 171, 172, 173; Congregational polity in, 237; divine authority in government of, 16; first settlers' backgrounds affecting organization in, 258n.1; Gorton captured by, 31; Harvard College, 171, 173, 179, 253; institutional variety in, 246, 310n.4; land banks in, 123; Lawful Money of New England, 189; leadership of,

250–51; legislating for towns and proprietors of common lands, 250; Misquamicut claims of, 94–95; new town promoters from, 82, 83; Phips as royal governor of, 60; Plymouth, 39, 40, 42, 249; on proprietary syndicates, 282n.1; in regional monetary system, 125; Rhode Island acquiring territory from, 193

Massachusetts Land Bank, 214

Mayhew, John, 173

Meeting for Sufferings, the (Quakers), 229

Mendon, 147

Mercantile law, 44–45

Mercury (newspaper), 203

Meshanticut, 76–77, 79

Miantonomi, 84, 141, 266n.41

Micarter, John, 68

Middletown, 144, 163, 195–96, 198, 242

Migratory fish, 128

Militias: under charter of 1663, 52; and the colonial government, 41; after Dominion of New England, 60–61; elite companies chartered, 214–16; General Assembly asserting its power over, 118–19; in Newport, 30; partisanship in choice of officers, 203; Providence establishing, 20; in Providence Plantations, 44; train bands, 118, 119

Mills: becoming autonomous, 41; becoming private associations, 207; colonial government regulating, 224; companies operating, 304n.48; General Assembly regulation of, 127–28, 129; and partisan politics, 203; in Portsmouth, 27; in Providence, 21; as self-regulating, 224; town regulation of, 14, 68–69

Ministry. *See* Clergy

Mishawomet (Shawomet) Purchase, 18, 33, 42, 75, 76, 150

Misquamicut, 95, 138, 144

Misquamicut company, 94–96, 146, 197

Money: Lawful Money of New England, 189, 190, 204, 238; old-tenor pounds, 204, 238. *See also* Paper money

Monopoly privileges, 245

Mumford, John, 142, 145

Mumford, Stephen, 102, 275n.2

Narragansett, 93, 174, 175, 176, 177–78

Narragansett country: proprietary syndicates in northern, 96–98; proprietary syndicates in southern, 93–96; term's meaning, 265n.41

Narragansett Indians: Canonicus, 84, 141, 266n.41; in charter of 1663, 50; disintegration of, 84; elimination of, 75, 76, 84; and Harris land claim, 73; Miantonomi, 84, 141, 266n.41; "Narragansett country" derived from, 265n.41; Narragansett Proprietors' mortgage on lands of, 73, 88–89, 92, 141, 279n.16, 282n.5; new towns created from land of, 82, 83–84; and Providence Grand Purchase, 17; settlers limited by, 39; United Colonies of New England threatening war against, 42

Narragansett Proprietors, 88–93; and Connecticut, 88, 89, 92, 93, 140, 141; and Harris land claim, 74; mortgage on Narragansett Indian lands, 73, 88–89, 92, 141, 279n.16, 282n.5; in northern Narragansett country, 96, 97; reorganization of 1677, 92; royal commissions backed by, 132; as a special and important case, 138; uniformity and discipline desired by, 98–99; and the "vacant lands," 140–43; Warwick claimed by, 75

Natural law, 16, 258n.4

Naval force, 118

Newdigate, Nathaniel, 120, 139

New England Yearly Meeting (Quakers), 107

New Hampshire, 246, 251, 310n.2

New Jersey, 250

New Netherland, 248

Newport: in the Aquidneck commonwealth, 29–31; baptism by total immersion in, 22; Baptists in, 28, 32, 178–79, 180, 228, 235; as capital of Aquidneck commonwealth, 31, 32; as capital of colonial government, 53; in central authority's extension, 8; chartered institutions sought by, 223; charter for, 131; in charter of 1644, 42; Church of England in, 173, 174, 175–76; Coddington in founding of, 25; and College of Rhode Island, 218,

Newport *(continued)*
219, 304n.45; colonial authority in, 6,
40; and colonial economic development policy, 125, 126, 135, 280n.40;
Colony House, 171, 279n.38; commercial center development in, 154–
56; commercial expansion of, 10,
114–15, 153, 187, 277n.1; commons
in, 69, 70–72, 144; conflicts over land,
65; Congregationalists in, 171–73,
235–37; after Dominion of New England, 60, 61; Easton's Point, 108, 181,
238; fire companies in, 163, 199; fort
built for harbor of, 118; founding of,
28–32; Friendship Club, 217–18,
242, 243; highway regulation in, 67; in
Jamestown's founding, 84, 85, 88;
land allocated for favored
occupations, 70; in land division, 145,
146, 148; and larger landholdings, 64;
Long Wharf, 155, 169, 208, 212–13,
224, 301n.11; lotteries in, 210, 211;
magistrates under charter of 1663, 51;
market in, 199; Masons in, 210, 211,
218, 301n.12; meeting of May 1,
1689, 58–59; merchants as a ruling
class, 136; the *Mercury,* 203; Middletown separated from, 195, 242; non-
Whites in, 159; officials increasing in,
66; as oligarchic, 31, 32; original compact of, 28–29; overseers of the poor
in, 167; political apathy in, 244; political power decreasing in, 187;
predominance wanes, 200, 201;
Quakers in, 105, 107, 108, 229, 238,
307n.14; quarantine procedures in,
196; Redwood Library, 214, 216–17,
224, 242, 243; representatives at General Assembly under charter of 1663,
49; as satellite of Boston, 277n.1;
schools, 31, 32, 70, 198; Seventh Day
Baptists in, 102, 104; split in, 163;
town officials of, 164; Trinity Church,
173, 175–76, 231–33; variety of institutions in, 208; wharves built in, 155;
the whole territory as serving, 249;
workhouse in, 198
Newport Artillery Company, 215–16,
224
Newport Tories, 116, 119, 132, 134, 140,
174

New Shoreham: deputies sent to General Assembly, 55; establishment of,
84, 85–87; General Assembly to subsidize port for, 201; a harbor planned
for, 87; as self-contained, 100; wardens as justices of the peace, 278n.19
New towns, 82–100; Middletown, 144,
163, 195–96, 198, 242; promoters of,
82; proprietary institutions in, 82–83;
after 1738, 195–96; shared ownership
of land as basis of, 82. *See also* East
Greenwich; Jamestown; Kingstown;
New Shoreham; Westerly
New York, 249, 252
Niantics, 141, 266n.41
Nichols, Benjamin, 190
Nicholson (Nickelson), Joseph, 107
Ninigret, 141, 143
Nongovernmental organizations, 211–
23; consent in, 242–43; as
subsidiaries to town government,
197–99
Non-Whites, 159
North Carolina, 248, 252
Northern Narragansett country, 96–98
North Kingstown, 162, 177

Oaths of office, 52
Old-tenor pounds, 204, 238
Ordination, 228, 305n.6, 309n.1
Original towns: colonial government
created by, 15, 40; communal ideal
disintegrating in, 64–81; custom and
innovation in, 13–39; town charters
for, 212, 302n.13. *See also* Newport;
Portsmouth; Providence; Warwick
Orphans, 166
Overseers of the poor, 167

Pacifists, 52, 59, 119, 295n.48
Paine, John, 289n.45
Palmes, Edward, 59
Paper money: abandonment of, 186–87;
in economic development, 125–26;
eighteenth-century versus modern,
254; and the imperial government,
134; issuance of, 116, 122, 191; keeping in circulation, 124; Massachusetts
leading in, 250, 251; Newport merchants opposing, 280n.40; payments
on first loans in, 188–89

Parishes: in the Church of England, 174, 175, 226, 227, 242, 252; in the communal idea, 13; Providence repudiating the traditional, 21; as rejected or failing in Rhode Island, 207

Park, Joseph, 173

Parliamentary charter of 1644, 41–45; central authority as strong in, 241; as failing to create a higher jurisdiction, 6; general acceptance achieved by, 5; as leaving the inhabitants to create their own institutions, 40; Williams obtaining, 20, 42, 259n.11

Particular courts, 30

Parties, political, 202–4, 250, 311n.13

Partnerships, 242, 244

Pawtuxet: establishment of, 17; freedom to choose its jurisdiction, 44; and Harris land claim, 72, 73; Massachusetts' claim to, 20, 33, 47; proprietary syndicates in, 78; Warwick as suspicious of, 35; in Westconnaug land division, 147

Peddlars, 126

Penn, William, 252

Pennsylvania, 248, 250, 252

Pequots, 94, 266n.41

Perpetual Council (Jamestown), 85

Pesthouses, 196, 198

Pettaquamscut, 93, 143–44

Pettaquamscut purchasers, 92, 93, 144, 173, 177

Pew taxes, 231, 232, 233, 235, 236

Philosophical Society, 216

Phips, Sir William, 60, 61

Plymouth (Massachusetts), 39, 40, 42, 249

Pocasset. *See* Portsmouth

Political apathy, 244

Political parties, 11, 202–4, 250, 311n.13

Poor, the (paupers): almshouses, 198; Anglican parishes taking responsibility for, 252; the drifting poor, 130; the franchise denied to, 243; Indians as, 159; overseers of the poor, 167; town councils taking responsibility for, 166–67; workhouses, 196, 198, 242, 253

Port fees, 126

Portsmouth: in Aquidneck commonwealth, 25, 29; Boston covenant of 1638, 23–24; as "branch or Limb" of the colony, 158; central control of ferries opposed in, 127; colonial authority in, 6, 40; commerce regulated by, 27; commercial center development in, 154, 156–57; commercial use of commons restricted, 69; commons in, 69, 70–72, 144; conflicts over land, 144; after Dominion of New England, 60; under Dominion of New England, 58; ferry service established in, 27; founding of, 23–28; General Court of Election of 1647, 43; in Jamestown's founding, 84, 88; in King Philip's War, 55; land allocated for favored occupations, 70; and larger landholdings, 64; magistrates under charter of 1663, 51; name changed to Portsmouth, 25; non-Whites in, 159; officials increasing in, 66; as Pocasset, 23; Quakers in, 105, 183; recording divisions of the commons, 67; road development in, 127, 162; town officials of, 164

Post road, 127

Potowomut, 75, 76, 96, 98

Poverty. *See* Poor, the

Predestination: Baptists and, 102, 103, 178, 229, 235, 309n.36; Gorton on, 36; Newport town church on, 32; Providence founders accepting, 21

Privy council, 122, 134, 197

Probate, 67, 121, 165, 166, 193, 289n.45

Property ownership: absentee ownership, 144, 145, 149; church property, 170, 238; in the communal ideal, 37; for ecclesiastical ends, 185; government regulation making safer, 224; institutional solidarity as flowing from, 99; law as embracing, 38. *See also* Land; Proprietary syndicates

Property qualification: for freemanship, 129, 159; for voting, 129, 159, 244

Property taxes, 53–54, 117, 122–23, 131

Proprietary syndicates, 77–80; assertions of corporative powers as failing, 207–8; commercial-mindedness of, 140; in conflicts over undivided land, 137–52; corporative attributes of, 212, 302n.13; as corrosive to public

Proprietary syndicates *(continued)* life, 137; Massachusetts laws on, 282n.1; Massachusetts leading in, 250; Misquamicut company, 94–96, 146, 197; in new towns, 82–83; Pettaquamscut purchasers, 92, 93, 144, 173, 177; quasi-governmental capacities of, 99–100; regulation of, 113, 115; Westconnaug purchase, 97, 138, 144, 146–48, 285n.29. *See also* Narragansett Proprietors

Providence: balking at reimbursing Clarke, 54; Baptists in, 22, 178, 179, 234–35, 242; in charter of 1644, 41, 42; Church of England in, 174; and College of Rhode Island, 218, 219, 234; and the colonial government, 40; Combination of 1638, 17; commercial center development in, 154, 157–58; commercial development of, 187; commercial use of commons restricted, 69; conflicts over land in, 65, 72–75, 148–50, 269n.30; Congregationalists in, 173, 227, 233–34; democracy in, 264n.27; under Dominion of New England, 58; economic ambitions of, 10; elite military companies in, 215; excluding newcomers, 56; fire companies in, 199; founding of, 15–23; the *Gazette*, 203; Harris land claim, 55, 72–74, 138, 269n.30; invitation to join Aquidneck commonwealth, 31; in King Philip's War, 55; King's Church, 232, 308n.26; land allocated for favored occupations, 70; and larger landholdings, 65; library in, 211, 217, 301n.12; lotteries in, 210, 211, 301n.12; magistrates under charter of 1663, 51; market in, 199; Newport's primacy challenged by, 10, 187; paperwork growing in, 66; post road to Westerly, 127; proprietary syndicates in, 78; recording divisions of the commons, 67; road maintenance in, 163; sergeants for, 164; water companies in, 221; in Westconnaug land division, 147; workhouse in, 198
Providence Cession, 18
Providence Country Troop of Horse, 302n.24

Providence Grand Purchase, 17, 74
Providence Plantations, 42
Proxy voting, 51
Public records, 66–67, 105, 164
Public utilities, 127, 223, 304n.58
Puritans, 13, 21, 22, 89, 254

Quakers, 104–9; on Aquidneck Island, 105, 108; Barclay's *An Apology for the True Christian Divinity*, 184; clergy, 106, 181, 183, 184; denominationalism in, 227, 229–31; in early eighteenth century, 181–84; effective religious polities developed by, 7; Greenwich Monthly Meeting, 182, 183, 294n.41; and incorporation, 11, 226, 237–39; land acquired by, 108, 111, 181, 293n.39; Meeting for the Sufferings, 229; men and women meeting separately, 107–8, 182, 275n.8, 294n.45; New England Yearly Meeting, 107; in Newport, 105, 107, 108, 229, 238, 307n.14; organization of, 101, 104, 111, 114, 181–82, 242–43; in Portsmouth, 105, 183; pyramids of assemblies of, 105, 182–83, 243; Rhode Island Monthly Meeting, 181, 182, 238; Rhode Island Quarterly Meeting, 182; schools, 183, 229–30, 307n.14; select meetings, 183, 231; separating themselves from secular society, 101, 105; on slavery, 230; a social matrix provided by, 41; the spiritual revitalization, 226; and traditional Christianity, 9; trusteeships used by, 238, 240, 309n.49; in Warwick, 183
Quarantine, 167–68, 196
Quarter courts, 30
Queen Anne's War, 118, 191
Quidnesset (Aquidnesset), 88, 89, 93, 141

Rawson's Fountain Society, 221–23
Records: church, 179–80, 181, 227; public, 66–67, 105, 164
Redwood, Abraham, 216
Redwood Library (Newport), 214, 216–17, 223–24, 242, 243
Referendum, 43, 45, 53
Regulatory agencies, 254

Religion: Great Awakening, 187, 226, 227–28, 239, 305n.2; Jews, 101–2, 109, 243, 244, 248; tolerance, 185, 252. *See also* Christianity; Religious institutions; Religious liberty

Religious institutions: charters of incorporation for, 226, 231–37; church organization in late colonial period, 226–40; church property, 170, 238; coercion by, 113; denominationalism, 227–31; in early eighteenth century, 170–85; fitting into larger frameworks of space and time, 170, 185; government support sought by, 208; ideas in the planning of, 6; in the late seventeenth century, 101–11; lotteries for, 210–11; pew taxes, 231, 232, 233, 235, 236; social responsibilities undertaken by, 244. *See also* Christianity; Church and state; Clergy; Town churches

Religious liberty: becoming a tradition, 255; becoming permanent, 38; and charter of 1644, 241; in charter of 1663, 50; churches in the legal structure without compromising, 226, 231; colonial government for protecting, 40, 42, 205, 208; and the Dominion of New England, 57; equal protection of churches for, 115; formation of new churches allowed by, 226; and the Great Awakening, 238; James II confirming, 59; and Providence church charters, 233; Rhode Island founders agreed on, 15; and shared authority between church and government, 251; as sole collective purpose in early Rhode Island, 46; and Trinity Church's petition for a charter, 232

Religious tolerance, 185, 252

Restoration, 42, 48, 247

Rhode Island: in the British Empire, 132–34; custom and innovation in the original towns, 13–39; in Dominion of New England, 56–58; external pressure leading to coalescence of, 39; first period of colonial development, 5–6; fourth period of colonial development, 9–12; in last decades of eighteenth century, 241–55; map of territory around Narragansett Bay,

1636–1657, 18–19; Massachusetts followed by, 250–51; Massachusetts territory acquired by, 193; other English colonies compared with, 246–54; population growth in from 1738, 296n.2; in regional monetary system, 125; second period of colonial development, 6–7; third period of colonial development, 7–9; a tradition created by, 255; urban dwellers as proportion of population, 252–53. *See also* Colonial government; New towns; Original towns; Parliamentary charter of 1644; Rhode Island founders; Royal charter of 1663

Rhode Island founders: as all coming from cities, 258n.1; communal ideal in establishing their settlements, 13–15; and English traditions, 245–46; justifying what they did, 5, 245, 254; as lacking experience of English governmental institutions, 262n.1; new communities created by, 5; planning everything for themselves, 2

Rhode Island Monthly Meeting (Quakers), 181, 182, 238

Rhode Island Quarterly Meeting (Quakers), 182

Richmond, 227–28

Rights. *See* Individual rights; Land rights

Roads: colonial government in creation of, 127; colonial policy after 1738, 201; driftways, 288n.33; General Court in maintenance of, 44; post road, 127; proprietary syndicates creating, 151; town councils laying out, 167, 196; town government in maintenance of, 67; town meeting responsibility for, 35, 161, 162–63

Rowland, David Sherman, 233

Royal charter of 1663, 48–53; as a constitution, 255; endorsement of 1690s, 132; land disputes leading to plans to annul, 137; as new relationship with the monarchy, 7, 62; resuming government under in 1689, 59–61, 116, 267n.67; the towns in the formulation of, 40

Rutman, Darrett B. and Anita H., 310n.7

Sabbatarians. *See* Seventh Day Baptists
Sacraments, 38, 171
St. Paul's Church (Narragansett), 175, 176, 177
Sands, John, 87
Sanford, John, 27
Sanford, Peleg, 61
Schools: Church of England, 176; corporate privileges for building, 220–21; land reserved for support of, 144; Middletown school committee, 195; in Newport, 31, 32, 70, 198; Newport Congregationalists establishing, 172; parents' associations for operating, 243; Quaker, 183, 229–30, 307n.14; religious institutions operating, 244; town management of, 198–99
Scotch-Irish, 248
Secret ballot, 43
Selectmen, 158, 287n.19
Separation of church and state, 6, 7, 27, 251
Separatists, 21
Sergeants, 164
Servitude, bound, 69, 159, 244
Seven Mile Line, 78, 79, 147
Seventh Day Baptists, 102–4; affinities with other Baptists, 103, 275n.4; cosmopolitan framework of, 101; elders' importance to, 305n.6; land secured by, 178; novel ecclesiastical structures of, 111, 180
Shawomet (Mishawomet) Purchase, 18, 33, 42, 75, 76, 150
Six Principle Baptists: as bulk of the Rhode Island flock, 180; denominationalism developing in, 227; in East Greenwich, 227; in general association of Baptist Churches, 228–29; incorporation sought by, 235; and Johnston Baptists' lottery, 301n.11; laying on of hands by, 22, 178; in Newport, 178, 179, 228
Slavery, 159, 184, 230, 243
Slave trade, 159, 230
Smallpox, 167–68, 196, 202
Smith, Richard, 59, 88, 266n.46
Smith, Richard, Jr., 88
Smithfield, 294n.41
Social contract, 16, 254
Social hierarchy, 13, 14, 38, 247

Society for Promoting the Gospel in New England, 173
Society for the Propagation of the Gospel in Foreign Parts (S.P.G.), 174–78, 231
Society of Friends. *See* Quakers
Soul liberty, 101, 246
South Carolina, 250
Southern Narragansett country, 93–96
Southertown, 94
South Kingstown: Baptist land ownership in, 292n.28; corruption in, 161; non-Whites in, 159; in Pettaquamscut purchase, 93; in Quaker Greenwich Monthly Meeting, 294n.41; quarantine procedures in, 196; roads in, 162, 196; town council functions in, 167
Stanton, Daniel, 197
Stanton, Joseph, 96
Status, 242
Stennet, Edward, 275nn. 2, 4
Stiles, Ezra, 235–37, 306n.6
Superior Court of Judicature Court of Assize and Goal Delivery, 121, 193–94, 298n.25
Swine, 21, 162

Tanning, 21
Taverns (inns), 14, 27, 41, 68, 165, 207
Taxes: under Dominion of New England, 58; excise on wine and liquor, 54; and paper money's abandonment, 186–87; parties fighting over, 203; pew taxes, 231, 232, 233, 235, 236; property taxes, 53–54, 117, 122–23, 131; resistance to, 113, 122
Ten Rod Road, 162
Thompson, Elias, 197
Thurston, Edward, 190, 238
Tolerance, religious, 185, 252
Tories, 116, 119, 132, 134, 140, 174
Toskeunk, 76, 79
Town boundaries, 131
Town charters: under charter of 1663, 52; for Newport, 131; of the original towns, 212, 302n.13; for Providence, 20; in Providence Plantations, 44, 45; for Warwick, 35
Town churches: in Newport, 28, 31–32; in Portsmouth, 23, 27–28; in Providence, 15, 21–22; in Warwick, 36–37

Town clerks, 20, 164

Town councils: boards of selectmen contrasted with, 158, 287n.19; colonial regulation of, 130; as common to New England, 15; in early eighteenth century, 165–68; functions of, 120; as gaining in importance over town meetings, 9, 153, 158, 165; judicial competence of, 121; in local defense, 278n.7; and the poor, 166–67; in Portsmouth, 26; as probate courts, 165, 166; probate procedure in, 67; in Providence, 20; in Providence Plantations, 44; quarantine powers of, 167–68; in road development, 127, 196; after 1738, 195, 196; size of, 165; standardization of, 165; as taking shape in the first two decades, 38

Town courts: under charter of 1663, 52, 66; in Newport, 29; Providence establishing, 20, 21, 259n.12

Towne, the (Warwick). *See* Four Mile Common

Town government: admitting inhabitants by, 130, 158–60; basic design of, 38; changes in later seventeenth century, 66–70, 80–81; clerks, 20, 164; colonial government centralization affecting, 8–9; colonial regulation of, 9, 129–31; in commercial center development, 10, 154–58; control of land separated from, 65, 80–81; disintegration as tendency in, 64; diversity of, 242; under Dominion of New England, 57; in early eighteenth century, 153–69; Newport establishing, 28–32; other colonies' compared with Rhode Island's, 252; policies and political organization, 200–204; Portsmouth establishing, 24–27; Providence establishing, 20–21; Rhode Island founders setting up, 5; after 1738, 186, 194–97; specialized officers for, 163–64, 289n.40; standardization of, 112–13; subsidiaries of, 197–99; in Warwick, 34, 35, 37. *See also* Town councils; Town courts; Town meetings

Town meetings: colonial regulation of, 130; as common to New England, 15; in early eighteenth century, 160–64;

in East Greenwich, 160, 161; fixed calendar for, 66, 160; as foundation of town government, 14; in Newport, 30, 160; in Providence, 20, 56, 160; as routinized, 161, 195; after 1738, 195, 196–97; as taking shape in the first two decades, 38; town councils gaining in importance over, 9, 153, 158, 165; voting rights controlled by, 159

Town watches, 278n.7

Trade (commerce): colonial regulation of, 126, 156; commercial center development, 154–58; government policy regarding, 205; government regulation making safer, 224; markets, 155, 199; mercantile law, 44–45; Newport's commercial expansion, 10, 114–15, 153, 187, 277n.1; Penn's Free Society of Traders, 252; Portsmouth promoting and regulating, 27; Providence's commercial expansion, 187; slave trade, 159, 230; town government in promotion of, 195

Train bands, 118, 119

Transportation: aimless policy after 1738, 201; colonial efforts at improving, 126–27. *See also* Bridges; Ferries; Roads

Treasury bills, 123

Trinity Church (Newport), 173, 175–76, 231–33

Trusteeships, 238, 240, 309n.49

United Colonies of New England, 42, 84

Usury, 202

"Vacant lands," Narragansett Proprietors and the, 140–43

Vane, Sir Henry, 29

Vaughan, William, 94, 97

Vendue masters, 126, 194, 280n.41

Veto power, 134, 282n.66

Vice-admiralty courts, 194, 249, 298n.25

Virginia, 13, 246–48, 250, 252, 253

Voting: property qualification for voting, 129, 159, 244; proxy voting, 51; secret ballot, 43. *See also* Franchise

Walton, John, 179

Wanton, Governor, 236, 308n.26

Wanton, John and William, 116, 123
Ward, Samuel, 202, 203, 204, 220,
    304n.45
Warden, Gerald B., 263n.17
War of Jenkins' Ear, 188, 296n.14
Warren, 219
Warwick: balking at reimbursing Clarke,
    53–54; on bicameralism, 265n.32;
    birth records in, 67; in charter of
    1644, 41, 42; and the colonial govern-
    ment, 40; commons in, 69; conflicts
    over land, 65, 75–77, 150; diverse
    population of, 35; after Dominion of
    New England, 60; under Dominion
    of New England, 58; economic regu-
    lation in, 35–36; fishing policy in,
    128; founding of, 33–37; General
    Assembly of August 31, 1654 in, 46;
    and Harris land claim, 55, 72, 73, 138;
    on itinerancy of governmental organs,
    53; magistrates under charter of 1663,
    51; Micarter fulling mill, 68; non-
    Whites in, 159; Quakers in, 183; Sha-
    womet Purchase, 18, 33, 42, 75, 76,
    150; town officials of, 164; workhouse
    in, 198. *See also* Four Mile Common
Warwick, Robert Rich, earl of, 34, 42, 43
Warwick Neck, 34, 35
Watches, town, 278n.7
Water companies, 221–23
Weirs, 128
Westconnaug purchase, 97, 138, 144,
    146–48, 285n.29
Westerly: Baptists in, 180; Congrega-
    tionalists in, 173; after Dominion of
    New England, 59; under Dominion
    of New England, 58; establishment
    of, 95–96; gaining territory, 100;
    General Assembly to subsidize port
    for, 201; post road from Providence,
    127; quarantine procedures in, 196;

rejoins Rhode Island, 96; road main-
    tenance in, 163; Stanton commons'
    claim in, 197; town officials of, 164;
    undivided lands assigned to individu-
    als, 146; and the "vacant lands" dis-
    pute, 141, 142
West Greenwich, 142
Wharton, William, 133–34
Wheelwright, John, 27, 28
Whipple, John, Jr., 127
Wightman, Daniel, 179, 293n.35
William, King, 7, 60
William and Mary, College of, 253
Williams, John, 87
Williams, Joseph, 147
Williams, Robert, 263n.18
Williams, Roger: baptism of, 22; on cor-
    porations, 301n.3; in founding of
    Providence, 15–17, 20–22; and Har-
    ris land claim, 72–73, 74, 269n.30;
    and Jamestown's founding, 271n.2; on
    natural law, 16, 258n.4; parliamentary
    charter obtained by, 20, 31, 42,
    259n.11; as President of Providence
    Plantations, 46, 47; on reimbursing
    Clarke, 54; religious views of, 21–22;
    village-mindedness of, 277n.1
Wine and liquor, excise on, 54
Winthrop, John, 28
Winthrop, John, Jr., 49, 53, 89
Withey, Lynne, 277n.1
Women: the franchise denied to, 243,
    244; as lottery directors, 301n.11;
    Quaker men and women meeting
    separately, 107–8, 182, 275n.8,
    294n.45; rights of free inhabitants for,
    159
Workhouses, 196, 198, 242, 253

Yale College, 179, 214

UNIVERSITY PRESS OF NEW ENGLAND publishes books under its own imprint and is the publisher for Brandeis University Press, Dartmouth College, Middlebury College Press, University of New Hampshire, Tufts University, and Wesleyan University Press.

Library of Congress Cataloging-in-Publication Data

James, Sydney V., 1929–1993.
    The colonial metamorphoses in Rhode Island : a study of institutions in change / by Sydney V. James; edited by Sheila L. Skemp and Bruce Daniels.
      p.   cm. — (Revisiting New England)
    Includes bibliographical references and index.
    ISBN 1–58465–017-6 (cl. : alk. paper)
    1. Rhode Island—History—Colonial period, ca. 1600–1775. 2. Associations, institutions, etc.—Rhode Island—History—17th century. 3. Associations, institutions, etc.—Rhode Island—History—18th century. I. Skemp, Sheila L. II. Daniels, Bruce Colin. III. Title. IV. Series.
F82.J33   2000
974.5'02—dc21   99–39782